Contemporary Essays on Style

Contemporary Essays on Style

rhetoric, linguistics, and criticism

GLEN A. LOVE **MICHAEL PAYNE**
University of Oregon

SCOTT, FORESMAN AND COMPANY

In Francis Christensen's essay "A Generative Rhetoric of the Paragraph," quoted material was reprinted with permission from the following:

(Pp. 40, 45, 46, 49, 50) Reprinted by permission of the publishers from J. Bronowski, *The Common Sense of Science,* Cambridge, Mass.: Harvard University Press. Used also by the permission of Heinemann Educational Books Ltd.

(Pp. 42-43) From pp. 56-57 *On Living in a Revolution* by Julian Huxley. Reprinted by permission of Harper & Row, Publishers.

(Pp. 43-44) From *The Origins and Development of the English Language* by Thomas Pyles. © 1964 by Harcourt, Brace & World, Inc., and reprinted with their permission.

(Pp. 48, 49, 50) Copyright 1947 by C. Day Lewis. Reprinted by permission of Harold Matson Company, Inc.

PREFACE

This book provides for students of language and literature a comprehensive sampling of the most productive recent commentary on the theory and analysis of prose style. Its purpose is:

1. to make conveniently available to students at all levels of English studies the important articles on style which have heretofore remained scattered throughout scholarly books and periodicals;

2. to make clear to students of English that during the past decade significant progress has been made in defining the concept of "style," a term which has had wide currency in English studies but which is too seldom defined precisely;

3. to provide the means for the student to examine his own prose style in a more sophisticated and critical fashion, even to the point of leading him to alter his own writing performance in light of his increased awareness:

4. to enable the student to become a more sensitive reader of both literary and nonliterary prose;

5. to enhance, for the student of English, his understanding of the methods and presuppositions of rhetoric, linguistics, and criticism.

At this time, perhaps no other subject than style can provide an area of convergence for the disciplines of rhetoric, linguistics, and criticism, all of which rest rather uneasily under the umbrella of "English."

Essays have been chosen for this book on the basis of their currency, significance, comprehensibility, and interest to the nonspecialist as well as the specialist. Nearly all of the works chosen are from the 1960's, a few are from the 1950's. None is dated earlier than 1951. By choosing only contemporary articles, we have hoped to provide a true forum in which writers reflect an awareness of the same central problems as well as one another's attempts to deal with those problems (although it has become apparent that there is less awareness of a shared tradition among the critics than there is among the rhetoricians and linguists). Further, by picking recent works, it has been possible to avoid the sorts of ethereal pronouncements and grand generalities about style which have, with a few exceptions, composed the corpus of statements on style in the past.

As for the criteria of significance and readability, it should be said that the essays are chosen not only for their negative virtues, the avoidance of lofty impressionism in the presence of style, but also for their significance as actual demonstrations of analytical and theoretical work in prose style. In Noam Chomsky's terms, descriptive and explanatory adequacy have been preferred to merely observational adequacy. In a few cases, significant works directed at highly specialized audiences (usually linguists writing for other linguists) have been judged inappropriate for inclusion here because of their difficulty for the nonspecialist reader. The standards of comprehensibility and interest to the general college audience have been applied not only to the selection of essays for inclusion but also in their arrangement within each of the three sections. Introductory notes to each of the essays attempt, whenever possible, to relate the works to one another by calling attention to common problems, theoretical disputes, contrasting methods of analysis, and the like. Thus, we believe the reader will find that the book may be read as more than a collection of random statements; that it approaches a continuity of statement about the current state of the study of prose style.

GLEN A. LOVE   MICHAEL PAYNE

The University of Oregon *Eugene, Oregon*

CONTENTS

PART ONE

Style
and Rhetoric

MONROE C. BEARDSLEY

Style and Good Style

Monroe C. Beardsley is currently professor of philosophy at Swarthmore. In such books as Thinking Straight *(1950; 3rd. ed., 1966) and* Aesthetics: Problems in the Philosophy of Criticism *(1958) he has done more than perhaps any other professional philosopher to help bridge the gap between English studies and the study of philosophy. The article that follows is a clear statement of the view that style and meaning—form and content —are inseparable.*

Recently I had occasion to look over a couple of manuscripts that had been pretty heavily copy-edited for the press. The copy-editors had very different suggestions for ideas about the ideal direction in which to mould the hapless works that had come their way, but one thing they did thoroughly agree upon: namely, that the authors did not know how to write, and would be helpless without an editor. The main trouble was apparently not grammar, or punctuation, or consistency of capitalization, but style.

Reading these manuscripts, comparing the harshly-cancelled original sentences with the neatly-written substitutes between the lines, led me to reflect again on the puzzling nature of style—a quality so evident to the sensitive reader, and yet so difficult to lay hold of and to talk sensibly about. It brought home to me the paradox of the situation in which one person undertakes to improve the style of something written by another. *A* writes his piece of discursive prose, say, and shows it to *B*. *B*, the style-improver, may be a copy-editor or a teacher correcting a composition by a student, or may even be *A* himself at some later time. How is it possible for *B* to improve *A*'s work? It can't be that *A* has failed to say what he wanted to say, because if he hasn't said it, how does *B* know what it is? And if *A has* said what he wanted to say, what can be wrong with the style?

Whether or not this is a real paradox, and, if so, how deep it goes, is one of the questions that I shall be trying to answer. Evidently it calls for a careful consideration of the nature of style: what style is precisely, and what it means to change the style of a sentence.

It's just as well for us to recognize at the start that there are several very different concepts of style, or uses of the term. I will distinguish the three main ones briefly, so as to get my bearings.

First, there is the concept of *a* style (that is, the distinctive style of an author or a particular work). When we think of *a* style, in this sense, we have in mind, no doubt, certain recurrent features of the writing. *A* style is a set of stylistic features. To escape a futile circularity in this definition, we

From *Reflections on High School English: NDEA Institute Lectures 1965,* ed. Gary Tate (Tulsa: University of Tulsa, 1966), pp. 91-105. Reprinted by permission of Gary Tate and the author.

must go on to say what a stylistic feature is—that is, what features of a discourse count as elements of style, and which do not.

Second, there is the concept a *good style*. The style-improver claims to make the style better, and presumably is guided by some criteria of evaluation. He must be able to say what is a fault of style, and why it is a fault, and how that fault can be eliminated—without creating some other fault.

Third, there is the concept of style itself—a part or aspect of the discourse, somehow distinguishable from what is called the substance or content.

The first concept will not concern us here; it is of aesthetic interest and importance, but we can set it aside. My chief attention will be on the second concept. My aim is to look at certain problems about style from the point of view of the style-improver—especially of the teacher who hopes not only to improve particular pieces of work by his students, but also to give them some guiding principles, or at least teach them a knack, so that they may become, as far as may be, their own style-critics.

Because of the special point of view I am adopting, I feel free to use the term "good style" in a modest way. When I speak of good style in this context I do not mean excellence or distinction—style that can claim special aesthetic merit. I mean only *not-bad style,* that is, style that is free of faults. It may seem over-generous to award this commendation to what may, at its best, pass unnoticed; but I think experienced teachers will agree with me that to achieve good style, even in the modest sense, is no mean feat. And it is no small ambition for a teacher or copy-editor to set himself the task of eliminating stylistic faults and helping others eliminate the faults in their own writing.

But in order to inquire what good style, or better style, is, I must lay the groundwork by giving, in summary, my answer to the third, and most fundamental question: what is style itself?[1] There are, then, three parts to my discourse: I shall consider what style is, and what good (or better) style is, and I shall discuss some of the practical consequences.

I

Many charming, clever, and memorable things have been said about style —most of which turn out to be highly misleading when subjected to analysis. One of the best things was said by Pascal, in his twenty-third *Pensée*, and I would like to take it as my text: "Words differently arranged have a different meaning, and meanings differently arranged have different effects."[2] When this double-barrelled aphorism is properly understood (that is, when I have gotten through telling you how *I* want to construe it), it sums up concisely the two theses I shall defend here, and it contains the two truths (the *only* two really general and fundamental truths) about style. Anyone who grasps

---

[1]The view sketched here has been formulated more precisely and fully in my *Aesthetics: Problems in the Philosophy of Criticism* (New York: Harcourt, Brace and World, 1958), pp. 221-27. How much I have learned from, and relied upon, William K. Wimsatt, Jr., will be evident to anyone who has read his essay on "Style as Meaning" in *The Prose Style of Samuel Johnson* (New Haven: Yale University, 1941; paperbound 1963).
[2]Trans. W. F. Trotter (New York: Modern Library, 1941), p. 11.

their implications, and follows them out consistently in practice, will find that the consequences are far-reaching.

The clearest way to say what style is, I think, is to say what a *difference* in style is. Take two sentences or parts of sentences, S_1 and S_2. We say that they differ in style when two things are true about them. First, they differ to some extent in *meaning*. And second, the difference is not on the plane of overt or explicit meaning, but on the plane of covert or implicit meaning. The distinction between explicit and implicit meaning is one that requires a certain amount of analysis to elucidate, but let me say in a general way what sorts of things I have in mind, and leave it to the examples to clarify the distinction. Implicit meaning includes what we would ascribe to the connotations rather than to the plain dictionary sense of a word, and it includes what we would consider to be merely suggested, or hinted, or intimated by a sentence rather than to what the sentence plainly states.

It is relatively easy to see what we are talking about when we compare two similar English expressions with respect to their style. If they don't differ at all in meaning, there is no difference in style (but this, as Pascal says, is almost impossible, for if there are different words, or the same words in a different order, there is almost certain to be some difference in meaning, however small and subtle). If the meanings differ in some explicit way, there is no difference in style. It follows from this analysis that the concept of style is inherently comparative, and therefore variable with the context of concern. To isolate a particular stylistic feature in any discourse is always to think of a particular element of implicit meaning in terms of which that discourse might differ from some other one. This is the first of my two theses, then: that style is detail of implicit meaning.

To clarify and support this thesis I require a few examples. And I will take them from a book on style that is regarded by many people with great affection and respect—the E. B. White revision of William Strunk, Jr.'s *The Elements of Style*.[3] I'm not choosing this as a bad example; when I speak critically of it, I do so more in sorrow than in anger. I can only say: what a pity that even so sound and sensible a book is so confused! In the final chapter, contributed by White, the view of style I have been sketching above is clearly stated and subscribed to: "Style has no such separate entity; it is non-detachable, unfilterable" (p. 55)—in other words, it is inseparable from meaning. But unfortunately the logical implications of this thesis are seldom kept in view.

Consider first the advice to use the active voice rather than the passive voice or constructions based on the verb "to be." "Many a tame sentence of description or exposition," say Strunk and White (p. 14), "can be made lively and emphatic by substituting a transitive in the active voice for some such perfunctory expression as *there is,* or *could be heard.*" Here is a clear-cut example of stylistic advice: how to make your sentence more lively and emphatic. Now take a look at some of their examples. The first one is this:

---

[3]New York: Macmillan, 1959.

Don't say "There were a great number of dead leaves lying on the ground;" but say "Dead leaves covered the ground." Granted there is a significant difference in style here. But isn't that a difference of meaning? For one thing, there are more leaves in the second sentence. The second one says that the ground was covered; the first one only speaks of a "great number." Stylistic advice is a rather odd sort of thing if it consists in telling students to pile up the leaves in their descriptions. Suppose the student brings the corrected paper back to his instructor and says, "Pardon me. You told me to say the leaves covered the ground, but actually they didn't; there was quite a bit of ground showing through. Still, there *were* a great many. Do I get a lower grade just for telling the truth?" What answer can the conscientious style-expert give to that?

Now, you may say, well it's not as if the student had used an exact number. Suppose he wrote, "There were 261 leaves on the ground," and his instructor commented in the margin: "Don't say there were 261; say there were 893—that will be more effective." This would of course be telling the student to lie. Since this difference in meaning would be explicit, the change from 261 to 893 would not be a change in style. But isn't the change from "a great many leaves" to "covered the ground" a kind of lie, too—or at least a considerable exaggeration? Naturally it is more lively and emphatic, but is it honest? True, the deception will be partially concealed, because it is conveyed implicitly rather than explicitly, but that does not make it less reprehensible.

Take another example that Strunk and White use to illustrate the same rule about liveliness and emphasis. Don't say "The reason he left college was that his health became impaired;" say "Failing health compelled him to leave college." What's the difference here? Again, it is a difference in meaning—in the picture of the situation that is conjured up by the different words and different grammar. In the one case, the health grew worse, and finally after some indecision, he left college—though health was not necessarily the sole consideration. The second sentence implies worse health: it left the student no choice. Naturally it is a more dramatic story. But is this what stylistic advice is all about? Are Strunk and White saying, "Never mind about the exact truth; always try to make things as dramatic as possible, provided you don't get caught in any explicit and easily detectable misstatements"?

The same sort of question can be raised about a great many of the Strunk-White examples. "Put statements in a positive form," they urge—"Make definite assertions" (p. 14). For instance, don't say "He was not very often on time," but rather "He usually came late." Now it seems to me that if I were asked about so-and-so's punctuality I might very well reply, "He was not very often on time," if I wanted to be careful not to overstate the matter, or to suggest that so-and-so came *very* late, or that he was deliberate and inconsiderate in coming late, etc. I am saying precisely what I want to mean, and ought to mean. What right has anyone to tell me *not* to mean this?

One more example: "Use definite, specific, concrete language," say

Strunk and White (p. 15). If you take this seriously, it means, "Don't write philosophy, because that will require abstract language." But here is one of their examples: don't say "A period of unfavorable weather set in;" say "It rained every day for a week." But this is like the leaves example; the second sentence gives us a higher rainfall.

My immediate purpose is not to question the advice given, though I suppose some of my skepticism has already emerged. I am coming to the question of good style shortly. My argument is that a difference of style is always a difference in meaning—though implicit—and an important and notable difference of style is always a sizeable difference in meaning. Some of the Strunk-White examples involve so considerable and obvious a change that it is questionable whether they are really stylistic changes. For example: don't say "He did not think that studying Latin was much use;" say "He thought the study of Latin useless" (p. 14). Now being useless (i.e., having no use at all), and not being of much use, are clearly different things. If anybody advised me to say the second after I had said the first, I would be rather annoyed—I would tell him not to go putting words in my mouth. I don't think that studying Latin is much use; but I would certainly not want to say that it is useless. I'm afraid our style-advisers got carried away on this one.

I can't resist one more example—this one not from Strunk and White but from a religious publication via the filler-spaces in *The New Yorker*.

> Words that sound happy put your reader in the right frame of mind to say "yes" to your request. Remember that a negative word or an unfriendly expression should never be used if there is a positive way to express the same thought. You might say: "We regret that we are unable to supply you with the item ordered. Is there another item which we may send you on the same subject?"
>
> But your reader-reaction will be 100 per cent improved if you rephrase that sentence to read: "Fortunately for you, although the specific item you ordered is out of print, we have another which might serve your purpose."

Nothing could be plainer than that this change of style is a radical change in meaning. None of us would countenance such a bland invitation to write "words that sound happy" in order to con the subnormal reader into the appropriate "reader-reaction"—so that he gets the impression that you are practically doing him a favor by not sending him the item he ordered. But we encourage this sort of confusion when we speak of style as though it *were* detachable and manipulable independent of meaning—when we define style as the "how" of writing vs. the "what"—when, in short, we lose sight of the fact that style is nothing but meaning. That is what encourages people to entertain the absurd idea that, as this writer says, there is both a "positive" and a "negative . . . way to express the same thought."

II

Now, if we are agreed about what style is, we can go on to the second question: what is *good* (i.e., not-bad) style? I assume that there are such things as *faults* of style—or at least there are pieces of discourse that are faulty *in* style—and so the basic question is what such a fault may be. Then the absence of such faults will be goodness of style.

There is one sort of problem about good style that I want to make sure we set aside here. A person who accepted a dinner invitation at the White House in a long Faulknerian sentence, or who wrote a letter of condolence in early Hemingwayese, has no doubt committed some sort of error involving style. The error is not an error *of* style, I think, but an error in the choice of style; the result is not bad style, necessarily, but *inappropriate* style. It is a lack of decorum. In fact, it is just the sort of error that one might commit if he took some of the Strunk and White advice too earnestly. "The latter sentence [the one not recommended] is less direct, less bold, and less concise," they say at one point (p. 13). But what kind of reason is this? In effect, they are saying, "Always write so as to *appear* like a bold, decisive, forthright sort of person. Never mind how you actually feel, or what the occasion is; just act bold."

What I am concerned with, then, is stylistic fault, and again I take my cue from Pascal. "Meanings differently arranged have different effects"—or, as I should put it, when meanings are combined, some combinations are better than others. But there are different ways of being better. When explicit meanings are wrongly combined, you get a logical fault (this is oversimplifying somewhat, but take it as a first approximation). The trouble with a sentence like "He married his widow's younger sister" is that it describes a logical impossibility. There's nothing wrong with the style. Freedom from logical error is good logic—though of course it may not be great cogency. But suppose the fault lies in the way explicit meanings are combined with *implicit* meanings. Then we have a fault of style. My second thesis is that such a fault is also a logical fault, though its locus is different from ordinary explicit logical error. In short, good style is logical congruity of explicit and implicit meaning. When what a sentence suggests or hints, and what its words connote, bear out the implications of the explicit meaning of the sentence, we have no fault of style; but when there is a clash, something must be remedied. And since we take the explicit meaning as primary, we think of the implicit meaning as what requires to be altered, so we say that the style is bad—just as we say that the hat is too small for the head, rather than that the head is too large for the hat.

As Wimsatt puts it (paperbound ed., p. 10), "Bad style is not a deviation of words from meaning, but a deviation of meaning from meaning."

To prove this thesis would be more of a task than I could undertake here —it is, in fact more of a task than anyone has ever undertaken. But a few examples will show how it can be supported, and you can test it further on your own favorite examples of horrible style.

My examples will come, again, from Strunk and White—and it is a tribute to their slim volume that it yields so many provocative examples. "Place the emphatic words of a sentence at the end," they advise at one point, in boldface italics (p. 26). "The proper place in the sentence for the word or group of words that the writer desires to make most prominent is usually the end." This puts the cart before the horse. It is not correct to say that the emphatic words of a sentence should be placed at the end; it is correct to say that whatever words *are* placed at the end of an English sentence will thereby be given emphasis. In all practical discussions of style, it is essential to distinguish two kinds of things that can be said. They are related as the factual and the evaluative, the *is* and the *ought.*

The first kind of statement is what might be called a *stylistic fact,* or a rhetorical fact. For example, "Whatever you place at the end of a sentence will tend to be emphasized." Or, "In general, the active voice carries with it a tone of greater assurance and decisiveness than the passive voice." Many inexperienced writers make mistakes because they do not grasp these facts about the very nature of English constructions. And the teacher can help a great deal merely by pointing these things out. "Look, by placing this at the end, you implicitly claim that it is more important than what you put earlier. Is this what you want to claim?" Or, "Look; here you use the passive voice; the active voice would make the sentence more direct and forthright. Which do you prefer?" In this way, a teacher sensitizes his students to stylistic facts so that they become more and more aware of exactly what they *are* saying, implicitly. But there is no call for the Strunk-White imperative here. The instruction is in the conditional form, like instruction in checkers, gardening, golf, or winemaking: "If you do such-and-such, then such-and-such a meaning will result." Strunk and White's second sentence can be taken in this conditional form.

So there are stylistic facts; are there also *stylistic rules,* or recommendations? There may be, as I said, rules of appropriateness: such-and-such is the accepted style for a thank-you note. But what more can we say? What reason can we give for condemning style, quite apart from what the writer wished to do? Some of the Strunk-White examples of poor style break down at once if we suppose a different context. Take the first example under the sentences just quoted. They reject this sentence: "Humanity has hardly advanced in fortitude since that time, though it has advanced in many other ways." They substitute: "Humanity, since that time, has advanced in many other ways, but it has hardly advanced in fortitude." Suppose you wrote the first sentence, and your copy-editor substituted the second one. Couldn't you simply reply that the first one says exactly what you want to say? From this reply there is no appeal. The second sentence, but not the first one, suggests that what is important is the lack of advance in fortitude. As far as style is concerned, one sentence is no better than the other; they simply say (implicitly) different things, and the question is (or ought to be) which is true.

But when Strunk and White condemn one sentence and praise the other, it is clear that they are making a hidden assumption. They are thinking of the sentence in the context of a sort of Baconian essay on the subject of fortitude. It's not easy to illustrate this assumption very briefly. But imagine something like this foreshortened context:

> Man is a miracle, or many miracles; but the most miraculous fact about him is his fortitude, his capacity to endure and to survive incredible hardships. Think of the conditions under which neolithic man kept going—the winters, the wild animals, the long distances of his migrations. Humanity has hardly advanced in fortitude since that time, though it has advanced in many other ways.

Here if we feel a slackness at the end, and a sort of betrayal of expectations, we can affirm a fault of style. For the end of the last sentence implicitly denies what the first sentence quite explicitly states: namely, that fortitude is the important topic under discussion. So there is a logical conflict after all, and this is the stylistic fault. Note that it is quite independent of the writer's intention and the reader's antecedent desires: it is internal to the discourse itself.

Compare another example that illustrates the same principle, though Strunk and White place it under the heading of active vs. passive voice. They cite: "I shall always remember my first visit to Boston," and continue "This is much better than 'My first visit to Boston will always be remembered by me'" (p. 13). But what's wrong with the latter sentence? If we look for the relevant stylistic fact, we find that it is the same one just considered. Putting the personal pronoun at the end rather than at the beginning of the sentence gives it an emphatic position, and the emphasis is increased by the unusual syntax. Compare these two analogous sentences:

(1) The police department will always remember my first visit to Boston.
(2) My first visit to Boston will always be remembered by the police department.

It would be silly to say that in this case the passive voice makes the second sentence "less direct, less bold, and less concise." I suppose it is less direct, but it is more dramatic and striking, because of its ominous overtones.

So it is not the active-passive difference that is important here. The difference is that the second sentence given by Strunk and White ("My first visit to Boston will always be remembered by me") implicitly claims that there is something noteworthy about *my* remembering it, as opposed to somebody else's remembering it. It says, in effect, "Others may forget it, but *I* certainly won't." Now this suggestion in itself can't make the sentence stylistically bad. One could invent a context in which it would be better than the sentence Strunk and White recommend. But they are tacitly thinking of it as in a context where the main topic under discussion has been, or is to be, the trip itself, its causes and consequences. And in *this* context, the implicit suggestion that there is something significant about *my* remembering it rather than somebody else introduces an irrelevant point. In effect, the sentence says, "It is important that *I* remember it," but the context shows that it is *not* important, because it has no logical bearing upon the other matters at hand.

At one point in their book, Strunk and White come close to making this point explicitly. They begin unpromisingly by giving advice that verges upon complete nullity. First they state their rule: "Use the active voice" (p. 13) —just like that, in so many words. But a little later they say, "This rule does not, of course, mean that the writer should entirely discard the passive voice, which is frequently convenient and sometimes necessary." All we need now is some explanation of how to tell when it is convenient and when necessary —but the much-praised conciseness of *The Elements of Style* naturally prevents them from pausing to give any such explanation. However, their example and comment are important. Compare "The dramatists of the Restoration are little esteemed today" with "Modern readers have little esteem for the dramatists of the Restoration." The authors add, "The first would be the preferred form in a paragraph on the dramatists of the Restoration; the second, in a paragraph on the tastes of modern readers." Excellent; right to the point. The difference in style is a difference in what is suggested about the focus of attention in the whole discourse. And the rightness or wrongness of the style depends on how that suggestion actually comports with the remainder of the discourse.

Some people may be puzzled by this sort of talk about style. In order to show what style is, and what good style is, you have to work out the implicit meanings and state them baldly for examination. Then they are no longer implicit, of course, and the explication of them may seem forced and artificial. But implicit meanings can be understood and can be stated explicitly; and that is the only way to exhibit their connections or divergences. This is what I call style-analysis. And it is essential if our discussions of style are not to degenerate into murky rhapsody or painfully misleading aphorism.

Perhaps I am stacking the cards too much for my second thesis by choosing examples that have already been selected, or constructed, to illustrate particular stylistic faults. So let me venture out of the laboratory for a brief field trip in the outside world of prose. My first specimen is one that came to hand not long ago in a book review by Elizabeth Janeway. She referred to the author of this book[4] as "a mistress of nearly impenetrable prose," and offered the following sample:

> The tyranny of happiness forms the nucleus of the defense apparatus employed by the woman who does not quite dare to break out, though restless, but who must continually seek a validation for her way of life.

---

[4]Edith de Rham, *The Love Fraud*, (New York: Clarkson N. Potter, 1965); see *The New York Times*, March 28, 1965.

Now granted this would be much clearer if we had a context in which "the tyranny of happiness" was defined. But even with that explanation on hand, there would still be stylistic trouble. And that comes largely because the connotations of the words are constantly working against the basic logical pattern proposed by the very same words. They are also working against each other.

We are told that the woman does not "dare to break out" of something (I suppose, the frustrations of her second-class status as married woman); she is compelled to "seek a validation" for her way of life. So far, so good, though we could follow the logical order of relationships better if the sequence of phrases in the sentence reflected that order. The next step—which would be clearer if it followed rather than preceded the end of the sentence—is to note that in order to find that validation, the woman requires a "defense apparatus." But "defense" is hardly the *mot juste* here, since it suggests some sort of enemy or attack, and leads us to look around in the context for hints as to what it is—only to return empty-handed. Then the "defense apparatus" is said to have a "nucleus," and again we try to fit the connotations into the picture—if there is a nucleus it holds things together, or is the center, or is surrounded by other material, etc. No apparatus that is readily conceivable has, in the strict sense, a nucleus—though it may have a most important part. Finally (but this is put first), the nucleus is said to be formed by the tyranny of happiness. Is it the tyranny itself, or the acceptance of such tyranny, or some theory about such tyranny, or something else, that the woman relies on for her validation? The syntax, apparently elliptical, claims a causal connection that is unwarranted by the rest of the context, as far as we have it here. And that is the secret of its failure—as style.

It is always interesting, and often instructive, to see what reviewers pick out as objectionable in the style of the books they review. Recently Joseph Epstein, reviewing a book[5] in the *New Republic* (June 5, 1965), wrote:

> Although every so often Coser will get off a cleanly barbaric sentence like "Geographical dispersion shades into or overlaps with functional differentiation," he occasionally achieves a graceful prose style and almost always commands a forceful one.

This example suggests many reflections—more than I will try to tease out now. It is just the sort of sentence of which Strunk and White would be likely to say: "Avoid abstract nouns. Be concrete. Be definite. Be forceful." But the trouble does not lie in the abstract nouns, I think, and they would not even obtrude on our attention if it weren't for the *active* and *concrete* verbs between them—namely "shades into" and "overlaps with." It is the connotations of these words that throw us off and leave us baffled when we try to figure out what is the exact relationship between geographical dispersion and functional differentiation that is being asserted.

---

[5]Lewis Coser, *Men of Ideas* (New York: Free Press, 1965).

Last week, in a hotel in Denver, I found a booklet containing information about restaurants and other tourist attractions.[6] One of the items read as follows:

LE PROFIL—1560 Sherman St. (222-0758).
Richly adorned and unique of its kind, here dinner is an experience. French and Continental cuisine with an air of Paris sophistication is skillfully prepared and served with care. This is truly a swish dining emporium. The atmosphere is relaxed but polished.

I'm sure any composition teacher would itch to get at this piece of prose; it exhibits such a fascinating range of defects. But I pass by the dubiously attached modifier and the curious redundancy in the first sentence, and what philosophers would call a "category mistake" in the second sentence (I mean that it is not strictly the cuisine but the food that is served). These certainly introduce meanings that distract from the basic order of thought —they strew logical red herrings along the path of sense. But my favorite sentence is the third. "Truly a swish dining emporium"! It would be hard to find two words whose connotations—whose whole ambiences of meaning —are more at odds with one another.

III

I promised some concluding remarks on practical applications, but as I look back it seems to me that I have drawn the practical consequences pretty much as I went along. However, it may be well to summarize my argument concisely, and take one more look to see whether other useful points emerge.

The steps of my argument are these. (1) Different words or a different order of words make different meanings—at least, they do if they make a difference in style, because style is detail of implicit meaning. (2) Therefore, if the teacher advises a change of words, or of word order, he is recommending a different meaning. And if he says one stylistic feature is better than another, he is saying that it is better to mean one thing rather than another. (3) No meaning as such is better than any other, considered solely from the stylistic point of view. (Of course there are moral and political and religious and other criteria in terms of which it is better to mean one thing rather than another.) (4) Therefore, if a change of meaning betters the style, that betterment must lie in the relationships of meanings. (5) The objective relationships that meanings have to each other are logical; meanings are compatible or incompatible, they are connected by causation, implication, coordination, subordination, etc. (6) Therefore, faults of style must be faults of logic; and good style must be compatibility of implicit and explicit meaning.

The practical problem for the writer is that of managing his implicit meanings so that they do not impede or divert or conceal or obstruct his explicit meanings. It is a continuous tactical problem. The strategy of writing is

---

[6] *Colorado Guestguide*, Vol. 7, 1965 summer edition, p. 8.

large-scale organization of meanings—the main steps of the argument, explicit logical relationships. What is left is management of the small-scale, subtler, and under-the-surface meanings to make them carry the thought forward, adding details on the side (so to speak), but details that fit in and enrich the thought—and perhaps show how the writer looks upon his own argument: how confident or doubtful he is, how detached or involved, how serious or playful, and so on.

A teacher who fully realizes that to change style is always to change meaning will never take his role as style-critic lightly, I think. He will shy away from simple absolute rules. He will not speculate about intentions, but focus on the discourse itself, and the way its parts work, or do not work, together. His main effort will be to help his pupils understand what I have called stylistic facts, so that they can become sensitive and discerning readers of their own work. And above all when he is faced with a hard writing-problem, he will insist that the sovereign remedy is to think out the logical connections clearly, and then make sure that the syntax and diction mirror those connections as clearly as possible.

I think I have time to play around with one final example from Strunk and White—or rather from White's concluding chapter—and to draw another moral from it. The moral (to state it first) is that the doctrine of style as meaning and of good style as logical relevance has a liberating effect on the style-critic (the teacher or copy-editor); if he really accepts the doctrine, and all its consequences, he should become tolerant of very different styles and undictatorial about his own recommendations.

White has some fun with variations on Thomas Paine: "These are the times that try men's souls." And the last and most outrageous variation is this: "Soulwise, these are trying times." White raises the question what is wrong with this—but he wisely makes no attempt to answer this question. Less wisely, no doubt, I rush in to fill the gap. Because it may seem that here, at any rate, is a stylistically bad sentence whose stylistic badness has nothing to do with logic, and therefore a sentence that can be rejected out of hand without taking into account relationships of meaning at all. Now of course, this sentence is a comedown from the original, and we can see how it differs and why it differs. "Trying times" and "times that try men's souls" are far from synonymous—a situation can be trying, in the modern sense, without constituting a real trial of one's whole self. And the "X-wise" construction has taken on foundation-board and executive-level overtones, besides its native vagueness and indeterminateness. "Soulwise, these are trying times" is flippant in tone, not deeply concerned. It reminds me of a crazy line from an S. J. Perelman television script: "A man in my position doesn't have as much freedom, choicewise."

But now suppose young Tom Paine were to bring you the first installment of a political piece he is writing, called *The American Crisis*. You open it up and read the first sentence: "Soulwise, these are trying times." Somehow it won't do. But what can you tell him? First, you can help him see the relevant stylistic facts, so that he knows exactly what he has said, explicitly and implicitly. You cannot prove to him, I think, that his sentence in itself is bad style. It might make an excellent beginning of a piece by Perelman. But, second, you can ask what kind of book this sentence is to be the beginning of—you can read further into the context. If the next sentence says, explicitly, that these times are not for the summer soldier and the sunshine patriot, but call for deep commitment and solemn purpose, then you can tell him that, in this context, the first sentence is bad style. For it says, implicitly, that the situation is not serious and that the writer does not care deeply about what is happening.

Let us suppose that, armed with this new insight, Tom Paine goes away to meditate. If you have helped him discern the logical jarring in his discourse, and have made him want to eliminate it, you have done your job. The rest is up to him. But of course if he returns the next day saying, "I've got it! Listen to this: 'These are the times that try men's souls,'" then you can congratulate yourself, as well as him. Unfortunately, few of our students are likely to come up to this level. So we had better be content with the more limited purpose of showing what is wrong, and why. But—and this is my parting plea—when we give reasons to argue that the style is faulty, let us make sure that we give *good* reasons. For bad reasons are worse than none at all.

LOUIS T. MILIC

Theories of Style
and Their Implications
for the Teaching of Composition

Louis T. Milic teaches English at Columbia where he is an Associate Professor in the Teachers College. He has written several essays on style and composition and has recently published A Quantitative Approach to the Style of Jonathan Swift *(1968). The article reprinted here takes exception to the organic theory of style to which Beardsley subscribes. Milic believes that in order to teach writing at all one must assume that style and meaning can be considered separately. This means the effective writer is one who chooses carefully among alternative utterances: "The writer intends to express something (idea) and he struggles with possibilities until he finds the formulation which best expresses it."*

From *College Composition and Communication,* XVI (May 1965), 66-69, 126. Reprinted with the permission of the National Council of Teachers of English and Louis T. Milic.

In the teaching of English, the term *style* comes up far too often, I think. The teacher tinkers with the student's style in something like the way an old-fashioned doctor, an empiric, tinkered with his patient's organs, using surgery, bleeding, and drugs, haphazardly and without reference to a general theory of health or illness. The net result is often that ascribed by Lesage to the famous Dr. Sangrado, who reduced many a healthy man to the last extremity. The precise applicability of this analogy I shall not insist on pointing out, but therapy old and new has always required theoretical foundation if it was to be useful to more than one patient.

A theory of style, therefore, would seem to be an important need for any teacher of composition, though this is hardly ever made clear. In fact, a teacher of composition (like any teacher) must also have a theory of learning, but in this too it is unlikely that the beginner at least has much idea of what his theory is or could state it formally. Those who undertake the teaching of composition in college have not usually had courses in educational psychology or learning theory, behaviorist or other. Yet they obviously operate on the basis of some intuitive theory of how learning takes place. The sources of this intuition have a rather unscientific and disorderly appearance. The most potent is surely imitation of one's own learning experience and of one's own teachers. A certain amount of theory is also quarried from commonplaces with the force of received truths: practice makes perfect; if you don't work hard, how do you expect to learn, etc. Information may be picked up from one's colleagues or articles in *Harpers* about the sorry state of American education or in *College English* about the dangers of teaching machines and programmed instruction.

There is no guarantee that this miscellaneous collection of data could profitably be replaced by systematic training in the psychology of learning: teachers required to take such courses are not notably more successful than their untrained colleagues. It is probable that the ingredients of the theory informally held by most teachers, consisting of demonstration, repetition and examination, are as effective as anything more sophisticated would be, in view of our more or less general ignorance of the factors constituting the process of learning. Since it is not certainly known what would be better than intuition, it is perhaps just as well that time is not wasted on acquiring methods that might prove fallacious. Surely, the main reason why theory is at a discount here is that students, almost regardless of the obstacles interposed by the teacher, cannot be prevented from learning. It is in their natures to learn and this is just as true in composition as in other subjects, as was evidenced in one experiment which showed that students taking physics instead of composition improved as much in composition in their first term in college as students exposed to the regular freshman course. But this should not be taken to imply that students cannot be helped to learn faster or better.

If we are to take the Kitzhaber report seriously, nothing can help; there is no agreement on what good composition is, nor what the subject matter of courses ought to be, nor about the texts, teachers, grades or anything else, except that the level of writing must be brought up. In view of the seriousness of the situation, I am reluctant to call attention to what seems to me a fundamental deficiency of all the approaches to this problem. No consistent theory of style seems to underlie the several efforts to teach composition. By this I mean that the relationship of thing to idea and idea to word is left unexpressed, to be interpreted according to the fashion of the moment. Whatever interpretation is favored, the consequences are formidable for the related question: to what extent and by what means can the writing behavior of the student be influenced to change. It is obvious that the choice between a stylistic monism and dualism will give vastly different answers and consequently imply vastly different strategies for dealing with our patients.

Though I may be accused of being precipitous in thinking of a college freshman as possessed of a mind and personality in some degree formed, I am speaking advisedly. The problem is clearly different in the earlier formative stages, in grammar school and in high school, when the material is still plastic. But in college we have on our hands a rather intractable entity, chock-full of habits with the force of a dozen years of practice. Thus, in a sense, the problem may be insoluble before we address ourselves to it.

There are only three real theories of style, though there has been much embroidery on the basic fabric. The most familiar is the theory of ornate form, or rhetorical dualism. From the classical rhetoricians who originated it to the rhetoricians of the moment who are still using it, this dualism view has always implied that ideas exist wordlessly and can be dressed in a variety of outfits, depending on the need for the occasion: the grand style, the plain style, the middle style and the low style and the like.

A second theory, the individualist or psychological monism, which finds its most common expression in the aphorism that the style is the man, may have originally sprung from Plato's conception of the *vir bonus,* the good man whose goodness would express itself equally in graceful dancing and graceful expression. The modern version is perhaps descended from Montaigne, who claimed to write in the way that was natural for him, following his own bent, and disdaining affectation. Brought wholly up-to-date, it means that a writer cannot help writing the way he does, for that is the dynamic expression of his personality, illustrated in his handwriting, his walk and all his activity.

The most modern theory of style, Crocean aesthetic monism, is an organic view which denies the possibility of any separation between content and form. Any discussion of style in Croce's view is useless and irrelevant, for the work of art (the composition) is a unified whole, with no seam between meaning and style. Thus, in the organic view, there is no style at all, only meaning or intuition. It is an elegant solution which has been widely adopted by enthusiasts quite unaware, it seems, that it left them nothing to do. It is so widespread that those who practice it hardly find it necessary even to say that style is not an isolable quality.

Now, how do these recondite theories affect us as teachers of composition? Although the connection between the dabblings of our freshmen and the ideas of Plato and Croce may seem remote, the implications of these theories have important consequences for the teaching of composition. It is in the nature of basic theories to generate implications and for opposed theories to produce contradictory implications. Thus it is evident that eclecticism will not really work and that a choice among these theories must be made by the teacher of composition. He cannot espouse one theory and teach on the basis of another, or, like many a handbook of composition, a conflation of all three.

If the teacher adopts the theory of ornate form, he must be prepared to accept—even to hail enthusiastically—its inevitable implications. The theory is based, as everyone knows, on the belief in the separate existence of content and form. Like any frankly dualistic view, it has attracted the disapproval of those who espouse a hard (or positivist) line. That is, though you can see words, you cannot see ideas or content. If you cannot see (feel, hear, etc.) content, you have no proof that it exists. What you cannot prove the existence of, they say, you have no business theorizing about. Yet, despite its unprovability and perhaps its scientific unsoundness, the dualistic theory has many attractions and advantages. But its implications must be accepted or at least accounted for.

To begin with, the disjunction of content and form permits a belief in a real intended meaning behind every utterance. The writer intends to express something (idea) and he struggles with possibilities until he finds the formulation which best expresses it. Because this seems to many to correspond with every writer's experience, it is readily accepted by everyone, including the critically naive, who proceed to sew it onto one of the monistic theories. Pedagogically, this makes it possible to enjoin the student to clarify his thought (without reference to the possible difficulty that this may be impracticable without the aid of language), to make it logical, before actually embodying it in words. The inelegancies and errors which occur can be treated as correctable by consulting the intended meaning. Correction and revision are done according to some absolute standard of rightness perhaps related to the hierarchy of styles: casual, informal, formal, ceremonial (also known as levels of usage). And if revision and correction are done sufficiently long and diligently, the expression of the intended meaning can become complete. It can reach the point where the reaction of a reader would be "There seems to be no other way to say it."

It should be evident that this theory of style corresponds pretty well with the practices of the old rhetoric. The theory of rhetorical dualism justifies certain classroom procedures. Students can be encouraged to write imitations of Swift, Addison, Johnson, Macaulay, Shaw or E. B. White. They can be set to write the same paper in a variety of styles, from the low to the grand. They can be taught the mysteries of anaphora, brachylogia, hypallage and epichireme. Their compositions can be tested for the suitable presence of the seven parts, from exordium to peroration. But, conversely, emphasis on subject and on personality must be excluded. Students should not be told to write naturally, to express their personalities, that is, because such a concept contradicts the fundamental assumptions of the theory of ornate form. Nor should any particular attention be paid to the substance of the writing for the theory explicitly denies any link between substance and form except for logic. The uniformity of the writing of the students which might result must be taken as a vindication of the theory and not as an evil consequence.

If the second theory, the individualist, is espoused, the field of activity is greatly narrowed. In Plato's view, the only route to the improvement of the student's writing (or dancing) is through the general enhancement of his soul. If we wish the writing to be good—Plato believes in an absolute standard—the writer must be a good person. Nothing else will avail. Thus courses in composition would become largely courses in spiritual self-improvement, perhaps with ethics, religion and psychotherapy as significant components. In the more modern version of this theory, that style is the expression of the student's mind and personality, there is not much more to do. We can exhort him to eschew mannerism and to write naturally, to express himself fully and to be as grammatical as possible while doing it. But what if the student's personality, fully expressed, leads to contortion, gibberish or paranoia? What is left except to throw up our hands? It is evident that under the influence of this theory we cannot urge the student to adopt another personality or to write more naturally than he does when his natural writing is not bearable. None of the usual tactics used in composition courses have any real bearing here except perhaps finding a subject on which the student can perform competently.

Croce's organic theory of style leaves us even more completely helpless, inasmuch as it explicitly disavows any segmentation between the subject and its form. Croce will have no truck with devices of rhetoric or anything which casts the least shadow on the integrity of expression. The consequence of the disappearance of style which results is that discussion of the student's writing must consist almost exclusively of its philosophy, so to speak. The emphasis which this theory forces on us is the dominance of the subject. For if there is no form, we cannot discuss, much less improve, the student's means of expression. The powerful trend to the study of linguistics and substantive matters in composition courses of late years may find its source in the unconscious adoption of this unitary view. If we cannot teach rhetoric, we must still teach something, but since miscellaneous social and topical subjects have produced no improvement, perhaps the final recourse to the subject matter of the language itself will succeed. Thus the proponents of the linguistic readers have in a way solved the Crocean paradox. Substance cannot be separated from form but if the substance *is the form* we can have the best of both worlds, writing exclusively about form. However ingenious this solution may seem, there is very little evidence that it has succeeded in improving the level of performance in English composition, if a nascent counter-trend to the linguistic approach is any guide, not to mention the shortage of qualified instructors.

Louis T. Milic 19

It is unfortunately true that composition theory has been going in circles for the last two or three decades and that the level of composition among freshmen has been declining. Those who refer to the good old days are usually rebuffed with sociological facts, such as the greater percentage of students in college now compared to half a century ago. As the base broadens, the average must go down. This is doubtless true, but it is not the entire answer. That, I believe, must be sought in an unhappy confusion in the minds of the teachers of composition. These unfortunates, beginning some three or four decades ago, threw rhetoric into the wastebasket, partly under the stimulus of the new Crocean discovery and partly under the influence of factors which also resulted in the dismissal of Latin from the curriculum, and were left with nothing to teach. Until about 1920, composition texts were rhetorics. After that, they became almost everything else, with results that have horrified all observers. The combination of the individualist theory—Write naturally!—and the organic theory—Content and form are inseparable!—has become a talisman so powerful that only scorn is reserved for those who would profess to doubt its magic power. In fact, it is considered a truth so self-evident that it hardly needs to be stated and thus it underlies the thinking of all or nearly all those who teach composition by any method, even the new rhetoricians.

The welter of theories and panaceas currently ornamenting the composition scene results, I believe, from this fundamental theoretical unsoundness: form cannot be taught by those who do not believe in it and the creative expression of personality cannot be interpreted as a reasonable compromise between form and substance. If we want to teach something in our composition classes, it may be that we must return to some form of rhetoric, which is honestly and unashamedly concerned with form and not with content. It seems to have evaded the scrutiny of interested parties that the decline in composition has not been a feature of educational systems still backwardly tied to old-fashioned rhetorical methods, including Italy, France, Germany, Spain and England. Perhaps there is a lesson in this.

A distinction may need to be made, also, between the best theory of style for teaching composition and the best theory for analyzing literary works. For teaching, a dualistic theory seems to be essential, at least in the early stages, until the maturing of the literary personality has had an opportunity to influence the student's style. For analysis, the problem is somewhat different. A fusion of expressive and unconscious theories seems to conform to the general practice. Writers, that is, write in a certain way because they select the most effective artifices of expression, but also because they are unconsciously bound to the requirements of individual personality.

The monistic view of style, therefore, cannot be allowed to infect the teaching of our subject, for it vitiates all the available pedagogical resources of rhetoric. In the college composition course, which represents for most students their first formal training in rhetoric, an awareness must be instilled of the existence of alternatives, of different ways of saying the same thing, of the options that the language offers. In this task, the perhaps exhausted vein of the old rhetoric may need a transfusion from the new. To aid instruction in the mechanism of expression, a systematic study of linguistics (rather than a helter-skelter travelogue) may also have a significant place. At the moment, however, only the direction of the journey is clear: the details of the itinerary are waiting to be discovered.

WINSTON WEATHERS

The Rhetoric of the Series

Winston Weathers teaches English at the University of Tulsa. His recent book The Strategy of Style *(1967), written with Otis Winchester, is an expansion of the theory of style presented in "The Rhetoric of the Series." In his essay Weathers defines style as "the art of choosing." In this sense his theory coincides with Milic's. But in examining series construction in formal terms of length, punctuation, and use of conjunctions, Weathers is also concerned with style as meaning. His argument thus stands between Beardsley's organic and Milic's dualistic theories.*

Style is the art of choosing, and one of our tasks, as writers and teachers of writing, is to identify as many compositional choices as possible. Our comprehension—and practice—of style improves as we organize verbal locutions and construction into areas of choice and indicate how the choice within any given area is to be made. Any such exercise seems valid, even if our conclusions are not always definitive or absolute.

I would like to discuss in this article so simple a construction as the series. "I went to the store and bought bread, milk, butter, and eggs." Nothing could be more common than that. And yet the stylist must be concerned with it. For style actually begins with the simple constructions—and if we cannot organize and interpret the simple things, how can we hope to have anything like a serious rhetoric that embraces more complicated structures and devices?

I would begin by noting that the series—as the result of the number of items it contains, the presence or absence of conjunctions within it, and the degree of parallelism in its presentation—functions rhetorically in a number of different but simultaneous ways. By manipulating the series in three different areas at once, the writer can determine what sort of intellectual

From *College Composition and Communication*, XVII (December 1966), 217-221. Reprinted with the permission of the National Council of Teachers of English and Winston Weathers.

or emotional appeal he wishes to make to his audience, and can add to the actual meaning of the series—via implications about the duration of the series, the individuality of the items, the importance of the series as a whole. Creating the basic rhetorical effect by series length and then modulating that effect by the use of conjunctions and parallelism, the writer achieves an overall effect appropriate to the content and meaning of his essay.

First of all, the length of the series. Surely every writer has asked himself and every style-conscious reader has asked the writer: Why did you present a series of three illustrations rather than two, why four events rather than three, why two rather than five?

And the answer is that the writer can construct one of three kinds of series in terms of length, each kind having its own particular rhetorical quality. He can write the two-part series and create the aura of certainty, confidence, didacticism, and dogmatism. He can write the three-part series and create the effect of the normal, the reasonable, the believable, and the logical. He can write the four-or-more part series and suggest the human, emotional, diffuse, and inexplicable.

Let us look at these possibilities.

When Arnold Bennett, in *An Author's Craft,* describes a dog's encounter with a London fire engine, "He glances casually at a . . . vermilion construction . . . whizzing towards him on four wheels, preceded by a glint of brass and a wisp of steam," Bennett has chosen a two-part series ("glint of brass and wisp of steam") because the two-part series creates the effect of massive, abrupt, and final summary. The effect would have been different had he said, "whizzing towards him on four wheels, preceded by a glint of brass, a wisp of steam, and a thunder of engines." The sense of the abrupt and total would have been diminished. Likewise, Swift uses the two-part series when he says that the hides of young children "will make admirable gloves for ladies, and summer boots for fine gentlemen." Surely juvenile skins would make more things than that—say lampshades?—but Swift chose two, not three, not four items for his series, since the effect he desired, consciously or unconsciously, was that of the two-part series alone: the effect of "nothing more need be said."

This sense of finality and totality is closely related, of course, to the authoritarian tone. Consider the use of the two-part series by the didactic Mr. Fowler in *A Dictionary of Modern English Usage:* "A sentence or a passage [two-part series] is rhythmical if, when said aloud, it falls naturally into groups of words each well fitted by its length and intonation [two-part series] for its place in the whole and its relation to its neighbours [two-part series]. Rhythm is not a matter of counting syllables and measuring the distance between accents [two-part series]. . . ." In this authoritarian passage, Fowler has used four separate two-part series.

There is indeed something abrupt and unquestionable in the two-part that is the secret of its effect.

But when the writer chooses the three-part series, he is seeking the effect of something more reasonable, ordinary, and more truly representative. The three-part series, the most frequently used, is the norm, for it has the touch of the common and understandable about it. It has the aura of the true and believable sample. One hears this when Chesterton says, "I liked the quality of brownness in October woods, or in beer, or in the peat-streams of the North." The sense of abruptness and finality in the two-part series is gone; the sense of the reasonable and even logical has been added. If Chesterton had said, "I liked the quality of brownness in October woods or in beer" there would have been an either-or quality to the series, a greater sense of an unbending position. With the three-part series he softens the list, expands its dimensions just enough to make it reasonable.

This use of the normative three-part series is clearly seen in this passage from Thoreau: "That age will be rich indeed when . . . the Vaticans shall be filled with Vedas and Zendavestas and Bibles, with Homers and Dantes and Shakespeares." Thoreau's very breaking up of a longer series into two distinct three-part series is revealing. And the same predilection for the normative series is seen in this Thoreau passage: "It is time that villages were universities and their elder inhabitants the fellows of universities. . . . Shall the world be confined to one Paris or one Oxford forever? Cannot students be boarded here and get a liberal education under the skies of Concord? Can we not hire some Abelard to lecture to us? Alas. . . . we are kept from school too long."

The effect of the three-part series is normality and reasonableness, and it is related distantly to the syllogism. But when the writer creates the third kind of series, of four-or-more parts, he achieves another effect: that of plethora, abundance, the unlimited, or what Professor Corbett calls in his *Classical Rhetoric for the Modern Student,* the "weighty and exhausting." At times the effect is extended to that of the diversity that is confusion. With this longer series, the writer moves from the certainty of the two-part, from the reasonableness of the three-part, to the more complicated emotional realism of the catalogue.

Dostoevsky, for instance, wrote in a letter to his brother Mihail: "There remains in me my heart and the same flesh and blood which can also love, and suffer, and desire, and remember, and this, after all, is life." Dostoevsky's four-part series does contribute to the effect of life, just as Bartolomeo Vanzetti's five-part series contributes to the effect of emotion in a letter to Dante Sacco: "You shall know, when you will be able to understand this tragedy . . . how good and brave your father has been with you . . . during these eight years of struggle, sorrow, passion, anguish, and agony." Being a series of life and emotion, the four-part becomes the series of plea and petition also, as for example in Shelley's attempt to persuade Keats to come to Italy: "I spare declamation about the statues, and the paintings, and the ruins, and in a greater piece of forebearance, about the mountain streams, fields, the colours of the sky, and the sky itself." All in all, the catalogue series suggests a world human, pluralistic, and emotional.

By using these three different kinds of series the writer can achieve different rhetorical effects—and he can adapt his writing to his subject and audience. In fact, each series may lend itself to a particular kind of writing, to certain broad areas of utterance.

Consider that a writer, recording and arranging the words of a divine figure, may tend to use the two-part series, as in this Biblical passage that J. Middleton Murry says "stirs your depths": "Come unto me, all ye that labour and are heavy laden [two-part series], and I will give you rest. Take my yoke upon you, and learn of me [two-part series]; for I am meek and lowly [two-part series] in heart; and ye shall find rest unto your souls. For my yoke is easy, and my burden is light [two-part series]." This use is appropriate, for, being a series of confidence, certainty, even dogmatism, it meets the very conditions of religious and apocalyptic statement.

But if the writer is a political leader, concerned with making his own position tenable, reasonable, and acceptable to followers, he may tend to use the three-part series. Julius Caesar's famous, "I came, I saw, I conquered," is a choice made, no doubt, out of many possibilities. Caesar could have written, "I came and I conquered," but that suggests dogmatism and tyranny. He could have written, "I came, I saw, I fought, I conquered, I claimed, and I kept," but that suggests something less than heroic, filled as it is with busyness, even confusion. Caesar obviously chose the three-part series because it avoids the extremes of more-than-human certainty on the one hand and a kind of emotional pleading on the other. Or consider Lincoln's "of the people, by the people, for the people." His choice of the three-part series suggests a desire to create the effect of the believable and judicious selection. Milton, in a passage Murry describes as "irresistible," uses the three-part series in discussing matters of state: "When complaints are freely heard, deeply considered, and speedily reformed, then is the utmost bound of civil liberty attained. . . ."

But yet, what if the leader of a people is not trying to make reasonable new ideas or events that have already taken place or his own actions? What if he is trying to persuade, convince, and speak to the emotions? He may move on to the four-or-more-part series, as Winston Churchill does in his famous "blood, sweat, toil, and tears." How different the effect if Churchill had said, "blood, sweat, and tears," how much more ordinary and common; how much different had he said, "blood and tears," how definite and complete, with no more possible sacrifices to be made.

Any one writer, of course, can make a demonstration of all three possibilities as his subject matter changes. Bacon does this when he uses the two-part series to achieve the didactic effect for which he is noted; to imply, "This is the way it is, you don't have to question it." "Truth may perhaps come to the price of a pearl, that showeth best by day; but it will not rise to the price of a diamond or carbuncle, that showeth best in varied lights." But Bacon can move on to the three-part series to make his statements less didactic, more reasonable, as he does when he writes on the subject of studies: "Studies serve for delight, for ornament, and for ability. . . . Crafty men condemn studies, simple men admire them, and wise men use them." Obviously Bacon knew that in talking about studies, a potentially unpopular subject, one might well take less a dogmatic tone, more a reasonable one. And when Bacon deals with subjects of emotional nature, or certain subjects and aspects of human behavior, somehow beyond the reasonable, he can move to the catalogue series: "Groans and convulsions, and a discolored face, and friends weeping, and blacks, and obsequies, and the like show death terrible." Or "Revenge triumphs over death; love slights it; honor aspireth to it; grief flieth to it; fear pre-occupieth it." The mystery of death seems to deserve the longer list of items.

I realize that these interpretations of rhetorical effect are open to discussion. Yet I think this is part of our task as writers and stylists—to venture forth with at least proposed interpretations; we can always refine and polish, or even change. To leave rhetorical devices blank and unevaluated is to avoid the whole matter and to leave style in as nebulous a condition as ever.

Writers do, of course, manipulate more than the length of the series. Whatever the basic rhetorical effect achieved through length, modulation can occur by manipulation of conjunctions and parallelism.

Looking at the use of conjunctions, we observe that the writer works from a norm—if he has no reason to do otherwise, he constructs his series with the normal single conjunction: "blood, sweat, toil, and tears." From this norm, he can go in either of two directions—he can add conjunctions or omit them.

When the writer omits conjunctions, he adds to the series an implicit statement: "in a hurry," or "all at once." When Priestly says, "If . . . in July 1914 . . . everybody, emperors, kings, archdukes, statesmen, generals, journalists had been suddenly smitten with an intense desire to do nothing . . . then we should all have been much better off than we are now," he is saying, via asyndeton, that everybody all at once, without debate, in a hurry, would have done so and so. Likewise, when H. Caudwell says of the artist, "His nature leads him constantly to explore, constantly to seek new aspects of truth," the omission of the conjunction suggests the idea of simultaneity, of two things occurring at once. But asyndeton suggests also integrity, not only that a number of things are happening at once, but that a number of things are really one thing: one act, quality, or person. That is why Caesar said, "I came, I saw, I conquered." If Caesar had said, "I came, I saw, and I conquered," he would have lost the effect of a single integrated act. If he had said, "I came, and I saw, and I conquered," he would have created the effect of separated, even isolated events. And, in addition, he would have created the effect of slow rather than rapid time.

Caesar's decision not to use polysyndeton suggests what the stylistic effect of the many conjunctions is. Polysyndeton adds to the series the statement "and in no hurry" or "these things definitely occurred one after the other." A good example is from Lewis Mumford: "Time-keeping passed into time-serving and time-accounting and time-rationing." With time as his subject, Mumford appropriately chose to add the effect of slow time by the use of polysyndeton. Or consider this example from Yeats' *Autobiography:* "My first memories are fragmentary and isolated and contemporaneous, as though one remembered some first moments of the Seven Days." Here again, the writer is dealing with the very subject of time's passing, of memory of the past, and to support that subject he adds the modulation of polysyndeton.

Polysyndeton also moves a series into separateness, making increasingly discrete and clear the various items. When Swift says, "They are every day dying and rotting, by cold, and famine, and filth, and vermine, as fast as can be reasonably expected," he has included in the series not only the idea that death is taking place over a long period of time, but he is making sure the reader is aware of each single way of dying. If Swift had said they are dying "by cold, famine, filth, and vermine," he would have reduced the discrete quality of each item; and if he had said "by cold, famine, filth, vermine" he would have suggested not multiplicity of the problems, but that the problems were all of one simple, contained category.

If a writer does not wish to suggest either simultaneity or great duration or does not wish to suggest either the singleness or multiplicity of his ideas, then he will use the normal single conjunction. But as he wishes to add any of these ideas to the basic rhetorical effect of his series, he can take advantage of conjunction modulation.

Likewise, the writer can manipulate parallel structure of the series in order to say something about the importance of the series as a whole. Parallelism is the propriety of the series, but the writer, without disturbing that propriety, can establish choices that will determine the degree of intensity, emphasis, and significance that he wishes the series to have. Perfect parallelism creates the greatest emphasis—it is the device a writer uses to say "this series is to be especially noticed" or "this series is to be read on a high level of consideration." Then, as the writer wished to de-emphasize his series or to relieve it of its obviousness, he moves away from perfect parallelism.

Manipulation of parallelism is primarily a matter of interrupting the parallelism or of diversifying the length of the various elements put into parallel relationship. The writer can construct exact parallelism, as Lewis Mumford does when he says, "The modern industrial regime could do without coal and iron and steam." The series of "coal and iron and steam" is presented in exact word-for-word parallelism. But in another series in the same essay, Mumford chooses to reduce the impact of such parallelism: "In its relationship to determinable quantities of energy, to standardization, to automatic action, and finally to its own special product, accurate timing, the clock has been the foremost machine in modern techniques." This is a four-part series with each of the items of different length: "determinable quantities of energy" [four words: a syntax of adjective, noun, adjectival prepositional phrase]; "standardization" [one word]; "automatic action" [two words: adjective, noun]; and "its own special product, accurate timing" [six words: three adjectives, a noun, a two-word appositive]. Note also that there is an interruption between the third and fourth items with the word "finally."

This process of interruption and diversification can be extended to the point that the parallelism is almost entirely muted or disguised, with the

author, in effect, removing the series from the spotlight—though in his manipulations, the writer cannot move so surely from one category to another, as he can with length or conjunctions. With parallelism the writer is dealing with degrees rather than categories and is moving along a spectrum. Nevertheless we might suggest that the writer generally makes his choice from among perfect parallelism; moderately interrupted and diversified parallelism; and extremely interrupted and diversified parallelism. This at least helps suggest three basic possibilities.

This then is the outline of a proposed rhetoric of the series. With choices to be made concerning the number of items in a series, the use of conjunctions, and the degree of parallelism, the writer can construct for himself a paradigm of a least twenty-seven possible presentations. Establishing these twenty-seven choices, the writer is in a better position to make the particular selection he needs in order to say what he really wants to say. The paradigm has probably always existed in the unconscious of the successful stylist, but for the sake of pedagogy, if nothing else, we need to bring this paradigm (and all such paradigms) out into the open, present it to the writer and would-be writer, and help him make more than hit-and-miss stylistic decisions.

All we really say to the student of writing now about the series is that series do exist, that a series of equal ideas should be presented in compound, co-ordinate form, that parallelism is the proper structure for so doing, etc. I don't believe we say much about the choices that can be made and why they should be made.

I offer this paper as prolegomenon in that direction.

FRANCIS CHRISTENSEN

A Generative Rhetoric of the Sentence

Francis Christensen is professor of English at the University of Southern California. He has recently published Notes Toward a New Rhetoric *(1967), a collection of essays for composition teachers. The article reprinted here, like Weathers' essay on the series, approaches the problem of form and content by demonstrating the relationship within the sentence between*

"A Generative Rhetoric of the Sentence" from *Notes Toward a New Rhetoric* by Francis Christensen. Copyright © 1967 by Francis Christensen. Reprinted by permission of Harper & Row, Publishers, and the National Council of Teachers of English.

grammatical structures and meaning. Following this approach, Professor Christensen formulates four principles of what he calls "generative rhetoric": (1) that composition is essentially a process of "addition"; (2) that "direction of movement" is a basic principle in sentence modification; (3) that "levels of abstraction" correspond to the layers of grammatical structure of a sentence; and (4) that "texture" (or style) is produced by "addition," "direction of movement," and "levels of abstraction."

If the new grammar is to be brought to bear on composition, it must be brought to bear on the rhetoric of the sentence. We have a workable and teachable, if not a definitive, modern grammar; but we do not have, despite several titles, a modern rhetoric.

In composition courses we do not really teach our captive charges to write better—we merely *expect* them to. And we do not teach them how to write better because we do not know how to teach them to write better. And so we merely go through the motions. Our courses with their tear-out work books and four-pound anthologies are elaborate evasions of the real problem. They permit us to put in our time and do almost anything else we'd rather be doing instead of buckling down to the hard work of making a difference in the student's understanding and manipulation of language.

With hundreds of handbooks and rhetorics to draw from, I have never been able to work out a program for teaching the sentence as I find it in the work of contemporary writers. The chapters on the sentence all adduce the traditional rhetorical classification of sentences as loose, balanced, and periodic. But the term *loose* seems to be taken as a pejorative (it sounds immoral); our students, no Bacons or Johnsons, have little occasion for balanced sentences; and some of our worst perversions of style come from the attempt to teach them to write periodic sentences. The traditional grammatical classification of sentences is equally barren. Its use in teaching composition rests on a semantic confusion, equating complexity of structure with complexity of thought and vice versa. But very simple thoughts may call for very complex grammatical constructions. Any moron can say "I don't know who done it." And some of us might be puzzled to work out the grammar of "All I want is all there is," although any chit can think it and say it and act on it.

The chapters on the sentence all appear to assume that we think naturally in primer sentences, progress naturally to compound sentences, and must be taught to combine the primer sentences into complex sentences—and that complex sentences are the mark of maturity. We need a rhetoric of the sentence that will do more than combine the ideas of primer sentences. We need one that will *generate* ideas.

For the foundation of such a generative or productive rhetoric I take the statement from John Erskine, the originator of the Great Books courses, himself a novelist. In an essay "The Craft of Writing" *(Twentieth Century English,* Philosophical Library, 1946) he discusses a principle of the writer's craft, which though known he says to all practitioners, he has never seen

discussed in print. The principle is this: "When you write, you make a point, not by subtracting as though you sharpened a pencil, but by adding." We have all been told that the formula for good writing is the concrete noun and the active verb. Yet Erskine says, "What you say is found not in the noun but in what you add to qualify the noun . . . The noun, the verb, and the main clause serve merely as the base on which meaning will rise . . . The modifier is the essential part of any sentence." The foundation, then, for a generative or productive rhetoric of the sentence is that composition is essentially a process of *addition*.

But speech is linear, moving in time, and writing moves in linear space, which is analogous to time. When you add a modifier, whether to the noun, the verb, or the main clause, you must add it either before the head or after it. If you add it before the head, the direction of modification can be indicated by an arrow pointing forward; if you add it after, by an arrow pointing backward. Thus we have the second principle of a generative rhetoric—the principle of *direction of modification* or *direction of movement*.

Within the clause there is not much scope for operating with this principle. The positions of the various sorts of close, or restrictive, modifiers are generally fixed and the modifiers are often obligatory—"The man who came to dinner remained till midnight." Often the only choice is whether to add modifiers. What I have seen of attempts to bring structural grammar to bear on composition usually boils down to the injunction to "load the patterns." Thus "pattern practice" sets students to accreting sentences like this: "The small boy on the red bicycle who lives with his happy parents on our shady street often coasts down the steep street until he comes to the city park." This will never do. It has no rhythm and hence no life; it is tone-deaf. It is the seed that will burgeon into gobbledygook. One of the hardest things in writing is to keep the noun clusters and verb clusters short.

It is with modifiers added to the clause—that is, with sentence modifiers— that the principle comes into full play. The typical sentence of modern English, the kind we can best spend our efforts trying to teach, is what we may call the *cumulative sentence*. The main clause, which may or may not have a sentence modifier before it, advances the discussion; but the additions move backward, as in this clause, to modify the statement of the main clause or more often to explicate or exemplify it, so that the sentence has a flowing and ebbing movement, advancing to a new position and then pausing to consolidate it, leaping and lingering as the popular ballad does. The first part of the preceding compound sentence has one addition, placed within it; the second part has 4 words in the main clause and 49 in the five additions placed after it.

The cumulative sentence is the opposite of the periodic sentence. It does not represent the idea as conceived, pondered over, reshaped, packaged, and delivered cold. It is dynamic rather than static, representing the mind thinking. The main clause ("the additions move backward" above) exhausts the mere fact of the idea; logically, there is nothing more to say. The additions stay with the same idea, probing its bearings and implications, exemplifying it or seeking an analogy or metaphor for it, or reducing it to details. Thus the mere form of the sentence generates ideas. It serves the needs of both the writer and the reader, the writer by compelling him to examine his thought, the reader by letting him into the writer's thought.

Addition and direction of movement are structural principles. They involve the grammatical character of the sentence. Before going on to other principles, I must say a word about the best grammar as the foundation for rhetoric. I cannot conceive any useful transactions between teacher and students unless they have in common a language for talking about sentences. The best grammar is the grammar that best displays the layers of structure of the English sentence. The best I have found in a textbook is the combination of immediate constituent and transformation grammar in Paul Roberts's *English Sentences.* Traditional grammar, whether over-simple as in the school tradition or over-complex as in the scholarly tradition, does not reveal the language as it operates; it leaves everything, to borrow a phrase from Wordsworth, "in disconnection dead and spiritless." *English Sentences* is oversimplified and it has gaps, but it displays admirably the structures that rhetoric must work with—primarily sentence modifiers, including relative and subordinate clauses, but, far more important, the array of noun, verb, and adjective clusters. It is paradoxical that Professor Roberts, who has done so much to make the teaching of composition possible, should himself be one of those who think that it cannot be taught. Unlike Ulysses, he doesn't see any work for Telemachus to work.

Layers of structure, as I have said, is a grammatical concept. To bring in the dimension of meaning, we need a third principle—that of *levels of generality* or *levels of abstraction.* The main clause is likely to be stated in general or abstract or plural terms. With the main clause stated, the forward movement of the sentence stops, the writer shifts down to a lower level of generality or abstraction or to singular terms, and goes back over the same ground at this lower level.[1] "He has just bought a new car, a 1963½ Ford, a Galaxie, a fastback hardtop with four-on-the-floor shift." There is no theoretical limit to the number of structural layers or levels, each at a lower level of generality, any or all of them compounded, that a speaker or writer may use. For a speaker, listen to Lowell Thomas; for a writer, study William Faulkner. To a single independent clause he may append a page of additions, but usually all clear, all grammatical, once we have learned how to read him. Or, if you prefer, study Hemingway, the master of the simple sentence: "George was coming down in the telemark position, kneeling, one leg forward and bent, the other trailing, his sticks hanging like some insect's thin legs, kicking up puffs of snow, and finally the whole kneeling, trailing figure coming around in a beautiful right curve, crouching, the legs shot forward

---

[1]Cf. Leo Rockas, "Abstract and Concrete Sentences," CCC, May 1963. Rockas describes sentences as abstract or concrete, the abstract implying the concrete and vice versa. Readers and writers, he says, must have the knack of apprehending the concrete in the abstract and the abstract in the concrete. This is true and valuable. I am saying that within a single sentence the writer may present more than one level of generality, translating the abstract into the more concrete in added levels.

and back, the body leaning out against the swing, the sticks accenting the curve like points of light, all in a wild cloud of snow."

This brings me to the fourth, and last, principle, that of texture. *Texture* provides a descriptive or evaluative term. If a writer adds to few of his nouns or verbs or main clauses and adds little, the texture may be said to be thin. The style will be plain or bare. The writing of most of our students is thin —even threadbare. But if he adds frequently or much or both, then the texture may be said to be dense or rich. One of the marks of an effective style, especially in narrative, is variety in the texture, the texture varying with the change in pace, the variation in texture producing the change in pace. It is not true, as I have seen it asserted, that fast action calls for short sentences; the action is fast in the sentence by Hemingway above. In our classes, we have to work for greater density and variety in texture and greater concreteness and particularity in what is added.

I have been operating at a fairly high level of generality. Now I must downshift and go over the same points with examples. The most graphic way to exhibit the layers of structure is to indent the word groups of a sentence and to number the levels. Since in the narrow columns of this journal indentation is possible only with short sentences whose additions are short, I have used it with only the first three sentences; the reader is urged to copy out the others for himself. I have added symbols to mark the grammatical character of the additions: SC, subordinate clause; RC, relative clause; NC, noun cluster; VC, verb cluster; AC, adjective cluster; Abs, absolute (i.e., a VC with a subject of its own); PP, prepositional phrase. With only a few exceptions (in some the punctuation may be questioned) the elements set off as on a lower level are marked by junctures or punctuation. The examples have been chosen to illustrate the range of constructions used in the lower levels; after the first few they are arranged by the number of levels. The examples could have been drawn from poetry as well as from prose. Those not attributed are by students.

1

1 He shook his hands,
   2 a quick shake, (NC)
      3 fingers down, (Abs)
         4 like a pianist. (PP)—Sinclair Lewis

2

   2 Calico-coated, (AC)
   2 small bodied, (AC)
   2 with delicate legs and pink faces (PP)
      3 in which their mismatched eyes rolled wild and subdued, (RC)
1 they huddled,
   2 gaudy motionless and alert, (AC)
   2 wild as deer, (AC)
   2 deadly as rattlesnakes, (AC)
   2 quiet as doves. (AC)—William Faulkner

3

1 The bird's eye, / , remained fixed upon him;
  2 bright and silly as a sequin (AC)
1 its little bones, / , seemed swooning in his hand.—Stella Benson
  2 wrapped . . . in a warm padding of feathers (VC)

4

(1) The jockeys sat bowed and relaxed, moving a little at the waist with the movement of their horses$^{2\text{-VC}}$.—Katherine Anne Porter

5

(1) The flame sidled up the match, driving a film of moisture and a thin strip of darker grey before it$^{2\text{-VC}}$.

6

(1) She came among them behind the man, gaunt in the gray shapeless garment and the sunbonnet$^{2\text{-AC}}$, wearing stained canvas gymnasium shoes$^{2\text{-VC}}$.—Faulkner

7

(1) The Texan turned to the nearest gatepost and climbed to the top of it, his alternate thighs thick and bulging in the tight jeans$^{2\text{-Abs}}$, the butt of his pistol catching and losing the sun in pearly gleams$^{2\text{-Abs}}$.—Faulkner

8

(1) He could sail for hours, searching the blanched grasses below him with his telescopic eyes$^{2\text{-VC}}$, gaining height against the wind$^{2\text{-VC}}$, descending in mile-long, gently declining swoops when he curved and rode back$^{2\text{-VC}}$, never beating a wing$^{2\text{-VC}}$.—Walter Van Tilburg Clark

9

(1) The gay-sweatered skaters are quicksilvering around the frosty rink, the girls gliding and spinning$^{2\text{-Abs}}$, the boys swooping and darting$^{2\text{-Abs}}$, their arms flailing like wings$^{3\text{-Abs}}$.

10

(1) He stood at the top of the stairs and watched me, I waiting for him to call me up$^{2\text{-Abs}}$, he hesitating to come down$^{2\text{-Abs}}$, his lips nervous with the suggestion of a smile$^{3\text{-Abs}}$, mine asking whether the smile meant come, or go away$^{3\text{-Abs}}$.

11

(1) Joad's lips stretched tight over his long teeth for a moment, and (1) he licked his lips, like a dog$^{2\text{-PP}}$, two licks$^{3\text{-NC}}$, one in each direction from the middle$^{4\text{-NC}}$.—Steinbeck

12

(1) We all live in two realities: one of seeming fixity$^{2\text{-NC}}$, with institutions, dogmas, rules of punctuation, and routines$^{3\text{-PP}}$, the calendared and clock-

wise world of all but futile round on round[4-NC]; and one of whirling and flying electrons, dreams, and possibilities[2-NC], behind the clock[3-PP].— Sidney Cox

13

(1) It was as though someone, somewhere, had touched a lever and shifted gears, and (1) the hospital was set for night running, smooth and silent[2-AC], its normal clatter and hum muffled[2-Abs], the only sounds heard in the whitewalled room distant and unreal[2-Abs]: a low hum of voices from the nurse's desk[3-NC], quickly stifled[4-VC], the soft squish of rubber-soled shoes on the tiled corridor[3-NC], starched white cloth rustling against itself[3-NC], and outside, the lonesome whine of wind in the country night[3-NC], and the Kansas dust beating against the windows[3-NC].

14

(1) The beach sounds are jazzy, percussion fixing the mode[2-Abs]—the surf cracking and booming in the distance[3-Abs], a little nearer dropped barbells clanking[3-Abs], steel gym rings, flung together[4-VC], ringing[3-Abs], palm fronds rustling above me[3-Abs], like steel brushes washing over a snare drum[4-PP], troupes of sandals splatting and shuffling on the sandy cement[3-Abs], their beat varying[4-Abs], syncopation emerging and disappearing with changing paces[5-Abs].

15

(1) A small negro girl develops from the sheet of glare-frosted walk, walking barefooted[2-VC], her bare legs striking and coiling from the hot cement[3-Abs], her feet curling in[4-Abs], only the outer edges touching[5-Abs].

16

(1) The swells moved rhythmically toward us irregularly faceted[2-VC], sparkling[2-VC], growing taller and more powerful[2-VC], until the shining crest bursts[3-SC], a transparent sheet of pale green water spilling over the top[4-Abs], breaking into blue-white foam as it cascades down the front of the wave[5-VC], piling up in a frothy mound that the diminishing wave pushes up against the pilings[5-VC], with a swishmash[6-PP], the foam drifting back[5-Abs], like a lace fan opened over the shimmering water as the spent wave returns whispering to the sea[6-PP].

The best starting point for a composition unit based on these four principles is with two-level narrative sentences, first with one second-level addition (sentences 4, 5), then with two or more parallel ones (6, 7, 8). Anyone sitting in his room with his eyes closed could write the main clause of most of the examples; the discipline comes with the additions, provided they are based at first on immediate observation, requiring the student to phrase an exact observation in exact language. This can hardly fail to be exciting to a class: it is life, with the variety and complexity of life; the workbook exercise is death. The situation is ideal also for teaching diction—abstract-concrete, general-specific, literal-metaphorical, denotative-connotative. When the sentences begin to come out right, it is time to examine the additions for their grammatical character. From then on the grammar comes to the aid of the writing and the writing reinforces the grammar. One can soon go on to multi-level narrative sentences (1, 3, 9-11, 15, 16) and then to brief narratives of three to six or seven sentences on actions that can be observed over and over again—beating eggs, making a cut with a power saw, or following a record changer's cycle or a wave's flow and ebb. Bring the record changer to class. Description, by contrast, is static, picturing appearance rather than behavior. The constructions to master are the noun and adjective clusters and the absolute (13, 14). Then the descriptive noun cluster must be taught to ride piggy-back on the narrative sentence, so that description and narration are interleaved: "In the morning we went out into a new world, a glistening crystal and white world, each skeleton tree, each leafless bush, even the heavy, drooping power lines sheathed in icy crystal." The next step is to develop the sense for variety in texture and change in pace that all good narrative demands.

In the next unit, the same four principles can be applied to the expository paragraph. But this is a subject for another paper.

I want to anticipate two possible objections. One is that the sentences are long. By freshman English standards they are long, but I could have produced far longer ones from works freshmen are expected to read. Of the sentences by students, most were written as finger exercises in the first few weeks of the course. I try in narrative sentences to push to level after level, not just two or three, but four, five, or six, even more, as far as the students' powers of observation will take them. I want them to become sentence acrobats, to dazzle by their syntactic dexterity. I'd rather have to deal with hyperemia than anemia. I want to add my voice to that of James Coleman (*CCC*, December 1962) deploring our concentration on the plain style.

The other objection is that my examples are mainly descriptive and narrative—and today in freshman English we teach only exposition. I deplore this limitation as much as I deplore our limitation to the plain style. Both are a sign that we have sold our proper heritage for a pot of message. In permitting them, the English department undercuts its own discipline. Even if our goal is only utilitarian prose, we can teach diction and sentence structure far more effectively through a few controlled exercises in description and narration than we can by starting right off with exposition (Theme One, 500 words, precipitates *all* the problems of writing). The student has something to communicate—his immediate sense impressions, which can stand a bit of exercising. The material is not already verbalized—he has to match language to sense impressions. His acuteness in observation and in choice of words can be judged by fairly objective standards—is the sound of a bottle of milk being set down on a concrete step suggested better by *clink* or *clank?* In the examples, study the diction for its accuracy, rising at times to the truly imaginative. Study the use of metaphor, of comparision. This verbal virtuosity and syntactical ingenuity can be made to carry over into expository writing.

But this is still utilitarian. What I am proposing carries over of itself into the study of literature. It makes the student a better reader of literature. It helps him thread the syntactical mazes of much mature writing, and it gives him insight into that elusive thing we call style. Last year a student told of re-reading a book by her favorite author, Willa Cather, and of realizing for the first time *why* she liked reading her: she could understand and appreciate the style. For some students, moreover, such writing makes life more interesting as well as giving them a way to share their interest with others. When they learn how to put concrete details into a sentence, they begin to look at life with more alertness. If it is liberal education we are concerned with, it is just possible that these things are more important than anything we can achieve when we set our sights on the plain style in expository prose.

I want to conclude with a historical note. My thesis in this paragraph is that modern prose like modern poetry has more in common with the seventeenth than with the eighteenth century and that we fail largely because we are operating from an eighteenth century base. The shift from the complex to the cumulative sentence is more profound than it seems. It goes deep in grammar, requiring a shift from the subordinate clause (the staple of our trade) to the cluster (so little understood as to go almost unnoticed in our textbooks). And I have only lately come to see that this shift has historical implications. The cumulative sentence is the modern form of the loose sentence that characterized the anti-Ciceronian movement in the seventeenth century. This movement, according to Morris W. Croll[2], began with Montaigne and Bacon and continued with such men as Donne, Brown, Taylor, Pascal. Croll calls their prose baroque. To Montaigne, its art was the art of being natural; to Pascal, its eloquence was the eloquence that mocks formal eloquence; to Bacon, it presented knowledge so that it could be examined, not so that it must be accepted.

But the Senecan amble was banished from England when "the direct sensuous apprehension of thought" (T. S. Eliot's words) gave way to Cartesian reason or intellect. The consequences of this shift in sensibility are well summarized by Croll:

> To this mode of thought we are to trace almost all the features of modern literary education and criticism, or at least of what we should have called modern a generation ago: the study of the precise meaning of words; the reference to dictionaries as literary authorities; the study of the sentence as a logical unit alone; the careful circumscription of its limits and the gradual reduction of its length; . . .[3] the attempt to reduce grammar to an exact science; the idea that forms of speech are

---

[2]"The Baroque Style in Prose," **Studies in English Philology: A Miscellany in Honor of Frederick Klaeber** (1929), reprinted in A. M. Witherspoon and F. J. Warnke, **Seventeenth-Century Prose and Poetry,** 2nd ed. (1963). I have used the latter, and I have borrowed from Croll in my description of the cumulative sentence.
[3]The omitted item concerns punctuation and is not relevant here. In using this scale, note the phrase "what we should have called modern a generation ago" and remember that Croll was writing in 1929.

always either correct or incorrect; the complete subjection of the laws of motion and expression in style to the laws of logic and standardization—in short, the triumph, during two centuries, of grammatical over rhetorical ideas. (p. 1077)

Here is a seven-point scale any teacher of composition can use to take stock. He can find whether he is based in the eighteenth century or in the twentieth and whether he is consistent—completely either an ancient or a modern—or is just a crazy mixed-up kid.

FRANCIS CHRISTENSEN

A Generative Rhetoric
of the Paragraph

An extension of the method proposed in "A Generative Rhetoric of the Sentence," the essay below deals with the structure of the paragraph. In this essay the thesis sentence is considered the equivalent in the paragraph to the main clause (the highest level of abstraction) in the sentence, and the other sentences in the paragraph are equivalent to modifiers in the sentence. This is one of a series of essays on paragraph analysis which appeared in College Composition and Communication *during 1965 and 1966. The May 1966 issue of that journal includes a "Symposium on the Paragraph" in which Professor Christensen replies to his critics.*

In my article "A Generative Rhetoric of the Sentence" (*CCC*, October 1963), I said that the principles used there in analyzing the sentence were no less applicable to the paragraph. My purpose here is to make good that claim, to show that the paragraph has, or may have, a structure as definable and traceable as that of the sentence and that it can be analyzed in the same way. In fact, since writing that paper, I have come to see that the parallel between sentence and paragraph is much closer than I suspected, so close, indeed, that as Josephine Miles put it (in a letter) the paragraph seems to be only a macro-sentence or meta-sentence.

The chapters on the paragraph in our textbooks are so nearly alike in conception that one could almost say that, apart from the examples, the only striking difference is in the choice of *indention* or *indentation*. The prescription is always the same: the writer should work out a topic sentence and then choose one of the so-called methods of paragraph development to substantiate it. The topic sentence may appear at the beginning or at the end of the paragraph or anywhere in between, or it may be merely "implied," a sort of ectoplasmic ghost hovering over the paragraph. Besides this, some books speak of "paragraph movement"—chronological (as in narrative), spatial (as in description), logical (as in discursive writing). If the movement is logical, it may be inductive or deductive or a combination of the two, and some books offer diagrams, as systems analysts use flow charts, to picture the thought funneling down from the topic sentence or down to it.

This prescription for writers and the analysis it is based on are even more unworkable than the conventional treatment of the sentence as simple-compound-complex, with emphasis on the complex, or as loose-balanced-periodic, with emphasis on the periodic. I doubt that many of us write many paragraphs the way we require our charges to write them or that we could find many paragraphs that exemplify the methods of development or the patterns of movement.[1]

First, the methods of paragraph development. These methods are real, but they are simply methods of development—period. They are no more relevant to the paragraph than, on the short side, to the sentence or, on the long side, to a run of several paragraphs or to a paper as long as this or a chapter. They are the topics of classical rhetoric. They are the channels our minds naturally run in whether we are writing a sentence or a paragraph or planning a paper. There is no point in restricting a class (as for a whole semester in a freshman course I once taught) to a single method of development until the last week, when we reached what the textbook called a "combination of methods." It is almost impossible to write a paragraph without employing a combination of methods or to find paragraphs that do not.

In another article ("Notes Toward a New Rhetoric: II. A Lesson from Hemingway," *College English*, October 1963), I maintained that in representational (or narrative-descriptive) writing, where the aim is to *picture* actions and objects, there are only three methods of development, of description, as I called them, only three things one can do to present an image. These methods are to point to (1) a quality or attribute or to (2) a detail or (3) to make a comparison. A single sentence may exemplify all three: "The gypsy was walking out toward the bull again, walking heel-and-toe, insultingly, like a ballroom dancer, the red shafts of the banderillos twitching with his walk"—Hemingway. These methods are exactly parallel to the methods of development or support in discursive writing. The great difference is that in representational writing the methods are so few and in discursive writing so many. In either kind of writing the methods of description or develop-

---

[1] In this article I propose to deal only with the paragraphs of discursive writing and to exclude from these the short introductory and transitional and concluding paragraphs.

ment are hard to discern except in the light of what may be called a "structural analysis."

In the light of such a structural analysis, most paragraphs are like the sentences I called "cumulative." They exemplify the four principles proposed for the rhetoric of the sentence. Let us think of the topic sentence as parallel to the base clause of a sentence and the supporting sentences as parallel to the added single-word modifiers and clusters and subordinate and relative clauses. (1) Then it is obvious that there could be no paragraphs without *addition*. (2) When a supporting sentence is added, both writer and reader must see the *direction of modification* or *direction of movement*. Discerning the direction is easier in the sentence because the sentence is self-contained and the elements added differ in form from the base clause. The direction of movement in the paragraph is explained below. The failure to see the relation of each upcoming sentence to what has gone before is probably one source of the difficulty many people have in reading. (3) When sentences are added to develop a topic or subtopic, they are usually at a lower *level of generality*—usually, but not always, because sometimes an added sentence is more general than the one it is added to. (4) Finally, the more sentences the writer adds, the denser the *texture*. The paragraphs our students write are likely to be as thin-textured as their sentences, and teachers can use this structural analysis of the paragraph to *generate* paragraphs of greater depth.

I have arranged the details of this approach to the paragraph under nine headings.

1. THE PARAGRAPH MAY BE DEFINED AS A SEQUENCE OF STRUCTURALLY RELATED SENTENCES.

By a sequence of structurally related sentences I mean a group of sentences related to one another by coordination and subordination. If the first sentence of a paragraph is the topic sentence, the second is quite likely to be a comment on it, a development of it, and therefore subordinate to it. The third sentence may be coordinate with the second sentence (as in this paragraph) or subordinate to it. The fourth sentence may be coordinate with either the second or third (or with both if they themselves are coordinate, as in this paragraph) or subordinate to the third. And so on. A sentence that is not coordinate with any sentence above it or subordinate to the next above it, breaks the sequence. The paragraph has begun to drift from its moorings, or the writer has unwittingly begun a new paragraph.

2. THE TOP SENTENCE OF THE SEQUENCE IS THE TOPIC SENTENCE.

The topic sentence is comparable to the base clause of a cumulative sentence. It is the sentence on which the others depend. It is the sentence whose assertion is supported or whose meaning is explicated or whose parts are detailed by the sentences added to it. In the examples that follow, it will always be marked 1, for the top level.

3. THE TOPIC SENTENCE IS NEARLY ALWAYS THE FIRST SENTENCE OF THE SEQUENCE.

The contrast between deductive and inductive, or between analytic and synthetic as it is sometimes put, seems to have led us to assume that the one kind of movement is as common as the other and that the topic sentence therefore is as likely to appear at the end as at the beginning. The many scores of paragraphs I have analyzed for this study do not bear out this assumption. Except as noted in point 7 below, the topic sentence occurs almost invariably at the beginning. In fact, I do not have clear-cut examples of topic sentences in the other theoretically possible positions. Readers may check their own actual practice and mine in this piece.

In connected writing, the topic sentence varies greatly in how explicit it is in designating the thesis of the paragraph. Sometimes it is quite explicit; sometimes it is a mere sign pointing to the turn the new paragraph is going to take. Sometimes it is the shortest sentence of the paragraph; sometimes it is not even a grammatically complete sentence. It seems to me that these differences are irrelevant, provided only that the reader gets the signal and the writer remembers the signal he has called.

4. SIMPLE SEQUENCES ARE OF TWO SORTS—COORDINATE AND SUBORDINATE.

Here the parallel between sentence and paragraph becomes fully evident. In analyzing the rhetoric of the sentence, I described what I called the two-level and the multilevel sentence. Here is an example of each and a paragraph exactly parallel in structure with each. The two sets of terms seem to me necessary to put the emphasis where it is needed in teaching and to avoid conflict with the use in grammar of *coordination* and *subordination*.

A. TWO-LEVEL SENTENCE

1 [Lincoln's] words still linger on the lips—
  2 eloquent and cunning, yes,
  2 vindictive and sarcastic in political debate,
  2 rippling and ribald in jokes,
  2 reverent in the half-formed utterance of prayer.—Alistair Cooke

A. COORDINATE SEQUENCE PARAGRAPH

1 This is the essence of the religious spirit—the sense of power, beauty, greatness, truth infinitely beyond one's own reach, but infinitely to be aspired to.
  2 It invests men with a pride in a purpose and with humility in accomplishment.
  2 It is the source of all true tolerance, for in its light all men see other men as they see themselves, as being capable of being more than they are, and yet falling short, inevitably, of what they can imagine human opportunities to be.

Francis Christensen   *39*

2 It is the supporter of human dignity and pride and the dissolver of vanity.

2 And it is the very creator of the scientific spirit; for without the aspiration to understand and control the miracle of life, no man would have sweated in a laboratory or tortured his brain in the exquisite search after truth.

Dorothy Thompson, "The Education of the Heart"

B. MULTILEVEL SENTENCE

1 A small negro girl develops from the sheet of glare-frosted walk,
2   walking barefooted,
3   her brown legs striking and recoiling from the hot cement,
4   her feet curling in,
5   only the outer edges touching.

B. SUBORDINATE SEQUENCE PARAGRAPH

1 The process of learning is essential to our lives.
2   All higher animals seek it deliberately.
3   They are inquisitive and they experiment.
4   An experiment is a sort of harmless trial run of some action which we shall have to make in the real world; and this, whether it is made in the laboratory by scientists or by fox-cubs outside their earth.
5   The scientist experiments and the cub plays;
      both are learning to correct their errors of judgment in a setting in which errors are not fatal.
6   Perhaps this is what gives them both their air of happiness and freedom in these activities.

J. Bronowski, The Common Sense of Science (Vintage), p. 111.

The analytical procedure for discovering the structure is really quite simple. There is no problem in locating the base clause of a sentence, and one can assume—provisionally (see 6 and 7 below)—that the first sentence of a paragraph is the topic sentence. Then, going sentence by sentence through the paragraph, one searches in the sentences above for likenesses —that is, for evidences of coordination. In both sets of two examples, the second element is *unlike* the first one; it is different and so it is set down as subordinate—that is, it is indented and numbered level 2. With the third element the two sets part company. In the examples marked A, the third element is *like* the second, it is parallel to the second, and so it is set down as coordinate. The clearest mark of coordination is identity of structure at the beginning of the sentence. The fourth element is like both the second and third; and the fifth is like the second, third, and fourth. All the elements marked 2 have the same relation to one another; they are siblings. And because of this, they all have the same immediate relation to level 1, the base clause or topic sentence; they are all children of the same mother. In the examples marked B, on the other hand, the third element is *unlike* the second, and of course unlike the first; the fourth is unlike the third or any other above it, and so on. Search as you may, you will find no signs of parallelism. So, instead of two generations, there are five in the sentence and six in the paragraph. No element after the second is related immediately to level 1; it is related to it only through all of the intermediate generations.

The fact that there are two kinds of sequence makes all the difference in what we can say about the paragraph.

It should be evident how we must treat the methods of development or support. In the coordinate sequence, all the coordinate sentences employ the *same* method—in this paragraph they enumerate the *results* or *effects*. In the subordinate sequence, every added sentence may, and likely will, employ a *different* method. There is no theoretic limit to the number of levels, and the lists of methods in our textbooks are far from exhausting the whole range of what we may say in discursive writing to develop or support a topic.

It should be evident, also, that we need two separate sets of yardsticks for measuring such things as unity, coherence, and emphasis. Take coherence, for example. The repetition of structure in A is all that is necessary to join sentence to sentence at the same level. Any connectives other than the simple *and* for the last member would be an impertinence—*again, moreover, in the same vein, in addition* would be a hindrance rather than a help. But repetition or structure *is* necessary; like things in like ways is one of the imperatives of discursive writing. Any attempt to introduce variety in the sentence beginnings, by varying the pattern or by putting something before the subject, would be like trying to vary the columns of the Parthenon. In a subordinate sequence, just as clearly, repetition of structure must be avoided. Each added sentence, being different in the method of development, must be different in form. In a subordinate sequence, the problems of unity, coherence, and emphasis are altogether different—and more difficult.

Another paragraph will illustrate two other points. First, a writer sometimes intends a coordinate sequence but, like the dog that turns around once or twice before he settles down, takes, and sometimes wastes, a sentence or two before he begins his enumeration. (For other examples see paragraphs E, J, and O.) Second, the coordinate sentences need not be identical in structure; they need only be like enough for the reader to place them. In this paragraph it is evident that all three sentences at level 3 present *examples*.

C. COORDINATE SEQUENCE

1 He [the native speaker] may, of course, speak a form of English that marks him as coming from a rural or an unread group.

  2 But if he doesn't mind being so marked, there's no reason why he should change.

    3 Samuel Johnson kept a Staffordshire burr in his speech all his life.

    3 In Burns's mouth the despised lowland Scots dialect served just as well as the "correct" English spoken by ten million of his southern contemporaries.

3 Lincoln's vocabulary and his way of pronouncing certain words were sneered at by many better educated people at the time, but he seemed to be able to use the English language as effectively as his critics.

Bergen Evans, *Comfortable Words,* p. 6

5. THE TWO SORTS OF SEQUENCE COMBINE TO PRODUCE THE COMMONEST SORT —THE MIXED SEQUENCE.

Simple sequences, especially coordinate ones, are not common. More often than not, subordinate sentences are added to add depth to coordinate sequences, and coordinate sentences are added to emphasize points made in subordinate sequences. The resulting mixed sequences reveal their origin as derived from either coordinate or subordinate sequences.

My justification for the term *generative* lies here. The teacher can, with perfect naturalness, suggest the addition of subordinate sentences to clarify and of coordinate sentences to emphasize or to enumerate. With these additions the writer is not padding; he is putting himself imaginatively in the reader's place and anticipating his questions and resistances. He is learning to treat his subject home.

D. MIXED SEQUENCE—BASED ON COORDINATE SEQUENCE

1 The other [mode of thought] is the scientific method.
  2 It subjects the conclusions of reason to the arbitrament of hard fact to build an increasing body of tested knowledge.
  2 It refuses to ask questions that cannot be answered, and rejects such answers as cannot be provided except by Revelation.
  2 It discovers the relatedness of all things in the universe—of the motion of the moon to the influence of the earth and sun, of the nature of the organism to its environment, of human civilization to the conditions under which it is made.
  2 It introduces history into everything.
    3 Stars and scenery have their history, alike with plant species or human institutions, and
    nothing is intelligible without some knowledge of its past.
      4 As Whitehead has said, each event is the reflection or effect of every other event, past as well as present.
  2 It rejects dualism.
    3 The supernatural is in part the region of the natural that has not yet been understood, in part an invention of human fantasy, in part the unknowable.
    3 Body and soul are not separate entities, but two aspects of one organization, and
    Man is that portion of the universal world-stuff that has evolved until it is capable of rational and purposeful values.

4 His place in the universe is to continue that evolution and to realize those values.
Julian Huxley, *Man in the Modern World* (Mentor), pp. 146-47.

This paragraph suggests careful calculation of what could be left to the
reader and what must be made more explicit. Huxley took a chance on the
first two items. What he added to the third made it a two-level sentence. The
sentences he added to the last two made the paragraph a mixed one. He was
under no obligation to expand all five items equally. The writer's guide is
his own sense of what the reader must be told. In our classes we must work
to develop this sense. The difference is often the difference between self-
expression and communication.

     E. MIXED SEQUENCE—BASED ON COORDINATE SEQUENCE
1 An obvious classification of meaning is that based on scope.
1 This is to say, meaning may be generalized (extended, widened) or it may
     be specialized (restricted, narrowed).
  2 When we increase the scope of a word, we reduce the elements of its
      contents.
    3 For instance *tail* (from OE *taegl)* in earlier times seems to have
       meant 'hairy caudal appendage, as of a horse.'
      4 When we eliminated the hairiness (or the horsiness) from the mean-
        ing, we increased its scope, so that in Modern English the
        word means simply 'caudal appendage.'
      4 The same thing has happened to Danish *hale,* earlier 'tail of a cow.'
        5 In course of time the cow was eliminated, and in present-day
          Danish the word means simply 'tail,' having undergone a
          semantic generalization precisely like that of the English
          word cited;
        the closely related Icelandic *hali* still keeps the cow in the
        picture.   •
    3 Similarly, a *mill* was earlier a place for making things by the process
       of grinding, that is, for making meal.
      4 The words *meal* and *mill* are themselves related, as one might
        guess from their similarity.
        5 A mill is now simply a place for making things: the grinding has
          been eliminated, so that we may speak of a woolen mill, a
          steel mill, or even a gin mill.
    3 The word *corn* earlier meant 'grain' and is in fact related to the word
       grain.
      4 It is still used in this general sense in England, as in the "Corn
        Laws," but
        specifically it may mean either oats (for animals) or wheat (for
        human beings).

    4 In American usage *corn* denotes maize, which is of course not at all what Keats meant in his "Ode to a Nightingale" when he described Ruth as standing "in tears amid the alien corn."

  3 The building in which corn, regardless of its meaning, is stored is called a barn.

    4 *Barn* earlier denoted a storehouse for barley; the word is in fact a compound of two Old English words, *bere* 'barley' and *aern* 'house.'

      5 By elimination of a part of its earlier content, the scope of this word has been extended to mean a storehouse for any kind of grain.

      5 American English has still further generalized by eliminating the grain, so that *barn* may mean also a place for housing livestock.

      Thomas Pyles, *The Origins and Development of the English Language,* pp. 306-07.

Here the development has proceeded so far that the four coordinate sentences (level 3) have become in effect subtopic sentences. The paragraph could be subdivided, making them the topic sentences of a series of paragraphs. The long paragraph looks well on a book page; the shorter paragraphs would look more palatable in narrow newspaper columns. Either way, the effect would not be essentially different.

The problem of a reader tackling a long paragraph like this is to identify the coordinate sentences. He reads one 3rd-level sentence and then some sentences explaining it as an example of semantic generalization. He must be aware when he has come to the end of that explanation and must then shift his attention back to level 3. He must recognize the direction of movement. The first three 3rd-level sentences are easy to spot because like things have been put in like ways: the italicized words chosen as examples have been made the grammatical subject or apposed to the subject. But the opportunity to make a deft transition led the author to vary the pattern for the fourth. I have seen readers stumble at this point, and I have seen some make Danish *hale* parallel to the four English words.

F. MIXED SEQUENCE—BASED ON COORDINATE SEQUENCE

1 This is a point so frequently not understood that it needs some dwelling on.

  2 Consider how difficult it is to find a tenable argument that *thrown,* say, is intrinsically better than *throwed.*

    3 We can hardly say that the simple sound is better.

      4 For if it were, we would presumably also prefer *rown* to *rowed, hown* to *hoed, strown* to *strode,* and we don't.

    3 Nor can we argue convincingly that *throwed* should be avoided because it did not occur in earlier English.

    4 Many forms which occurred in earlier English cannot now be used.

    5 As we mentioned earlier, *holp* used to be the past tense form of
        help; helped was incorrect.
    5 But we could not now say "He holp me a good deal."
  2 As for "me and Jim," the statement that *I* should be used in the subject
      position begs the question.
    3 One can ask why *I* should be the subject form, and
      to this there is no answer.
      4 As a matter of fact, *you* was at one time the object form of the
          second person plural, *ye* being the subject form.
      4 But no one objects now to a sentence like "You were there."

Paul Roberts

I have included this paragraph to illustrate further the kind of clues that
mark coordination: at the first level 3, *we can hardly say: nor can we argue;*
at level 5, *used to be: now;* at the second level 4, *was at one time: now.* At
level 2 there are no verbal clues; the reader just has to recognize that "me
and Jim" is another example like "throwed" to illustrate the point that needs
dwelling on.

G. MIXED SEQUENCE—BASED ON SUBORDINATE SEQUENCE

1 The purpose of science is to describe the world in an orderly scheme or
    language which will help us to look ahead.
  2 We want to forecast what we can of the future behaviour of the world;
      particularly we want to forecast how it would behave under several
        alternative actions of our own between which we are usually trying
        to choose.
    3 This is a very limited purpose.
      4 It has nothing whatever to do with bold generalizations about the
          universal workings of cause and effect.
      4 It has nothing to do with cause and effect at all, or with any other
          special mechanism.
      4 Nothing in this purpose, which is to order the world as an aid to
          decision and action, implies that the order must be of one kind
          rather than another.
        5 The order is what we find to work, conveniently and instruc-
            tively.
        5 It is not something we stipulate;
          it is not something we can dogmatise about.
        5 It is what we find;
          it is what we find useful.

J. Bronowski, *The Common Sense of Science*, pp. 70-71.

This would be a simple five-level sequence but for the repetition at levels
4 and 5. It is a fair guess that the desire for rhetorical emphasis generated
these additions. With five statements there could be five 5th-level sen-

tences, but the author has chosen to put them in three groups. This is a matter of paragraph punctuation (see 9 below).

(see 9 below)

H. MIXED SEQUENCE—BASED ON SUBORDINATE SEQUENCE

1 Science as we know it indeed is a creation of the last three hundred years.
    2 It has been made in and by the world that took its settled shape about 1660, when Europe at last shook off the long nightmare of religious wars and settled into a life of inquisitive trade and industry.
        3 Science is embodied in those new societies;
        it has been made by them and has helped to make them.
            4 The medieval world was passive and symbolic;
            it saw in the forms of nature the signatures of the Creator.
            4 From the first stirrings of science among the merchant adventurers of the Renaissance, the modern world has been an active machine.
                5 That world became the everyday world of trade in the seventeenth century, and
                the interests were appropriately astronomy and the instruments of voyage, among them the magnet.
                5 A hundred years later, at the Industrial Revolution, the interest shifted to the creation and use of power.
                    6 This drive to extend the strength of man and what he can do in a day's work has remained our interest since.
                        7 In the last century it moved from steam to electricity.
                        7 Then in 1905, in that wonderful year when . . . he published papers which made outstanding advances in three different branches of physics, Einstein first wrote down the equations which suggested that matter and energy are interchangeable states.
                        7 Fifty years later, we command a reservoir of power in matter almost as large as the sun, which we now realize manufactures its heat for us in just this way, by the annihilation of its matter.
                            J. Bronowski, *The Common Sense of Science*, pp. 97-98

Conventionally, the "movement" of this paragraph might be called chronological; but it is only roughly so—it leaps, and at levels 4, 5, and 7 it lingers. Note the marks of coordination: level 4, *the medieval . . . passive: the modern . . . active;* level 5, *the seventeenth century: a hundred years later;* level 7, depending on *since* at level 6, *in the last century: then in 1905: fifty years later.*

The first sentence at level 4 ("The medieval world . . .") is interesting because the topic sentence limits the time to "the last three hundred years." One could easily read through levels 1-5 skipping "The medieval world . . ." The sentence has been inserted—extralogically and extrachronologically— in order to set up a contrast. Such inserted sentences are fairly common and were at first very puzzling to me. Occasionally, also, one encounters and is puzzled by a parenthetic sentence. Such sentences should be set off by parentheses, but all sentences so set off are not extrasequential.

6. SOME PARAGRAPHS HAVE NO TOPIC SENTENCE.

I. PARAGRAPH WITHOUT TOPIC SENTENCE

2 In Spain, where I saw him last, he looked profoundly Spanish.

   3 He might have passed for one of those confidential street dealers who earn their living selling spurious Parker pens in the cafés of Málaga or Valencia.

      4 Like them, he wore a faded chalk-striped shirt, a coat slung over his shoulders, a trim, dark moustache, and a sleazy, fat-cat smile.

      4 His walk, like theirs, was a raffish saunter, and everything about him seemed slept in, especially his hair, a nest of small, wet serpents.

   3 Had he been in Seville and his clothes been more formal, he could have been mistaken for a pampered elder son idling away a legacy in dribs and on drabs, the sort you see in windows along the Sierpes, apparently stuffed.

2 In Italy he looks Italian; in Greece, Greek:

   wherever he travels on the Mediterranean coast, Tennessee Williams takes on a protective colouring which melts him into his background, like a lizard on a rock.

2 In New York or London he seems out of place, and is best explained away as a retired bandit.

   3 Or a beach comber: shave the beard off any of the self-portraits Gauguin painted in Tahiti, soften the features a little, and you have a sleepy outcast face that might well be Tennessee's.

                Kenneth Tynan, *Curtains*

The three sentences marked level 2 are clearly coordinate. But there is no superordinate sentence to umbrella them; that is, there is no level 1, no topic sentence. With paragraphs such as this the topic can usually be inferred from the preceding paragraph. But sometimes the topic sentence is actually part of the preceding paragraph, arbitrarily and illogically separated. Or, as in J, the preceding paragraph *is* the topic sentence; the two paragraphs of J constitute a single sequence. The basic pattern here is like that of B; but with the series of three examples disjoined, they stand alone in a paragraph that has no topic sentence.

J. TOPIC SENTENCE IN PRECEDING PARAGRAPH

1 The mystical artist always sees patterns.

   2 The symbol, never quite real, tends to be expressed less and less realistically, and

   as the reality becomes abstracted the pattern comes forward.

¶3 The wings on Blake's angels do not look like real wings,
    nor are they there because wings belong to angels.
  4 They have been flattened, stylized, to provide a curving pointed
    frame, the setting required by the pattern of the composition.
3 In Hindoo art and its branches, stylization reaches its height.
  4 Human figures are stylized far beyond the point of becoming a
    type;
    they too are made into patterns, schematic designs of the human
    body, an abstraction of humanity.
3 In the case of an Eastern rug all desire to express any semblance of
  reality has gone.
  4 Such a work of art is pure decoration.
    5 It is the expression of the artist's final withdrawal from the
    visible world, essentially his denial of the intellect.

                 Edith Hamilton, *The Greek Way* (Mentor), p. 33.

7. SOME PARAGRAPHS HAVE SENTENCES AT THE BEGINNING OR AT THE END THAT DO NOT BELONG TO THE SEQUENCE.

Occasionally a paragraph has one or more introductory (I) or transitional (T) sentences before the sequence begins. And occasionally one has a sentence or more added after the sequence has run its course; that is, the first of such sentences is not coordinate with any sentence above it or subordinate to the one next above it. They are related to the sequence, but are not a part of it; they form a conclusion (C). To save space, I have quoted only enough to establish that the sentences so marked are extrasequential.

K. PARAGRAPH WITH INTRODUCTION
I1 If you are at the beach, and you take an old, dull, brown penny and rub it
    hard for a minute or two with handfuls of wet sand (dry sand is no
    good), the penny will come out a bright gold color, looking as clean
    and new as the day it was minted.
1 Now poetry has the same effect on words as wet sand on pennies.
  2 In what seems an almost miraculous way, it brightens up words that
    looked dull and ordinary.
    3 . . .

                 C. Day Lewis, *Poetry for You,* pp. 8-9.

Most of the examples of what I would call introductory sentences are like this in offering a comparison. The comparison is not carried through the paragraph, but is used only as a starter.

L. PARAGRAPH WITH TRANSITION
T1 So far I've been talking about some of the world-shapes out of which
    poetry is built.
  T2 But images, metaphors, and similes are not the only things which may
    go to make the pattern of a poem.

1 There are meter and rhyme.
2 You may be surprised that I have not put meter first . . .

C. Day Lewis, *Poetry for You,* p. 33.

Transitions from paragraph to paragraph are ordinarily embedded in the topic sentence, as a single word or a phrase, a subordinate clause, or the first part of a compound sentence. But sometimes, as here, they take a full sentence or more.

The first sentence of a paragraph may even be a major transition. It may be the topic sentence of a series of paragraphs or even the thesis sentence of an article.

M. PARAGRAPH WITH CONCLUSION

1 When we follow the growth of science, we come to understand how that movement has been probing for these unifying concepts.
  2 Look at the movement of biology since the days of Ray and Linnaeus: . . . .
  2 Look at chemistry, from Dalton's law. . . .
  2 Look at the march of physics to unity: . . .
    3 We have seen this lead to the creation of energy from matter; to a picture of space as closed but possibly expanding; and now . . . .
C1 Science is a process of creating new concepts which unify our understanding of the world, and
the process is today bolder and more far-reaching, more triumphant even than at the great threshold of the Scientific Revolution.

J. Bronowski, *The Common Sense of Science,* pp. 132-33.

Concluding sentences are rather rare, and some of them, like this one, round off a sequence of paragraphs rather than the one they are joined to. Such concluding sentences are ordinarily at a higher level of generalization than the sentences they follow, and those who take the most general sentence to be the topic sentence may take them for topic sentences. They may say that the paragraph has two topic sentences, fore and aft.

8. SOME PARAGRAPHING IS ILLOGICAL.

[N.]
1 Rhymes, as you know, generally come at the end of lines.
  2 They are put there because it helps to create and make clear the musical pattern of the stanza:
  the ear learns to expect a rhyme, just as it expects a beat, at certain definite intervals, and
  it's pleased when it finds one there.
1 But you may get a rhyme in the middle of a line, too: and
some poets are extremely skilful in making assonances and other sound-echoes all over the poem.
  2 This often done by the use of alliteration.

3 For example,
    I hear lake water lapping with low sounds by the shore.
  ¶4 Those three 'l's' make a pleasant liquid sound:
    the sound here, in fact corresponds with the sense.
  4 So it does in
      Dry clashed his armour in the icy caves,
    where the hard 'c' of 'clashed' and 'caves' seems to dry one's
      mouth up when
    one speaks the line aloud.
                    C. Day Lewis, *Poetry for You,* pp. 35-36.

The two sentences marked 1 are clearly coordinate. One has to say, then, that the paragraph is compound (a reasonable solution; there are such paragraphs), or that the first two sentences are introductory or transitional, or that the paragraphing is simply illogical, breaking up a short sequence.

Paragraphing at level 4 is even more illogical. It breaks up a sequence at the most unexpected point. Perhaps the tired teacher will sigh "If gold rusts. . . ."

On the other hand, many a run of four or five paragraphs totaling 500-600 words can be analyzed as a single sequence, with the paragraph divisions coming logically at the subtopic sentences. This is the consummation we should work for.

9. PUNCTUATION SHOULD BE BY THE PARAGRAPH, NOT BY THE SENTENCE.

                            o.
1 This brings me to the third failing of eighteenth century science, which I
    find most interesting.
  2 A science which orders its thought too early is stifled.
    3 For example, the ideas of the Epicureans about atoms two thousand
        years ago were quite reasonable; but
      they did only harm to a physics which could not measure temperature
        and pressure and learn the simpler laws which relate them.
  3 Or again, the hope of the medieval alchemists that the elements might
      be changed was not as fanciful as we once thought.
    4 But it was merely damaging to a chemistry which did not yet
        understand the composition of water and common salt.
            J. Bronowski, *The Common Sense of Science,* p. 47

This is a minor example of punctuating without an eye to the paragraph as a whole. The two sets at level 3 are the same in intent and, except for the punctuation, the same in form. Likes have been put in unlike ways.

Paragraph punctuation usually involves the choice of whether to make compound sentences or not. In paragraph G the same author wisely grouped five coordinate statements into three sentences, sorting them out on the basis of content. Paragraph E does not really have two topic sentences, and a semicolon would avoid that appearance. I have taken it as a rule that a sentence that merely restates another is on the same level with it. If this is a bad rule, then all the numbers for level should be raised one. In paragraph P the effects of repetition and balance would be obscured if the sentences were not punctuated as compound.

P.

1 Nowhere, at no time, have there been five and a half years so alternately
  wondrous, compelling, swift and cruel.
2 As the Sixties began, our aspirant astronauts had yet to enter space;
    now, they practice giant steps to the moon.
2 Then, jet travel was a conversation piece;
    now, we change the flight if we've seen the movie.
2 Then, we were about to be swamped by a recessionary wave;
    now, riding history's highest flood of prosperity, we are revising our
    assumptions about the inevitability of ebbs in our economic life.
2 Then, our Negroes were still marshaling their forces;
    now, they have marshaled the conscience of mankind.
2 Then, we were arguing over the fitness of a Roman Catholic to be
    President;
    now, we subdue the nightmare of his murder.
2 Then, a Southerner in the White House seemed politically unthinkable;
    now, a Southerner builds with the most emphatic mandate we have
    ever bestowed.
2 Then, John Birch was an unknown soldier, actresses still wore clothes
    at work, and dancing was something a man and woman did together.
                                              Leonard Gross, *Look*, 6/29/65

*   *   *

Is the paragraph a logical entity, a sequence of structurally related sentences, or is it a visual unit, with the first line indented and the last line left incomplete? Clearly it is both and the two jostle; sequences are broken up because writers don't recognize them or because they want their paragraphs to look all of a size. This lack of "register" between the logical and the visual has kept us from making sense of the paragraphs we encounter in our reading. The problem is the same as that of sentences that are fragmentary or run together. These atypical units do not compel us to deny or disregard grammatical relations or to assert that the sentence is a myth.

I'd like to claim that the paragraph that submits to this kind of structural analysis is thereby a good paragraph and the only good paragraph. But I only claim that the structural relations I have disclosed are real (they were discovered by induction), and I urge my readers to discover them for themselves. The teacher who thinks that writing is an art and that art cannot be taught, that the teacher can only inspire and then keep out of the way, will not find anything he can use. But the teacher who believes, as I do, that the only freedom in any art comes from the mastery of technique, may find here the means both to kindle and restrain.

CARL H. KLAUS

Reflections on Prose Style

*Carl H. Klaus is a member of the English department at the University of
Iowa. He is the editor of* Style in English Prose *(1968). "Reflections on
Prose Style," the introduction to his book, argues that style is both the personal character of the writer himself and the author's deliberate use of
language. Professor Klaus' point of view provides a workable alternative
to the exclusive definition of style as* either *personality* or *linguistic choice.
The substance of his argument is an application of his theory to specific
passages by Franklin, Hobbes, and others, by which the author demonstrates the utility of his theory for students of both composition and literature.*

Style is the man; style is not the man. Both statements are true, and this
paradox suggests the complex and apparently contradictory ideas that
emerge in any discussion of expository prose style. The complexity arises
because style is a term that may refer to several different, even if related,
entities, much as "democracy" can refer to a form of government, or a state
governed by democratic principles, or the spirit of political equality. The
entities change, but the term remains the same.

When we say, for example, that style is the man, we are trying to account
for the origin of particular habits of language by attributing them to the
special personal character of the writer himself. Puttenham takes this approach in *The Arte of English Poesie:*

> For if the man be grave, his speech and style is grave; if light-headed,
> his style and language also light; if the mind be haughty and hot, the
> speech and style is also vehement and stirring; if it be cold and tem-
> perate, the style is also very modest; if it be humble, or base and meek,
> so is also the language and style.

At this distance in time, Puttenham may strike us as being somewhat too
confident in his simple equations, but he does represent a perennially recurrent, and valid, framework for the understanding of prose style.

Style may also describe the deliberate use of language, the self-conscious
process of composing, to achieve specific purposes and calculated effects.
When style appears in this context, the discussion frequently turns to forces
outside the writer, as in Chesterfield's stylistic advice to his son:

> Your business is negotiation abroad, and oratory in the House of
> Commons at home. What figure can you make, in either case, if your

style be inelegant, I do not say bad? Imagine yourself writing an office-letter to a secretary of state, which letter is to be read by the whole Cabinet Council, and very possibly afterward laid before Parliament; any one barbarism, solecism, or vulgarism in it, would, in a very few days, circulate through the whole kingdom, to your disgrace and ridicule.

In this passage, Chesterfield has quite deliberately shifted the emphasis from style as a feature of the writer's personality, an outgrowth of the man as he is, to style as an assumed manner, a manipulation of language, adopted by policy for a specific audience or occasion.

In yet another sense, style may refer to the written product itself, the configurations of language it displays, quite apart from the character of the writer or the nature of his purposes. In discussions of this kind, style is usually taken to mean the qualities that result from particular kinds of diction, figures, and sentence designs. In the beginning of his essay "On Familiar Style," Hazlitt clearly limits himself to this sense of the term:

It is not easy to write a familiar style. Many people mistake a familiar for a vulgar style, and suppose that to write without affectation is to write at random. On the contrary, there is nothing that requires more precision, and, if I may so say, purity of expression, than the style I am speaking of. It utterly rejects not only all unmeaning pomp, but all low, cant phrases, and loose, unconnected *slipshod* allusions. It is not to take the first word that offers, but the best word in common use; it is not to throw words together in any combinations we please, but to follow and avail ourselves of the true idiom of the language.

Style so conceived maintains a separate identity, independent of the writer or his purposes, and Hazlitt strongly implies its autonomy when he personifies familiar style, telling us that "It utterly rejects not only all unmeaning pomp, but all low, cant phrases, and loose, unconnected *slipshod* allusions."

Hazlitt, of course, does not persist in discussion style as if it were autonomous, any more than Chesterfield confines himself exclusively to style as policy, or Puttenham to style and the man, for these concepts of prose exposition are by no means incompatible. They will appear together with different emphases in almost every commentary on style. These three approaches to style do not even encompass all of the possible conceptions implied by the term. But they can serve as useful points of reference in a discussion of style, for prose exposition is a process of communication involving a writer, an audience, and a piece of writing. The more we know about each participant in the process, the more we know about style.

The writer is, perhaps, the most incomprehensible participant in the process, for the mental operations that manifest themselves in prose statement are not finally knowable even by the writer himself. We ponder some words, while others spring suddenly to mind—apparently from nowhere. We labor over some sentences, while others come ready-made. But differences such as these can rarely be explained to our satisfaction. Past verbal experience will account for some of the difference, as will our mood, or temperament, when writing, not to mention a whole range of other influences we might name; but we cannot finally define and distinguish the mental processes that produce the words quickly in one case, painfully in another. Probably, we cannot retrace the mental steps, the verbal choices, we go through, even when we ponder over a single word. Knowing so little about ourselves in this respect, it hardly seems conceivable that we should be able to speculate about others, and in a sense we acknowledge that mystery when we say that style is the man. And as there are many men, so there are many styles, and many mysteries.

But even while we may not be able to intrude fully upon the privacy of our own minds, or upon the privacy of others', we do know some things about ourselves and about other men. We know our own convictions, more or less, and we know equally well the habitual ways in which we view experience and respond to it. The sum of this is that we know something about our life style, and prose style is inevitably an outgrowth of the way we live. To a lesser extent we know the same about other men. Of Chesterfield and Thoreau, for example, we know enough to say they were radically different men in almost all respects. Chesterfield, a man of the world, a member of the aristocracy, systematic in the pursuit of elegance and so sophisticated in the dissimulations of court intrigue and political negotiation that it seemed to be his second nature; Thoreau, a recluse, who deliberately isolated himself from society for two years, preferring the simplicity of nature at Walden Pond to the complexity of life at Concord, scorning the shams of men for the truth of his idealistic vision. The contrast is dramatic—so dramatic, in fact, that it carries over into the style and content of their remarks about style, enabling us, even before we are told, to distinguish Chesterfield from Thoreau in the following two passages:

> Style is the dress of thoughts; and let them be ever so just, if your style is homely, coarse, and vulgar, they will appear to as much disadvantage, and be as ill received as your person, though ever so well proportioned, would, if dressed in rags, dirt, and tatters. It is not every understanding that can judge of matter; but every ear can and does judge, more or less of style: and were I either to speak or write to the public, I should prefer moderate matter, adorned with all the beauties and elegancies of style, to the strongest matter in the world, ill-worded and ill-delivered.

> I fear chiefly lest my expression may not be *extra-vagant* enough, may not wander far enough beyond the narrow limits of my daily experience, so as to be adequate to the truth of which I have been convinced. *Extra vagance!* it depends on how you are yarded. The migrating

buffalo, which seeks new pastures in another latitude, is not extravagant like the cow which kicks over the pail, leaps the cowyard fence, and runs after her calf, in milking time. I desire to speak somewhere *without* bounds; like a man in a waking moment, to men in their waking moments; for I am convinced that I cannot exaggerate enough to lay the foundation of a true expression.

The first is carefully designed to emphasize the comparison between style and clothes. The initial sentence, for example, is constructed according to an elaborate balance, in which "homely, coarse, and vulgar" are neatly paralleled with "rags, dirt, and tatters." The second sentence betrays a similar intricacy of design, the first two clauses using roughly corresponding word order to point up the contrast between judging matter and judging style, and the remaining material similarly balanced to emphasize the contrast between "moderate matter, adorned" and "the strongest matter . . . ill-worded."

The second makes its force not so much through syntax, through the careful, even elaborate, arrangement of words, phrases, and clauses, as through the power of a single word and the meanings that can be wrung out of it. "Extravagant" is the word, and we encounter it more often than we think: *"extra-vagant," "Extra vagance,"* and "extravagant" are not the only occurrences, for the obsolete meaning of "extravagant" is "straying beyond bounds," which is related to its Latin origin, "to wander outside." Recognizing these facts, we suddenly discern the word again in the first sentence, "may not wander far enough beyond," and again in the fourth sentence, *"without* bounds," and even earlier in the third sentence in "leaps the cowyard fence."

If we had to make an identification at this point, we would have little difficulty in attributing the first to Chesterfield and the second to Thoreau, for the first is elegant, even fussy, in its intricately designed sentences, while the second disdains such fashionable controls, playing outlandishly with language to assert its meaning. Further examination of the passages merely confirms the relation between the styles and the men. Chesterfield draws his metaphor from social experience in his concern with clothes and dress, Thoreau draws his from the activities of nature in his images of the "migrating buffalo" and the "cow which kicks over the pail." Finally, of course, we should note the contrasting values, in Chesterfield's concern with "elegancies of style" and Thoreau's concern with "the truth of which I have been convinced." In every detail, then, these two passages are a direct reflection of the men who wrote them.

But even as these passages reveal both men in their styles, they also disclose both men adopting distinctive stylistic identities for themselves. Chesterfield is rather explicitly concerned with an advantageous appearance, more especially an elegant one; and his preference for "moderate matter" elegantly adorned, rather than "the strongest matter in the world, ill-worded," clearly indicates that style is for him a matter of policy. He does not wish to be "ill-received," and he will compromise thought for a favorable reception. Thoreau, to be sure, is not willing to sacrifice thought; in fact he, quite in contrast to Chesterfield, is concerned that his style be "adequate to the truth." Yet his moral convictions commit him, as he sees it, to a stylistic policy no less deliberate than Chesterfield's: his style must be "extravagant like the cow which kicks over the pail, leaps the cowyard fence, and runs after her calf, in milking time." One might argue, of course, that their stylistic credos represent decisions typical of each man, that the calculated stylistic appearances are extensions of the real men. Even so, one would have to acknowledge that both men have specific purposes in mind, and that as accomplished writers both men are moved as much by conscious decisions as by unconscious psychological impulses. These decisions, having been formulated once and acted upon repeatedly, may well become so habitual as to seem part of each man, but it is important to recognize that they are deliberately acquired capacities rather than innate qualities. Thus if style is the man, it is only so in a fairly complicated sense, certainly more complex at least than the one implied by Puttenham. And it may well be that style is always to some extent an invention of the writer, a fiction, that conceals the man as surely as it reveals him.

The difficulty of establishing a direct and precise relationship between style and the man will become evident after we look at the following passages:

> About this time I met with an odd volume of *The Spectator*. It was the third. I had never before seen any of them. I bought it, read it over and over, and was much delighted with it. I thought the writing excellent, and wished, if possible, to imitate it.

> Forasmuch as the enemies of America, in the parliament of Great Britain, to render us odious to the nation, and give an ill impression of us in the minds of other European powers, have represented us as unjust and ungrateful in the highest degree; asserting on every occasion, that the colonies were settled at the expence of Britain; that they were, at the expence of the same, protected in their infancy; that they now ungratefully and unjustly refuse to contribute to their own protection . . .

> There is in every village a vacant dwelling, called the strangers' house. Here they are placed, while the old men go round from hut to hut, acquainting the inhabitants, that strangers are arrived, who are probably hungry and weary; and every one sends them what he can spare of victuals, and skins to repose on.

> Be studious in your profession, and you will be learned. Be industrious and frugal, and you will be rich. Be sober and temperate, and you will be healthy. Be in general virtuous, and you will be happy.

We might very well attribute these four passages to four different writers, and with good reason, for they seem to represent four rather different styles, both in diction and sentence design. The first is quite simple and unsophisticated in manner: the diction plain and unaffectedly colloquial—"About this time," "read it over and over"; the syntax uncomplicated and straightforward, working in terms of simple sentences, simple coordination, and a minimal amount of subordination, to produce an effect that seems quite spontaneous in its abrupt movement from one personal statement to another. The second is altogether different in its magisterial and oratorical qualities: the diction formal and legalistic—"Forasmuch as," "render us odious," "in the highest degree," "at the expence of the same"; the syntax extremely complicated and contrived, working in terms of a periodic sentence which suspends the main clause by piling up a series of subordinate clauses and phrases, so numerous that we eagerly seek the chief meaning of the statement. The third strikes a rough balance between the first two, neither so simple as the first, nor so complex as the second: the diction relaxed at one moment—"the old men go round from hut to hut"—slightly more formal the next—"acquainting the inhabitants that strangers are arrived"; the syntax straightforward, rather than periodic, but depending nonetheless on the complexity of a technically "loose" sentence in which the chief meaning is formulated in the initial clause and then qualified or amplified by a series of subordinate phrases and clauses that develop out of one another, so that the sentence seems to be a limitlessly expandable entity. The final passage, studiously aphoristic, has almost no stylistic affinities with the other three: the diction heavily adjectival in its insistence on qualities of behavior— "frugal," "learned," "industrious," "sober"; the syntax highly schematic, depending on balanced clauses within each sentence, and parallelism among the sentences to produce a cumulative sense of design and pattern. Given four passages so different in style, one could hardly believe they were written by a single man, and yet they were. All are by Benjamin Franklin.

In view of this perplexing situation, one might well be moved to ask which one of these styles *is* the man; and the answer of course would be that all of these styles are the man, the corollary of which is that no single one of them fully represents Franklin, that none of these styles is the man. Each of them is in a sense an invention of Franklin, a fictional personality he creates to meet the needs of a different purpose, audience, or occasion. The first passage, for example, is from his *Autobiography,* and this fact alone will tell us a great deal about why the style is so simple, straightforward, and apparently unaffected. The autobiographical form allows a first-person narrative, as other forms do not, and the personal history in turn often presumes that the writer is honestly telling all, concealing nothing, about himself. In order to achieve this sense of authenticity, Franklin chooses a style that sounds as uncontrived, as frank, as honest, as he would like us to think he is at that moment in the narrative. But the simplicity of this passage is as deliberately contrived, as artificial, as the complexity of the second passage. The second is so different in style because the occasion, the purpose, and the audience are so different. In this passage, from the *Proposed Vindication and Offer from Congress to Parliament,* Franklin is writing on behalf of the Congress of the United States to the Parliament of England, and these circumstances immediately require that he adopt a lofty and impersonal manner. As part of the diplomatic negotiations between the Colonies and Great Britain, the document further requires that Franklin write as if he were preparing the legal brief for a case in international law, as he does in this introductory statement, systematically formulating the claims of "the enemies of America, in the parliament of Great Britain," each of which he will answer in his "vindication." The third passage comes from yet a different context, not a state paper, but a pamphlet about the Indians, called *Remarks Concerning the Savages of North America.* The title is ironic, for Franklin is trying to dispel the prejudices of his countrymen about the Indian natives:

> Savages we call them, because their manners differ from ours, which we think the perfection of civility; they think the same of theirs.
> Perhaps, if we could examine the manners of different nations with impartiality, we should find no people so rude, as to be without any rules of politeness . . .

Since he recommends "impartiality," he is compelled himself to assume the manner of an impartial observer, much like a scientist, or more specifically, an anthropologist, and this purpose accounts for the straightforward, but deliberate manner in which he fully explains the hospitable behavior of the Indians. The fourth passage, of course, is an instance of Franklin the moralist, and it comes from the end of a letter of advice to a young man who sought Franklin's opinions on early marriages; these circumstances readily explain why Franklin adopts the aphoristic manner. Here he can be amiably didactic, as he cannot in the other contexts, because the circumstances permit such a tone, because the recipient of the letter has granted him that privilege. The style of each of these four passages, then, projects a distinctly different personality, and each personality is, in a sense, artificial, created by Franklin to meet a complex of realities existing as much outside of him as within him.

If this concept of style seems to compromise the writer's integrity, we need only imagine the folly of ignoring it—we need only imagine Franklin writing the statement to Parliament or the pamphlet on the Indians in the very simple and personal style of the *Autobiography.* The results would be very incongruous indeed, as incongruous as the spectacle of someone attending a formal church wedding in his bathrobe. We dress for the occasion, and it is no less true that we write for the occasion. Each set of conditions calls for a certain kind of verbal behavior, and the stylistic response if it is to be appropriate and effective must come within those conventional limits. The limits are not narrowly prescriptive—they allow for a wide range of verbal alternatives, and choosing among them the writer authenticates himself in the personality he assumes and the voice he projects. It must be acknowledged, for example, that no other man would have chosen to write in the same way as Franklin did in each of the four passages, and that Franklin's orderly and systematic cast of mind is manifest throughout the stylistic variation among the four passages. But even as we can see Franklin in the unchanging man, we can also see Franklin adjusting himself to meet a changing series of circumstances, public as well as private. Tentatively, then, we might say that style is the result of a complex set of mental activities, beginning within the man, moving out to the world, as private purposes become shaped by the exigencies of public communication, and returning once again to the man, when the writer chooses the precise form in which to accommodate himself to the world and its conventions.

It would be foolish, of course, to assume that the process is quite so clear-cut, or that the writer behaves quite so deliberately at every point in the act of writing, but it is clear that considerations of purpose do make themselves felt at a fairly high level of consciousness, and that having chosen a purpose the writer has also chosen a style, or has had a style chosen for him. This influence is probably nowhere more clearly seen than in the prose style of scientific discourse. The scientist, whether he be Bacon, or Hobbes, or Sprat, prefers plainness and precision, rather than ornateness and eloquence, and the reasons for that preference are fairly obvious. But the preference is so important that it has become a stylistic prescription for anyone engaged in scientific enquiry. As early as the seventeenth century, for example, the scientists of the Royal Society established a stylistic credo for themselves which Sprat extols in his history:

> It will suffice my present purpose to point out what has been done by the Royal Society towards the correcting of its excesses in natural philosophy, to which it is, of all others, a most professed enemy.
>
> They have, therefore, been most rigorous in putting in execution the only remedy that can be found for this extravagance, and that has been a constant resolution to reject all the amplifications, digressions, and swellings of style, to return back to the primitive purity and shortness, when men delivered so many things almost in an equal number of words. They have exacted from all their members a close, naked, natural way of speaking—positive expressions, clear senses, a native easiness—bringing all things as near the mathematical plainness as they can, and preferring the language of artisans, countrymen, and merchants, before that of wits or scholars.

Certainly the most telling detail is their desire to bring "all things as near the mathematical plainness as they can," for style according to such an ideal is judged by its proximity to numerical and symbolic notation. Hobbes' prose is exemplary of the plain and spare style in scientific discourse:

> When a body is once in motion, it moves (unless something else hinder it) eternally, and whatsoever hinders it cannot in an instant, but in

time and by degrees, quite extinguish it. And as we see in the water, though the wind cease, the waves give not over rolling for a long time after, so also it happens in that motion which is made in the internal parts of a man then when he sees, dreams, etc.

Adjectives have been relentlessly pared away, so that the entire emphasis here is upon the simple noun and the activity it performs. Figurative statements, such as the comparison between movement in the water and motion within man, have illustrative and explanatory, rather than imaginative, functions. Scientific style thus disdains the suggestiveness and ambiguity of metaphor in favor of precise and unambiguous definition. But if we move away from scientific to meditative prose, where the emphasis is not on the idea alone, but on the emotional and imaginative impact of the idea, the style becomes metaphoric, ornate, and self-consciously rhythmical, as in Taylor's reflections on "the vanity and shortness of man's life":

Death meets us everywhere, and is procured by every instrument, and in all chances, and enters in at many doors; by violence and secret influence, by the aspect of a star and the stink of a mist, by the emissions of a cloud and the meeting of a vapour, by the fall of a chariot and the stumbling of a stone, by a full meal or an empty stomach, by watching at the wine or by watching at prayers, by the sun or the moon, by a heat or a cold, by sleepless nights or sleeping days, by water frozen into the hardness and sharpness of a dagger, or water thawed into the floods of a river, by a hair or a raisin, by violent motion or sitting still, by severity or dissolution, by God's mercy or God's anger; by everything in providence and everything in manners, by everything in nature and everything in chance.

The metaphoric pressure of the statement is immediately announced in the personification of death as the unfriendly and unwanted visitor who "enters in at many doors," and the metaphor is extended when the doors, the entryways, become the agencies of death. The statement is certainly not concise in any ordinary sense. The idea of the sentence is exhausted in the material preceding the first semicolon, and the sentence might well be concluded at that point without really altering or diminishing the truth of the statement. The exemplifications that follow can be construed only as a means of giving imaginative and emotional force to the idea through the cumulative impact of the details, expressed as they are in a series of pairs that develop the insistent rhythm of balance. Incremental repetition, then, is the stylistic principle working through the passage, and it is clearly the result of a purpose quite different from that of scientific explanation. Taylor is not unique in this respect; the style is not simply a function of the man; it is as much a result of the meditative impulse, which produces similar rhetorical qualities, for example, in the style of Donne:

We study health, and we deliberate upon our meats, and drink, and air, and exercises, and we hew and we polish every stone that goes to that building; and so our health is a long and a regular work: but in a minute a cannon batters all, overthrows all, demolishes all; a sickness unprevented for all our diligence, unsuspected for all our curiosity; nay, undeserved, if we consider only disorder, summons us, seizes us, possesses us, destroys us in an instant.

Once again the statement develops metaphorically beginning with the implicit comparison between the health of the body and the structure of a building, and the metaphor as in the Taylor passage not only expresses the idea—of mortality—but also evokes a range of associated feelings. Once again, too, the style depends on repetition, in the piling up of parallel verbs, and the repetition, as in the Taylor passage, produces a rhythm which emphasizes the emotional impact of the metaphor. Scientific discourse and meditation are not, of course, the only purposes that manifest themselves in distinctive prose styles. Journalistic commentary, historical presentation, propaganda, literary criticism, autobiography—every purpose tends to have certain special stylistic conventions associated with it, and these will inevitably affect any man who seeks to communicate with other men, for such are the means of giving public currency to private convictions.

When understood in this sense, it becomes clear that style may well be an unintentional extension of a man's original impulse for writing, that having chosen a purpose a man has also, unknowingly perhaps, committed himself to a certain kind of style. If this is the case, then in some sense style does not originate within the man; it exists apart from him, as an inheritance, a legacy, that shapes his conceptual ends as surely as he does. Style is formative, then; it determines the man as much as he determines it. If this concept seems paradoxical we need only recall that one first learns to communicate by appropriating the forms of expression available within his environment, that imitation, consciously or unconsciously, is the means by which any man begins to develop verbal facility. Educational psychologists may well propound this notion as if it were peculiarly innovative, but we can discover the principle in schoolmasters as far back as Ascham (not to mention others who preceded him):

. . . all languages, both learned and mother tongues, be gotten and gotten only by *imitation*. For as ye use to hear, so ye learn to speak. If ye hear no other, ye speak not yourself, and whom ye only hear, of them ye only learn.

And, therefore, if ye would speak as the best and wisest do, ye must be conversant where the best and wisest are. But if you be born or brought up in a rude country, ye shall not choose but speak rudely. The rudest man of all knoweth this to be true.

The consequences of this simple principle are momentous. To begin with, it explains why we can turn to any single century, such as the sixteenth, and find recurrent stylistic qualities among most of the writers who lived during that period. An educated man of the sixteenth century, for example, will favor schematically designed sentences because he has been raised on the classical rhetoricians and trained to imitate Gorgias and Isocrates, Cicero and Quintilian, whose styles embody elaborate principles of syntactic design. We are not surprised, then, when we come upon the ornateness of Lyly's intricately balanced phrases and clauses, or the majesty of Hooker's periodic sentences, or the alertness of Bacon's aphoristic style. But styles do not persist in prose any more than they do in dress. They change, and they change as often as not when they fail to be in keeping with the deepest convictions of the men who inherit them. Thus if we turn to the seventeenth century, we will find writers disdaining the ingenious symmetries of classical oratory, as does Burton, who claims that it is "not my study or intent to compose neatly, which an orator requires, but to express myself readily and plainly as it happens." Or we can hear such a writer as Bunyan speaking out against the dishonesty of ornate style:

> I could . . . have stepped into a style much higher than this in which I have here discoursed, and could have adorned all things more than here I have seemed to do: but I dare not: God did not play in convincing of me; the Devil did not play in tempting of me; neither did I play when I sunk as into a bottomless pit, when the pangs of hell caught hold upon me: wherefore I may not play in my relating of them, but be plain and simple, and lay down the thing as it was . . .

Burton and Bunyan—and other seventeenth century writers as well—reject the earlier style because they are convinced that it fails to express the reality of their experience, and believing an extemporaneous style is more authentic they create a tradition as influential as that of the sixteenth century.

Whether we favor one tradition or another is finally irrelevant. What does matter is the influential nature of our stylistic heritage, for language is the basis of thought, and it follows from this truth that inherited forms of expression will inevitably perpetuate the forms of thought associated with them. Herein lies the most profound reason for a study of prose style. When we recognize that it can ultimately shape our beliefs and the beliefs of other men, we assume the responsibility of mastering style lest we be mastered by it. Ascham recognized this truth four hundred years ago:

> For mark all ages, look upon the whole course of both the Greek and Latin tongue, and ye shall surely find that when apt and good words began to be neglected, and properties of those two tongues to be confounded, then also began ill deeds to spring, strange manners to oppress good orders, new and fond opinions to strive with old and true doctrine, first in philosophy and after in religion, right judgment of all things to be perverted . . .

Orwell has reformulated it for our time:

> Now, it is clear that the decline of a language must ultimately have political and economic causes: it is not due simply to the bad influence of this or that individual writer. But an effect can become a cause, reinforcing the original cause and producing the same effect in an intensified form, and so on indefinitely. A man may take to drink because he feels himself to be a failure, and then fail all the more completely because he drinks. It is rather the same thing that is happening to the English language. It becomes ugly and slovenly because our thoughts are foolish, but the slovenliness of our language makes it easier for us to have foolish thoughts. The point is that the process is reversible. Modern English, especially written English, is full of bad habits which spread by imitation and which can be avoided if one is willing to take the necessary trouble. If one gets rid of these habits one can think more clearly, and to think clearly is the first step toward political regeneration: so that the fight against bad English is not frivolous and is not the exclusive concern of professional writers.

If we are indifferent to style, we sacrifice our freedom to think and "think more clearly." If we care about style, we can most truly be ourselves. Style in this sense is the man.

ROBERT WADDELL

Formal Prose and Jargon

Robert Waddell taught English at Columbia University. He is the author of Grammar and Style *(1951), from which the following discussion of jargon has been selected. In this selection Professor Waddell objects to jargon largely because of the ambiguity of its meaning. His objection, then, introduces a different way of considering the interdependence of style and meaning than has appeared in the previous essays. It should be clear, however, that Waddell is not disparaging the legitimate use of specialized terminology. All rigorous disciplines have their unique styles, largely because the careful use of terminology within a given context sharpens meaning rather than blurs it. But too often, as Waddell points out, jargon is unnecessarily substituted for a clear, plain style.*

From *Grammar and Style* by Robert Waddell. Copyright 1951 by Robert Waddell. Reprinted by permission of Holt, Rinehart and Winston, Inc.

Almost any society requires for its important personages and for official, academic, and ceremonial purposes some sort of formal or special style of language—usually something several sizes larger than everyday speech, dressier and more dignified. The royal *we* and the kind of language that goes with it is one such formal style—available only to royalty. In various languages at various times and for various purposes formal styles have been of many sorts. Some have been so ponderous or fine spun that they conveyed very little at all except that the user was a man of exalted position capable of using such language. Others, like that of the eighteenth-century English gentleman and man of letters have been polished, graceful, and eminently clear. In twentieth-century English we are badly off. Our most popular formal style is a graceless standardized jargon offensive to anyone with any taste or feeling for the values of language.

As we have just observed, the eighteenth-century style was one of the best. As was pointed out in Chapter 1, [not printed here] it was the style of a relatively small aristocratic class, in which most of the scholars were gentlemen and many of the gentlemen were scholars. Being assured about their own good breeding, learning, and positions in society, these men could afford to write as they pleased, without prescribed rules and formulas, and trusting to their own sense of fitness and propriety to produce a style appropriate to their purposes and the demands of the occasion. Yet since they shared certain assumptions about manners, reason, and good taste, there is a common quality of lucidity, gracefulness, and ease about almost all their writing on whatever occasion, frivolous or grave, formal or informal. Though more or less standardized in many of its qualities, the eighteenth-century style was nevertheless personal and highly flexible. For illustration, let us glance at Johnson's famous letter to Lord Chesterfield. Although Chesterfield is insulted as a snob and meddlesome opportunist, the language remains dignified and polite from beginning to end.

To the Right Honorable the Lord of Chesterfield
7th February, 1755.
My Lord,

I have been lately informed, by the proprietor of *The World* that two papers, in which my Dictionary is recommended to the public, were written by your Lordship. To be so distinguished is an honor, which, being very little accustomed to favors from the great, I know not well how to receive, or in what terms to acknowledge.

When, upon some slight encouragement, I first visited your Lordship, I was overpowered like the rest of mankind, by the enchantment of your address, and could not forbear to wish that I might boast myself *Le vainqueur du vainqueur de la terre;*—that I might obtain that regard for which I saw the world contending; but I found my attendance so little encouraged, that neither pride nor modesty would suffer me to continue it. When I had once addressed your Lordship in public, I had exhausted all the art of pleasing which a retired and uncourtly scholar can possess. I had done all that I could; and no man is well pleased to have his all neglected, be it ever so little.

Seven years, my Lord, have now past, since I waited in your outward rooms, or was repulsed from your door; during which time I have been pushing on my work through difficulties, of which it is useless to complain, and have brought it at last to the verge of publication, without one act of assistance, one word of encouragement, or one smile of favor. Such treatment I did not expect, for I never had a patron before. . . .

Is not a patron, my Lord, one who looks with unconcern on a man struggling for life in the water, and, when he has reached ground, encumbers him with help? The notice which you have been pleased to take of my labors, had it been early, had been kind; but it has been delayed till I am indifferent, and cannot enjoy it; till I am solitary, and cannot impart it; till I am known, and do not want it. I hope it is no very cynical asperity not to confess obligations where no benefit has been received, or to be unwilling that the public should consider me as owing that to a patron, which providence has enabled me to do for myself.

Having carried on my work thus far with so little obligation to any favorer of learning, I shall not be disappointed though I should conclude it, if less be possible, with less; for I have been long wakened from that dream of hope, in which I once boasted myself with so much exultation, my Lord,

your Lordship's most humble
most obedient servant,
Sam. Johnson.

The nineteenth century, as we also observed in Chapter 1, [not printed here] found the eighteenth-century style inappropriate or even impossible for many of its purposes. Many men of letters, especially those we call Romanticists, felt hampered by the polish and restraint and developed instead highly individual styles of their own. The great nineteenth-century middle class, educated chiefly in piety and practicality, untrained in the eighteenth-century manners, ease, and lucidity, and indeed somewhat suspicious of eighteenth-century irony, elegance, and wit, found the eighteenth-century formal style unmanageable. Unequipped with, or at any rate unable to trust entirely, their own sense of propriety and good taste, they required something more standardized and less slippery, something they could depend upon for solid businesslike dignity without having to bother about the little complexities and nuances of the particular occasion. For the style they wanted, the nineteenth-century middle class looked not to the eighteenth-century aristocracy, but to their own institutions of power and authority —chiefly to government, to corporate wealth, and to a new source—science, which in the nineteenth century was acquiring enormous prestige.

The language of government is much influenced by the ancient style of the law, which is technical, repetitious, abstract, and impersonal to an exasperating degree—and for good reasons. It is the endeavor of the law to set down exactly and beyond possibility of misunderstanding or evasion whatever may be the current notions of justice as they work themselves out in thousands of kinds of personal relations and particular circumstances. To do so it must use a tediously complicated language, which no lawyer will attempt to defend on aesthetic grounds and which, for any purpose but its own, is atrocious.

The language of business and corporate wealth derives partly from the plain, bare language of ordinary commerce and bookkeeping, partly perhaps from the technical language of accountants and economists and from the language of the law, and partly from the banker's and the businessman's own good opinions of themselves. Obviously the custodians of large accumulations of money and masonry require a style sufficiently impressive to assure investors that their cash is in good hands. At best this style is dull, abstract, and somewhat ponderous.

The language of science and technology is dry, technical, and impersonal; originally it was designed to report on and explain dispassionately the composition and behavior of matter under various conditions.

These three styles are well enough suited for their own special purposes. But they are scarcely suitable for any others—especially those involving most human activities and feelings. The eighteenth-century style—even at its most formal—had always behind it a man who felt personally responsible for what he was saying. But responsibility in our three institutional styles can at best be fixed on the government, nature, or the law of supply and demand and at worst on nothing at all. The common element in these styles is their rigid impersonality. There is no way to insult Lord Chesterfield in any of them.

Yet it was precisely the impersonality of these styles that recommended them to nineteenth-century middle-class democracy. Tocqueville remarks that one of the major tendencies in an equalitarian and competitive society is that toward uniformity and conformity. Whether to ward off envy or contempt, men tend to behave, at least in public, exactly alike. And an impersonal style in writing makes all men equal on paper, whatever the actual differences in birth, wealth, brains, or breeding may be. It is a kind of lowest common denominator of style. It reveals no personality and gives nobody away. It is utterly "safe."

But from the legal, scientific, and financial styles, the nineteenth century learned almost nothing about precision or exactness in law, science, or finance, or in anything else. It learned only that a certain wordy complexity sounded official and important, that a profusion of seemingly technical terms sounded authoritative and scientific, and that dullness was a kind of guarantee for dignity.

The more this sort of language came to be admired by the public, the more its original practitioners came to admire it themselves and the more they improved upon it. Bureaucrats striving to sound like administrative offices and to impress the public, their superiors, and each other developed a complicated officialese that has become in our day incomprehensible except through the most diligent effort. Politicians, undersecretaries, "spokesmen," and candidates for public office found it easier and easier to talk in vague pseudo-official generalities when "considerations of policy" made it "unfeasible" to say anything plainly in public. Businessmen developed a kind of staccato, "efficient" jargon, in which, for example, any sort of acquaintance or personal communication is called a *contact* (which word also becomes a verb).[1] And the style kept on spreading from politics and business to formal journalism, education, academic research, social service, engineering, medicine, religion—wherever men who wished to sound technical, authoritative, and official could employ it.

As much to blame as anyone for the development and diffusion of this formal jargon are the social scientists—economists, sociologists, and psychologists. Their intention was to achieve the impersonal objectivity and precision of the natural sciences. They could not really adapt the mathematical and controlled experimental techniques of the natural sciences to their own subject matter. But they did borrow a very technical sounding vocabulary and a habit of theorizing about the "natural" laws of economic and other social activity.

Of the theories thus produced many were harmless; many were extremely useful and suggestive. A few of them, in their impersonal ignoring of humanity and human values, were pernicious and dangerous. To talk about "labor" as a commodity is within limits a useful way to discuss and clarify certain problems, but when this sort of abstraction leads the theorist into thinking of the laborer as a commodity, he is in serious moral difficulties—and so is the laborer. The danger is no less when the laborers themselves and their bosses and intellectual advocates begin thinking of themselves as Labor, with only unitary desires and functions. Or when all business activity, honest and otherwise, is lumped under the word Capital and identified with Enterprise or Freedom—or with Tyranny and Oppression.

Economists and other social scientists have retreated from the more extravagant positions of this nineteenth-century social "science," with the exception of certain fanatics who have adopted them as religions and of certain wily or indignant opportunists who use them to blow dust into the eyes of the innocent.

But the style the social scientists adopted in the course of this scientific spree still survives in full bloom, often with the effect of making good political or economic theory unreadable or even incomprehensible. The vocabulary cribbed from the natural sciences consisted of mathematical *factors,* astronomical *phases,* chemical *reactions,* physical *forces,* and similar words. To the use of such technical terms there can be no reasonable objection so long as they are really technical, that is, so long as they name and define

---

[1]Businessmen have lately become aware of their more egregious stylistic follies, and the "Yrs. of the 15th ult. received and contents noted" sort of thing has disappeared, except perhaps in commercial backwaters.

notions otherwise obscure or confused. So used they make discourse more precise rather than less so. But by too many writers these words and others like them (such as *aspect, case, feature, function,* and *phenomenon*) were used so vaguely that they came to mean nothing in particular and almost anything in general. Strung together with connectives like *in connection with* and verbs all in the passive voice (like those in scientific experimental reports) they became simply a jargon, a jargon that for windy vagueness and pretentious abstraction is a marvel.

It should not be inferred from the foregoing that all social scientists, businessmen, and government officials invariably write in the flabby jargon here decried. Most of them, in fact, write English of one sort or another. But enough of them use enough jargon to give it wide currency in learned journals, official directives, annual reports, and other impressive publications. Enough to give the unwary and inexperienced writer the notion that *this* formality is something special (as indeed it hideously is) to be distinguished from what seems to him mere ordinary and intelligible English.

Furthermore, the social scientists, bureaucrats, and businessmen are by no means the only writers who have developed pretentious and ugly jargons. In literary criticism, philosophy, music, theology, psychiatry, and other dignified pursuits, certain practitioners affect highly special and sometimes meaningless ways of saying things (or of saying nothing). Most of these jargons, however, have never caught the public fancy. It is the jargon of the sociologist, the bureaucrat, the businessman, and the professional educator who calls himself an educationist that the innocent public finds impressive and tries to imitate.

Let us examine, to see what it's like, a passage or two written wholly or partly in the popular public jargon we have been discussing. First, a bit of routine bureaucratic prose from a State Department release of 1943 about a victory concert somebody had thought up for the day when victory should arrive. After listing a program consisting of compositions representing each of the allied nations and concluding with the choral finale of Beethoven's "Ninth Symphony" and "Old Hundred,"[2] the release continues:

> While developing the above outline, various aspects were taken into consideration, particularly with regard to the playing of the chorale finale of Beethoven's "Ninth" which is considered by many to be the greatest piece of music of the whole era of republicanism and democracy.
>
> It was recalled that in Germany the words to Schiller's poem, "Ode to Joy," used therein with reference to the brotherhood of man, were changed and finally banned by Government decree; hence the playing of this part of the "Ninth" would seem exceptionally appropriate for this occasion.

---

[2]"Old Hundred" is the tune sung in most Protestant churches to the words "Praise God from whom all blessings flow," etc.

In closing the program it is suggested that reference might be made to the task that still lies ahead for the people of the United States and of the other United Nations in helping to rebuild the world. The tune "Old Hundred" included in the above outline, sung with organ accompaniment by a choral group, might be appropriate in this connection—*The New York Times.*

The tone of these paragraphs is unassuming, even gentle. They are addressed to the general public, not simply to other bureaucrats, and they seem modestly intended to win public approval for the concert proposed, and so they are written partly in English. But let us look at the jargon.

The first paragraph begins with a dangling elliptical clause: *While developing the above outline.* We never find out who developed the outline, because the main sentence has a passive verb and no suitable subject for the clause. The passive is perhaps jargon's best loved and most frequently used device, and so jargon is always full of dangling modifiers.

Next we have the subject of the sentence, *various aspects*—aspects of what, we are never told. Aspects of the outline perhaps, or of the developing. These *aspects*—we now come to the verb and presumably to the main point of the sentence—these various aspects *were taken into consideration* . . . ! A safer and more meaningless statement could scarcely be imagined. They were taken into consideration particularly *with regard to* the playing of the finale of Beethoven's "Ninth," whatever that means. The last clause, which bluntly asserts that the finale *is considered by many to be the greatest* . . . , is perhaps recklessly forthright, but otherwise the paragraph is a miracle of caution. It says nothing whatever. But perhaps we can scratch some crumb of meaning from the second paragraph.

It was recalled (we are not told by whom) *that in Germany the words to Schiller's poem "Ode to Joy," used therein* . . . . Wherein? In the symphony maybe. But: *used therein with reference to the brotherhood of man.* This probably means that the words "Alle Menschen werden Brüder," and so on, which *are* used in the poem and are indeed used *with reference to* the brotherhood of man, as our writer so vaguely puts it, were changed and finally banned by the Nazis. . . . *hence* [our cautious soul continues], *the playing of this part of the "Ninth" would seem exceptionally appropriate for this occasion,* though it is a little hard for the unpracticed reader of jargon to see why until it occurs to him that for this occasion the words will be restored in defiance of and triumph over the Nazis. But for a writer of jargon to display any hint of such powerful and unseemly human emotions is, of course, out of the question. Let us plod on.

In closing the program [a dangling gerund phrase this time], *it is suggested* [by nobody in particular] *that reference might be made* [again, nobody in particular will make it; it will simply *be made,* or rather *might be made*—no sense in sticking one's neck out] *to the task that still lies ahead*—and we continue in astonishingly plain English to the end of the sentence. And on into the next, until we discover that "Old Hundred" *might be appropriate,* which seems marvelously timid for so innocuous a suggestion, *in this connection.* In what connection? Then we remember that this is jargon, and that in jargon *connection* means absolutely anything, anything at all. Here it probably refers to the reference to the task that lies ahead, though certainly it does not matter much what it refers to.

For this sort of genteel, bureaucratic pussyfooting, there is sometimes (though not here) some excuse. The bureaucrat is seldom personally responsible for what he writes; half a dozen others may have a hand in it. His writing is the writing of an office, not a man; and perhaps the head of the office demands verbiage by the ream in order to impress his colleagues or Congress or some higher-up. It is, furthermore, not even safe to make requests, give orders, or explain things directly and simply; some Congressional snooper is always waiting to pounce and make headlines by "investigating" something, demanding dismissals, or cutting appropriations. Better play it safe, muffled, and quiet. But in developing this protective coloration for ticklish and intricate matters, the bureaucrat gets into the habit of making his meaning almost invisible even on the most innocuous occasions.

The passage quoted above is an example of how jargon can make even the simplest matters vague and obscure. The following sentence, from a Veterans Administration poster, shows how it can make complete nonsense:

> Student veterans—if your dependency status has changed, submit proof of this additional dependency now to your regional V. A. office.

In English *dependency status* means state of dependency. Therefore: if your state of dependency has changed, that is, if you are either more or less dependent than you were, send proof of *additional dependency to* . . . . But things will never come out even this way. Fortunately the cartoon on this poster—a young man wheeling a baby carriage—was perfectly clear.

Let us try a piece of business jargon. This is from an article (1944) on the postwar prospects of the rubber manufacturing industry:

> If income does rise, the rise will make feasible a vast expansion of car manufacturing, which in turn will increase the tire industry. Plans for full employment will undoubtedly insure greater stability of this income. This income will be reduced by taxes, and then the expansion of production will be bottled up or slowed up. On the other hand there will be new car markets, if modernization attempts in China, Latin America, and other backward areas are successful. The hope for this is small in view of the fact that reeducation of the people and building a network of better roads takes years to effectuate. Balancing these facts, it seems improbable that the market will increase at a faster rate than the rate of the pre-war decade.
>
> On the other hand, there is an increasing belief that the rubber volume consumed in automobile usage will decrease. There have been predictions made of new synthetic tire life expectancy 50%-100%

greater than the present natural rubber tire. Also a tubeless tire invention would save about 7% of the rubber content and the rubber thickness of the tire could be thinned. Thus synthetic rubber will be used in cases where natural rubber is impracticable.

Observe, first, the heavy preponderance of abstract nouns, such as *rise, expansion, stability, trend, rate, belief, usage, expectancy,* and *cases.* Note also the colorless adjectives *feasible, greater, impracticable,* and the useless infinitive *to effectuate.*

Second, look at the verbs: *does rise, will make feasible, will increase, will insure, will be bottled or slowed up, will be reduced, are, will be, takes, is, will increase, seems, will decrease, is, have been made, would save, could be thinned, is, will be used.* Not a vivid, concrete, visible action in the lot, except for *will be bottled up* and *could be thinned,* and they are both passive.

Third, note the jerky, awkward noun-noun constructions: *modernization attempts, rubber volume, automobile usage, tire life expectancy, tire invention, rubber thickness,* and others.

Fourth, note the blurriness: *increase the tire industry* (or will it only increase the production of tires?); *There is an increasing belief* (what is an increasing belief? or does this mean only that more and more people believe?); *synthetic rubber will be used in cases* (or will it be used in tires?).

Finally, observe the grammar: the dangling *Balancing these facts* and the illogical comparison *synthetic tire life expectancy 50%-100% greater than the present natural rubber tire.*

Let us finish this little survey with some academic jargon:

E. Bus. 155—*Methods and Materials in Distributive Education* (Work Experience Program). A study of effective procedures for establishing work experience and cooperative training programs in both the distributive and office occupations.—From a university catalogue.

"In conformity with the preceding point, if all the interacting parties (in marriage, in minority-majority groups, in different occupational, religious, political, economic, racial, ethnic and other interacting groups and persons) view the given overtly similar (or dissimilar) traits: A, B, C, D, N (physical, biological, mental, socio-cultural) as negligible values or as no values at all, as comprising even no similarity (or dissimilarity), such overt similarities-dissimilarities are innocuous in the generation of either solidarity or antagonism." This is a "scientific" way of saying that if we are unconcerned about our differences or similarities, they are not the sources of friendship or hostility.— Sidney Hook, review of P. A. Sorokin's *Society, Culture, and Personality,* in *The New York Times Book Review.*

And finally a miscellaneous collection from a single issue of a learned journal in sociology.

. . . concludes with proposed action program which has as its ultimate objective the wiping out of residential segregation. [That is, . . . *proposed program designed to wipe out residential segregation.*]

This volume . . . represents the result of a great deal of work. [It couldn't *be* the result, could it? Or possibly: *represents a great deal of work?*]

GROUP B consisted primarily of professional people with a mean college education, diversified interest areas (including intellectual-aesthetic fields) . . . [and] patterns of high creativity in participation activities . . . . Life aspirations approximated "self-realization" and personal satisfaction aims . . . . [Note the suspicious quotation marks around *self-realization*—a mere subjective delusion, probably.]

Life-goals approximated middle class social mobility aspirations.

A search . . . failed to reveal any published validity (or even reliability) figures for several of these short questionnaires.

. . . questions . . . sometimes included personality inventory items which are of questionable value.

. . . happiness adjustment items . . . . questions selected on other than an armchair basis . . . . marital prediction situations . . . . [And so on endlessly.]

That human beings should write like this! Yet this horrible prose would be unimportant or merely pathetic if it were only the private affair of the specialists who make it. But the desperate eagerness of many of us to be ourselves scientific and to sound on occasion official has led us to identify the jargon of the clumsiest scientific writers with science itself and the worst officialese with authority. An inexperienced writer can imitate it easily since it is all made of standard parts; hence, whenever he wishes to assume the toga of formality and authority, his prose sprouts *factors, aspects,* and *situations* like dandelions in May.

For the writer who is afraid of his own direct, aggressive impulses and of what people may think, jargon provides protection in muffling anonymity. For the writer who hates or fears people or who wishes to evade the problem presented by humanity's complicated untidiness, and its differences, violences, affections, whims, prickly egotisms, and feelings of all sorts, jargon is invaluable. With jargon he can vaporize concrete complexity and disorder into a uniform gray fog; he can disinfect the universe of man. In jargon nobody ever does anything, feels anything, or causes anything; nobody has an opinion. Opinions are had; causes result in; factors affect. Everything is reduced to vague abstraction. The writer can even abolish himself, for jargon never sounds as though anybody had written it; it seems simply to come about, as from a machine, and it talks mechanically of things that come about, through some indistinct interaction of forces.

We can exhibit this monstrosity in grammatical detail in a kind of parody of English grammar. This will be an idealized version abstracted from the juiciest and most popular usages of bureaucratic, sociological, and other sorts of official and pseudo-scientific prose. (No one, of course, has ever written jargon in the classically pure form here given. Even jargon by the most expert practitioners is contaminated with bits and shreds of plain English.)

GRAMMAR OF BASIC JARGON
I. Vocabulary

1. NOUNS

absence	field*	personnel
addition	formula	phase
adjustment	function	phenomenon
advantage	guide	picture§
aid	ideology	portion
appearance	impact	presence
application	increase	rate
area*	indication	reaction
aspect	influence	reference
basis	instance	result
behavior†	item	role†
case	lack	side‡
category	level	situation*
character†	line‡	solution
class	maximum	standpoint
condition	measure	state
criterion	medium	status
data	method	tendency
decrease	minimum	term
element	motivation	trend
extent	nature	type
facility	need	unit
fact	objective	utilization
factor	orientation	value
feature	outlook	viewpoint

---

*Area, field, and situation must never be used in a geographical sense in reference to places. Areas and fields are broad general abstract categories (e.g., the area of home economics; the criminology field) and are especially elegant when subdivided into branches. A situation is the general orientation of factors in a case, the significant totality of relevant data; when a situation arises, it usually has to be remedied.

†Behavior, character, role are used only in abstract reference (e.g., the indeterminate character of the data). Never to be used in reference to human beings (who, if they exist, should not be thought of as having characters—a vague and unsatisfactory term at best—but rather as belonging to personality type). Reference in these terms to the personages, i.e., the personnel, of fiction and drama is also obscure and obsolete. If personal reference is unavoidable, character should be confined to adjectival use, as in character structure, and the other terms should be used as follows: pre-adolescent group behavior rather than behavior of children; Hamlet role rather than role of Hamlet.

‡Used only abstractly: along economic lines; the military side of the situation.

§In part equivalent to outlook, in part to situation; usually referred to as the total picture (and often to be remedied). Never used to refer to a pictorial reproduction such as a photograph or two-dimensional representational art work.

2. PRONOUNS

it   there

3. VERBS

Class 1. Commonest Verb

is

Class 2. Regular Verbs

accomplish	effectuate	motivate
acquire	eliminate	necessitate
add	eventuate	obtain
assist	evidence	occur
balance	expedite	orient
base	exist	outweigh
become	facilitate	position
class	function	precede
classify	implement	promote
compose	include	prove
comprise	increase	represent
concern	initiate	result
contact	insure	state
contribute	integrate	structure
culminate	involve	term
decrease	locate	typify
effect	maintain	utilize

Class 3. Vaporized Common Verbs and Verb Phrases

arise	embrace	provide
begin	follow	reach
bring	form	serve
build	lend	speed

bring about	come to the	make for
bring forth	fore	play a part
bring in, out	enter in	spring up
come about	fall under	take place
come into	give rise to	take steps to
contact with	lie in	

4. ADJECTIVES

absent	advantageous	available
additional	apparent	better
adequate	approximate	broad

detrimental	major	positive
dynamic	maximal, -um	predominant
efficient	minimal, -um	present
essential	minor	primary
existent	moderate	prime
expedient	multiple	salient
favorable	necessary	satisfactory
feasible	numerous	so-called
functional	objective	static
great	optimal, -um	superior
indicative	outstanding	ultimate
initial	over-all	unique
integral	partial	unitary

(And, of course, participles like *added, conditioned, increased, predominating.*)

5. MODIFYING PHRASES

as far as ―― is concerned	in origin, of a ―― origin
for the most part	in this respect
from a ―― viewpoint	in this regard
in appearance, of a ―― appearance	in a ―― sense
in aspect, of a ―― aspect	in scope, of a ―― scope
in many cases	of great advantage
in character, of a ―― character	of great value
in a ―― condition	on a large scale
in the ―― line	on a ―― basis
in many instances	to a great degree
in a ―― manner	to a great extent
in nature, of a ―― nature	with few exceptions

6. CONNECTIVES

along with	in conjunction with
as a result of	in connection with
as regards	in the event that
as to (whether)	in the line of
associated with	in reference to
in association with	in regard to
due to	in relation to
due to the fact that	in such a manner that
from the standpoint of	in terms of
in the capacity of	in that
in the case of	in view of

in view of the fact that	relative to
on the basis of (*or* that)	respecting
on the part of	subsequent to
on the style of	to the extent that
other than	with reference to
pertinent to	with regard to
previous to	with respect to
prior to	with a view to
regarding	with the result that

Note: Adverbs, being obsolete, have been omitted from the vocabulary. Only a few indicating frequency or degree survive: *greatly, extremely, primarily, ultimately,* and the like. Others are replaced by adjective-noun constructions (e.g., *was given a favorable reception* for *favorably received*) or by prepositional phrases (e.g., *equal in a physical respect* for *physically equal*).

II. RULES

NOUNS

1. Never use a concrete noun in its original concrete sense.
2. Use one of the Ten Basic Nouns of Jargon in every sentence, if possible. The Ten Basic Nouns are: *aspect, case, character, condition, factor, feature, instance, nature, phase, situation.*

VERBS

3. Avoid verbs wherever possible: for example, use *prior to the Vanderpool committee investigation* rather than *before the Vanderpool committee investigated.*
4. In the main sentence, where a verb is unavoidable, use the most colorless verbal construction. Use *to be* as much as possible. Never say, for example, *believe* or *emphasize;* use *have the belief* or *put the emphasis on.*
5. Use all transitive verbs in the passive voice. Avoid mentioning the agent who performs the action, that is, the subject of the active voice.
6. Always use vaporized common verbs in a vague abstract sense, never in the original concrete sense. For example: this situation *arises* . . . ; religion *was begun* by man as a solution for . . . ; devaluation *will bring* or *make for* better trade relations . . . ; the field *embraces* both electronics and chemistry . . . ; factors *provide* or *give rise to* a new outlook . . . ; radar *falls under* the heading of electronics; *speed* moral reorientation; *build* confidence.
7. Where verbs are unavoidable, use dignified latinate terms; avoid vulgar informality. Use *state* for *say, imbibe* for *drink, ensue* for *follow,* and so on.

8. Avoid using simple adjectives in the vulgar manner. Whenever possible use nouns instead or prepositional phrases. For example, *psychological research* is flat and tasteless; prefer *psychology research* or *research of a psychological character*.

9. Avoid placing adjectives before the nouns they modify; put them after the nouns in prepositional phrases: e.g., *of a detrimental nature.* Avoid simple adjectives as complements: turn them into prepositional phrases (The quarrel was *of a feudal rather than a religious nature*), or turn them into noun objects of colorless verbs (e.g., the presentation *has compactness;* not *is compact*).

10. Always insert the category of modification to which a simple adjective complement belongs: e.g., rectangular *in shape;* efficient *in operation;* steel blue *in color;* gigantic *in size.* Otherwise, the reader has to pause to figure this out.

11. Avoid using nouns in old-fashioned prepositional phrases to modify other nouns. Place them directly before the other nouns like old-style adjectives: *economy purposes; control method; competition sphere; transportation facilities; personality traits; population increase; situation significance; group situation; air worthiness requirements.*

CONNECTIVES

12. Avoid old-fashioned simple connectives like *because, before, of,* or *as.* Always prefer *due to the fact that, prior to, in connection with, in a manner similar to,* and similar forms.

About the language outlined in this grammar of jargon, there are three or four things we may observe. The first is the heavy preponderance of nouns (the list of nouns in jargon could be extended almost indefinitely beyond the vocabulary given above; the list of verbs and adjectives could not). Many of the verbs and adjectives are only the same nouns in different grammatical functions. And all abstract! Jargon does not dramatize or describe anything concretely. It is concerned only to name and label things and then to indicate, very foggily, certain kinds of relations between them.

These relations constitute the second point worth noticing—the pseudo-scientific air of jargon. Most of the vocabulary is concerned with four apparently technical but really very simple, even basic, ideas or ways of thinking.

1. Many of the words indicate little more than mere occurrence or non-occurrence: *absence, presence, appearance, condition, data, element, fact, item, lack, phenomenon, situation, state; is, exist, enter in, lie in, occur, eliminate; apparent, essential, positive.*

2. Another group is devoted to classification: *category, class, area, field,*

line, character, nature, orientation, phase, role; classify, comprise, include, embrace, typify, fall under.

3. A large group is used for measurement of one sort or another: *addition, decrease, increase, extent, level, majority, maximum, rate; add, approximate, balance, culminate, precede, outweigh; broad, great, initial, moderate, outstanding, partial, predominant, primary, superior, ultimate.*

4. A fourth group is devoted to what we shall here call abstract lubrication: Do the factors in a case slither together in a comforting way? Then use words like *adjustment, aid, function, influence, medium, motivation, solution, trend; assist, effectuate, facilitate, expedite, ensure, maintain, make for, result, utilize; adequate, available, efficient, favorable, feasible, satisfactory.* But if things are not so satisfactory, tack *dis-, in-, mal-, non-,* or *un-* onto the same words. The only sign of life in jargon is this unctuous, flabby, mush-mouthed eagerness that everything shall be, in a broad general way, smooth and well greased. Nobody has to work for anything; things simply *tend, function, combine,* and *result in.* Everything must turn out to be *easy, available,* and *expedient*—or at very least *favorable* or *adequate.*

These four ways of thinking—take them honestly—are important and even essential to any kind of thought whatever, especially to scientific thought, which specializes in them. But in jargon none of them are actually performed in a precise or illuminating manner. They are only blurrily suggested; jargon goes vaguely through the motions. It all sounds very technical, and there is much clatter and hum from what we are meant to believe is scientific machinery. But the scientific results are very meagre. And so are any other results. Jargon is quite without means of suggesting much about color, tone, or visible motion. It cannot deal vividly with feeling, temper, opinion, or personality. It cannot indicate relations in simple, exact, or familiar terms, and it is helpless to cope with precise details. The universe of jargon is a dusty, gray, general fog, in which various factors may be said to exist. Jargon is concerned only to assert this existence and to classify it (more or less), and check the oil.

A third characteristic of jargon is its verbal inefficiency. It never uses one word where three or four will do. It never says *if,* it says *in the event that;* it never says *because,* it says *due to the fact that;* it does not say *in, by, of, for,* or *about,* it says *in connection with* and *with respect to.* These phrases are not only several times longer than the English equivalents but also much less precise. Jargon seldom commits itself to any single meaning in particular; instead it evasively alludes to any meaning that is vaguely relevant or possible in the context. The heavily worked phrases *for the most part* and *in many cases* (or *instances*) are examples of this inclusive . ambiguity:

> *For the most part* college students have little trouble in getting rides. [Does this mean *most students* have little trouble? Or that *students usually* have little trouble? It means neither—not exactly. The writer couldn't make up his mind. It means both—more or less.]

Engineers in the past have failed *in many instances* in designing the highway for speed and safety. [*Many engineers? Engineers have often?*]

Experimenters in the past, in treating heat transfer from vapor to cooling water, have devoted their efforts to steam and water, *with the exception of a very few cases*. [*Cases* of what? experimenters? efforts? steam and water? And what would any of these mean anyway?]

The single verbal economy that jargon can boast of is the plentiful use of nouns as adjectives, which cuts down on prepositions. But the saving in words is lost many times over through clumsiness and obscurity. The use of noun-adjectives is common in English (*stone* wall, *morning* paper, *business* letter, etc.), but it is usually confined to relatively short nouns, and the relation between noun-adjective and noun modified is usually clear and simple (time, place, purpose, composition, etc.). But in jargon, the longer the noun-adjective the better; and its relation to the noun modified can be anything—or, better yet, everything. Consider the sociologist's phrase *happiness adjustment*. Does this mean adjustment *to* happiness? *in* happiness? *for* happiness? or what? It means none of these, and all of them. It means, with beautifully sweeping vagueness, *adjustment in connection with happiness*.

A fourth, and pitiful, characteristic of jargon is its shuffling pace and arhythmic gait. Since a sentence in jargon is almost nothing but nouns, noun-adjectives, and other noun constructions strung together with relatively meaningless connectives (and somewhere or other at least an *is* among them to make things grammatically legal), there is little reason for it to stop anywhere in particular: it can pad itself out rearward with *in relation to*'s and other prepositional phrases until it runs out of breath. Since such a sentence is never trying to dramatize anything and since almost everything in it is as emphatic as everything else, there is no need for it to have a special shape, length, or pattern. Its parts are not very clearly distinguishable. Its subordinate clauses, for example, rarely begin with simple subordinate conjunctions like *since* or *before,* but rather with long prepositional phrases like *in view of the fact that* which looks simply like more nouns and prepositions among the many nouns and prepositions already in the sentence. Or the clause becomes a noun construction—*prior to the committee's investigation of the charge* instead of *before the committee investigated the charge.* Its precious noun-adjective is its only change of pace. It sometimes likes to pile up three or four of them, as we might in a parody of the sociologist's phrase mentioned above: *pre-high school age group happiness adjustment factors.* Slap something like this into the middle of the ordinary sentence in jargon and the sentence is galvanized into a series of spastic mechanical jerks, very welcome after the somnolent slow plodding of the paragraphs or pages preceding. . . .

Language like this, besides being feeble and obscure, is morally reprehensible because it is irresponsible. For jargon, which lacks all sharpness, clarity, and force, is beautifully designed, as George Orwell points out, "to make lies sound truthful and murder respectable, and to give an appearance of solidity to pure wind."[3] The apprentice writer who imitates it through laziness, incompetence, or gullibility, has of course no thought of murder or of any deception, but in using it he casts his vote for deceptive vagueness, abstract inhumanity, graceless bad manners, and confusion of thought. He becomes in effect a support and a willing listener to those who use this sort of language to bulldoze and deceive; through him the muddy vagueness spreads. For as Orwell continues, "an effect can become a cause, reinforcing the original cause and producing the same effect in intensified form, and so on indefinitely. A man may take to drink because he feels himself to be a failure, and then fail all the more completely because he drinks. It is rather the same thing that is happening to the English language. It becomes ugly and inaccurate because our thoughts are foolish, but the slovenliness of our language makes it easier for us to have foolish thoughts. The point is that the process is reversible. Modern English, especially written English, is full of bad habits which spread by imitation and which can be avoided if one is willing to take the necessary trouble. If one gets rid of these habits one can think more clearly, and to think more clearly is a necessary first step towards political regeneration: so that the fight against bad English is not frivolous and is not the exclusive concern of professional writers."

The writer who writes well writes like himself. For the apprentice writer this means first of all sorting himself out from the anonymous public background, examining the scene about him and his own manifold relations to it, judging his own and others' values, accepting, rejecting, changing his mind, but always trying to see the object as it really is to him—which may or may not have anything to do with what it is generally said to be.

His first writing about these preliminary efforts may be plain, bald, and inadequate, but if it is honest it will display individuality and perhaps even a blunt charm. With practice this individuality becomes clearer and more assured. This is not to say that the writer need be concerned at all with "expressing himself" all over the page; the writer entirely preoccupied with himself is more often than not a bore; there are other subjects. It is in attempting to report accurately his own observations and convictions and in honestly trying to make others see and agree that the writer's personality most naturally and pleasingly exhibits itself—quite by the way—as a kind of unearned increment to the rewards of writing honestly—as style, in a word, or the beginnings of style.

---

[3]"Politics and the English Language," *New Republic,* June 17, 1946. Orwell illustrates the respectability of murder as follows: "Consider for instance some comfortable English professor defending Russian totalitarianism. He cannot say outright, 'I believe in killing off your opponents when you can get good results by doing so.' Probably, therefore, he will say something like this: 'While freely conceding that the Soviet regime exhibits certain features which the humanitarian may be inclined to deplore, we must, I think, agree that a certain curtailment of the right to political opposition is an unavoidable concomitant of transitional periods, and that the rigors which the Russian people have been called upon to undergo have been amply justified in the sphere of concrete achievement."

The man who can write a decent informal style can with a little patience develop a responsible formal style, and his example may encourage others— to the vast improvement of our intellectual, moral, and political thinking. Oceans of bilge by and for the intellectually limited and the irresponsible will continue to surround us. Which provides all the more reason for the honest and intelligent to cultivate accuracy in observation, lucidity and force in statement, and good manners in persuasion.

EDWARD P. J. CORBETT

A Method of Analyzing Prose Style with a Demonstration Analysis of Swift's *A Modest Proposal*

Edward P. J. Corbett is professor of English at the Ohio State University. He is the author of Classical Rhetoric for the Modern Student *(1965). The following article consists of a compilation of techniques for analyzing prose style taken "from the ancient rhetoricians and from modern expositors of verbal strategies" and an application of those techniques to Swift's essay.* Professor Corbett thus provides a concise explanation and demonstration of the rhetorical function of style. Even though the subject of this stylistic analysis is a famous literary work, the method used in the analysis can be applied to any essay to determine the rhetorical function of its style.*

Most of us teachers have felt rather frustrated in our efforts to analyze prose style, either for ourselves or for our students in the classroom. This frustration has been brought on not only by a certain vagueness about what style is but also by the lack of a technique for analyzing prose style. As a result, we content ourselves in the classroom with enunciating such general, subjective labels for a particular author's style as "vigorous," "urbane," "ponderous," "curt," "mannered," "jaunty," "explosive," and that favorite all-purpose epithet "smooth-flowing." Some of us may have arrived at the point where we feel confident enough to designate more specific features of a prose style, such as the preponderance of Latinate diction, the mannerism of balanced sentence structure, or the high proportion of concrete images.

From *Reflections on High School English: NDEA Institute Lectures 1965,* ed. Gary Tate (Tulsa: University of Tulsa, 1966), pp. 106-124. Reprinted by permission of Gary Tate and the author.
*The text of Swift's *A Modest Proposal* is included in Appendix A. p. 293.

But usually by the time we have gone that far, we have exhausted our resources for describing prose style, and we spend the rest of the class period discussing the ideas of the essay under consideration.

The New Criticism, especially as it was presented in Brooks and Warren's influential textbook *Understanding Poetry,* gave us teachers a technique for analyzing the verbal strategies of a poem. Consequently, we feel very secure when we come to analyze poetry for or with our students. What we need now is comparable training in a method of analyzing prose style.

What would lay the groundwork for the development of such a method would be a number of descriptions of prose style comparable to the descriptions of English grammar that we have had from modern linguists. It is surprising how few of these studies have been produced. At the end of the last century, Edwin H. Lewis's *The History of the English Paragraph* (University of Chicago Studies, 1894), L. A. Sherman's *Some Observations upon Sentence-Length in English Prose* (University of Nebraska Studies, 1892), and G. W. Gerwig's *On the Decrease of Predication and of Sentence Weight in English* (University of Nebraska Studies, 1894) presented statistical studies of several prose stylists. In this century, we have had a few stylistic studies of specific authors, such as Warner Taylor's *The Prose Style of Johnson* (Madison, 1918), Zilpha E. Chandler's *An Analysis of the Stylistic Techniques of Addison, Johnson, Hazlitt and Pater* (Iowa City, 1928), and W. K. Wimsatt's *The Prose Style of Samuel Johnson* (New Haven, 1941).[1] Very shortly, I understand, Mouton of the Hague will publish Louis Milic's study of Jonathan Swift's style.

As more of these stylistic descriptions appear, we will gain a basis for more valid generalizations about English prose style, and we may find that we have to relinquish some of our illusions about how certain writers create their stylistic effects. Such studies will also help us to develop techniques for analyzing style and to prepare textbooks for the classroom. Those of us who are interested in doing something with style in the classroom are looking forward to the publication of textbooks on style now being prepared by such teachers as Richard Ohmann, Francis Christensen, Winston Weathers and Otis Winchester, Harriet Sheridan, and Josephine Miles.

I will outline here a procedure for analyzing prose style. There will be very little in this proposed method that is original. I have merely brought together what I have learned about style from the ancient rhetoricians and from modern expositors of verbal strategies. After I have outlined the various features of style that one might look for in studying any prose piece, I will illustrate the method with a fairly detailed analysis of one of the most anthologized prose essays in English literature, Jonathan Swift's *A Modest Proposal.*

Any stylistic analysis must start out, I think, with some close observa-

---

[1] We must not forget, of course, the pioneering work that Morris W. Croll did in the 1920's on sixteenth and seventeenth-century English prose style. These studies will soon be published in a single volume.

tion of what actually appears on the printed page. One might, for instance, sense that a particular author uses a great many short sentences. Now, sentence-length is one of the features that can tell us something about an author's style. But it should be obvious that we cannot make a tenable generalization about an author's characteristic sentence-length until we have determined, by some rather tedious counting and tabulating, just how long or short his sentences are. Such a procedure would make counters and measurers of us all—"a slide-rule method," to use Leslie Whipp's term,[2] that we humanistically trained teachers may find repellent—but this is a necessary step if we are to learn something about style in general and about style in particular.

If teachers and students survive the tedium of such counting and tabulating, they will then have a chance to bring to bear their aesthetic sensibilities. The next step in the procedure—and a more significant step—is to relate what the statistics reveal to the rhetoric of the piece being analyzed. Determining the length of a prose sentence is much like scanning a line of verse. Just as it is fairly easy to determine that a particular line of verse is written in iambic pentameter, so it is easy to determine that a particular sentence in prose is, say, twenty-one words long. But so what? The more important consideration is the function of that meter or that sentence-length. What contribution does this meter or this sentence-length make to the effect that the writer was seeking to produce? Here is where our judgment or our aesthetic sensibility or our rhetorical sense will have an opportunity to exercise itself. And it is here, in our relating of fact to function, that we will experience a perceptible growth in our powers of analysis and criticism.

A note of caution should be raised at this point. Inductive logic has taught us that the strength of a generalization rests partly on the number of observed facts. Just as one swallow does not make a summer so a prevalent stylistic feature observed in a single piece of prose does not necessarily constitute a characteristic of the author's style. An author's style may change as his subject-matter or his purpose or his audience changes. Moreover, his style may have evolved over a period of time, and the stylistic feature that we have observed in this particular prose piece may be a mannerism that he eventually outgrew. True, certain characteristics of an author's style will be fairly constant, but we would be wise to withhold any generalizations about those constants until after we have studied a reasonably large body of a man's prose. All that we may be able to conclude from our inductive study of a single essay is that this particular stylistic device is a feature of this particular prose piece. But of course even that limited generalization represents some gain in our knowledge of an author's style.

Another caution is that we must be careful in our effort to relate fact to function. Dr. Johnson, you recall, said about Pope's celebrated doctrine of

---

[2]See Leslie T. Whipp and Margaret E. Ashida, "A Slide-Rule Composition Course," *College English*, XXV (October, 1963), 18-22.

suiting sound to the sense, "This notion of representative metre, and the desire of discovering frequent adaptations of the sound to the sense, have produced, in my opinion, many wild conceits and imaginary beauties." We can indeed become excessively ingenious in our efforts to make a stylistic feature fit a rhetorical function. The pitfalls of such speculation, however, should not discourage us from at least making the attempt. Even a strained speculation about the aptness of a particular stylistic feature is better than leaving an observed fact hanging in mid-air. We can later revise or reject our forced speculation when our knowledge or skill grows. If I may indulge in a platitude, nothing ventured, nothing gained.

With these general observations and cautions about the method in mind, we can now look at a listing of some of the objectively observable features of style. These features will be considered under the three main heads of words, sentences, and paragraphs.

What is there that we can observe about words or, to use the more common rhetorical term, diction? Well, we can seek to determine whether an author's diction is predominantly general or specific; abstract or concrete; formal or informal; polysyllabic or monosyllabic; common or special; referential or emotive. Judgments about the either-or will be more subjective in some cases than in others. We can, for instance, determine precisely the proportion between monosyllabic and polysyllabic diction; but since the difference between, say, formal and informal diction is relative, our judgments about some words on this score will necessarily be subjective. Making allowances for those subjective judgments, however, we still can determine, in cases of relative difference, the general tenor of a man's diction. After studying the diction of an A. J. Liebling piece on boxing, for instance, we would find it fairly easy to conclude that although Mr. Liebling adroitly mixes formal and informal words, his diction is predominantly informal.

The frequency of proper nouns in a piece will also tell us something about a man's style. In the readability formula that Rudolf Flesch devised several years ago, the incidence of proper nouns was one of the factors that enhanced the readability of prose. Then too there will always be some few words in an essay that will tell us a great deal about an author's period, milieu, range of interest, education, and bias. We would do well to look for such indicative words.

Studying the diction of a prose piece from these various angles will help us to determine the "weight" of a man's style and to account for the effect that a man's style creates. Sometimes, for instance, when we get the general impression that a man's style is heavy and opaque, we are surprised to learn, after a close study of the diction, that the peculiar texture of his style has *not* been produced by his choice of words. And that kind of revelation is a real gain for us, because then we know that we will have to look elsewhere for the cause of the ponderous effect.

In moving on from a study of word-choice to a study of words in collocation, we find that the most fruitful syntactical unit to study is the sentence. What can we look for when we study the sentences in a prose piece? For one thing,,we can study the length of sentences (measured in number of words). Once the total number of sentences and the total number of words are known, we can, by a simple exercise in long division, figure out the average sentence-length. We can then get an idea of variations of sentence-length by tabulating the percentage of sentences which *exceed,* and the percentage which *fall short of,* the average by a specified number of words.

One can also make a study of the *kinds* of sentences in a prose piece. One can tabulate the grammatical types of sentences (simple, compound, complex, compound-complex); or the rhetorical types (loose, periodic, balanced, antithetical); or the functional types (statement, question, command, exclamation). In studying varieties of sentence patterns, one can look at such things as inversions of normal word-order, the frequency and kinds of sentence-openers (infinitive, gerund, or participial phrases; adverb clauses; absolute constructions; expletive patterns; conjunctive words and phrases); and the methods and location of expansion in the sentences.

Although tropes (words with transferred meanings) could be observed when we are studying diction, and schemes (unusual sentence patterns) could be observed when we are studying sentences, it is probably better to make a separate step of recording figures of speech. Under tropes we would be noting such things as metaphor, simile, synecdoche, metonymy, irony, litotes, oxymoron, antonomasia. Under schemes we would be noting such things as anaphora, apposition, parallelism, antithesis, chiasmus, climax, anastrophe. The study of schemes and tropes can reveal a great deal about the degree of vividness, vivacity, and ornateness in an author's style.

The rhetoric of the next largest unit, the paragraph, has been one of the most neglected aspects of stylistic study. Modern rhetoric books have paid a great deal of attention to the topic sentence, to the various methods of developing paragraphs, and to the qualities of unity, coherence, and emphasis, but a study of these aspects does not reveal very much about a man's style. Perhaps the reason why classical rhetorics did not deal at all with the paragraph is that classical rhetoric was concerned primarily with spoken discourse. Paragraphing of course is a typographical device to punctuate units of thought in written discourse only, and this kind of punctuation often reveals no more about a man's style than the punctuation used within sentences. But there must be an approach to the study of the paragraph that would reveal something about style, and perhaps Professor Francis Christensen's projected book on the rhetoric of the sentence and paragraph will provide the approach that will yield significant information about the style of the paragraph.

As a beginning, meanwhile, we can look at such things as the length of paragraphs (measured in number of words and/or number of sentences), the various levels of movement or development in the paragraph, the means of articulating sentences within the paragraph, and the transitional devices used between paragraphs. By observing the length of paragraphs and the modes of development and articulation, we will get a sense of the density, pace, and readability of an author's style.

The tabulation of objectively observable items, such as I have been outlining, might be called the stage of "gathering the data." It is a wearisome, time-consuming inductive exercise, but it is a necessary stage if our generalizations about a man's style are to be at all tenable. Needless to say, one does not have to look at *all* of the features in every stylistic analysis, and one does not have to follow the order outlined above. Sometimes concentration on a few salient features will bring us closer to the essence of a man's style than will an exhaustive analysis. Style is a complex of many linguistic devices cooperating to produce a peculiar effect, but it may not always be necessary to expose all of the linguistic devices in order to account for the effect.

Let me recommend one fruitful practice for this gathering of the data. You might try copying out by hand long passages of the essay or even the entire essay. You will be amazed at the number of additional things you will detect about a man's style when you write out his text. From my experience with transcribing a text, I would estimate that by copying you will detect at least three times as many features as you will by merely reading and rereading the text. In gathering the data for my analysis of Swift's *A Modest Proposal,* I detected some of the most significant features of his style only after I had laboriously copied out the entire text of the essay.

Gathering the data is a prelude for the more important, the more difficult stage—relating this data to the author's rhetorical strategies. It does not take much intelligence to gather the data; it takes only patience and accuracy. But it does take intelligence and perhaps a good measure of imagination to be able to see the rhetorical function of a particular stylistic feature.

The "why" of any stylistic feature can be answered only in relation to something else—the subject-matter or the occasion or the genre or the author's purpose or the nature of the audience or the ethos of the writer. To be able to relate stylistic features to their rhetorical function then, we must have a secure knowledge of the essay we are analyzing. As a minimum, we must know its purpose, its thesis, and its organization. In addition, we may need to know something about the author, something about the situation that prompted the essay, something about the audience to whom the essay was directed. We should be able to gain a good deal of this kind of knowledge from internal evidence alone. But we may find it helpful to resort to external sources in order to supplement what internal evidence tells us. So we may have to turn to biographical reference works, to literary histories, to critical articles. The point is that the more profound our understanding of the essay is, the easier it will be to relate a stylistic feature to its rhetorical function.

Before launching into my analysis of *A Modest Proposal,* let me suggest some follow-up exercises. Once your students have done an analysis of one or more stylistic features of an essay, they can be asked to study another essay by the same author. They may discover thereby that an author's style changes noticeably as his subject-matter or his purpose or his audience changes. The value to your students of such an observation will be the realization that an author must be in command, not of one style but of many styles. Next, you may want to direct your students to study another author, either from the same period or from a later period, preferably an author writing on a similar subject or with a similar purpose. Such comparisons can make meaningful to the students Buffon's famous statement, "Style is the man." And such comparisons can also make the students aware that styles change not only as the subject or genre or audience or purpose changes but as the period changes. Twentieth-century style in general is distinctively different from seventeenth-century style, and it will represent a real gain in the students' education if they come to realize that the radical changes in modern man's way of life have had a marked influence on the dominant style of the age.

Eventually, students should be turned loose on an analysis of their own prose style. This exercise may well be the most fruitful one for the students. They will be fascinated not only by what they learn about their own style but also by what they learn from comparing their style with that of professional writers. Let us hope that the students will be intelligent enough to recognize that the differences between their style and other authors' styles do not mean that their style is necessarily inferior to the styles of the other authors.

The best themes I have received from students during my teaching career have been those written by freshmen who were asked to comment on what they had learned from a series of stylistic studies. One of the reasons why these themes were fascinating enough to keep me up until 2:00 in the morning reading them was, I think, that the students were writing from a body of specific knowledge that they themselves had derived inductively. In other words, the problem of invention having been solved for them, the students had something to say—and somehow, for the first time, they were finding apt words to say what they had to say. Try this with your students. You may for the first time in your teaching career become excited about a batch of themes.

I have gone on long enough now about a general procedure for analyzing prose style. The method should become more meaningful for you as I apply it to a specific piece of prose—in this case, Jonathan Swift's famous satirical essay *A Modest Proposal.*

I might begin this stylistic analysis by defining what kind of discourse *A Modest Proposal* is, since genre makes its own demands on the kind of style that an author will employ. With reference to the literary genres, *A Modest Proposal* can be classified as a satire, and with reference to the four forms of discourse, satire must be classified as argumentation. If we were using the classical rhetorician's three kinds of persuasive discourse to further specify what type of argumentation we have here, we would classify *A Modest Proposal* as an instance of "deliberative" discourse, since Jonathan Swift is bent on changing the attitude of the propertied class toward the Irish poor and ultimately on moving this class to take some action that would remedy the lot of the poor.

In 1728, a year before *A Modest Proposal* was published, there had been a devastating famine in Ireland caused by three successive failures of the harvest. This famine had aggravated the misery of a people that had already been reduced to abject poverty by years of heavy taxation, repressive laws, and absentee landlordism. As Louis A. Landa has pointed out,[3] Swift hoped to expose the contradiction between a favorite maxim of the mercantilist economic writers—namely, that people are the riches of a nation—and the practice of reducing the majority of subjects to a condition of grinding poverty. The prevalence of the poverty was plain to see, and there had been no lack of proposals, from the political economists, of ways to remedy the condition of the poor. But the ruling class and the absentee landlords were not listening; battening on the revenues from the land, they were not much concerned about the condition of the peasants who were producing their wealth. Swift was determined to get their ear. He would shock them into attention. And he would shock them into attention with a monstrous proposal presented by means of two of his favorite satiric techniques—using a mask and using irony.

To make his use of the mask or *persona* effective, Swift must create a character who is consistent, credible, and authoritative. This must be a character who, in a sense, "sneaks up" on the reader, a character who lulls the reader into expecting a sensible, practicable solution of the Irish problem and who, even after he has dropped his bombshell, maintains his pose and his poise. This character will exert a curious kind of ethical appeal—a man who at the beginning of the essay gives the impression of being serious, expert, and well-meaning but who gradually reveals himself to be shockingly inhuman and naive. The character that eventually emerges is that of a fool whose insanity becomes, as Martin Price puts it, "a metaphor for the guilt of responsible men."[4]

One of the consequences of this use of a *persona* is that the style of the essay will not be Swift's style; rather it will be a style appropriate to the character that Swift has created. True, some of the characteristics of Swift's style will be present; no author can entirely submerge his own style, except perhaps when he is engaged in writing a parody of another author's style. But if Swift does his job properly, the message of the essay will be conveyed to us in a style that differs, at least in some respect, from the style that Swift displays when he is speaking in his own voice.

One of the respects in which the style of *A Modest Proposal* differs noticeably from Swift's usual style is the sentence-length. The average sentence-length in this essay is 56.9 words per sentence. And we note some

---

[3]See Louis A. Landa, "*A Modest Proposal* and Populousness," *Modern Philology*, XL (1942), 161-170 and "Swift's Economic Views and Mercantilism," *Journal of Literary History*, X (1942), 310-335.

[4]Martin Price, *Swift's Rhetorical Art* (New Haven: Yale University Press, 1953), p. 88.

remarkable variations above and below that average. Although 46% of his sentences are composed of less than 47 words, almost 30% of his sentences are longer than 67 words (see Appendix for additional statistics on sentence-length). It is interesting to compare this sentence-length with that in two other works where Swift used a *persona*. In studying 200 paragraphs of *Gulliver's Travels* and 100 paragraphs of *A Tale of a Tub,* Edwin Herbert Lewis discovered the average sentence-length to be 40.7 words—almost 50% shorter than the average sentence in *A Modest Proposal.*[5] What has happened to the "conciseness" that Herbert Davis says is the most distinctive quality of Swift's style?[6] What has happened of course is that in *A Modest Proposal* we are listening to a man who is so filled with his subject, so careful about qualifying his statements and computations, so infatuated with the sound of his own words, that he rambles on at inordinate length.

We note this same tendency to qualify and ramify his thoughts in other characteristics of the proposer's sentence structure. We note this, for one thing, in his frequent use of parentheses. Sometimes the parenthetical matter throws in a gratuitous aside—"(as I must confess the times require)"; or editorializes—"(although indeed very unjustly)"; or qualifies a statement —"(I mean in the country)"; or insinuates an abrupt note of ethical appeal— "(it would, I think with humble submission, be a loss to the public)." Interpolated gestures like these, especially when they are as frequent as they are in this essay, betray a man who is unusually concerned for the accuracy of his statements and for the image he is projecting to his audience.

Something of the same tendency is evident in the many absolute constructions in the essay. Most of these occur at the end of fairly long sentences— e.g. "the charge of nutriment and rags having been at least four times that value" (para. 7); "their corn and cattle being seized and money a thing unknown" (para. 33). These trailing-off phrases create the effect of a thought suddenly remembered and desperately thrown in. What is clever, though, about Swift's use of these trailing-off phrases, placed as they are in an emphatic position, is that in many cases they carry the real sting of the sentence. Here is that topsy-turviness of values that constitutes one of the main strategies of the essay—important things couched in ironical terms or hidden away in weak structures.

This tendency to ramify, qualify, or refine statements is evident too in the proposer's habit of compounding elements. I am referring not so much to the common eighteenth-century practice of using doublets and triplets, of which there are a conspicuous number in *A Modest Proposal,* as to the proposer's habit of stringing out words and phrases beyond the common triad, so that we get the effect almost of an exhaustive cataloguing of details or qualifiers. I am referring to instances like these:

---

[5]Edwin H. Lewis, *History of the English Paragraph* (Chicago: University of Chicago Press, 1894), pp. 35-36.
[6]Herbert Davis, "The Conciseness of Swift," *Essays on the Eighteenth Century Presented to David Nichol Smith* (Oxford: at the Clarendon Press, 1945), pp. 15-32.

stewed, roasted, baked, or boiled (para. 9)

of curing the expensiveness of pride, vanity, idleness, and gaming in our women (para. 29)

equally innocent, cheap, easy, and effectual (para. 32)

by advancing our trade, providing for infants, relieving the poor, and giving pleasure to the rich (para. 33)[7]

What is observable about the proposer's amplifications is that his epithets are rarely just synonymous variations, such as the displays of *copia* that were common in Anglo-Saxon poetry and Euphuistic prose. In a phrase like "innocent, cheap, easy, and effectual," each adjective adds a distinct idea to the predication.

Along with this heavy compounding, Swift occasionally uses the scheme of polysyndeton—e.g. "in the arms or on the back or at the heels" (para. 2); "dying and rotting by cold and famine and filth and vermin" (para. 19). Multiplying conjunctions like this has the effect of further stringing out the list. Swift sometimes adds to the compounded elements the scheme of alliteration, as in the just-quoted "famine and filth and vermin" or in the triplet "parsimony, prudence, and temperance" (para. 29). In these examples, we get the impression of a man who is beginning to play with words. In the only other conspicuous use of alliteration, "in joints from the gibbet" (para. 18), our impulse to laugh at this sporting with words is suddenly restrained by our realization of the horror of the image. At other times, Swift will reinforce the compounding with the scheme of climax, as in the two or three examples in the first paragraph of the essay, or with the scheme of anticlimax, as in the example quoted above from paragraph 33.

Although all of this compounding is done within the framework of parallelism, parallelism is not a characteristic of the proposer's style or of Swift's style in general. But Swift demonstrates that he knows how and when to use parallel structure. In paragraph 29, the key paragraph of the essay, he lays out his long enumeration of "other expedients" on a frame of parallel structure. The list is long, the list is important, and Swift wants to make sure that his readers do not get lost in this maze of coordinate proposals.

Another thing that the long rambling sentences and the frequent compounding might suggest is a "spoken" style. If one compares spoken style with written style, one notes that spoken style tends to be paratactic—a stitching together of coordinate units. We have just observed this kind of rhapsodic structure in the word and phrase units of *A Modest Proposal*, but when we look at the kinds of grammatical sentences (see Appendix), we observe a marked predominance of the subordinate structures that typify a sophisticated written style. Over half of the sentences are complex, and

---

[7]There is nothing in *A Modest Proposal* that approaches the crushing catalogue of words in Book IV of *Gulliver's Travels:* "Hence it follows of necessity that the vast numbers of our people are compelled to seek their livelihood by begging, robbing, stealing, cheating, pimping, forswearing, flattering, suborning, forging, gaming, lying, fawning, hectoring, voting, scribbling, star-gazing, poisoning, whoring, canting, libelling, free-thinking, and the like occupations."

almost a third of the sentences are compound-complex. Although there are five simple sentences in the essay, there is not a single compound sentence, which is the commonest structure in extemporaneous spoken discourse. So although the essay may give the impression of a certain colloquial ease, this impression is not being produced by the syntax of the sentences.

Further evidence of a calculated literary style is found in the proposer's inclination to periodic structure. As Walter J. Ong said in a recent article on prose style, "Oral composition or grammatical structure is typically non-periodic, proceeding in the 'adding' style; literary composition tends more to the periodic."[8] We see this periodic structure exemplified in a sentence like the first one of paragraph 4: "As to my own part, having turned my thoughts, for many years, upon this important subject, and maturely weighed the several schemes of other projectors, I have always found them grossly mistaken in their computations." No one *speaks* a sentence like that; sentences like that are produced by someone who has time to plot his sentences.

This tendency to delay the main predication of the sentence is most pronounced within another structural pattern that is so common in the essay as to be a mannerism. I refer to the proposer's habit of putting the main idea of the sentence into a noun clause following the verb of the main clause. These noun clauses follow either personal structures like "I am assured by our merchants that . . . ," "I have reckoned that . . . ," "he confessed that . . ." or impersonal structures like "it is not improbable that . . ." and "it is very well known that . . . ." There are at least nineteen instances like these, where the main idea of the sentence is contained in the noun clause. And frequently the proposer further delays the main idea by making us read almost to the end of the noun clause before he gives us the main predication. A prime example of this is the final sentence of paragraph 18:

> Neither indeed can I deny, that if the same use were made of several plump young girls in this town, who, without one single groat to their fortunes, cannot stir abroad without a chair, and appear at the playhouse and assemblies in foreign fineries, which they will never pay for, the kingdom would not be the worse.

Reading a sentence like this, we wonder whether the man will ever get to the point, and in this case, when the point is finally reached, we find that it is deflatingly anti-climactic.

This tendency toward periodic structure is evidence not only of a deliberate written style but of a habit of the *persona* that suits Swift's rhetorical purpose. I suggested earlier that part of Swift's rhetorical strategy is to create a character who will, as it were, "sneak up" on the reader. The frequent use of periodic structure is one of the ways in which the proposer "sneaks up" on the reader.

---

[8]Walter J. Ong, "Oral Residue in Tudor Prose Style," *PMLA*, LXXX (June, 1965), 149.

And we see this same tactic in the early paragraphs of the essay. In the first two paragraphs we see the long, leisurely, meandering sentences in which the proposer, in a matter-of-fact tone, describes the present condition of the poor. There is further dawdling in paragraph 4, where in two rambling sentences he seeks to establish his credentials with his audience. Then in paragraph 6, the second longest paragraph of the essay, we are subjected to a litany of cold, hard figures or "computations." In the short paragraph 9, we hear the disturbing sputter of a lighted fuse as the proposer retails the testimony of his American acquaintance about what a delicacy a year-old child is. Then in paragraph 10, after the expenditure of almost a thousand words on preliminaries (almost a third of the essay), the proposer drops his bombshell. Nor does his pace become any more frenetic from this point on. He continues to "leak out" information, testimony, and arguments.

The noticeable periodic structure of many of the sentences, then, is part of Swift's strategy of sneaking up on the audience, of disarming the reader in order to render him more sensitive to the blow that will be delivered to the solar plexus. The proposer tells us in paragraph 27 that he is "studious of brevity." But he is not brief at all; he takes his own good time about dealing out what he has to say to his audience. This is not the curt Senecan amble; this is the rambling Ciceronian cadence. The Ciceronian cadence does not fit Jonathan Swift, of course, but it does fit the character he has created and does contribute to the rhetorical effectiveness of the essay.

We could pursue this discussion of sentences and schemes, but let us move on to a consideration of the diction of the essay. Let us see what a study of the diction tells us about Swift's strategies and about the proposer's style.

To begin with, we might advert briefly to the words and idioms that mark the essay as a product of the eighteenth century. One of the things that has often been remarked of Swift's style is that it is strikingly modern. As one of my students said to me. "When I'm reading Swift, I have the feeling that I'm reading George Orwell all over again." One of the reasons certainly for this impression of modernity is the diction and idiom. Swift uses very few words and idioms that are outdated. But he does use just enough dated words and expressions to prevent our getting the impression that we are reading the morning newspaper. I counted about a dozen idioms which were peculiar to the eighteenth century or were still current in the eighteenth century but are no longer current—expressions like "of towardly parts" (para. 6), "no gentleman would *repine* to give ten shillings" (para. 14), "I cannot be altogether *in* his sentiments" (para. 17) (see Appendix for additional examples). If one were attempting to date this piece from internal evidence, probably the two words that would be the best index of the period in which this essay was written would be *shambles* (para. 16) and the *chair* (para. 18) in which the plump young girls ride about town. The *OED* would tell us that in the eighteenth century *shambles* meant "a place where meat is sold," "a slaughter house" and that *chair* designated a means of transportation. Expressions like these give the essay its Augustan flavor, but aside from these, the diction and idiom are remarkably modern.

The Appendix carries a note about the monosyllabism of the essay. Only about one-third of the nouns in the first ten paragraphs are monosyllabic, and I suspect that there is a much higher percentage of polysyllabic, Latinate diction in *A Modest Proposal* than we will find in most of Swift's other prose works, especially in that prose where he is speaking in his own voice. This polysyllabic diction is appropriate of course for the kind of pedantic character that Swift has created in *A Modest Proposal*. The proposer wants to pass himself off on his audience as a man who has indulged in a great deal of scientific, scholarly study of the problem, so as to enhance his authority—"having turned my thoughts, for many years, upon this important subject, and maturely weighed the several schemes of other projectors" (para. 4).

The mathematical and mercantile terminology is also contributing to the image of the dedicated investigator and the political arithmetician. Besides the many figures cited, there are repeated uses of words like "compute," "reckon," "calculate," "shillings," "pounds," "sterling," "accounts," "stock," "commodity," *"per annum."* By putting jargon like this in the mouth of his proposer, Swift is making him talk the language of the other political economists who had turned their attention to the problem. We might say of the cold-bloodedness with which the proposer delivers himself of these terms that it represents his disinterested endeavor to propagate the worst that is known and thought about the problem in the Anglo-Irish world.

The most notable of the lexical means that Swift uses to achieve his purpose is the series of animal metaphors (see the Appendix). Charles Beaumont has pointed out that Swift is here employing the ancient rhetorical device of diminution, the opposite effect of amplification.[9] Swift first reduces his human beings to the status of animals and then to the status of food furnished to the table when these animals are slaughtered. So we pass from animal images like "dropped from its dam" and "reserved for breed" to such slaughtered-animal images as "the carcass," "the fore or hind quarters," and "the skin of which, artificially dressed." We feel the impact of these metaphors when we realize that Swift is suggesting that the Anglo-Irish landlords were treating human beings no better than they treated their domestic animals. The proposer points up this inhuman treatment when he says, in paragraph 26, that if his proposal were adopted, "men would become as fond of their wives, during the time of pregnancy, as they are now of their mares in foal, their cows in calf, or sows when they are ready to farrow."

Another trope that Swift uses to achieve diminution is litotes—the opposite trope to hyperbole. Here are four prominent examples of litotes or

---

[9]See Charles Allen Beaumont, "A Modest Proposal," *Swift's Classical Rhetoric* (Athens, Ga.: University of Georgia Press, 1961), pp. 15-43. After my own gathering of data, it was reassuring to me to discover that I had noted many of the same stylistic features that Beaumont had found.

understatement. In paragraph 2, the proposer refers to the burden of the prodigious number of beggar children as "a very great additional grievance." In paragraph 17, he speaks of the practice of substituting the bodies of young lads and maidens for venison as "a little bordering on cruelty." At the end of the periodic sentence in paragraph 18, he says that "the kingdom would not be the worse" if the bodies of plump young girls were sold as a delicacy for the table. The most notable example of litotes in the essay—and the one that serves as the chief tip-off to the irony of the essay—is found in the first sentence of the key paragraph 29: "I can think of no one objection that will possibly be raised against this proposal, unless it should be urged that the number of people will be thereby much lessened in the kingdom." The frequent use of litotes fits in well with the proposer's tendency to underplay everything.

The proposer not only underplays his proposal (note "a modest proposal") and his arguments to justify the proposal but also underplays his emotions. One has a hard time of it finding emotionally freighted words in the essay. Only in paragraphs 1 and 5 do I find conspicuous clusters of what I. A. Richards calls "emotive words":

> paragraph 1: Melancholy, all in rags, helpless infants, dear native country, crowded
> paragraph 5: abortions, horrid practice, murdering their bastard children, alas, tears and pity, poor innocent babes, savage and inhuman breast

The only other place in the essay where I sense the proposer losing a tight rein on his emotions is in his outburst in paragraph 18 against the plump young girls of the town, and in this instance, the anger simmering under these words is, I suspect, the emotional reaction of the clergyman Swift rather than of the worldly proposer. And this is the one place in the essay where I feel that Swift momentarily drops the mask and speaks in his own voice.

Swift considerably enhances the emotional impact of his message by this underplaying. And the other trope that is responsible for the emotional power of the essay is irony. As I remarked before, irony is an over-arching device for the entire essay: the proposer means what he says, but Swift does not. Irony, however, is a prevalent device within the essay too. I counted at least fifteen instances of words being used ironically. Rather than weary you with the entire catalogue, let me quote a few representative examples (the ironical words are italicized):

> will make two dishes at an *entertainment* for friends (para. 10)
> the fore and hind quarters will make a *reasonable* dish (para. 10)
> will make admirable gloves for *ladies* and summer boots for *fine gentlemen* (para. 14)
> some *scrupulous* people might be apt to censure (para. 17)

The horror of this irony hits us all the harder when we realize that the proposer, in his naivety, intends his words to be taken literally. These are the places where I can almost see Swift grinning through the lines of print.

Swift does something with words in this essay that I had not noticed him doing in any of his other prose works. He repeats key words so that they almost become motifs in the essay. The Appendix lists some of these repeated words and records the frequency of repetition. Note particularly the repetitions and variations of the words *child* and *parent*. Swift realizes that the proposal violates one of the most fundamental of human relations—the child-parent relation. When this violation of the normal child-parent relation is joined with a suggestion of cannibalism, a practice that almost universally offends the sensibilities of mankind, we get a proposal of the utmost monstrosity. And if Swift can get his audience to react violently enough to the revolting proposal, there is hope that they will resort to some of the "other expedients" for a solution to the problem of poverty. Basically that is his main rhetorical strategy in the essay.

I cannot wholly account for the rhetorical function of the repetition of the kingdom-country-nation diction. Swift may be seeking to emphasize that the poverty of the people is a problem of national scope, one in which the welfare of the entire nation is crucially involved. Hasn't this been the theme that President Johnson has been urging in his efforts to promote his Poverty Program? Another explanation may be that Swift is suggesting that just as, on the domestic level, the normal child-parent relationships have broken down, the kingdom-citizen relationships have broken down on the national level.

This kind of repetition of key words and phrases is a device that we have come to associate with Matthew Arnold's style. Anyone who has read Arnold's prose extensively knows how effective this tactic can be for purposes of exposition. Although repetition is not a mannerism of Swift's style in general, we can appreciate the emotional effect that Swift achieves in this argumentative piece with these drumbeat repetitions. These insistent repetitions keep bringing us back to the full implications of the modest proposal.

Before this exhaustive analysis becomes prostratingly exhausting, I had better bring it to a quick conclusion. Maybe a good way to conclude this study is for me to quote two estimates of Swift's style and then to ask you which of these two estimates seems to be, in the light of the foregoing analysis, the more just.

The first quotation is from Dr. Johnson's *Life of Swift:*

> For purposes merely didactic, when something is to be told that was not known before [his style] is in the highest degree proper, but against that inattention by which known truths are suffered to lie neglected, it makes no provision; it instructs, but does not persuade.

There is no denying that Swift's style does achieve an "easy and safe conveyance of meaning," but do you find Dr. Johnson's denial of persuasive value in Swift's style too harsh? Perhaps you are more disposed to accept Coleridge's judgment on Swift's style: "The manner is a complete expression of the matter, the terms appropriate, and the artifice concealed."

But maybe it is unfair to ask you to choose between these two estimates, for one of my points has been that in this essay we are observing not so much Swift's style as a style that Swift has created for his modest proposer. And who, after all, remembers this essay for its style? This analysis has revealed, I hope, that there is considerable stylistic artifice in *A Modest Proposal,* but hasn't this essay become memorable mainly because of the monstrousness of the proposal and the cleverness of the ironical form? As a matter of historical fact, Swift did *not* succeed in persuading his audience to do something about a lamentable situation. But he did succeed in producing a great piece of literature.

APPENDIX

Some Statistics on Swift's *A Modest Proposal*

3474 words
  33 paragraphs
  61 sentences   (For this study, a sentence is defined as a group of words beginning with a capital letter and ending with some mark of terminal punctuation.)

Average number of words per paragraph 105.2
Average number of sentences per paragraph 1.84
  18 one-sentence paragraphs
   7 two-sentence paragraphs
   4 three-sentence paragraphs
   3 four-sentence paragraphs
   1 five-sentence paragraph (#29)

Shortest paragraph #8 (20 words)—a transitional paragraph (other transitional paragraph, #20, is 34 words long)
Longest paragraph #29 (289 words)—"other expedients" (a key paragraph)

Average number of words per sentence 56.9
Number of sentences 10 words or more *above* average 18
Percentage of sentences above average 29.5%
Number of sentences 10 words or more *below* average 28
Percentage of sentences below average 45.9%
Longest sentence .... 179 words (para. 32)
Other long sentences: 164 words (para. 6); 141 words (para. 29); 119 words (para. 18); 109 words (para. 4); 102 words (para. 13)
Shortest sentence .... 11 words (last sentence of para. 27)
  (other short sentence: first sentence of transitional paragraph #20)

34 Complex sentences
18 Compound-complex sentences
 5 Simple sentences (paragraphs 4, 19, 20, 27)
 4 Elliptical or incomplete sentences (paragraphs 10, 29 (two), 31)

REPEATED WORDS

child (children) 25	} 33	kingdom 13	} 27		
infants 6		country 9			
babes 2		nation 5			

		the year 6	} 16
mother 6	} 20	one year old 1	
parents 7		annually 3	
breed (breeders) 7		solar year 2	
		per annum 4	

number 7	} 15	food 7	} 19
compute 5		flesh 4	
reckon 2		carcass 5	
calculate 1		plump 3	

propose 5	} 9	gentlemen 5	} 12
proposal 4		persons of quality 2	
		beggars 5	

SWIFT'S *A MODEST PROPOSAL*

Diction or idiom peculiarly eighteenth-century

(The number in parentheses refers to the paragraph in which the expression occurs.)

(6) of *towardly* parts
(10) increas*eth* to twenty-eight pounds
(13) fish being a *prolific* diet
(14) no gentleman would *repine* to give ten shillings
(16) *shambles* may be appointed
(16) dressing them hot from the knife
(17) the *want* of venison . . . for *want* of work and service
(17) I cannot be altogether *in* his sentiments
(18) who came from *thence, above* twenty years ago
(18) without a *chair*
(19) and I have been desired to employ my thoughts what course may be taken
(19) But I am not *in the least pain upon* that matter
(19) and thus the country and themselves are *in a fair way* of being delivered from the evils to come
(25) bring great *custom* to taverns where the *vintners* will certainly be so prudent

(26) emulation among the married women, *which* of them could bring

(32) to reject any offer, proposed by wise men, *who* [which?] shall be found equally innocent, cheap, easy, and effectual

ANIMAL IMAGERY

 (3) at the *heels* of their mother

 (4) a child just *dropped* from its *dam*

(10) reserved for breed

(10) more than we allow to sheep, black-cattle, or swine

(10) therefore one *male* will be sufficient *to serve* four *females*

(10) to let them *suck* plentifully . . . to render them plump and fat for a good table

(10) the fore or hind quarter

(14) for the *carcass* of a good fat child

(15) flay the *carcass* . . . the skin of which, artificially *dressed*

(16) as we do roasting pigs

(26) men would become as fond of their wives, during the time of their pregnancy, as they are now of their mares in foal, their cows in calf, or sows when they are ready to farrow

(27) propagation of swine's flesh

(27) the great destruction of pigs

(27) fat *yearling* child

MONOSYLLABISM

In the first ten paragraphs of the essay, there are 1127 words; of these, (60%) 685 are monosyllabic. But since a good many of these monosyllabic words are pronouns, prepositions, conjunctions, or auxiliary verbs, we get an unreliable estimate of Swift's diction. If we look at the nouns only, we get a different picture. In these same ten paragraphs, there are 204 nouns. Of these, 73 are monosyllabic (36%), 131 are polysyllabic. If we regard only the substantive words in these paragraphs, we get, for Swift, an unusually high number of polysyllabic words.

PART TWO

Style
and Linguistics

ARCHIBALD A. HILL

Correctness and Style
in English Composition

Archibald A. Hill teaches linguistics at the University of Texas. He has written Introduction to Linguistic Structures *(1958) and several informative essays about the relation between linguistics and literary criticism. In the following article Professor Hill argues the relevance of linguistic studies to problems of correctness and style in writing. He emphasizes that correctness is appropriateness to a particular dialect, whereas style is a concern for appropriate and effective choices between utterances within a given dialect. His essay is a clear indication of how the linguist's treatment of style differs from the rhetorician's.*

The teacher of English is often accused by students of language of being unable to modify his teachings in accord with facts of usage no matter how well proved, and the linguist in turn seems to those of us who have to struggle with freshmen to be a wild libertarian who would accept the most shapeless writing on the ground that all linguistic forms are equally good. Perhaps, as with other disputes, some of the differences may be resolved if the basic terms are more clearly defined.

I shall begin with correctness, giving a few well-worn statements of what it is not.

Correctness is not logic, since all languages are largely illogical. English says, "I see him," as if sight were a positive act of will comparable to that in "I hit him." Yet all of us know enough optics to realize that, if there is any action involved, it starts with *him* and reaches and affects *me*. Languages which happen, like Eskimo, to avoid this particular illogicality fall into others as great.

The basis of correctness is not beauty inherent in the forms used. Beauty in linguistic forms is due to the associations they arouse. Such a form as "goil" is ugly only if the hearer happens to dislike Brooklyn. To realize the truth of this statement, one has only to consider variants where we have no such associations. If a child in the New Mexican pueblo of Santa Clara puts the sentence, "I am going to town," in the form *bupiyeummang,* the "ugly" pronunciation is immediately corrected to *bupijeummang.* The Tewa parents are not being merely arbitrary; they are objecting to an unacceptable dialect. I doubt if any English speaker can seriously maintain that he finds one Tewa form more beautiful than the other.

The basis of correctness is not history; such a belief would contradict the results of linguistic science. Further, the belief that older forms are

From *College English*, XII (1951), 280-285. Reprinted with the permission of the National Council of Teachers of English and Archibald A. Hill.

better than newer can readily be reduced to an absurdity. If only old forms are right, then we do not speak English but bad Old English—or bad Indo-Hittite.

Equally certainly correctness is not the result of an authoritative ruling by an individual or a book. A neat example of this last view is the statement of a columnist who once said that 98 per cent of Americans mispronounced a given word, since they failed to follow dictionary recommendations. Actually such a statement demonstrates that 2 per cent of America mispronounces the word or that the dictionaries had better catch up on usage.

A final view once widely held is that anything which is impossible in Latin is incorrect in English. The view hardly needs denial, baleful as its lingering influence may be on the analysis of English grammar. At least, no one would now seriously maintain that "Oh, father!" is a vocative case, incapable of being split into two words.

I can start my positive exposition with a quotation which puts clearly the idea that the composition teacher has a double task. Most of what will follow will be merely an attempt to sharpen the distinction set up in the quotation.

> Competence . . . has to do with the organization of ideas . . . with putting words together . . . in such a way as to convey meaning easily and clearly. Decency may be regarded as the manners of discourse, and bears the same relation to speaking and writing that good table manners have to eating. The schoolboy who declares, "We ain't goin' to have no baseball team this year" is using language with competence, for his meaning is perfectly clear, but he is not using it with decency.[1]

For these terms I should like to substitute "correctness" and "style." Any form is correct if it is current in the dialect—to be defined, of course, beforehand—that the writer is using. A form is incorrect only if it has no such currency. It follows that it is possible to be incorrect in the use of other dialects than the rather vaguely defined Standard Written English with which teachers concern themselves. Professor Thorpe's schoolboy was using language incorrectly if he was speaking in the formal atmosphere of the schoolroom; but, if he was speaking to playmates across the tracks, he was speaking correctly enough. A more serious illustration is that the English department of one of our leading universities was recently taken to task because its training did not equip graduates to communicate with workmen. The point was well taken: it is as serious an error to use the forms of Standard English where they are socially out of place as it is to use Gullah in the pages of a learned article. Incorrectness can result also, not merely from the use of a dialect in an inappropriate situation, but as well from the mixture of dialects or the improper imitation of a dialect. Readers of Galsworthy

---

[1] Clarence D. Thorpe (ed.), *Preparation for College English* (Ann Arbor: University of Michigan Press, 1945), p. 12 n.

may remember that he sometimes makes an American character say sentences like, "If you've gotten a sense of humour, you've gotten it jolly well hidden up." Such sentences are grossly un-American at the same time that they are un-British; they are therefore incorrect.

The second term was "style." If forms A and B both occur in a given dialect, it is impossible to say that either is incorrect in that dialect. It may, however, be possible to show that A is better than B in the particular context in which it occurs. Such an evaluation will be based on the positive qualities of the passage under criticism; that is, A is better than B if it is clearer, more in accord with artistic conventions, or fits better with the structure of the utterance in which it falls. It should be stated emphatically that good and bad style are both possible in any dialect—Professor Thorpe's schoolboy was speaking with excellent style, since his statement left no doubt of the vigor of his denial. It should also be pointed out that, if a stylistic variant is condemned in one passage, it is by no means implied that it should be condemned elsewhere.

A third form of variant also exists. These are the indifferent variants. If A and B both exist, and no stylistic reason can be found for preferring one over the other, the variation is indifferent. The existence of indifferent variants is of some importance, since somehow the idea has gotten abroad that, if there are two ways of saying a thing, one must always be better than the other. English teachers are all too often called on to adjudicate between six and a half-dozen, though to devote effort to such decisions can only falsify what we so much need to tell our students.

From these rather generalized examples we can pass to discussion of variants such as actually appear in student themes. We will begin with variants which involve correctness, the first group of them springing from insufficient knowledge of the way in which writing represents the forms of speech. It is characteristic of these forms that, if read aloud with normal pronunciation, they immediately become acceptable Spoken English.

He couldn't *of* had a worse introduction.

Sentences like this have a sort of currency in dialect writing but have no currency in Standard Written English. The mistake consists in selecting the wrong spelling for a weak form which is homonymous for *have* and *of*. It is odd that the reverse mistake as in "a pair *have* shoes" seems never to occur.

Rooms for *Tourist*.

This is a type of form which is common in much of the South. What is back of it is an assimilation of -*sts* to -*ss* or simply to -*s*. It occurs at all levels of regional speech, and even teachers of English use it quite unconsciously. The mistake can be explained to students by giving the conditions under which the assimilation occurs and by pointing out that written forms do not recognize the change.

The next group of variants are incorrect because they employ local or social dialect forms not found in the Standard language.

Youse had better not do it.

This sentence will be recognized as belonging to uncultured New York City speech. Its badness, however, is altogether the result of its lack of currency in standard dialects of any type—it cannot be condemned as illogical or out of keeping with the structure of the language, since it makes a contrast between singular and plural just as other pronouns do, and since it is parallel to the southern *you all*.

I want this *doing* immediately.

This sentence is not likely to occur in compositions by American students, but it is nonetheless instructive, since we are likely to think of anything British as all right. The form is northern British local dialect, which finds its way into occasional printed books, among them those of Hall Caine. It is certainly not correct in this country. Another local sentence type is the southern "I *might could* do it," which is common enough in colloquial speech, but which I have never seen in print. The sentence should be rejected in compositions, acceptable as it may be in less formal situations.

The next group of incorrect variants arises from an unsuccessful attempt to use the forms or vocabulary of a standard dialect and are thus comparable to the mistakes made by foreigners.

This phone broken. Do not *uses*.

This sentence appeared on a sign put up by a colored janitor in a government building. The writer presumably used a type of dialect in which the present forms of verbs are without variation. Knowing that an *-s* appears in many forms where he would not use it, he corrected a little too much.

Modern culture is *sadistic*. Its music, painting, and literature are all sad.

In these sentences from a doctoral examination it is amusing to watch what starts out to be a provocative statement evaporate into a merely unfortunate attempt at elegance. The mistake is parallel to the student habit of describing modern poetry as "mystic" under the belief that this word is a critical term meaning "hard to understand."

A final type of incorrect variation is of rather common occurrence in student themes. This is contamination of one construction by another, with consequent production of variants lacking currency. A convenient if somewhat mentalistic explanation is to say that the writer intended one construction and then shifted his intention to another. Readers can readily supply other examples than the one which follows.

There are *a points* which I can make. . . .

The author of this phrase has mixed *are a few points* with *are points,* producing a mistake which at first sight seems quite improbable for a native speaker.

Our next group of variants are correct but are examples of bad style. All but the first are actual examples of composition.

John met Jack, and *his* wife spoke to *him.*

In English, as in many languages, we have no way of distinguishing the reference of pronouns when there are two nouns of the same class, so that ambiguity often results. The sentence above must be condemned as bad style, though similar sentences can be found by the hundreds in all sorts of writing.

Record the pronunciation on the lists in capital letters.

This sentence is drawn from a set of directions made up by a professor of English, who will, I hope, pardon my use of it. The sentence seems clear enough, but unfortunately the intended meaning was: "Record the pronunciation of only those words which appear in capital letters on the lists." Such ambiguities pursue us all.

This factory is two miles beyond Lynchburg, going south.

This sentence is the only really bad example of our old friend the dangling participle which I collected in two sessions of theme-reading. You will note that I have called it bad style, not an example of incorrectness. First, it produces ambiguity, not perhaps of a sort dangerous to real understanding, but sufficient to give a comic effect. Thus the sentence has positive badness. Second, dangling participles are surprisingly common in Standard Written English, though the handbooks do not admit it. Generally, no matter what our rationalizations, we do not notice danglers unless the stylistic effect is bad.

The next sentence may strike the reader as wildly improbable, though it comes from an actual composition.

Mrs. Jackson devoted many years of endeavor to establishing and supporting a home where unfortunate women who had made mistakes (which they often sincerely regretted) could go to have their bastards.

The stylistic fault is obvious, since the final word comes with a distinct shock, the stronger for the vaguely elegant verbiage which precedes it.

The next variants are some which seem to me indifferent, though occasionally a particularly puristic handbook condemns one or more of them.

He *dove,* OR He *dived.*
It's *me,* OR It's *I.*
We carried it in a *burlap bag* (OR *croker sack,* OR *gunny sack*).
Let him do it if he *dares* (OR *dare*).

The first three of these are regional variants or are regional variants some-times crossed with social variation. Yet since both forms appear in Standard writing, no matter what the origin, none of them can be condemned as in-correct. The second set is perhaps the most interesting, since *It's I* seems to occur as the natural form around Boston, though elsewhere it is a school-mastered product not to be recommended. Shelley's line, "Be thou me, impetuous one!" is a helpful quotation in dealing with the overmeticulous, since, though it may be a trick, it is always possible to point out that no one would wish the line changed to "Be thou I." The last set shows variation between an older and a newer form, both of which occur in formal writing.

There follow some forms of wide currency, which seem to me also de-fensible stylistically, though they are nonetheless often condemned.

The mail is all delivered by plane, *which* is not only remarkably efficient, but is the chief weekly excitement.

This sentence violates the frequently expressed rule that *which* must have a definite antecedent. Yet vague antecedents are common in modern writ-ing and have been common at all periods of the language. There is no ambi-guity in the sentence above, and *which* seems a convenient device for avoid-ing a clumsily exact rephrasing. The sentence comes from the *Saturday Evening Post.*

We might assume that Standard Oil is going to sponsor a news program. *They* will select a commentator with political views which coincide with *their* own.

This example comes from a student theme discussed by a panel of English teachers, a majority of whom regarded the indefinite *they* as incorrect. The sentence is of a type similar to the one above, has wide currency, and is certainly convenient. The stylistic effect of *it* would be quite different in this passage, and some such periphrasis as "the board of directors of Stand-ard Oil" would be awkward. In the opinion of one person at least, illogical suppleness has always been one of the beauties of English.

I hope that I have by now given enough examples to make it clear that skepticism toward handbook rules does not mean undue libertarianism. To sum up, that part of a composition teacher's activity which concerns itself with correctness is grammar—normative grammar if he is telling students what to use; descriptive grammar if he is himself finding out what forms are current. That part of his activity which concerns the excellence of forms is a part of literary criticism. Both activities are difficult, and both important. On the one hand, it requires investigation rather than mere acceptance of authority to determine whether a given form is right or wrong. For instance, I recently wanted to know whether students should be graded down for writing "the table's leg" or "the story's climax." I went to a national periodical and found there about a hundred examples of both the -s genitive and the *of* phrase, about equally divided between living beings and inanimate objects. The handbook rule is clearly false, and students should not be corrected for genitives which break it. As for stylistics, on the other hand, it is not my task to try to cover the subject, though it is obvious that we must bring to the reading of themes the same sort of detailed analysis which we give to understanding the literature we teach. I am aware that teachers are overworked and that it is perhaps too much to expect them to devote even an hour a week to investigating usage, or that they criticize their themes in the same spirit in which they analyze a paragraph of Swift or Arnold. There is only one answer to such an objection, arrogant as the answer may sound. It is surely better, and in the long run easier, to find the facts and teach them than to rely on a merely convenient myth.

MARTIN JOOS

From *The Five Clocks*

Martin Joos is director of the Linguistic Center at the University of Toronto. He has edited Readings in Linguistics *(1957) and written* The English Verb: Form and Meanings *(1964). In* The Five Clocks, *the first part of which is presented here, Professor Joos discusses the five styles of English—frozen, formal, consultative, casual, and intimate—and identifies the contexts in which these styles are generally found. Joos' own style in this essay is whimsical and entertaining; the author has deliberately avoided the frozen and formal styles which are as often employed by linguists as by writers in any rigorous discipline.*

Ballyhough railway station has two clocks which disagree by some six minutes. When one helpful Englishman pointed the fact out to a porter, his reply was 'Faith, sir, if they was to tell the same time, why would we be having two of them?'

That more than one kind of English is likely to be in use at the same time and place is a notorious fact. So is sex, for that matter, or the weather. But our accommodations to those facts are not equally realistic. We have easily understood that evolution has so shaped our planet's flora and fauna that agriculture is best served by fluctuating weather and cyclical seasons. With a great deal more effort, we are coming to understand that sex is here to stay and may even have a sort of survival-value—that its seasons and its vagaries may conceivably be essential to the business of being human.

Long ago taught to give weather its highest praise by calling it 'seasonable,' we have been learning recently to treat sex with the same respect for facts. The intellectual gain is great, however few may value it. Much greater, some say, is the profit that comes from not sending children into adulthood with useless burdens of guilt.

English-usage guilt-feelings have not yet been noticeably eased by the work of linguistic scientists, parallel to the work done by the psychiatrists. It is still our custom unhesitatingly and unthinkingly to demand that the clocks of language all be set to Central Standard Time. And each normal American is taught thoroughly, if not to keep accurate time, at least to feel ashamed whenever he notices that a clock of his is out of step with the English Department's tower-clock. Naturally he avoids looking aloft when he can. Then his linguistic guilt hides deep in his subconscious mind and there secretly gnaws away at the underpinnings of his public personality. Freud or Kinsey may have strengthened his private self-respect, but in his social life he is still in uneasy bondage to the gospel according to Webster as expounded by Miss Fidditch.

Shall the porter speak up? Well, it isn't likely to do much good this year. But the porter is a sort of Court Fool and won't lose his job for speaking up once. And if enough of us speak up, travelers may learn to read clocks with more sympathy and self-respect.

The Ballyhough situation was simple. But English, like national languages in general, has five clocks. And the times that they tell are not simply earlier and later; they differ sidewise too, and in several directions. Naturally. A community has a complex structure, with variously differing needs and occasions. How could it scrape along with only one pattern of English usage? (Webster, of course!—Well, . . .)

It would be very little better served with a single range of usages, differing along the length of a single scale. And yet our public theory of English is all laid out along just such a single yardstick. (Webster is one Webster, and Miss Fidditch is his prophet.)

We have not yet learned to speak of English as we speak of the weather and agriculture, and as we are slowly learning to speak of sex and survival.

In the school folklore called 'grammar' for lack of effective challenge—a sort of numerology taught in high-schools instead of algebra, an astrology masquerading as astronomy in our colleges—we are bound to speak of English usage only in a simplistic way, like a proper Victorian maiden lady speaking of Men.

Ask a normal citizen to compare 'if they was to tell the same time' with 'if they were to tell the same time' and he will check by Miss Fidditch's tape: 'Bad, fair, good, better, best = Correct.' And that's about all. Oh yes; he will deplore the conditions which prevail, he will mutter that he too has sinned and fallen short of Webster, and he will be worried about his son's English. Then he will wander off into spelling-reform and Communism.

But now if you press him for a program, he will suggest installing a master-clock system. He will promise to speak up in the next P.T.A. meeting for more and better grammar teaching, like they had in Webster's day. What he doesn't know is that he himself has two English-usage clocks as adequately adjusted as any railroad-man's watch, for use on different occasions, plus three others that are more or less reliable depending on his experiences and the distances to his horizons. And he will be baffled by your lunacy if you casually say what linguists know: That he built and adjusted those clocks himself, with less help than hindrance from schooling.

What he does know is that his usage varies, as he thinks. The fact is that his several usages do not vary enough to matter, any one of them. They alternate with each other, like his pajamas and overalls and committee-meeting suit, each tailored so as not to bind and so that he finds the pockets without looking. And he has one master-clock to tell him when to change. (Tsk, tsk! Mixed metaphor!—Pray for me, Miss F.)

Then, when he happens to notice that the garments differ, he parrots her appraisals of better and worse. Finally he pleads 'No contest,' on the theory that he was surely wrong every time—that correctness is for teachers, who have the word from Webster. (Where did Webster get it from?—Excuse me, I'm busy.)

Bad, fair, good, better, best. Only the best is Correct. No busy man can be Correct. But his wife can. That's what women are for. That's why we have women to teach English and type our letters and go to church for us and discover for us that the English say 'Aren't I?' while we sinfully hunt golf balls in the rough on Sunday, and, when our partner finds two of them, ask 'which is me?' (Webster: colloq.—Professor K of Harvard: I speak colloq myself, and sometimes I write it.)

Only the porter . . . Only a few of us today are aware of the other scales of English usage. It is our business to consciously know about their social utility. We have to say 'consciously,' for, beneath their cant, the members of the community are unconsciously familiar with those other values: that is, in fact, what it means to 'be a member of' a community. The unaware familiarity is what makes the values effective and gives the individual his profit from them. The kids know that; that's why they don't listen to Miss

Fidditch—they have their eye on the main chance. (Where does it say how to sweet-talk in French—Who cares! She's [He's] American.)

Must usages differ? We might as well ask whether quadrupeds must have four legs and snakes have none. Each question is meaningful—to a believer in Original Sin. A scout from Mars would ask no such questions. He would take each usage as belonging to a current stage in a continuing evolution. And he would not confuse his research with a Golden-Age myth or a Progress theory—nor with a World-is-going-to-the-dogs fallacy either.

His basic research assumption would be: Since usage differences call for efforts to keep them under control, there must be rewards for the efforts. They must have survival-values. Then he would set about tabulating differences, efforts, and values. Rather soon, he would examine how the young advance toward better control and improved chances of survival. Example: 'Hi, Toots!'—'Don't be such a goof!' (Quiet there, Miss F. These are people preparing for examinations.)

Efforts and values are never perfectly in equilibrium. That is why usages change: they are constantly being readjusted to make up for the constant erosion that washes out the profits. In one word, a classical instance of homeostasis—a term which our scout learned at home on Mars from medical research and found useful in describing his native culture. Catabolism and metabolism. When you assume a fixed position, you're dead. Dead as Caesar or a Siberian mammoth. Or Webster.

When too many people had abandoned 'Ain't I?' we promptly used the tar-brush on 'Pleased to meet you.' To a social animal, the question of first importance always is 'What group am I in?' The second question is 'How do I stand within the group?' Only third are the message transactions, namely 'How are things changing within my group?' A poor fourth is 'How's the weather?'—matters of information. Fifth (earlier only for pedants) is 'How does my group rank among other groups?'—with respect to language usage, this is 'correctness.'

Among other things—among a great many others!—the scout from Mars must examine the match-up between the bad-to-best scale of English usage and the parallel scales of occasions, of moods, and of men. It would be foolish to assume in advance that they are just bad-to-best men. (You mean that the Good Guys don't always flaunt Webster and the Bad Guys don't always flout Webster?—Precisely.)

Our scout's report would contain a footnote pointing out that 'bad' is a word also used for an inedible egg, and that 'bad egg' is a personal epithet; also that 'the best butter' occurs in the literature. His chapter on the bad-to-best scale could be a fascinating one. But we have no right to assume that it would be the longest chapter, or the most important one in the scout's view. By trying hard to be as objective as a man from Mars, let's see how close we can come to reconstructing his report.

And Webster?—Complete in his Appendix. But we don't need to reprint it because it's in the Museum of Natural History. Or we could ask Miss Fidditch. We probably will anyhow.

HOW MANY CLOCKS?

Here are, in order of importance, four of the usage-scales of native central English:

AGE	STYLE	BREADTH	RESPONSIBILITY
senile	frozen	genteel	best
mature	formal	puristic	better
teenage	consultative	standard	good
child	casual	provincial	fair
baby	intimate	popular	bad

These four scales are essentially independent; relations among them are not identities. (But isn't the best English genteel?—That must be Miss Fidditch talking.)

Age. The frame within which all other scales develop. Though this is the most important of them all, we shall have very little to say about the age-scale of usage because nothing can be done about it directly, and that little will have to wait to near the end.

Style. Here are the five clocks to which we shall principally devote our attention. They may be called 'higher' and 'lower' for convenience in referring to the tabulation; but that doesn't mean anything like relative superiority. More later.

Breadth. This scale measures breadth of experience and of self-limitation. From popular English up to standard English, your experiences broaden your usages; and from there up to genteel you narrow them again to suit your personality. Nothing further.

Responsibility. Here at last is the actual usage-scale nearest to Miss Fidditch's mythical scale of excellence, and we borrow her scale-labels but not her meanings for them, eliminating her favorite synonym 'correct' for the top. More immediately.

Much as linguists hate to admit it, the responsibility scale does exist. It even has considerable though minor importance. Its importance is minor because we use it only in forming social clusters, momentary or lasting. If we have done a good job, the cluster is homogeneous on the responsibility scale, which holds it together as a social group. Then we can forget the responsibility-ratings of the group's members, because we are done using them: they are used only in first forming the group or in adding or dropping members. This responsibility scale needs to be cleared out of the way, to prevent confusion, before we consider the five clocks of style.

The reason why linguists dislike acknowledging the responsibility scale is that any acknowledgment of its existence is customarily taken as an endorsement of the 'quality' theory of usage which they of course reject. That

Martin Joos   111

quality theory holds that usages are intrinsically good or bad—that each usage is by itself absolutely good or absolutely bad, under a taboo-rule, without inquiring into what good or evil it performs in real life. For example, 'ain't' and 'hisself' are rated as bad English (or 'not English' to make the condemnation stronger by including a self-contradiction in it); and every essay at discussing their badness counts as an attempt to introduce poison into the water-supply. (What does Webster say? Well, that settles it, doesn't it? I don't see what good it would do to discuss the matter any further.)

Now those linguists are right to a certain extent. 'Ain't I?' has just as respectable an origin as 'Aren't we?'—and, ultimately, a more respectable origin than 'Aren't I?' as it is pronounced by most of those Americans who use it. Again, in view of everybody's 'myself, ourselves, yourself, your-selves' the bad minority's 'hisself, theirselves' would be more grammatical if logic governed grammar. Yet the origin and the logic don't matter; here the master rule has been known for centuries: Treason doth never prosper; what's the reason? Why, if it prosper, none dare call it treason. In short, the community's choice of what shall count as the norm and what shall be rated as 'bad' (in general, even by those who use it) apparently is an arbitrary choice, so that usage is never good or bad but thinking makes it so.

What, never? There is more to it than that. There is something about social living that creates a responsibility-scale of usage; and when we have examined the natural basis of that scale, we shall see why the folklore calls it a quality scale.

The community's survival depends on cooperation; and adequate co-operation depends on recognizing the more and the less responsible types of persons around us. We need to identify the natural burden-bearers of the community so that we can give them the responsibility which is heaviest of all: we make them responsible for cooperation itself. Then the majority of us can function carefree in our square and round niches, free of the burden of maintaining the cooperation-net which joins us all. Some few of us have a strong interest in cooperation-nets without much competence in them; we are placed as letter-carriers and writers and legislators and teach-ers and so on; and for those jobs we are selected by tests which discriminate between interest and talent in the maintenance of cooperation.

In any case, the community places us principally by language-use tests which measure us on the various usage scales. Conversely, each of us selects others. For the present, we are interested in just one scale, namely respon-sibility—a personality scale and a usage scale running quite accurately parallel to each other.

We start very early learning to use this scale. It would be an exceptionally foolish ten-year-old who trusted a well-groomed sharper in preference to a judge in a bathing-suit. And he selects the more responsible person prin-cipally by listening, for the same reason that an employer wants an inter-view with each job-seeker—an interview for which no handbook is needed, for the oral code is public property.

The oral code for responsible personalities is indeed in part arbitrary, conventional: 'himself,' not 'hisself.' But the convention has a natural base, and in a very simple way. Responsible language does not palter. It is explicit. It commits the speaker. The responsible speaker is under a sort of almost morbid compulsion to leave himself no way out of his commitment. The responsibility-dialect does not mumble; its grammar does not contradict itself; its semantics doesn't weasel. That is its basis; 'himself' and the rest are conventional, but they borrow their strength from the natural basis; they are overlays, but the basis is strong enough to overpower the illogicality of 'himself.'

Miss Fidditch's shibboleths are about half conventional overlays. Did she create them? No; the community did, on the theory that birds of a feather flock together. Through some historical accident—some random fluctuation in the distribution of 'himself' and 'hisself' among members of the community—it happened that 'himself' came to be regarded as relatively more common in the responsibility-dialect. It may not have been actually more common there, but the community at large at least thought it was, and that was enough. Flocking did the rest. Those young people who aspired to responsibilities (perhaps only subconsciously aspired) selected 'himself' (normally without awareness of what they were doing or why), while those who aspired to irresponsible lives selected 'hisself' if it was conventionally available to them.

If it was not, they instead selected effete usages. Vulgarity and effeteness use equivalent signals in our culture. Each supplies its fellowship with passwords. For the community at large, the passwords are signals saying 'No responsibilities wanted!' And we take them at their word—for this part of our communication-system—the more certainly because the whole code works subconsciously.

Miss Fidditch's mistake is in trying to work out the code consciously and logically, instead of simply listening to what clearly responsible people actually say. Sometimes, however, she does listen; and then if she tries to teach what she has learned, and if her more responsible pupils learn to speak that way, Miss Fidditch is apt to imagine that her teaching is what taught them. That is an illusion. Responsibility earns respect; therefore most people (not all!) try for a step higher on the responsibility scale of English usage: simply to earn the respect of others, even irresponsible persons will try this if they don't feel the danger in it. In any case, that is why usages once labeled 'bad' always dwindle and ultimately vanish. Not because Miss Fidditch banned them! The kids aren't listening to her; they listen to Uncle David who is an aviator and to Dr. Henderson, perhaps also to historical and fictional characters if the school is doing its proper job. Miss Fidditch is convinced that bad English is gaining ground; she is only looking for burglars under the bed; statistics says the opposite, item by item. (Don't cry, Miss Fidditch! Homeostasis will keep up your supply of bad English, never fear!)

Finally, the community prefers the center of the scale: 'good' usage, not 'best.' It routinely rejects morbidly honest candidates for office, and the best English counts as the disqualification that makes a teacher.

III

INFORMAL CLOCKS

Now for the Five Clocks that will concern us for the rest of this occasion— the five styles duly tabulated on page [111]. With a single exception, there is no law requiring a speaker to confine himself to a single style for one occasion; in general, he is free to shift to another style, perhaps even within the sentence. But normally only two neighboring styles are used alternately, and it is anti-social to shift two or more steps in a single jump, for instance from casual to formal. When the five styles have been separately and comparatively described, the details of shifting will be obvious.

We begin with 'good standard mature consultative style' because the readers of this report are presumably best at home there. The community itself, though its average age is in the 'mature' bracket, is best at home in the completely central 'good standard teenage consultative style,' used for replanning baseball and other matters of moment. To add to the confusion, your reporter is writing good standard mature formal style, with many borrowings from the consultative and casual styles, plus shreds and patches of frozen style placed with honest care.

On the next page there is a long sample of good standard mature consultative style. We know that it is genuine: it was recorded from a telephone line. Here it is copied from *The Structure of English,* by Charles Carpenter Fries, with fictitious names used for smoothness instead of giving only initials as in the book. One speaker's words are italicized. Quoting Fries: 'These oral reactions on the hearer's part do not interfere with the continuous flow of utterances of the speaker. They simply serve to give something of the hearer's reaction and to signal the fact that he is listening attentively to the speaker.'[1] In face-to-face consultation, some of these may be silent, consisting of nods and smiles and the like; but it is clear that the audible ones were not invented recently for telephone use, since they can all be documented from earlier printed books. In a lively conversation the total number of listener's insertions, audible and silent together, is likely to be much greater than what we find here, and the audible ones alone perhaps roughly as many as here, that is to say about one every six seconds.

      I wanted to tell you one more thing I've been
2 talking with Mr. Davis in the purchasing de-
      partment about our typewriters *yes* that order
4 went in March seventh however it seems that

---

[1]Charles Carpenter Fries, *The Structure of English* (New York: Harcourt, Brace & World, 1952), p. 50.

we are about eighth on the list *I see* we were
6 up about three but it seems that for that type
of typewriter we're about eighth that's for a
8 fourteen-inch carriage with pica type *I see* now
he told me that Royce's have in stock the
10 fourteen-inch carriage typewriters with elite
type *oh* and elite type varies sometimes it's
12 quite small and sometimes it's almost as large
as pica *yes I know* he suggested that we go
14 down and get Mrs. Royce and tell her who we
are and that he sent us and try the fourteen-
16 inch typewriters and see if our stencils would
work with such type *I see* and if we can use
18 them to get them right away because they have
those in stock and we won't have to wait *that's*
20 *right* we're short one typewriter right now as
far as having adequate facilities for the staff
22 is concerned *yes* we're short and we want to
get rid of those rentals *that's right* but they are
24 expecting within two weeks or so to be receiving—ah—to start receiving their orders on
26 eleven-inch machines with pica type *oh* and of
course pica type has always been best for our
28 stencils *yes* but I rather think there might be
a chance that we can work with elite type *well*
30 *you go over and try them and see what they're*
like and do that as soon as you can so that
32 *we'll not miss our chance at these*²

Consultative style is the easiest kind of English to describe, though that doesn't matter so much because we're not going to write its grammar here. Still, a few remarks may not be amiss. We see that 'we won't' [19] and 'we'll not' [32] are not synonymous: in the latter, 'will' is not negatived but only the following words are, so that the message is 'we'll surely get our chance at these.' We can see that 'oh' [11, 26] acknowledges receipt of new informa- tion, 'I see' [5, 8, 17] certifies that it has been understood, 'yes' [3, 22, 28] approves the other's understanding of the situation, and 'that's right' [19- 20, 23] approves the other's decision. Such differences in meanings are so important in consultation that even face to face the listener's contributions will not remain entirely silent.

The two defining features of consultative style are: (1) The speaker sup- plies background information—he does not assume that he will be under- stood without it—such information as 'elite type varies' [11]. (2) The addressee participates continuously. Because of these two features, con-

---

²*Ibid.*, p. 51.

sultative style is our norm for coming to terms with strangers—people who speak our language but whose personal stock of information may be different.

But treating the listener as a stranger is hard work in the long run; therefore we sooner or later try to form a social group with him. Our most powerful device for accomplishing this is the use of casual style. Casual style is for friends, acquaintances, insiders; addressed to a stranger, it serves to make him an insider simply by treating him as an insider. Negatively, there is absence of background information and no reliance on listeners' participation. This is not rudeness; it pays the addressee the compliment of supposing that he will understand without those aids. On the positive side, we have two devices which do the same job directly: (1) ellipsis, and (2) slang, the two defining features of casual style.

The term 'slang' is used here in a strict sense, not in the loose popular sense which makes it a term of condemnation for anything and everything in language which is discountenanced: substandard usage, dialect, cant, jargon, or merely slovenliness. A dictionary definition (in Webster's New International Second Edition) includes 'cant' as one meaning of 'slang' and 'jargon' as a second, both of which we eliminate; the third meaning there is what we will follow: 'Language comprising certain widely current but usually ephemeral terms (especially coined or clipped words, or words used in special senses, or phrases, usually metaphors or similes) having a forced, fantastic, or grotesque meaning, or exhibiting eccentric or extravagant humor or fancy.' Examples: 'leather' is not slang but thieves' cant for 'wallet;' 'to be with it' is not slang but carny jargon; 'to be in the know' was slang in the sixteenth century but is now standard English; 'skiddoo' is dead slang; it is useless to quote live slang, because it is pretty certain to be dead before this page is read.

The purpose of ellipsis and the purpose of slang is the same; but they are opposite in their description and opposite in their history. Ellipsis is a minus feature and is very stable historically; slang is a plus feature and is absolutely unstable. Yet both signify the same: that the addressee, an insider, will understand what not everybody would be able to decipher.

Ellipsis (omission) makes most of the difference between casual grammar and consultative grammar. 'I believe that I can find one' is proper (though not required) in consultative grammar, but casual English requires a shorter form, say 'I believe I can find one' if not the still more elliptical 'Believe I can find one.' All the weak words of English can be omitted at the beginning of a casual sentence: 'Been a good thing if . . .' for 'It would have been a good thing if . . .' and similarly '[A] friend of mine . . .' or '[The] coffee's cold.' Some ellipsis is only phonological: 'Can I help you?' is consultative and 'C'n I help you?' is casual. Modern 'cute' from original 'acute' and 'fence' from 'defence' are two out of many words which originated in casual style and have since been promoted; similarly, 'Thank you' from 'I thank you' has been promoted all the way to formal style, while 'Thanks' from 'Many thanks' or 'Much thanks' (Shakespeare) has been promoted only to consultative. Aside from such little shifts in the tradition, ellipsis is stable: the elliptical expressions in use today can nearly all be found in Shakespeare, for instance 'Thanks.'

As an institution, slang is also ancient; but each individual slang expression is, on the contrary, necessarily unstable. The reason is obvious. Because the utility of any slang expression for classing the addressee as an insider (or excluding an unwanted listener as an outsider) depends on the fact—or at least the polite fiction—that only a minority of the population understands this bit of slang, each slang expression is necessarily ephemeral; for when that fiction has become transparent with age, its purpose is foiled, and then the useless slang is abandoned while new slang has to be created to take its place—not new slang of the same meaning, of course, but just enough new slang to maintain a normal supply. The abandoned slang is then 'dead slang,' a few items of which may still be resurrected as period-pieces for jocular or nostalgic employment, for instance 'kiddo' or 'for crying out loud.' (How awful!—That's life, Miss Fidditch.)

It's what is called 'half-life' in nuclear physics. The half-life of a slang expression is of the order of magnitude of one year, which implies that about one specimen in a thousand will survive for ten years, and thus become tough enough to last indefinitely; example: 'to be in the know.' When slang is created for use in literature, the slang is dignified by such titles as 'trope, simile, metaphor,'—and it is routinely rejected when outworn there also. (I can't believe it.—You don't have to, Miss F.)

Besides these two pattern devices—ellipsis and slang—casual style is marked by an arbitrary list of formulas, all very stable, which are learned individually and used to identify the style for the hearer's convenience. 'Come on!' has been one of these identifiers since before the time of Shakespeare (*The Tempest,* I, ii, 308); and all this while, every adult native speaker of English to whom it was addressed has unconsciously known that the speaker was using casual style and has reacted accordingly—and the speaker, without knowing why he did it, has used it to procure that reaction. It is all automatic, unconscious, just as the speaker of a falsehood is not aware that his motive for saying 'as a matter of fact' is to label it as false— a Freudian confession which is institutional in English. (I'm sure I never . . . —I believe you!)

Each style has its own list of such conventional formulas, which we may call 'code-labels' because they serve both to carry part of the message and to identify the style. The identifying function of a code-label is uniformly effective; its message-bearing function varies freely from nothing at all to a full message-fraction. Thus 'Come on!' means anything from 'Consider yourself among friends' to 'You're invited'; while 'Come on, cheer up!' means nothing but 'Cheer up because you're among friends.' There is of course a long list of casual code-labels, but 'Come on!' is one of the commonest.

Consultative code-labels include the standard list of listener's insertions 'yes [professorial for *yeah*], yeah, unhunh, that's right, oh, I see, yes I know' and a very few others, plus the 'well' that is used to reverse the rôles between listener and speaker. Another class of consultative code-labels consists of formulas for meeting that fluency problem which casual style evades by never tackling totally new topics; these are skeleton-keys for opening new doors without fumbling for the exact key which formal style will seek out at leisure. In our sample [pages 114-115] these skeleton-keys include the all-purpose noun 'thing' [line 1] for 'item, plan, problem, event, etc.,' the all-purpose preposition 'on' [25] for 'in, for, by, of, concerning, etc.,' and finally the counting-approximaters 'about' [5, 6, 7] and 'or so' [24], both meaning 'approximately' (a formal word). Other consultative code-label skeleton-keys exist, but our sample is enough to show how they work. In line 1, good casual style would have had 'something else' and stiff formal style perhaps 'a situation which has arisen.' A formal jokester may pretend to get a ludicrous picture out of 'I'd like to see you on a typewriter'; the trained social animal simply takes 'on' as a code-label for informal consultation.

Both colloquial styles—consultative and casual—routinely deal in a public sort of information, though differently: casual style takes it for granted and at most alludes to it, consultative style states it as fast as it is needed. Where there happens to be no public information for a while, a casual conversation (among men) lapses into silences and kidding, a consultative one is broken off or adjourned. These adjustments help to show what sort of rôle public information plays in the two colloquial styles: it is essential to them both.

Now in intimate style, this rôle is not merely weakened; rather, it is positively abolished. Intimate speech excludes public information. (Then how can it be language?—Let's see: it's *Miss* Fidditch, isn't it?)

Definition: An intimate utterance pointedly avoids giving the addressee information from outside of the speaker's skin. Example: 'Ready' said in quite a variety of situations, some of them allowing other persons to be present; note that this could be equivalent to either a statement or a question; the manner of saying it will be described in a moment. Another: 'Engh' or 'Cold' said at the family supper-table, but not to tell the speaker's wife that the coffee is cold—as it would tell her after we let Miss Fidditch expand the ellipsis for us: wrongly, for this is not an ellipsis. This tells the speaker's wife nothing about the coffee. How could it! She knows exactly how long since it was hot. If she had had to be told, the casual-style 'Coffee's cold' would have been used instead. After all, they both know the code. The point of any such utterance is simply to remind (hardly 'inform') the addressee of some feeling (unspecified, but that does not matter) inside the speaker's skin. (But I do wish they would speak like human beings!— What else?)

The systematic features of intimate style are two, just as in the other styles: (1) extraction; (2) jargon. Both are stable, once the intimate group (normally a pair) has been formed. Extraction has just been illustrated: the speaker extracts a minimum pattern from some conceivable casual sentence.

Extraction is not ellipsis. An elliptical sentence still has wording, grammar, and intonation. Intimate extraction employs only part of this triplet. Our printed 'Engh' represents an empty word, one that has no dictionary meaning but serves as a code-label for intimate style. (The parallel word in casual style, spelled 'unh,' has a different vocal quality.) There is, however, a message-meaning; this is conveyed by the intonation, the melody, with which 'Engh' is spoken. The speaker has extracted this intonation from a possible casual sentence, and that is all he uses of the grammatical triplet 'wording, grammar, intonation.' Again, our other example 'Cold' represents the word-identity alone, here spoken in a meaningless monotone; and the same is true of 'Ready.' In these instances, the triplet has been reduced to its first member, as 'Engh' reduced it to its last one, leaving the addressee to fill out the message—or, preferably, to comprehend it as it stands. (I couldn't.—Would you be so kind?)

Once more, this is not rudeness; this pays the addressee the highest compliment possible among mature people. Maturity implies some guardedness in public relations; here there is none, and the speaker is saying so. There is an exact discrimination between the inside and the outside of the speaker's skin; he makes this obvious, and pays the addressee the compliment of implying that she knows him inside and out. (Engh—It *is* . . . Miss Fidditch, isn't it?)

Intimate style tolerates nothing of the system of any other style: no slang, no background information, and so on. Any item of an intimate code that the folklore calls 'slang' is not slang but jargon—it is not ephemeral, but part of the permanent code of this group—it has to be, for intimacy does not tolerate the slang imputation that the addressee needs to be told that she is an insider. The imputations of all other styles are similarly corrosive. Accordingly, intimate codes, or jargons, are severely limited in their use of public vocabulary. Each intimate group must invent its own code. Somehow connected with all this is the cozy fact that language itself can never be a topic in intimate style. Any reaction to grammar, for instance, promptly disrupts intimacy. [S'mother time, M . . . F . . .]

NILS ERIK ENKVIST

From "On Defining Style"

Nils Erik Enkvist is Donner Professor of English Language and Literature at Åbo Akademi, Turku, Finland. Professor Enkvist's definition of style, like Hill's and Joos', emphasizes the importance of context in stylistic analysis. The selection below is part of a monograph in which Enkvist examines the function of style in teaching foreign languages. Thus, as he explains, " . . . I am here more interested in outlining procedures leading to an ultimately practical view of style and method of stylistic analysis than in building up a complete linguistic theory out of a perfect, logical progression of postulates."

The arrangement of [my] argument will be simple: I shall start with a definition, and see where it takes us. . . .

The style of a text is the aggregate of the contextual probabilities of its linguistic items.

Two terms, *aggregate* and *contextual,* still need a word of explanation. Style is the *aggregate* of frequencies of linguistic items in two different senses. First, style is the result of more than one linguistic item. For instance, a given word in a text only acquires stylistic significance by juxtaposition with other words. Therefore uncontextualized statistics on single items are of no stylistic significance. Texts longer than one sentence are involved at least in the norm. Secondly, the study of style must not be restricted to phonological or morphological or lexical or syntactic observations: it must be built up of observations made at various levels. Otherwise style merely turns into a sub-department of one of the established steps of linguistic analysis.[1] For example, in a scientific paper on *lepidoptera,* certain zoological terms will be found to have high frequencies; in another scientific paper on molluscs, these zoological terms related to butterflies may have low or zero frequencies; still the style of the two papers may be much the same, which only appears when the aggregate of data from levels other than the technical part of the lexis is brought into the comparison, and when both papers are compared with a contextually different norm.

Style is concerned with frequencies of linguistic items in a given context, and thus with *contextual* probabilities.[2] To measure the style of a passage,

"On Defining Style" by Nils Erik Enkvist from *Linguistics and Style,* published by Oxford University Press, 1964.

[1]See Martin Joos, 'The Isolation of Styles' in *Georgetown University Monograph Series on Languages and Linguistics* 12, Washington, D.C., 1960, pp. 109-10.

[2]The relationship between style and context appears, e.g., in Rolf Pipping, *Språk och stil,* Stockholm, 1940, where style is, under the influence of Sir Alan Gardiner's *Theory of Speech and Language* and Ph. Wegener's *Untersuchungen über die Grundfragen des Sprachlebens,* 1885, defined as a result of the speaker/writer's relationship with his public, subject, and linguistic inventory (p. 98).

the frequencies of its linguistic items of different levels must be compared with the corresponding features in another text or corpus which is regarded as a norm and which has a definite contextual relationship with this passage. For the stylistic analysis of one of Pope's poems, for instance, norms with varying contextual relationships include English eighteenth-century poetry, the corpus of Pope's work, all poems written in English in rhymed pentameter couplets, or, for greater contrast as well as comparison, the poetry of Wordsworth. Contextually distant norms would be, e.g., Gray's *Anatomy* or the London Telephone Directory of 1960.

An appeal to context here obviates the need for references to extralinguistic meaning; the context of a given text is presumably better accessible to objective, linguistic and sociolinguistic classification. Contextual relationships can be defined in many ways. Each text and each passage partakes of several contexts. Some of them are definable in formal, linguistic terms ('last couplet of a Shakespearean sonnet', 'text in rhymed pentameter couplets'). Others involve provenance, period and literary genre. Others must be based on context of situation, including the speaker, the listener, and their relationship and environment. In a study of Mr. Micawber's conversation with David Copperfield, one relevant contextual aspect is 'gentleman speaking to a boy'.[3]

Contexts, then, must be defined on several levels, and contextual components can be further classified into various, elaborate patterns.[4] To classify all categories of context *a priori* is impossible, not least because contexts vary from one language, culture and time to another.[5] All we can attempt is 'a limited theory of selection by sociophysical setting',[6] and we must be prepared to revise this limited theory to keep it up to date as changes in our modes of life suggest new, significant context categories. Such new categories often invite projection into the past as well; thus our constant revaluation of old literary texts may partly depend on recent shifts in context classification. Very tentative illustration is therefore the only purpose of lists of features in the contextual spectrum, such as this:

textual context
    linguistic frame
        phonetic context (voice quality, speech rate, &c.)

---

[3]In a working paper on 'Applied Linguistics in the Teaching of English as a Secondary Language' read at the Anglo-American Conference on English Teaching Abroad at Jesus College, Cambridge, in June, 1961, Mr. J. C. Catford defines 'registers' as 'sub-varieties of dialect (or idiolect) which correlate with the social rôle being played by the performer: e.g. one and the same individual may function socially as, say, a husband/father, as a member of a political party, as a professor of Zoology, &c., and he makes use of a range of *registers* appropriate to these different rôles.' Within the framework of the present essay, registers turn into a sub-variety of style.

[4]On such classifications, see, e.g. J. R. Firth, *Papers in Linguistics,* London, 1957, pp. 35-36, and Kenneth L. Pike, *Language in Relation to a Unified Theory of the Structure of Human Behavior,* Glendale, Calif., 1954-60, I.5, 52-55 and III.17.

[5]In the second part of this book, Spencer and Gregory recognize five major dimensions for placing a text: history, dialect, and field, mode and tenor of discourse.

[6]I quote from Jerrold J. Katz and Jerry A. Fodor, 'The Structure of a Semantic Theory', *Language,* XXXIX, 1963, p. 181.

phonemic context
morphemic context *(he sings/he singeth)*
syntactic context (including sentence length and complexity)
lexical context
punctuation, capitalization
compositional frame
    beginning, middle or end of utterance, paragraph, poem, play, &c.
    relationship of text to surrounding textual portions
    metre, literary form, typographical arrangement
extratextual context
    period
    type of speech, literary genre
    speaker/writer
    listener/reader
    relationship between speaker/writer and listener/reader in terms of sex, age, familiarity, education, social class and status, common stock of experience, &c.
    context of situation and environment
    gesture, physical action
    dialect and language

If items from this list, such as certain phonetic features or gesture, are included in the description of those linguistic features whose contextual spread we wish to study, they must of course be omitted from among the contextual features.

In the quest for meaningful norms of comparison, the first common-sense approach might be based on a question such as: 'With what texts, what types of communication and what responses occurring in what situations should the text or passage we wish to analyse be compared and contrasted in the first place?' In theory our answer will depend on the level of delicacy[7] we wish to aim at in our linguistic description of stylistic elements and in our grouping of contexts; in practice we must be prepared to give it *ad hoc.* The contextual elements must also be fitted into a hierarchy, whose most meaningful arrangement depends on the problem at hand. Roughly speaking, more inclusive contextual groupings are correlated with more comprehensive style categories.[8]

A thorough study of style should be built on the examination of texts that have a number of intersecting contextual relationships. Two questions are relevant here. First, what expressions are used in a given context? Secondly, in what contexts does a given expression occur? We should thus not only look into the differences between, say, conversational passages in Dickens and in Thackeray. We should also see in what situations a given

---

[7]See below, p. [128] n. 12.
[8]See below, pp. [127-130].

expression occurs in their works (and also in, say, modern English, presuming that the expressions of nineteenth-century novelists ought to be compared with modern idiom).

As the writer is here regarded as part of the context of what he writes, our definition will include all those stylistic elements that consist of personal idiosyncrasies and that constitute a stylistic idiolect.

According to this view, every passage has a constellation of contexts as well as a style. There is no styleless language. 'John is a boy', for instance, contrasts with the logician's 'John is a young male human' and with the doctor's 'John, o, 8 yrs.' All three are likely to appear in different contextual constellations. 'Please pass the salt' similarly contrasts stylistically with 'please give me ten milligrams of sodium chloride', which is likely to appear in a related, but different, situational context. In both sentences, A wants some salt from B; in the first sentence, he does so at the table, and in the second, in the laboratory. But 'please pass the salt' does not contrast stylistically with 'please pass the pepper', which is likely to occur in exactly the same situational context in the dining-room. In other words, the choice between *salt* and *sodium chloride* is stylistic, and that between *salt* and *pepper* non-stylistic. I shall return to this question on pp. [126-127] below.

In theory one may perhaps justify stylistic comparison of any texts. But these examples suggest that the most practical starting-point for analyses of style may well turn out to be the examination of frequencies of linguistic items in related, but different, contexts. If the contexts are very closely related, we run an initial risk of not finding style behind the pragmatics of our material. If the contextual relationship is very distant, the whole comparison may be too far-fetched to yield anything but trivial results. In other words, the initial comparison of the styles of the two texts becomes more difficult both if the texts are very similar and if they are very different. The difference between two texts may of course also be diachronic: thus the *Authorized Version* and the *Cambridge Bible* invite stylistic comparison not least because their time-bound context is different, even though the language of the 1611 Bible is regarded as part of living English.

Style, then, is a link between context and linguistic form. It follows that contextualization of the material is necessary if the foreign-language student is to acquire a grasp of its stylistic impact.[9]

There are three ways of measuring the predictability of linguistic items in a given context. First there is the classic method of literary critics to rely upon their experience or 'sense of style' when deciding what expressions are common and what expressions are not. Often, however, their assessments of frequencies are inextricably mixed with other considerations.

---

[9]In foreign-language teaching on TV, problems of contextualization come dramatically to the fore. See S. Pit Corder, *English Language Teaching and Television*, London, 1960, pp. 44ff. and *passim*.

Secondly, the frequencies in each constellation of contexts can be computed directly out of a corpus of texts, for instance with the aid of a computer. The probabilities in different contextual constellations can then be determined with the aid of statistical formulae. Detailed context analysis is a necessary prerequisite of this method. Thirdly, it is possible to give a group of informants a piece of text as a stimulus or frame, and then to ask them what linguistic item or items they expect to occur next to, or near, it.[10] Conversely, one might ask the informants to define the contexts in which a given expression is likely to appear. The number of correct guesses, or fulfilled expectations, gives a rough measure of the relative predictabilities of the items guessed at. This procedure necessitates an initial distinction between grammatical, non-stylistic and stylistic choice as well as some control of contextual factors before it allows an assessment of stylistic predictabilities. In practice, the informants must be carefully screened as to education, experience, and linguistic ability.

One important step is the grouping of linguistic items into those that function as style markers in a given context, and into those whose stylistic function is limited or nil. To recognize style markers, a study must be made of the distribution of linguistic items in different, but related, contexts.

Let us begin with a simple example. If a statement such as *As everybody knows, the earth is flat* is, in twentieth-century English, invariably found in jocular and humorous contexts, never in serious or scientific ones, it does possess stylistic value and might even serve as a style marker. If a person utters or writes it, we can safely predict he will be joking. If, on the contrary, this statement is found in a range of contexts from jocular to seriously scientific, it cannot serve as a style marker. The same applies to features at other levels of the linguistic spectrum. If a slow rate of speech is characteristic of the delivery of sermons, it can be regarded as part of pulpit style. More inclusive analysis may show that it, in fact, marks a more comprehensive style category such as 'solemn, formal public oratory'. To find examples of context-bound lexical elements is too simple to need illustration here.

We may now define style markers as those linguistic items that only appear, or are most or least frequent in, one group of contexts. In other words, style markers are contextually bound linguistic elements. Elements that are not style markers are stylistically neutral. This may be rephrased: style markers are mutually exclusive with other items which only appear in different contexts, or with zero; or have frequencies markedly different from those of such items.[11]

---

[10]This method was used by Iván Fónagy in 'Communication in Poetry', *Word*, XVII, 1961, 194-218.

[11]In 'Styles as Dialects', *Preprints of Papers for the Ninth International Congress of Linguistics*, Cambridge, Mass., 1962, Werner Winter writes: 'A style may be said to be characterized by a pattern of recurrent selection from the inventory of optional features of a language. Various types of selection can be found: complete exclusion of an optional element, obligatory inclusion of a feature optional elsewhere, varying degrees of inclusion of a specific variant without complete elimination of competing features.' (p. 214.)

ONE VIEW OF STYLE AS CHOICE

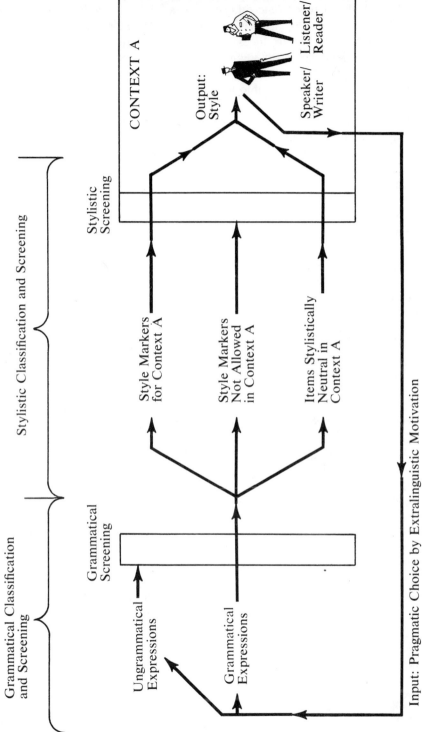

In the light of this, some otherwise meaningless repetitions of linguistic items acquire meaning as style markers. For instance, the swearing and cursing of a soldier introduces a stream of stylistically significant items—'style reminders'—into statements that would otherwise remain more neutral. The origin of slang can be sought in an effort to create and introduce new style markers unavailable in the existing inventory of linguistic items.

The concept of style markers is of course intimately linked with the view of style as choice discussed above . . . to which I shall now return by way of a digression. Stylistic choice, it will be seen, involves the choice of style markers, whereas non-stylistic choice involves selection from among stylistically neutral items. All neutral items are capable of occurring in the context at hand and within the style in question. Non-stylistic choice is thus contextually free, stylistic choice contextually bound. In practice, most utterances are composed of style markers as well as of stylistically neutral elements.

Thus, strictly speaking, the definition of style markers makes it superfluous to worry any longer about style as choice: stylistic choice is simply the context-bound use of style markers. By introducing style markers, our initial definition of style as the aggregate of contextual probabilities has sufficed to distinguish between stylistic and non-stylistic selection. Let us all the same discover if we can construct a model of style as choice, if only to see what difficulties we must face in doing so.

For one such model at least, we must, however reluctantly, introduce a fourth type of choice: pragmatic selection. By pragmatic choice I here mean the choice of a meaning for an utterance—or of 'something to say'—by extralinguistic motivation. Pramatic choice thus involves the decision of what a person wants to convey in his linguistic message. In encoding this message, the speaker may use both style markers and stylistically neutral elements. Now the four levels or types of selection—pragmatic, grammatical, stylistic, and non-stylistic—presumably form a sequential hierarchy of one kind or another. One interpretation of the successive phases of selection involved in our style model takes them in this order, and leads to a process illustrated in the diagram [p. 125].

Here the speaker/writer and listener/reader are both part of a given context, A. By extralinguistic motivation, the speaker (for short) wants to convey a message to the listener. This message is to begin with encoded grammatically: only grammatical items pass through the first screen, non-grammatical items being caught. Next, the grammatical items are screened stylistically by criteria determined by context A. This second screen passes all stylistically neutral items as well as the style markers bound to context A, but retains all style markers that cannot occur in context A. Only items screened grammatically and stylistically are thus capable of entering into the speaker's style.

What, then, is wrong with this model? It is, to begin with, not based on any psychophysiological considerations nor on any particular, full theory of linguistic description of language as a whole. Also, grammatical choice here occupies a higher hierarchic position than stylistic choice; the order of the two screens must be reversed if we wish to regard grammatical choice as hierarchically subordinate to stylistic, that is context-bound, selection. The grammar screen must then be placed within the context. This happens for example if we allow poetic contexts a grammar of their own, permitting constructions such as Cummings's *he danced his did*. I have here opted for grammatical priority because this situation is more relevant to foreign-language teaching, where all texts have presumably been first screened by grammatical considerations. (Stylistic screening is of course also concerned with the selection of grammatical style markers from among the grammatically permissible items.) Finally, a debatable feature of this model is its use of pragmatic choice and thus of prelinguistic meaning. The scheme becomes more defensible if we take for granted that, for a given individual, stylistic screening merely involves a selection from among all the grammatical structures known to that individual.

We may thus construct various more or less satisfactory models to illustrate the difference between grammatical, stylistic, and non-stylistic selection. But one of the main advantages in the definition of style as the aggregate of contextual probabilities is that it gives us a chance of bypassing such models in our actual stylistic analysis, which can be directly concerned with the operational comparison of frequencies of linguistic items in contextually related norms. The aim of stylistic analysis is the inventory of style markers and a statement of their contextual spread.

Let us illustrate this with yet another example. Mr N and Mrs N are sitting in front of the fire on a rainy day. N says, *What a beastly day!* Does the choice of this utterance have stylistic value, or is it stylistically neutral? It is, let us note, conditioned by the context 'N to Mrs N at home when it rains'.

The answer may be yes or no, depending on our choice of norms and levels in the contextual hierarchy against which the probability of N's utterance is matched. If we find that the utterance *What a beastly day!* is characteristic of N as opposed to B, who usually reacts to rain by asking Mrs B *Isn't this rain awful?*, it possesses stylistic value at one level by marking N's individual style, or stylistic idiolect, as different from B's on that same level. If it is shared by most members of N's social class, as opposed to another socially definable category of people who use other expressions in a similar context, it functions as a marker of a classbound style, but does not mark N's style as different from that of others of his own social class. If, again, *What a beastly day!* mostly occurs in N's fireside conversation, not in his shop-talk with other chartered accountants, it is characteristic of his familiar style or register. And so forth.

In spite of the downpour, N might conceivably also have said *What a lovely afternoon!*, presumably if he had a taste for irony. Now if N mostly reacts to rain by calling it *lovely,* whereas B, C, and D mostly call it *beastly,* this also separates N's individual style from those of B, C, and D. But N's individual taste for irony will not have sufficient weight to characterize the style of N, B, C, D and their peers as a group. The study of group usage naturally necessitates study of more than one informant.

Similar phenomena can be found in literary texts as compared with norms circumscribed by literary contexts. The interesting point is that in all these comparisons, the same linguistic element may appear as a style marker when matched against one norm, and as stylistically neutral when compared with another. This may lead to initial confusion. The general resolution of such problems must be sought in hierarchic levels of contexts and context-bound norms, and thus in the delicacy[12] of the analysis. As always, maximally delicate statements are meaningless because they merely reproduce the primary data in full. Therefore no stylistic analysis should start by studying linguistic behaviour in terms of absurdly detailed, transitory, and unique contextual constellations. We have to climb to higher rungs on the hierarchic ladder of contexts before we arrive at meaningful descriptions of styles.

So, when matched against the very low-level and delicate norm of 'Mr B to his wife at home when it rains', Mr N's use of *What a beastly day!* is stylistic if *(a)* it is contextually bound (for instance, provoked by rain), and *(b)* it has a much greater frequency in N's speech than in that of B. However, if we match N's utterance against higher, less delicate and more inclusive norms such as 'middle-class husbands to their wives' or 'middle-class people in familiar conversation', such frequency differences are likely to disappear as we stop paying attention to minute contextual details (in this case, rain) and simultaneously increase the range of the norm. But if N's *What a beastly day!* is matched against the frequencies in sermons, and if it proves to have a very low frequency in sermon contexts, it will have stylistic significance in marking N's fireside conversation as different from sermons. The linguistic description of utterances in stylistic analysis should similarly aim for suitable delicacy levels. Thus *What a beastly day!* can, at one such level, be regarded as a sentence with the intonation contour of an exclamation and with the structure *what a* + one of the adjectives *beastly, lovely, gorgeous, terrible, nasty, horrid,* &c., + substantive. It will of course be more meaningful to look for instances of this whole class of expressions than merely for the one sentence *What a beastly day!* All this, incidentally, agrees with common-sense views of style.

The norm, then, should be chosen so as to have a meaningful contextual relationship with the text whose style we are studying. The higher we climb on the hierarchic ladder of styles in our choice of contexts and levels of comparison, the fewer are the stylistic choices, the fewer the style markers, the larger and more inclusive the style categories, and the more numerous

---

[12] I have borrowed this extremely useful concept from Dr. M. A. K. Halliday's article 'Categories of the Theory of Grammar,' *Word,* XVII, 1961, p. 268, where it is defined as 'depth of detail' and as a 'cline running from a fixed point at one end (least delicate, or 'primary') to that undefined but theoretically crucial point (probably statistically definable) where distinctions are so fine that they cease to be distinctions at all, like a river followed up from the mouth each of whose tributaries ends in a moorland bog.'

the stylistically neutral choices and items. Therefore the delicacy of stylistic analysis—as indeed of all linguistic analysis—should be set at the level providing us with optimally meaningful results. If we go too high, for instance by defining the norm in terms of the language as a whole, we lose significant details; if we aim too low, we fail to see the forest for mere trees. All this should once again remind us of the importance of basing stylistic analyses on adequate materials, and of thus avoiding the excessively delicate—as well as excessively far-fetched—approaches warned against in section 4 above [not printed here].

To sum up: after the style markers in a sufficiently large number of texts have been compared with those in a sufficiently large number of suitably selected norms, and after the contextual ranges have been correspondingly widened, it becomes possible to formulate increasingly general and powerful descriptions of styles and style categories. We are then advancing along the cline from more delicate to less delicate statements, and gradually working up from the analysis and description of individual passages, texts and substyles to the determination of more inclusive categories of style.

Style being a matter of frequencies, not only of occurrence *versus* non-occurrence, absolute mutual exclusion is not the only distributional pattern with stylistic relevance. Statistical trends too provide us with many style markers.[13] For instance, the choice between active and passive constructions in English is one of those whose stylistic correlations can be expected to appear only, or largely, in statistical terms. As long as both types of construction are grammatical, the choice between them cannot be a matter of grammar. If the use of one or the other is contextually bound, the choice is stylistic. Thus the writer of an adventure story is likely to opt mainly for vigorous active constructions, whereas the scientist will prefer to report on his procedures by effacing his ego behind a passive. But even the scientist may occasionally emerge with a direct first-person sentence. If, on the other hand, the choice is dictated by emphasis (as *The Christians were eaten by lions* in a text on Christians, not lions), it becomes non-stylistic. This view is justified by the fact that passives occur over a very wide contextual spread in instances where the main subject of the passage would otherwise be hidden as the object of an active construction. The use of the passive for emphasis is therefore not strictly bound contextually. But even if the choice between actives and passives is sometimes non-stylistic, in English a high incidence of passive constructions functions as a very striking style marker. Sentence and clause length, sentence complexity, word length, and a host of other features may also yield statistical trends sufficiently context-bound for the marking of styles. At least in theory, strikingly low frequencies of certain linguistic items may similarly characterize definite style categories.

---

[13]See above, p. 21, first footnote; and Werner Winter, *op. cit.*, and especially 'Relative Häufigkeit syntaktischer Erscheinungen als Mittel zur Abgrenzung von Stilarten', *Phonetica*, VII, 1961, 193-216. Several papers in the past few years' files of *Voprosy Jazykoznanija* also present relevant data; see, e.g. S. I. Kaufman, 'Ob imennom kharaktere tekhnicheskoje stilja' in X, 1961: 5, 103-8.

The style markers that appear in the same text form a stylistic set for that text.

An example. In French we find that texts characterized by one contextual constellation (roughly, 'literary') use the *passé simple* as a narrative tense, mark questions by inversion *(Monsieur votre père vient-il?)*, and employ *nous*. Texts characterized by another contextual constellation (roughly, 'colloquial') avoid the *passé simple;* form questions with the aid of tags such as *est-ce que* and, in speech, intonation, but do not invert the word order; and use *on* instead of *nous*, with the verb in the third person singular.[14] In a suitably selected sample of two types of context-determined texts we shall find that these three items are mutually exclusive and that each text will use either Set I or Set II without mixing items from the two sets:

> Set I: *passé simple,* inverted questions, *nous*
> Set II: no *passé simple,* non -inverted questions, *on*

Within this sample, we may predict: if we find an instance of *passé simple,* we can expect the same text to have *nous* and inversion in questions, but not constructions such as *Il vient, ton père?* or *on* for the first person plural.

The style markers that are shared by a large number of texts within a range of related but different contexts form a major stylistic set. Those texts that share a major stylistic set belong to the same major style. Analysis of a sufficiently large number of texts covering the entire contextual spectrum of a given language will result in a definition of the major styles of that language. These can be labelled and defined, e.g. with terms that suggest important contextual categories or style markers. Thus in French we might make one major distinction between *passé-simple* style and non-*passé-simple* style. In English, the labels frozen, formal, consultative, casual, and intimate have been suggested for five major style categories.[15] It is worth a passing note that the most classic of all such categorizations—the distinction of three levels, *stylus gravis, mediocrus* and *humilis*—may well have owed its success through the centuries to its close links with a literary tradition permitting only three major contextual categories, whose main features could be summarized in Virgil's Wheel.

---

[14]There is of course no contradiction between the citing of this example (borrowed from André Martinet, *Eléments de linguistique générale,* Paris 1960. pp. 163 and 173) and the insistence on contextual relationship, voiced above. Even if *Monsieur votre père vient-il?* and *Il vient, ton père?* occur in contexts that are different in terms of the polarity between literary and colloquial situations, they have other contextual features in common. Thus both are questions inquiring about the arrival of the conversational partner's father. Comparable examples could be cited from a host of languages. I have, for instance, observed that in my own spoken Finland-Swedish I make a consistent contextual distinction between two styles, one with *skulle* and imperfect forms of the type *kallade,* and another with *sku* and *kalla.* In this instance the polarity is between formal and familiar speech.

[15]Joos, *op. cit.* In 'Entropija russkogo jazyka', *Voprosy Jazykoznanija,* XI, 1962: 6, 115-30, A. A. Piotrovskaja and co-workers distinguish between four major styles in Russian: conversational, belletristic, factual, and poetic. Conversational passages from Nekrasov, Babel, and Grossman come under conversational style.

In many contexts, styles can be expected to overlap. If in a given context different speakers use different styles, which they elsewhere agree in associating with the same contextual ranges, this context is stylistically ambiguous. For example, if, in situation A, one educated young man uses the more formal *yes, Sir* and another equally educated young man prefers the less formal *yes*, though there are other situations in which both agree in using either *yes, Sir* or *yes*, situation A is contextually ambiguous. Such overlaps are likely to increase towards the boundaries between the contextual areas of different styles, and may therefore give us clues to contextual and stylistic groupings.

An overlap of stylistic sets[16] within a given passage of text will first of all motivate a critical re-examination of the criteria by which these sets were obtained. If the method was sound, such an overlap is the result either of a mixture of styles, or, if further analysis shows that each set is consistently used in definite portions of the text, of one or several shifts of style.

Many literary effects are based on a shift of style, which may be defined as a switch from one stylistic set to another. In terms of our basic definition of style it involves a shift in the probabilities of the linguistic items of the text as measured against one and the same contextual norm. If, for instance, a clergyman delivering a sermon shifts from biblical idiom into colloquial English, this lowers the probabilities of his linguistic items as matched against biblical and pulpit norms. We might also regard the same change as a norm shift if for some reason we find it more expedient to match the probabilities, no longer against those of biblical English but against those of colloquial usage. But we must still remember the context (here, the pulpit). The intentional or unintentional use of a style marker or a stylistic set in an unambiguously alien context might be labelled as contextual transfer. It can be compared to the wearing of brown shoes with black tie; its effects vary from the striking through the humorous, the awkward and the rude to the disastrous.

A shift of style must not be confused with metaphor. Metaphor involves collocational shifts at the lexical level under specific semantic constraints, but without regard to such other contextual limitations as enter into style. Of course, given types of metaphors and their frequencies may function as important style markers, not least in poetry. If a given metaphor introduces a word from an alien stylistic set, it also involves a shift of style; if the metaphoric term is taken from the same stylistic set as the rest of the utterance, no shift in style will result.

In many types of texts, such as plays and novels, different passages often use different styles. The style of a narrative passage, for instance, may contrast with that of dialogue or interior monologue. Such shifts of style are obviously accompanied by shifts of context. The same holds true of the speech of different characters, the speaker being part of the context of what

---

[16]That is, stylistic sets already established by study of other texts.

he says. Those subvarieties of style which correlate with the varying social rôles of a given speaker or writer may be called registers.

Another distinction that should be kept in mind is that between style and dialect,[17] for instance in works mixing dialects, or dialects and standard language, for literary effect. If dialect is used only in readily definable contexts, it can most conveniently be regarded as a sub-variety of style; a shift of dialect thus turns into a shift of style. So in *Lady Chatterley's Lover,* Mellors's change from Standard English into dialect has obvious connexions with shifts in context and with stylistic features. The frequency of taboo words, for instance, is higher in the dialect passages. Mellors can also be said to employ two major registers, one dialect register and one Standard English register, which may perhaps be further subdivided by more detailed reference to the different social rôles with which his choice of idiom is linked.

There are many instances of situations in which even the choice of language within one and the same society has been more or less markedly context-bound. Obvious European examples include the use of Greek in the Roman Empire, of Latin in the Middle Ages and Renaissance, of French in England during the Middle-English period, of Danish in Norway, of Swedish in Finland at least before 1863, and of French among the upper classes of eighteenth-century Europe and pre-revolutionary Russia.

Even if the use of a second language is widespread and consistent enough to be bound by context, it can be dealt with by the principles and methods described above. The distinction between dialect and style can be approached in two ways. Either we define the material subjected to stylistic analysis as dialectally homogeneous and classify possible dialects as varieties of style, or we begin by grouping passages by dialect and proceed to separate stylistic analysis of each of the dialects that occur in our text. It is, however, always relevant to note possible correlations between context and dialect as well as between shift of context and shift of dialect.

One reason complicating a general discussion of style, dialect and language is that traditional distinctions between dialect and language are based on historical and cultural, not purely linguistic, developments and principles. Thus languages and dialects have very different status and prestige in different multilingual and multidialectal environments.

We may further distinguish between microstylistics and macrostylistics. Microstylistics is the study of style markers and stylistic sets within the sentence or within units smaller than the sentence, whereas macrostylistics is the stylistics of sentence sequences.

The study of features not statable in terms of contextual probabilities of linguistic items, style markers, stylistic sets and shifts of style is not the task of stylistics but of other levels of linguistic or literary analysis.

---

[17]See Werner Winter, 'Styles as Dialects', *Preprints of Papers for the Ninth International Congress of Linguists,* Cambridge, Mass., 1962, pp. 214-19.

RICHARD OHMANN

Generative Grammars and
the Concept of Literary Style

*Richard Ohmann teaches English and linguistics at Wesleyan University
and edits* College English, *a publication of the National Council of Teachers
of English. Among his books are* The Logic and Rhetoric of Exposition
(1963, with Harold C. Martin) and Shaw: The Style and the Man *(1962).
Like Archibald Hill, Professor Ohmann has done much to promote a common forum for the rhetorician, the linguist, and the critic. In the article
reprinted here Ohmann begins by listing the multiple approaches taken to
stylistic analysis in the past. But unlike Hill, Joos, and Enkvist—all of whom
advocate in the preceding essays a general, contextual theory of style—
Ohmann believes a workable theory of style must come from an adequate
theory of syntax which will "take into account the deeper structural features
of language." Noam Chomsky's theory of phrase structure-transformational
grammar provides Ohmann with such a syntactic theory, and Ohmann
develops a stylistic theory based upon what Chomsky and others have discovered about the deep structure of language.*

A style is a way of writing—that is what the word means. And that is almost
as much as one can say with assurance on the subject, which has been remarkably unencumbered by theoretical insights. Yet we know a good deal
more than that, in a way: the same way, roughly in which a native speaker
"knows" the grammar of English, although no existing grammatical analysis
gives a full and adequate account of his linguistic intuition. Readers familiar
with literature have what might sensibly be called a *stylistic* intuition, a
rather loosely structured, but often reliable, feeling for the quiddity of a
writer's linguistic method, a sense of differences between stretches of literary discourse which are not differences in content. In fact many readers
can tell, by skimming a batch of unfamiliar passages, not only that the differences are there, but who the authors are. Read the first few paragraphs
of a *New Yorker* story and you can often (without a surreptitious glance at
the end) identify it as a Cheever, an O'Hara, an Updike, or a Salinger, even
if the subject matter is uncharacteristic. Further evidence, if any is needed,
of the reliability of stylistic intuitions is the ability of some to write convincing parodies, and of others to recognize them as such. Thus the theorist
of style is confronted by a kind of task that is commonplace enough in most
fields: the task of explicating and toughening up for rigorous use a notion
already familiar to the layman.

But in stylistics the scholar has always had to make do with a theoretical

From *Word*, XX (December 1964), 423-439. Used by permission of the Linguistic Circle of New York,
Inc., and the author.

apparatus not far removed from that of the layman. And although many practitioners have plied their craft with great subtlety, a survey of their work leaves one far from certain what that craft *is*. For the attempt to isolate the cues one attends to in identifying styles and in writing stylistic parody has sprawled out into an almost embarrassing profusion of critical methods. And most of these methods, I believe, are interesting in inverse proportion to their emphasis on what we sense as style. The following list will suggest, but not exhaust, the multiplicity of approaches:

(1) What might be called "diachronic stylistics," the study of changes in national literary style from one period to the next. Clearly this approach presupposes a mastery of what might be called

(2) "Synchronic stylistics," or the study of this or that period style. Since the style of a period can only be the sum of linguistic habits shared by most writers of that period, synchronic stylistics presupposes in turn the ability to describe the style of a single writer. But there is little agreement upon how such description is to be managed; many methods compete for critical attention.

(3) Impressionism: the application of metaphorical labels to styles ("masculine," "limber," "staccato," "flowing," "involuted," etc.), and the attempt to evaluate (Swift's style is the best, or the most natural to English). This sort of criticism makes agreeable parlor conversation, records something of the critic's emotional response, and gives intuition its due, but little else can be said in its favor.

(4) The study of sound, especially of rhythm. This approach is capable of some rigor, but the more rigor (that is, the more strictly the critic attends to physical or to phonemic features), the less relevance to what we sense as style. For—let me state this dogmatically—in prose, at least, rhythm as perceived is largely dependent upon syntax, and even upon content, not upon stress, intonation, and juncture alone.

(5) The study of tropes. Attention to metaphor, antithesis, synecdoche, zeugma, and the other figures of classical rhetoric often proceeds from a desire to see the writer's style in terms of what he thought he was doing, and to this extent points away from a descriptive analysis of style, and toward the history or philosophy of rhetorical theory. Even when the studies of figurative language maintain a descriptive focus, they embrace only a small, though important, part of style, and liberally mixed with content, at that.

(6) The study of imagery. The fact that a writer favors images of disease, money, battle, or the like, is frequently of great interest, but imagery divorced from its syntactic embodiment is surely more a matter of content than of style.

(7) The study of what is variously called "tone," "stance," "role," and so on: roughly, the writer's attitude toward what he is saying, toward his reader, and toward himself, as suggested by his language. The critic in this vein infers, from the locutions on the printed page, a hypothetical live situa-

tion in which such language would be appropriate, and discusses the social and emotional features of that situation. This approach has unquestionably been fruitful. Its success depends on a highly developed sense of connotative meaning, both of words and of constructions, and this sense is something that many critics possess in abundance. Tone, however, like figurative language, is only a part of style, and the question remains in what measure tone itself is a product of formal linguistic features.

(8) The study of literary structure, which, like the study of tropes and tone, has flourished among the new critics. And to be sure, patterns of organization in a literary work are *related* to style (the way a novel is put together may have an analogue in the way a sentence is put together), but to consider structure a *component* of style, except perhaps in a short poem, stretches the meaning of the term "style" to its limits.

(9) The analysis of particular and local effects—a change of verb tense, or the placement of an interrogative, for instance, in a certain passage. Clearly, individual strategies of this sort fit more comfortably under the heading of *technique* than of style, for style has to do primarily with the habitual, the recurrent.

(10) The study of special idiosyncrasies, such as the omission of causal connectives from contexts where they usually appear. Such quirks are doubtless stylistic elements, and they can richly reward analysis, as a number of studies by Leo Spitzer have shown. But a few idiosyncrasies do not add up to a style, by any method of calculation.

(11) The study of a writer's lexicon, as pursued, for example, by Josephine Miles. Lexical preferences, unless seen in the context of a ramified system of word classes, are like imagery patterns, in that they reveal more about content than about style.

(12) The statistical study of grammatical features—abstract nouns, adjectives, subordinate clauses, questions, and the like. This method is without doubt pertinent, but significant results have been highly elusive. One reason is the crudeness of the categories which traditional grammar has made available to critics, whose knowledge of linguistics generally seems to lag by a few decades. (Linguists, by and large, have not busied themselves with stylistics.) Another reason, equally important, is the overwhelming inefficiency of the procedure, given the very large number of grammatical categories, and the lack of any grammatical system that relates them in meaningful, formally motivated ways. Without such a theory, a collection of counts is simply a collection of counts.

And indeed, the inability of these and other methods, in spite of many partial successes, to yield a full and convincing explication of the notion of style seems in general to follow from the absence of an appropriate underlying linguistic and semantic theory. A style is a characteristic use of language, and it is difficult to see how the *uses* of a system can be understood unless the system itself has been mapped out. It is no surprise, in other words, to find stylistics in a state of disorganization when syntax and semantics, upon which stylistics clearly depends, have themselves been hampered by the lack of a theory that is inclusive, unified, and plausible.

The situation in stylistics is understandably analogous to that in the philosophy of language,[1] though more muddled still. Just as philosophers have tended to concentrate on this or that discrete feature of language—words, or groups of words, or grammatical predication, or the relation of reference, or logical structure—in isolation from the rest, so analysts of style have talked about sound, tropes, images, diction, devices of conjunction, parallel structure, and so on, without any apparent sense of priority or centrality among these concerns. Thus, in a time when linguistic theory and practice have passed through at least one renaissance, the most serviceable studies of style[2] continue to proceed from the critic's naked intuition, fortified against the winds of ignorance only by literary sophistication and the tattered garments of traditional grammar. Especially damaging is the critic's inability, for lack of a theory, to take into account the deeper structural features of language, precisely those which should enter most revealingly into a stylistic description.

It is my contention that recent developments in generative grammar, particularly on the transformational model, promise, first, to clear away a good deal of the mist from stylistic theory, and, second, to make possible a corresponding refinement in the practice of stylistic analysis. In the remainder of this paper I hope to state a case for the first of these claims, and to make a very modest initial thrust toward documenting the second.

That Chomsky's formulation of grammatical theory is potentially useful should become apparent from an examination of the common sense notion of style. In general that notion applies to human action that is partly invariant and partly variable. A style is a *way* of doing *it*. Now this picture leads to few complications if the action is playing the piano or playing tennis. The pianist performing a Mozart concerto must strike certain notes in a certain order, under certain restrictions of tempo, in a certain relation to the orchestra, and so on. These limitations define the part of his behavior that is fixed. Likewise, the tennis player must hit the ball over the net with the racket in a way partly determined by the rules of the game (errors and cheating are not style). But each has a significant amount of freedom, beyond these established regularities: the tennis player, for instance, chooses from a repertory of strokes, shots, and possible placements (analogous, perhaps, to the linguistic resources of the writer or speaker), and he also has freedom of intensity, smoothness, flamboyance, etc. (as the writer or speaker has freedom in the use of paralinguistic resources like loudness and emphatic punctuation). The tennis player's use of these options, in so far as it is habitual or recurrent, constitutes his style. But the relevant division between fixed and variable components in literature is by no means

---

[1]See Jerrold Katz and Jerry Fodor, "What's Wrong with the Philosophy of Language?," *Inquiry* V (1962), pp. 197-237.

[2]William K. Wimsatt, *The Prose Style of Samuel Johnson* (New Haven, 1941), and Jonas Barish, *Ben Jonson and the Language of Prose Comedy* (Cambridge, Mass., 1960), to name just two of the best.

so obvious. What *is* content, and what is form, or style? The attack on a dichotomy of form and content has been persistent in modern criticism; to change so much as a word, the argument runs, is to change the meaning as well. This austere doctrine has a certain theoretical appeal, given the supposed impossibility of finding exact synonyms, and the ontological queerness of disembodied content—propositions, for instance—divorced from any verbal expression. Yet at the same time this doctrine leads to the altogether counterintuitive conclusion that there can be no such thing as style, or that style is simply a part of content.[3]

To put the problem more concretely, the idea of style implies that words on a page might have been different, or differently arranged, without a corresponding difference in substance. Another writer would have said *it* another *way*. For the idea of style to apply, in short, writing must involve choices of verbal formulation. Yet suppose we try to list the alternatives to a given segment of prose: "After dinner, the senator made a speech." A dozen close approximations may suggest themselves ("When dinner was over, the senator made a speech," "The senator made a speech after dinner," "A speech was made by the senator after dinner," etc.), as well as a very large number of more distant renderings ("The senator made a postprandial oration," "The termination of dinner brought a speech from the senator," etc.). Which ones represent stylistic variations on the original, and which ones say different things? We may have intuitions, but to support them is no trivial undertaking. Clearly it would help to have a grammar that provided certain relationships, formally statable, of alternativeness among constructions. One such relationship, for example, might be that which holds between two different constructions that are derived from the same starting point. And, of course, a generative grammar allows the formulation of precisely this sort of relationship.

In the phrase structure component, to begin with, there are alternate ways of proceeding from identically labeled nodes, alternate ways of expanding (or rewriting) a symbol. A verb phrase may be expanded[4] into a transitive verb plus a noun phrase, a copula plus an adjective, a copula plus a noun phrase, or any one of several other combinations.[5] The various possibilities for rewriting at this stage of the grammar account for some of the major sentence types in English, and since the structural meaning of, say, $V_t + NP$ differs considerably from that of $Be + Adj$, a writer's preference for one or another of these forms may be a stylistic choice of some interest.

But notice that the possibility of alternative routings in the phrase struc-

---

[3]For an earlier attempt by the present author to deal with this problem, see "Prolegomena to the Analysis of Prose Style," in *Style in Prose Fiction; English Institute Essays,* 1958, ed. Harold C. Martin (New York, 1959), pp. 1-24. [Reprinted herein, pp. 177-190.]

[4]I do not mean to suggest that a speaker or writer actually performs these operations. But the different possibilities of expansion in the grammar do offer an analogue to the choices open to the writer.

[5]Possibly some other order of expansion is preferable, such as the one Lees uses: $VP \rightarrow$ (Prev) Aux + MV. See Robert B. Lees, *The Grammar of English Nominalizations,* Part II, *International Journal of American Linguistics* XXVI 3 (1960), 5. If the grammar takes this form, then the choice I am speaking of enters only with the expansion of the main verb. Such questions are immaterial, however, to my point.

ture component does not really solve the problem of style in a satisfactory way. I have been looking for linguistically constant features that may be expressed in different ways. The difficulty with taking a unit like the verb phrase for such a constant is its abstractness, its lack of structure. The symbol VP merely stands for a *position* in a string at one level of description. Two different expansions of VP will both occupy the same position, but will not necessarily retain any structural feature in common. Nor will the sentences that ultimately result from the two derivations necessarily share any morphemes or even morphemes from the same classes. Thus, the rewriting of VP as $V_t + $ NP is part of a derivation that leads eventually to the sentence "Columbus discovered America," among others. But there is no kernel sentence corresponding (semantically) to this one which results from a derivation in which NP is rewritten Be + Adj. Sentences like "Columbus was brave," or possibly "Columbus was nautical" are about as close as one can come. And certainly they are not stylistically different expressions of the same thing, in the sense required for stylistics—not in the way that "America was discovered by Columbus" is. The phrase structure part of the grammar does not account for intuitively felt relationships of sameness and difference between sentences, for the possibility of saying one "thing" in two different ways. Perhaps this is one reason why almost no important work in stylistic criticism has evolved from the grammatical analyses of American linguists.

To be of genuine interest for stylistics, a grammar must do more than simply provide for alternate derivations from the same point of origin. There are at least three important characteristics of transformational rules which make them more promising as a source of insight into style than phrase structure rules. In the first place, a large number of transformations are optional, and in quite a different sense from the sense in which it is optional how VP is expanded. VP must *be* expanded by one of the various rules, or of course no sentence will result from the derivation. But an optional transformation need not be applied at all. Given a string or pair of strings so structured that a certain optional transformation can apply, failure to apply it will not keep the derivation from terminating in a sentence.[6] Thus "Dickens wrote *Bleak House*" is a sentence, as well as "*Bleak House* was written by Dickens," which has undergone the passive transformation. Likewise, "Dickens was the writer of *Bleak House*" is a sentence, one that comes from the same kernel string as the other two, via a different optional transformation: agentive nominalization.[7] Technically, transformations apply to underlying strings with certain structures, but for the purposes of this paper they may be thought of as manipulations—reordering, combination, addition, deletion—performed on fully formed sentences, rather than as ways of *getting* to parts of fully formed sentences from incomplete, abstract symbols

---

[6]This is simply to rephrase the definition of an optional transformation; see Noam Chomsky, *Syntactic Structures* ('s-Gravenhage, 1957), p. 45.
[7]Lees, *op. cit.*, p. 70 (transformation T47).

such as NP. Each application of a different optional transformation to a sentence results in a new sentence, similar in some ways to the original one. Thus a grammar with transformational rules will generate many pairs and limited sets of sentences, like the set of three sentences about Dickens, which belong together in an intimate structural way—not simply by virtue of being sentences. Many such sets of sentences will strike a speaker as saying "the same thing"—as being alternatives, that is, in precisely the sense required for stylistics.

A second and related reason why transformational happenings are relevant to style is the very fact that a transformation applies to one or more *strings,* or elements with structure, not to single symbols like VP, and that it applies to those strings by virtue of their structure. A transformation works changes on structure, but normally leaves *part* of the structure unchanged. And in any case, the new structure bears a precisely specifiable relationship to the old one, a relationship, incidentally, that speakers of the language will intuitively feel. Moreover, the transform retains at least some morphemes from the original string; that is, transformations are specified in such a way that "Columbus discovered America" cannot become, under the passive transformation, *"Bleak House* was written by Dickens," although this sentence has the same structure as the proper transform "America was discovered by Columbus." This property of transformations—their preserving some features from the original string—accounts for the fact that sets of sentences which are transformational alternatives seem to be different renderings of the same proposition.[8] Again, this is the sort of relationship which seems intuitively to underlie the notion of style, and for which only a transformational grammar offers a formal analogue.

The third value of a transformational grammar to the analyst of style is its power to explain how complex sentences are generated, and how they are related to simple sentences. Writers differ noticeably in the amounts and kinds of syntactic complexity they habitually allow themselves, but these matters have been hard to approach through conventional methods of analysis. Since the complexity of a sentence is the product of the generalized transformations it has gone through, a breakdown of the sentence into its component simple sentences and the generalized transformations applied (in the order of application) will be an account of its complexity.[9] And since the same set of simple sentences may usually be combined in different ways, a set of complex sentences may be generated from them, each of which differs from the others only in transformational history, while embodying the same simple "propositions." Such differences should be

---

[8]Notice that many such sets, including the three sentences about Dickens, will share the same *truth conditions,* to use the philosopher's term. This fact gives further encouragement to anyone who would treat transformational alternatives as different expressions of the same proposition.

[9]Since deletions and additions will probably have taken place in the course of the derivation, the complex sentence will naturally not contain all and only all of the linguistic elements contained in the component sentences. These must be reconstructed and supplied with appropriate hypothetical elements, but there is generally a strong formal motivation for reconstructing the component sentences in one way rather than another.

interestingly approachable through transformational analysis. So should major variations in type of compounding: self-embedding as against left- and right-branching, for example, or the formation of endocentric as against the formation of exocentric constructions. These deep grammatical possibilities in a language may well be exploited differently from writer to writer, and if so, the differences will certainly be of stylistic interest.

Let me summarize. A generative grammar with a transformational component provides apparatus for breaking down a sentence in a stretch of discourse into underlying kernel sentences (or strings, strictly speaking) and for specifying the grammatical operations that have been performed upon them. It also permits the analyst to construct, from the same set of kernel sentences, other non-kernel sentences. These may reasonably be thought of as *alternatives* to the original sentence, in that they are simply different constructs out of the identical elementary grammatical units.[10] Thus the idea of alternative phrasings, which is crucial to the notion of style, has a clear analogue within the framework of a transformational grammar.

But is it the *right* analogue? What I have called "transformational alternatives" are different derivatives from the same kernel sentences. The notion of style calls for different ways of expressing the same content. Kernel sentences are not "content," to be sure. Yet they *have* content, and much of that content is preserved through transformational operations. "Dickens was the writer of *Bleak House* and America was discovered by Columbus" says much the same thing, if not exactly the same thing, as "Dickens wrote *Bleak House;* Columbus discovered America." Of course some transformations import new content, others eliminate features of content, and no transformation leaves content absolutely unaltered. The analogue is not perfect. But it is worth remembering that other kinds of tampering with sentences (e.g., substitution of synonyms) also change content. And, to look at it another way, the most useful sense of "content"—*cognitive* content—may be such that transformations do generally leave it unaltered (and such that synonyms do exist).[11] In any case, transformational alternatives come as close to "different expressions of the same content" as other sorts of alternatives; moreover, they have the practical advantage of being accessible to formal, rather than to impressionistic, analysis. There is at least some reason, then, to hold that a style is in part a characteristic way of deploying the transformational apparatus of a language, and to expect that transformational analysis will be a valuable aid to the description of actual styles.

So much for theory and prophecy. The final proof must come, if it comes at all, from a fairly extensive attempt to study literary styles in the way I

---

[10]Of course the alternative forms need not be complete sentences, or single sentences. That is, the alternatives to sentence A may include (1) sentence B, (2) part of sentence C and (3) the group of sentences, D, E, and F. The most interesting alternatives to a given sentence often arrange the kernel material in units of different lengths.

[11]I owe this point and several others to correspondence and conversation with Noam Chomsky.

am suggesting. For a transformational analysis, however appealing theoretically, will not be worth much unless it can implement better stylistic descriptions than have been achieved by other methods—"better" in that they isolate more fully, economically, and demonstrably the linguistic features to which a perceptive reader responds in sensing one style to be different from another. The space available here will not suffice for a full scale demonstration, nor do I now have at my disposal nearly enough stylistic description to prove my case. Besides, the necessary grammatical machinery is by no means available yet (in fact, it is too early to say with certainty that Chomsky's plan for grammars is the right one—there are many dissenters). I shall use the rest of this paper merely to outline, by example, a simple analytic procedure that draws on the concept of grammatical transformations, and to suggest some virtues of this procedure.

My first specimen passage comes from Faulkner's story, "The Bear." It is part of a sentence nearly two pages long, and its style is complex, highly individual, and difficult—if it is read aloud, most hearers will not grasp it on first hearing. It is also, I believe, quite typically Faulknerian:

> the desk and the shelf above it on which rested the letters in which McCaslin recorded the slow outward trickle of food and supplies and equipment which returned each fall as cotton made and ginned and sold (two threads frail as truth and impalpable as equators yet cable-strong to bind for life them who made the cotton to the land their sweat fell on), and the older ledgers clumsy and archaic in size and shape, on the yellowed pages of which were recorded in the faded hand of his father Theophilus and his uncle Amodeus during the two decades before the Civil War, the manumission in title at least of Carothers McCaslin's slaves: . . .[12]

I propose to reduce the complexity of the passage by reversing the effects of three generalized transformations, plus a few related singular transformations:

(1) The relative clause transformation (GT19 in Lees' *The Grammar of English Nominalizations,* p. 89), along with the WH-transformations (Lees, T5 and T6, p. 39), the transformation which later deletes "which" and "be" to leave post-nominal modifiers (Lees, T58, p. 94), and the transformation which shifts these modifiers to prenominal position (Lees, T64, p. 98).[13]

(2) The conjunction transformation (Chomsky, *Syntactic Structures,* p. 36).

---

[12]William Faulkner, "The Bear," in *Go Down Moses* (New York: Modern Library, 1942), pp. 255-256.
[13]For another version of these transformations, see Carlota S. Smith, "A Class of Complex Modifiers in English," *Language* XXXVII (1961), pp. 347-348, 361-362.

(3) The comparative transformation, which, along with several reduction transformations and one order change,[14] is responsible for sentences like "George is as tall as John."[15]

Without this grammatical apparatus, the passage reads as follows:

> the desk. The shelf was above it. The ledgers$_1$ rested on the shelf. The ledgers$_1$ were old. McCaslin recorded the trickle of food in the ledgers$_1$. McCaslin recorded the trickle of supplies in the ledgers$_1$. McCaslin recorded the trickle of equipment in the ledgers$_1$. The trickle was slow. The trickle was outward. The trickle returned each fall as cotton. The cotton was made. The cotton was ginned. The cotton was sold. The trickle was a thread. The cotton was a thread. The threads were frail. Truth is frail. The threads were impalpable. Equators are impalpable. The threads were strong to bind them for life to the land. They made the cotton. Their sweat fell on the land. Cables are strong. The ledgers$_2$ were old. The ledgers$_2$ rested on the shelf. The ledgers$_2$ were clumsy in size. The ledgers$_2$ were clumsy in shape. The ledgers$_2$ were archaic in size. The ledgers$_2$ were archaic in shape. On the pages of the ledgers$_2$ were recorded in the hand of his father during the two decades the manumission in title at least of Carothers McCaslin's slaves. On the pages of the ledgers$_2$ were recorded in the hand of his uncle during the two decades the manumission in title at least of Carothers McCaslin's slaves. The pages were yellowed. The hand was faded. The decades were before the Civil War. His father was Theophilus. His uncle was Amodeus.[16]

There is some artificiality in this process, of course. The order of the reduced sentences is in part arbitrary. More important, the transformations I have reversed are not the last ones applied in the generation of the original construction; hence precisely the set of sentences (strings) above would not have occurred at any point in the derivation. Nonetheless, this drastic reduction of the original passage reveals several important things:

(1) The content of the passage remains roughly the same: aside from the loss of distinctions between "and" and "yet," "as ——— as" and "more ——— than," relative clauses and conjoined sentences, and the like, changes in content are minor. But the style, obviously, has undergone a revolution. In the reduced form of the passage there are virtually no traces of what we recognize as Faulkner's style.

(2) This denaturing has been accomplished by reversing the effects of

---

[14]Strong as cables → cable-strong.

[15]Lees, "Grammatical Analysis of the English Comparative Construction," *Word* XVII (1961), pp. 182-183. Carlota S. Smith, in "A Class of Complex Modifiers in English," offers a fuller treatment of such constructions, but Lees' simpler analysis is adequate for my present purposes.

[16]Subscripts mark differences in referent.

only three generalized transformations, as well as a few related singulary transformations. The total number of optional transformations involved is negligible as against the total number that apparently exist in the grammar as a whole. In other words, the style of the original passage leans heavily upon a very small amount of grammatical apparatus.

(3) Most of the sentences in the reduced version of the passage are kernel sentences. Most of the rest are only one transformation away from kernel sentences. Further reduction, by undoing any number of other transformations, would not change the passage or its style nearly so much as has already been done.[17]

(4) The three major transformations I have deleted have an important feature in common. Each of them combines two sentences that share at least one morpheme,[18] and in such a way that the transform may contain only one occurrence of that morpheme (or those morphemes), while preserving the unshared parts of the original sentences. That is to say, these transformations are all what might be called "additive." To put the matter semantically, they offer methods of adding information about a single "thing" with a minimum of repetition. Thus the two sentences "The threads were impalpable" and "The threads were frail" might be combined through any one of the three generalized transformations at issue here: "The threads which were impalpable were frail" (relative); "The threads were frail and impalpable" (conjunction); and "The threads were more frail than impalpable" (comparison). The three transforms are somewhat similar, both formally and semantically; and it seems reasonable to suppose that a writer whose style is so largely based on just these three semantically related transformations demonstrates in that style a certain conceptual orientation, a preferred way of organizing experience.[19] If that orientation could be specified, it would almost certainly provide insight into other, non-stylistic features of Faulkner's thought and artistry. The possibility of such insight is one of the main justifications for studying style.

The move from formal description of styles to critical and semantic interpretation should be the ultimate goal of stylistics, but in this article I am concerned only with the first step: description. My first example shows that the style of at least one short passage can be rather efficiently and informatively described in terms of a few grammatical operations. It might be objected, however, that the transformations I have concentrated on in destroying the style of the Faulkner passage are of such prominence in the grammar, and in the use of English, that *any* writer must depend heavily upon them. To show that this is not universally the case, it is sufficient to perform the

---

[17]Passives and pronouns are also fairly prominent here, but not enough to make them striking as stylistic features.

[18]Except that conjunction may also operate on two sentences with no common morphemes.

[19]It is apparently common for stylistic features to cluster like this in the work of an author. See my study, *Shaw: The Style and the Man* (Middletown, Conn., 1962), for numerous examples, and for an attempt to link style with cognitive orientation.

Richard Ohmann 143

same reductions on a characteristic passage from the work of another writer with a quite different style. Consider, therefore, the conclusion of Hemingway's story, "Soldier's Home":

> So his mother prayed for him and then they stood up and Krebs kissed his mother and went out of the house. He had tried so to keep his life from being complicated. Still, none of it had touched him. He had felt sorry for his mother and she had made him lie. He would go to Kansas City and get a job and she would feel all right about it. There would be one more scene maybe before he got away. He would not go down to his father's office. He would miss that one. He wanted his life to go smoothly. It had just gotten going that way. Well, that was all over now, anyway. He would go over to the schoolyard and watch Helen play indoor baseball.[20]

Reversing the effects of the relative and comparative transformations barely alters the passage: only the prenominal modifier "indoor" is affected. Removing the conjunctions does result in some changes:

> So his mother prayed for him. Then they stood up. Krebs kissed his mother. Krebs went out of the house. He had tried so to keep his life from being complicated. Still, none of it had touched him. He had felt sorry for his mother. She had made him lie. He would go to Kansas City. He would get a job. She would feel all right about it. There would be one more scene maybe before he got away. He would not go down to his father's office. He would miss that one. He wanted his life to go smoothly. It had just gotten going that way. Well, that was all over now, anyway. He would go over to the schoolyard. He would watch Helen play indoor baseball.

Notice that the reduced passage still sounds very much like Hemingway. Nothing has been changed that seems crucial to his style. Note too that although the revised passage is quite simple, none of the sentences is from the kernel. Hemingway is not innocent of transformations: he is relying on pronominalization, on a group of nominalizations, and, most notably, on a sequence of transformations responsible for what critics call the *"style indirect libre."* These transformations work this way:

(1) GT; quotation, or reported thought:

$$
\text{He} \left\{ \begin{array}{l} \text{thought} \\ \text{said} \\ \text{felt} \\ \text{etc.} \end{array} \right\} \text{NP}_\text{abst} \left. \begin{array}{l} \\ \\ \\ \\ \end{array} \right\} \rightarrow \text{He thought, "She has made me lie"}
$$
She has made me lie

---

[20] *The Short Stories of Ernest Hemingway* (New York, 1953), pp. 152-153.

(2) Indirect discourse (change of pronouns and of verb tense):

He thought, "She has made me lie"→ He thought that she had made him lie

(3) Deletion:

He thought that she had made him lie → She had made him lie[21]

The original passage, stripped of the effects of these transformations, reads as follows:

> So his mother prayed for him and they stood up and Krebs kissed his mother and went out of the house. He thought this: I have tried so to keep my life from being complicated. Still, none of it has touched me. I have felt sorry for my mother and she has made me lie. I will go to Kansas City and get a job and she will feel all right about it. There will be one more scene maybe before I get away. I will not go down to my father's office. I will miss that one. I want my life to go smoothly. It has just gotten going that way. Well, that is all over now, anyway. I will go over to the schoolyard and watch Helen play indoor baseball.

The peculiar double vision of the style, the sense of the narrator peering into the character's mind and scrupulously reporting its contents, the possibility of distance and gentle irony—all these are gone with the transformational wind.

To be sure, these transformations do not in themselves distinguish Hemingway's style from the styles of many other writers (Virginia Woolf, Ford Madox Ford, James Joyce, etc.). But it is interesting, and promising, that a stylistic difference so huge as that between the Faulkner and Hemingway passages can be largely explained on the basis of so little grammatical apparatus.

Up to this point, I have been exploring some effects on style of particular transformations and groups of transformations, and arguing that this method of description has, potentially, considerable value for literary critics. But there are at least two other ways in which transformational machinery will aid the analyst of style.

First, it has often been pointed out that constructions may be left-branching ("Once George had left, the host and hostess gossiped briskly"), right-branching ("The host and hostess gossiped briskly, once George had left"), or self-embedding ("The host and hostess, once George had left,

---

[21]Morris Halle (Massachusetts Institute of Technology) explained these transformations to me. He is treating them in a forthcoming article on Virginia Woolf's style, and I make no attempt here to put the rules in proper and complete form. It should be noted though, that there is at present no justification for the grammar to contain rule number three as a transformation, since the transform is already generated by other rules.

gossiped briskly"). Neither left- nor right-branching constructions tax the hearer's understanding, even when compounded at some length ("a very few not at all well liked union officials"; "the dog that worried the cat that chased the rat that ate the cheese that lay in the house that Jack built"). But layers of self-embedding quickly put too great a strain on the unaided memory ("the house in which the cheese that the rat that the cat that the dog worried chased ate lay was built by Jack"). Even a relatively small amount of self-embedding in a written passage can slow a reader down considerably.

With these preliminaries, consider the following sentence, which begins a short story:

> She had practically, he believed, conveyed the intimation, the horrid, brutal, vulgar menace, in the course of their last dreadful conversation, when, for whatever was left him of pluck or confidence—confidence in what he would fain have called a little more aggressively the strength of his position—he had judged best not to take it up.[22]

The style is idiosyncratic in the highest degree, and the writer is, of course, Henry James. His special brand of complexity is impossible to unravel through the method I pursued with Faulkner. A number of *different* transformations are involved. But notice that most of this complexity results from self-embedding. With the embedded elements removed the sentence is still far from simple, but the Jamesian intricacy is gone:

> She had practically conveyed the intimation in the course of their last dreadful conversation, when he had judged best not to take it up.

The following are the deleted sentences, with their full structure restored:

> He believed [it].
> [The intimation was a] horrid, brutal, vulgar menace.
> [Something] was left him of pluck or confidence.
> [It was] confidence in the strength of his position.
> He would fain have called [it that], a little more aggressively.

The embedded elements, in short, significantly outweigh the main sentence itself, and needless to say, the strain on attention and memory required to follow the progress of the main sentence over and around so many obstacles is considerable. The difficulty, as well as the Jamesian flavor, is considerably lessened merely by substituting left- and right-branching constructions for self-embedding, even though all the kernel sentences are retained:

---

[22]"The Bench of Desolation," *Ten Short Stories of Henry James,* ed. Michael Swan (London, 1948), p. 284.

He believed that in the course of their last dreadful conversation she had practically conveyed the intimation, a horrid, brutal, vulgar menace, which he had then judged best not to take up, for whatever was left him of pluck or confidence—confidence in the strength of his position, as he would fain have called it, a little more aggressively.

It seems likely that much of James's later style can be laid to this syntactic device—a matter of *positioning* various constructions, rather than of favoring a few particular constructions. The relevance of positioning to style is, to be sure, no news. But again, transformational analysis should clarify the subject, both by providing descriptive rigor and by making available a set of alternatives to each complex sentence.

Finally, styles may also contrast in the kinds of transformational operations on which they are built. There are four possibilities: addition, deletion, reordering, and combination. Of these, my final sample depends heavily on deletion. The passage is from D. H. Lawrence's *Studies in Classic American Literature,* a book with an especially brusque, emphatic style, which results partly from Lawrence's affection for kernel sentences. But his main idiosyncrasy is the use of truncated sentences, which have gone through a variety of deletion transformations. Here is the excerpt:

The renegade hates life itself. He wants the death of life. So these many "reformers" and "idealists" who glorify the savages in America. They are death-birds, life-haters. Renegades.

We can't go back. And Melville couldn't. Much as he hated the civilized humanity he knew. He couldn't go back to the savages. He wanted to. He tried to. And he couldn't.

Because in the first place, it made him sick.[23]

With the deleted segments replaced, the passage reads, somewhat absurdly, like this:

The renegade hates life itself. He wants the death of life. So these many "reformers" and "idealists" who glorify the savages in America [want the death of life]. They are death-birds. [They are] life-haters. [They are] renegades.

We can't go back. And Melville couldn't [go back]. [Melville couldn't go back, as] much as he hated the civilized humanity he knew. He couldn't go back to the savages. He wanted to [go back to the savages]. And he couldn't [go back to the savages].

[He couldn't go back to the savages] because, in the first place, it made him sick [to go back to the savages].

---

[23]D. H. Lawrence, *Studies in Classic American Literature* (New York: Anchor Books, 1955), p. 149.

One does not need grammatical theory to see that Lawrence is deleting. But the restoration of the full form which is allowed by the grammar does reveal two interesting things. First, there is a large amount of repetition in the original passage, much more than actually shows. Perhaps this fact accounts for the driving insistence one feels in reading it. Second, Lawrentian deletion is a stylistic alternative to *conjunction,* which can also take place whenever there are two sentences partly alike in their constituents. The reasons for Lawrence's preferring deletion to conjunction might well be worth some study.

And in general, study of that sort should be the goal of stylistic analysis. All I have done here is outline, briefly and in part informally, a fruitful method of stylistic *description.* But no *analysis* of a style, in the fuller sense, can get off the ground until there are adequate methods for the humble task of description. Such methods, I think, are provided by transformational grammar. Furthermore, I have argued, such a grammar is especially useful for this purpose in that it alone is powerful enough to set forth, formally and accurately, stylistic *alternatives* to a given passage or a given set of linguistic habits.

Now there is no reason to generalize from four passages to infinity, and in fact full stylistic descriptions of the work of even the four writers I have discussed would need to be far more elaborate than the sketches I have offered here. Moreover, many styles that readers perceive as distinctive are more complex in their syntactic patterns than these four. Finally, though syntax seems to be a central determinant of style, it is admittedly not the whole of style. Imagery, figures of speech, and the rest are often quite important. But to perform on various styles the kind of analysis I have attempted in this paper is to be convinced that transformational patterns constitute a significant part of what the sensitive reader perceives as style. Transformational analysis of literary discourse promises to the critic stylistic descriptions which are at once simpler and deeper than any hitherto available, and therefore more adequate foundations for critical interpretation. Not only that: if, as seems likely to happen, generative grammars with transformational rules help the linguist or critic to explicate convincingly the elusive but persistent notion of style, that achievement will stand as one more piece of evidence in favor of such grammars.

RICHARD OHMANN

Literature as Sentences

The following article is an extension of Richard Ohmann's previous essay, "Generative Grammars and the Concept of Literary Style." Professor Ohmann's discussion of deep and surface structures of sentences—in which he explains and to some extent simplifies Noam Chomsky's discussion of this topic in Aspects of the Theory of Syntax—*allows him to distinguish between form and content, style and meaning, much more specifically than the rhetoricians who have concentrated on the larger problem of rhetorical structure.*

Critics permit themselves, for this or that purpose, to identify literature with great books, with imaginative writing, with expressiveness in writing, with the non-referential and non-pragmatic, with beauty in language, with order, with myth, with structured and formed discourse—the list of defini-tions is nearly endless—with verbal play, with uses of language that stress the medium itself, with the expression of an age, with dogma, with the *cri de coeur,* with neurosis. Now of course literature is itself and not another thing, to paraphrase Bishop Butler; yet analogies and classifications have merit. For a short space let us think of literature as sentences.

To do so will not tax the imagination, because the work of literature in-dubitably *is* composed of sentences, most of them well-ordered, many of them deviant (no pejorative meant), some of them incomplete. But since much the same holds for dust-jacket copy, the Congressional Record, and transcripts of board meetings, the small effort required to think of literature as sentences may be repaid by a correspondingly small insight into literature as such. Although I do not believe this to be so, for the moment I shall hold the question in abeyance, and stay mainly within the territory held in com-mon by all forms of discourse. In other words, I am not asking what is special about the sentences of *literature,* but what is special about *sentences* that they should interest the student of literature. Although I employ the frame-work of generative grammar and scraps of its terminology,[1] what I have to say should not ring in the traditionally educated grammatical ear with out-landish discord.

First, then, the sentence is the primary unit of understanding. Linguists have so trenchantly discredited the old definition—"a sentence is a complete thought"—that the truth therein has fallen into neglect. To be sure, we de-limit the class of sentences by formal criteria, but each of the structures that qualifies will express a semantic unity not characteristic of greater or

From *College English,* XXVII (January 1966), 261-267. Reprinted with the permission of the National Council of Teachers of English and Richard Ohmann.
[1]I draw especially on Noam Chomsky, *Aspects of the Theory of Syntax* (Cambridge, Mass., 1965) and Jerrold J. Katz and Paul Postal, *An Integrated Theory of Linguistic Descriptions* (Cambridge, Mass., 1964).

lesser structures. The meanings borne by morphemes, phrases, and clauses hook together to express a meaning that can stand more or less by itself. This point, far from denying the structuralist's definition of a sentence as a single free utterance, or *form,* seems the inevitable corollary of such definitions: forms carry meanings, and it is natural that an independent form should carry an independent meaning. Or, to come at the thing another way, consider that one task of a grammar is to supply structural descriptions, and that the sentence is the unit so described. A structural description specifies the way each part of a sentence is tied to each other part, and the semantic rules of a grammar use the structural description as starting point in interpreting the whole. A reader or hearer does something analogous when he resolves the structures and meanings of sentences, and thereby understands them. Still another way to approach the primacy of the sentence is to notice that the initial symbol for all derivations in a generative grammar is "S" for sentence: the sentence is the domain of grammatical structure—rather like the equation in algebra—and hence the domain of meaning.

These remarks, which will seem truisms to some and heresy to others, cannot be elaborated here. Instead, I want to register an obvious comment on their relevance to literary theory and literary criticism. Criticism, whatever else it does, must interpret works of literature. Theory concerns itself in part with the question, "what things legitimately bear on critical interpretation?" But beyond a doubt, interpretation begins with sentences. Whatever complex apprehension the critic develops of the whole work, that understanding arrives mundanely, sentence by sentence. For this reason, and because the form of a sentence dictates a rudimentary mode of understanding, sentences have a good deal to do with the subliminal meaning (and form) of a literary work. They prepare and direct the reader's attention in particular ways.

My second point about sentences should dispel some of the abstractness of the first. Most sentences directly and obliquely put more linguistic apparatus into operation than is readily apparent, and call on more of the reader's linguistic competence. Typically, a surface structure overlays a deep structure which it may resemble but little, and which determines the "content" of the sentence. For concreteness, take this rather ordinary example, an independent clause from Joyce's "Araby": "Gazing up into the darkness I saw myself as a creature driven and derided by vanity." The surface structure may be represented as follows, using the convention of labeled brackets:[2] ^{S}[^{Adv}[V + Part ^{PP}[P ^{NP}[D + N]]] ^{Nuc}[N ^{VP}[V + N ^{PP}[P ^{NP} [D + N ^{Adj}[V + and + V ^{PP}[P + N]]]]]]]
The nucleus has a transitive verb with a direct object. In the deep structure, by contrast, the matrix sentence is of the form ^{S}[NP ^{VP}[V + Complement + NP]]: "I + saw + as a creature + me." It has embedded in it one sentence

---

[2]Each set of brackets encloses the constituent indicated by its superscript label. The notation is equivalent to a tree diagram. Symbols: S = Sentence, Adv = Adverbial, V = Verb, Part = Particle, PP = Prepositional Phrase, P = Preposition, NP = Noun Phrase, D = Determiner, N = Noun, Nuc = Nucleus, VP = Verb Phrase, Adj = Adjectival.

with an intransitive verb and an adverb of location—"I gazed up into the darkness"—and two additional sentences with transitive verbs and direct objects—"Vanity drove the creature," and "Vanity derided the creature." Since "darkness" and "vanity" are derived nouns, the embedded sentences must in turn contain embeddings, of, say "(Something) is dark" and "(Someone) is vain." Thus the word "vanity," object of a preposition in the surface structure, is subject of two verbs in the deep, and its root is a predicate adjective. The word "creature," object of a preposition in the surface structure, also has a triple function in the deep structure: verbal complement, direct object of "drive," and direct object of "deride." Several transformations (including the passive) deform the six basic sentences, and several others relate them to each other. The complexity goes much farther, but this is enough to suggest that a number of grammatical processes are required to generate the initial sentence and that its structure is moderately involved. Moreover, a reader will not understand the sentence unless he grasps the relations marked in the deep structure. As it draws on a variety of syntactic resources, the sentence also activates a variety of semantic processes and modes of comprehension, yet in brief compass and in a surface *form* that radically permutes *content*.

I choose these terms wilfully: that there are interesting grounds here for a form-content division seems to me quite certain. Joyce might have written, "I gazed up into the darkness. I saw myself as a creature. The creature was driven by vanity. The creature was derided by vanity." Or, "Vanity drove and derided the creature I saw myself as, gazer up, gazer into the darkness." Content remains roughly the same, for the basic sentences are unchanged. But the style is different. And each revision structures and screens the content differently. The original sentence acquires part of its meaning and part of its unique character by resonating against these unwritten alternatives. It is at the level of sentences, I would argue, that the distinction between form and content comes clear, and that the intuition of style has its formal equivalent.[3]

Sentences play on structure in still another way, more shadowy, but of considerable interest for criticism. It is a commonplace that not every noun can serve as object of every verb, that a given noun can be modified only by adjectives of certain classes, and so on. For instance, a well-defined group of verbs, including "exasperate," "delight," "please," and "astound," require animate objects; another group, including "exert," "behave," and "pride," need reflexive objects. Such interdependencies abound in a grammar, which must account for them by subcategorizing nouns, adjectives, and the other major classes.[4] The importance of categorical restrictions is clearest in sentences that disregard them—deviant sentences. It happens that the example from Joyce is slightly deviant in this way: in one of the

[3] I have argued the point at length in "Generative Grammars and the Concept of Literary Style," *Word*, 20 (Dec. 1964), 423-439. [Reprinted above.]

[4] Chomsky discusses ways of doing this in *Aspects of the Theory of Syntax*, Chapter 2.

underlying sentences—"Vanity derided the creature"—a verb that requires a human subject in fact has as its subject the abstract noun "vanity." The dislocation forces the reader to use a supplementary method of interpretation: here, presumably he aligns "vanity" (the word) with the class of human nouns and sees vanity (the thing) as a distinct, active power in the narrator's psyche. Such deviance is so common in metaphor and elsewhere that one scarcely notices it, yet it helps to specify the way things happen in the writer's special world, and the modes of thought appropriate to that world.

I have meant to suggest that sentences normally comprise intricacies of form and meaning whose effects are not the less substantial for their subtlety. From this point, what sorts of critical description follow? Perhaps I can direct attention toward a few tentative answers, out of the many that warrant study, and come finally to a word on critical theory. Two samples must carry the discussion; one is the final sentence of "The Secret Sharer":

> Walking to the taffrail, I was in time to make out, on the very edge of a darkness thrown by a towering black mass like the very gateway of Erebus—yes, I was in time to catch an evanescent glimpse of my white hat left behind to mark the spot where the secret sharer of my cabin and of my thoughts, as though he were my second self, had lowered himself into the water to take his punishment: a free man, a proud swimmer striking out for a new destiny.

I hope others will agree that the sentence justly represents its author: that it portrays a mind energetically stretching to subdue a dazzling experience *outside* the self, in a way that has innumerable counterparts elsewhere in Conrad. How does scrutiny of the deep structure support this intuition? First, notice a matter of emphasis, of rhetoric. The matrix sentence, which lends a surface form to the whole, is " # S # I was in time # S #" (repeated twice). The embedded sentences that complete it are "I walked to the taffrail," "I made out + NP," and "I caught + NP." The point of departure, then, is the narrator himself: where he was, what he did, what he saw. But a glance at the deep structure will explain why one feels a quite different emphasis in the sentence as a whole: seven of the embedded sentences have "sharer" as grammatical subject; in another three the subject is a noun linked to "sharer" by the copula; in two "sharer" is direct object; and in two more "share" is the verb. Thus thirteen sentences go to the semantic development of "sharer," as follows:

1) The secret sharer had lowered the secret sharer into the water.
2) The secret sharer took his punishment.
3) The secret sharer swam.
4) The secret sharer was a swimmer.
5) The swimmer was proud.
6) The swimmer struck out for a new destiny.
7) The secret sharer was a man.

8) The man was free.
9) The secret sharer was my second self.
10) The secret sharer had (it).
11) (Someone) punished the secret sharer.
12) (Someone) shared my cabin.
13) (Someone) shared my thoughts.

In a fundamental way, the sentence is mainly *about* Leggatt, although the surface structure indicates otherwise.

Yet the surface structure does not simply throw a false scent, and the way the sentence comes to focus on the secret sharer is also instructive. It begins with the narrator, as we have seen, and "I" is the subject of five basic sentences early on. Then "hat" takes over as the syntactic focus, receiving development in seven base sentences. Finally, the sentence arrives at "sharer." This progression in the deep structure rather precisely mirrors both the rhetorical movement of the sentence from the narrator to Leggatt via the hat that links them, and the thematic effect of the sentence, which is to transfer Leggatt's experience to the narrator via the narrator's vicarious and actual participation in it. Here I shall leave this abbreviated rhetorical analysis, with a cautionary word: I do not mean to suggest that only an examination of deep structure reveals Conrad's skillful emphasis—on the contrary, such an examination supports and in a sense explains what any careful reader of the story notices.

A second critical point adjoins the first. The morpheme "share" appears once in the sentence, but it performs at least twelve separate functions, as the deep structure shows. "I," "hat," and "mass" also play complex roles. Thus at certain points the sentence has extraordinary "density," as I shall call it. Since a reader must register these multiple functions in order to understand the sentence, it is reasonable to suppose that the very process of understanding concentrates his attention on centers of density. Syntactic density, I am suggesting, exercises an important influence on literary comprehension.

Third, by tuning in on deep structures, the critic may often apprehend more fully the build of a literary work. I have already mentioned how the syntax of Conrad's final sentence develops his theme. Consider two related points. First, "The Secret Sharer" is an initiation story in which the hero, through moral and mental effort, locates himself vis à vis society and the natural world, and thus passes into full manhood. The syntax of the last sentence schematizes the relationships he has achieved, in identifying with Leggatt's heroic defection, and in fixing on a point of reference—the hat— that connects him to the darker powers of nature. Second, the syntax and meaning of the last sentence bring to completion the pattern initiated by the syntax and meaning of the first few sentences, which present human beings and natural objects in thought-bewildering disarray. I can do no more than mention these structural connections here, but I am convinced that they supplement and help explain an ordinary critical reading of the story.

Another kind of critical point concerns habits of meaning revealed by sentence structure. One example must suffice. We have already marked how the sentence shifts its focus from "I" to "hat" to "sharer." A similar process goes on in the first part of the sentence: "I" is the initial subject, with "hat" as object. "Hat" is subject of another base sentence that ends with "edge," the object of a preposition in a locative phrase. "Edge" in turn becomes object of a sentence that has "darkness" as subject. "Darkness" is object in one with "mass" as subject, and in much the same way the emphasis passes to "gateway" and "Erebus." The syntax executes a chaining effect here which cuts across various kinds of construction. Chaining is far from the only type of syntactic expansion, but it is one Conrad favors. I would suggest this hypothesis: that syntactically and in other ways Conrad draws heavily on operations that link one thing with another associatively. This may be untrue, or if true it may be unrevealing; certainly it needs clearer expression. But I think it comes close to something that we all notice in Conrad, and in any case the general critical point exemplified here deserves exploration: that each writer tends to exploit deep linguistic resources in characteristic ways—that his style, in other words, rests on syntactic options within sentences (see fn. 3)—and that these syntactic preferences correlate with habits of meaning that tell us something about his mode of conceiving experience.

My other sample passage is the first sentence of Dylan Thomas' "A Winter's Tale":

> It is a winter's tale
> That the snow blind twilight ferries over
>   the lakes
> And floating fields from the farm in the
>   cup of the vales,
> Gliding windless through the hand
>   folded flakes,
> The pale breath of cattle at the stealthy
>   sail,
>
> And the stars falling cold,
> And the smell of hay in the snow, and
>   the far owl
> Warning among the folds, and the frozen
>   hold
> Flocked with the sheep white smoke of
>   the farm house cowl
> In the river wended vales where the tale
>   was told.

Some of the language here raises a large and familiar critical question, that of unorthodox grammar in modern poetry, which has traditionally received a somewhat facile answer. We say that loss of confidence in order and reason leads to dislocation of syntax, as if errant grammar were an appeal to the irrational. A cursory examination of deep structure in verse like Thomas', or even in wildly deviant verse like some of Cummings', will show the matter to be more complex than that.

How can deviance be most penetratingly analyzed? Normally, I think, in terms of the base sentences that lie beneath ungrammatical constructions. Surface structure alone does not show "the river wended vales" (line 10) to be deviant, since we have many well-formed constructions of the same word-class sequence: "machine made toys," "sun dried earth," and so on. The particular deviance of "the river wended vales" becomes apparent when we try to refer it to an appropriate underlying structure. A natural one to consider is "the river wends the vales" (cf. "the sun dries the earth"), but of course this makes "wend" a transitive verb, which it is not, except in the idiomatic "wend its way." So does another possibility, "NP + wends the vales with rivers" (cf. "NP + makes the toys by machine"). This reading adds still other kinds of deviance, in that the Noun Phrase will have to be animate, and in that rivers are too cumbersome to be used instrumentally in the way implied. Let us assume that the reader rejects the more flagrant deviance in favor of the less, and we are back to "the river wends the vales." Suppose now that "the vales" is not after all a direct object, but a locative construction, as in "the wolf prowls the forest"; this preserves the intransitivity of "wend," and thereby avoids a serious form of deviance. But notice that there is *no* transformation in English that converts "the wolf prowls the forest" into "the wolf prowled forest," and so this path is blocked as well. Assume, finally, that given a choice between shifting a word like "wend" from one subclass to another and adding a transformational rule to the grammar, a reader will choose the former course; hence he selects the first interpretation mentioned: "the river wends the vales."

If so, how does he understand the anomalous transitive use of "wend"? Perhaps by assimilating the verb to a certain class that may be either transitive or intransitive: "paint," "rub," and the like. Then he will take "wend" to mean something like "make a mark on the surface of, by traversing"; in fact, this is roughly how I read Thomas' phrase. But I may be wrong, and in any case my goal is not to solve the riddle. Rather, I have been leading up to the point that every syntactically deviant construction has more than one possible interpretation, and that readers resolve the conflict by a process that involves deep and intricately motivated decisions and thus puts to work considerable linguistic knowledge, syntactic as well as semantic.[5] The decisions nearly always go on implicitly, but aside from that I see no reason to think that deviance of this sort is an appeal to, or an expression of, irrationality.

---

[5] See Jerrold J. Katz, "Semi-sentences," in Jerry A. Fodor and Jerrold J. Katz, eds., *The Structure of Language* (1964), pp. 400-416. The same volume includes two other relevant papers, Chomsky, "Degrees of Grammaticalness," pp. 384-389, and Paul Ziff, "On Understanding 'Understanding Utterances,'" pp. 390-399. Samuel R. Levin has briefly discussed ungrammatical poetry within a similar framework in *Linguistic Structures in Poetry* (The Hague, 1962), Chapters 2 and 3.

Moreover, when a poet deviates from normal syntax he is not doing what comes most habitually, but is making a special sort of choice. And since there are innumerable kinds of deviance, we should expect that the ones elected by a poem or poet spring from particular semantic impulses, particular ways of looking at experience. For instance, I think such a tendency displays itself in Thomas' lines. The construction just noted conceives the passing of rivers through vales as an agent acting upon an object. Likewise, "flocked" in line 9 becomes a transitive verb, and the spatial connection Thomas refers to—flocks in a hold—is reshaped into an action—flocking —performed by an unnamed agent upon the hold. There are many other examples in the poem of deviance that projects unaccustomed activity and process upon nature. Next, notice that beneath line 2 is the sentence "the twilight is blind," in which an inanimate noun takes an animate adjective, and that in line 5 "sail" takes the animate adjective "stealthy." This type of deviance also runs throughout the poem: Thomas sees nature as personal. Again, "twilight" is subject of "ferries," and should thus be a concrete noun, as should the object, "tale." Here and elsewhere in the poem the division between substance and abstraction tends to disappear. Again and again syntactic deviance breaks down categorical boundaries and converts juxtaposition into action, inanimate into human, abstract into physical, static into active. Now, much of Thomas' poetry displays the world as process, as interacting forces and repeating cycles, in which human beings and human thought are indifferently caught up.[6] I suggest that Thomas' syntactical irregularities often serve this vision of things. To say so, of course, is only to extend the natural critical premise that a good poet sets linguistic forms to work for him in the cause of artistic and thematic form. And if he strays from grammatical patterns he does not thereby leave language or reason behind: if anything, he draws the more deeply on linguistic structure and on the processes of human understanding that are implicit in our use of well-formed sentences.

Most of what I have said falls short of adequate precision, and much of the detail rests on conjecture about English grammar, which at this point is by no means fully understood. But I hope that in loosely stringing together several hypotheses about the fundamental role of the sentence I have indicated some areas where a rich exchange between linguistics and critical theory might eventually take place. To wit, the elusive intuition we have of *form* and *content* may turn out to be anchored in a distinction between the surface structures and the deep structures of sentences. If so, syntactic theory will also feed into the theory of *style*. Still more evidently, the proper *analysis* of styles waits on a satisfactory analysis of sentences. Matters of *rhetoric*, such as emphasis and order, also promise to come clearer as we better understand internal relations in sentences. More generally, we may be able to enlarge and deepen our concept of literary *structure* as we are

---

[6]Ralph Maud's fine study, *Entrances to Dylan Thomas' Poetry*, (Pittsburgh, 1963), describes the phenomenon well in a chapter called "Process Poems."

increasingly able to make it subsume linguistic structure—including especially the structure of deviant sentences. And most important, since critical understanding follows and builds on understanding of sentences, generative grammar should eventually be a reliable assistant in the effort of seeing just how a given literary work sifts through a reader's mind, what cognitive and emotional processes it sets in motion, and what organization of experience it encourages. In so far as critical theory concerns itself with meaning, it cannot afford to bypass the complex and elegant structures that lie at the inception of all verbal meaning.

STEPHEN ULLMANN

Style and Personality

Stephen Ullmann is professor of French language and literature at Harvard. Two of his recent books are Style in the French Novel *(1964) and* Language and Style *(1964). Professor Ullmann has written several pioneer studies which combine linguistics and literary criticism. His work, however, does not proceed from a theory of phrase structure-transformational grammar as does Ohmann's. In the following essay Ullmann reëxamines Buffon's classical though often disparaged principle, "Style is the man himself."*

At a recent conference on 'Style in Language' it was suggested that the style of a person is as unique as his fingerprints.[1] The analogy is slightly misleading since one's fingerprints do not change whereas one's style may do so; moreover, one cannot alter one's fingerprints but one can adjust one's style to suit the circumstances; one can even modify it for purposes of parody, pastiche, or the need to portray a character through his speech. Nevertheless, Buffon's principle, 'Style is the man himself', is still widely held and has been echoed by many writers and thinkers. Schopenhauer described style as the 'physiognomy of the mind', and Flaubert as an 'absolute way of looking at things'. Proust believed that 'style for the writer, like colour for the painter, is a question not of technique but of vision',[2] and Gide declared: 'A new personality needs a new form to express itself sincerely. The sentence which is peculiar to us must be as difficult to bend as Ulysses' bow.'[3]

From *Review of English Literature*, VI (April 1965), 21-31. Reprinted by permission of Stephen Ullmann.
[1] *Style in Language*, ed. T. A. Sebeok, New York-London (1960), pp. 378 ff.
[2] "Le style pour l'écrivain, aussi bien que la couleur pour le peintre, est une question non de technique mais de vision', *Le Temps retrouvé*, Paris, Pléiade ed., vol. III (1961 impr.), p. 895.
[3] 'Une personnalité neuve ne s'exprime sincèrement que dans une forme neuve. La phrase qui nous est personnelle doit rester aussi particulièrement difficile à bander que l'arc d'Ulysse', *Nouveaux Prétextes*, Paris (1947), p. 169.

Most students of style would agree that there is an intimate connection between a writer's language and his personality, in the widest sense of that term. In order to study this connection more closely, modern stylistics has evolved a number of methods, five of which will be briefly discussed in this essay: statistical analysis; the so-called 'psychological' approach; typologies of style; the evidence of key-words; lastly, the interpretation of recurrent images. Since my own work in this field has mainly been concerned with French writers, most of the examples will be drawn from French literature.

I. STATISTICAL ANALYSIS

'Stylostatistics', as it is somewhat pretentiously called, has become very popular of late;[4] at the same time, the use of quantitative methods in a sphere where quality and context, aesthetic effects and suggestive overtones are of supreme importance, has aroused understandable misgivings. Yet even those who feel that detailed statistics are both unnecessary and undesirable in these matters would probably agree that a rough indication of frequencies would often be helpful. A distinguished French scholar has spoken, for instance, of Victor Hugo's 'abuse' of images from electricity in his later works, but has quoted a bare three examples of this tendency.[5] One would like to know whether there were dozens, scores or hundreds of such images, whether their number was significantly higher than in Hugo's earlier writings, and how his usage compared with that of his contemporaries. Another field where some numerical pointers could be useful is the distribution of a device of style in a whole work. A penetrating American critic has found, for example, that Camus's novel *L'Étranger* is singularly poor in images, but that there is a sudden efflorescence of bold and intense similes and metaphors in the scene where the narrator shoots an Arab on an Algerian beach.[6] This anomalous distribution is symptomatic of the narrator's state of mind as portrayed through his style. Dazed by the heat and glare of the sun, he is assailed by all kinds of hallucinations: the light reflected from the Arab's knife hits him on the forehead like a long flashing blade; he feels the 'cymbals' of the sun against his forehead while the burning sword scorches his eyelashes and thrusts into his aching eyes.[7] It is this imagery which suggests the only possible motivation for his crime: in his state of utter confusion, he apparently mistook the light reflected from the blade for the blade itself and pulled the trigger from some obscure instinct of self-defence.

Statistics may also help to establish the authorship, unity or chronology of certain works. This method, which classicists have applied for many years to the study of Plato's dialogues, has been widely discussed during the recent

---

[4] A useful survey will be found in Rebecca Posner's recent article, 'The Use and Abuse of Stylistic Statistics', *Archivum Linguisticum*, xv, 1963, pp. 111-39.

[5] F. Brunot, *Histoire de la langue française*, XIII, Part I (by Ch. Bruneau), Paris (1953), pp. 103 f. and p. 185, n. I, where there is a brief comparison between Hugo's and Michelet's usage.

[6] W. M. Frohock, 'Camus: Image, Influence and Sensibility', *Yale French Studies, ii*, no. 2, 1949, pp. 91-99, especially pp. 99 ff.

[7] For a detailed account see my book, *The Image in the Modern French Novel*, Oxford (1963), pp. 248 ff.

debate on the authenticity of St. Paul's epistles. The advent of computers has given a powerful impetus to this approach; yet even here there is a great danger of hasty conclusions disregarding the role of context and the complexities of literary creation. A recent article by two French linguists provides an example of these pitfalls.[8] Having noted that the frequency of adjectives rises steadily in Racine's plays from *Andromaque* to *Esther,* the authors point out that there is one exception: *Iphigénie* has fewer adjectives than might have been expected. They wonder, therefore, whether *Iphigénie* was not written earlier than is commonly believed; there is, it would seem, some external evidence to support this view. However that may be, the number of adjectives in the play need have no bearing whatever on the date of its composition: it may be connected with the dramatic structure of the work or may even be due to a temporary change in Racine's style. Numerical data are no more than a starting-point for the critic; they must be tested for qualitative differences and carefully examined in the light of the context and the whole situation before any conclusions can be drawn from them.

2. THE 'PSYCHOLOGICAL' APPROACH

The most influential exponent of this doctrine was the late Professor Leo Spitzer. Combining Croce's and Vossler's philosophy of language with some Freudian ideas, Spitzer evolved his famous theory of the 'philological circle', which he expounded in a long series of books and articles astonishingly wide in range, and especially in the volume *Linguistics and Literary History* (1948). The term 'philological circle' is rather unfortunate since it suggests that there is an element of circularity in the method,[9] whereas in fact there is none. It simply means an operation in three phases moving from the periphery to the centre and then back to the periphery. In the first place the critic, who must be equipped with 'talent, experience and faith',[10] will read and re-read the text until he is struck by some persistently recurring peculiarity of style. In the next phase, he will try to discover some psychological feature which would account for this peculiarity. In the final phase he will make the return journey to the periphery and look for further manifestations of the same mental feature. To take a concrete example, when reading Diderot, Spitzer noticed the frequency of a certain rhythmic pattern: 'a self-accentuating rhythm, suggesting that the "speaker" is swept away by a wave of passion which tends to flood all limits'.[11] The psychological explanation was clearly indicated: this rhythm was the linguistic expression of Diderot's nervous temperament which, 'instead of being tempered by style, was allowed to energize style'. Nor was it difficult to discover further manifestations of this temperament in Diderot's philosophy of mobility, his

---

[8]R. L. Wagner and P. Guiraud, 'La Méthode statistique en lexicologie', *Revue de l'Enseignement Supérieur,* 1959, no. I, pp. 154-9.
[9]Cf. R. A. Hall, Jr., *Idealism in Romance Linguistics,* Ithaca (1963), p. 73.
[10]L. Spitzer, *Linguistics and Literary History. Essays in Stylistics,* Princeton (1948), p. 27.
[11]ibid., p. 135.

efforts to transcend all rational boundaries. There was thus, in this author, a very neat correspondence between three different planes: his temperament, his philosophy and his style.

The 'philological circle' has been criticized on various grounds. Some observers objected to the intuitive nature of the method and to the slenderness of the linguistic evidence on which such far-reaching conclusions were built. Others pointed out that some peculiarities of style need have no psychological background: they may be mere mannerisms or tics. It has also been suggested that the sequence of events may not always be the one foreseen in the theory: 'many relationships professing to be thus established are not based on conclusions really drawn from the linguistic material but rather start with a psychological and ideological analysis and seek for confirmation in the language.'[12] In the final stages of his long career, Spitzer himself tended to move away from his earlier positions. In a lecture given a bare fortnight before his death,[13] he emphasized that the psychological approach could be more easily applied to modern literature than to earlier periods which often aimed at a more impersonal style. He also pointed out that 'psychoanalytical stylistics' was merely a special form of the 'biographical fallacy'. To correct these weaknesses, he recommended a truly 'structural' approach where 'stylistic analysis is subordinated to an interpretation of the work of art as a *poetic organism in its own right,* without any recourse to psychology'.[14]

3. TYPOLOGIES OF STYLE

On an even more ambitious scale, some critics have devised more or less elaborate typologies of style on psychological grounds. Some of these are centred on imagery and are inspired by Freudian or Jungian ideas: they posit a fundamental distinction between 'animizing' and 'de-animizing' images, classify metaphors according to the four elements—earth, water, air and fire—from which they are drawn,[15] etc. A French scholar distinguishes between two main classes of image-makers: the 'chemists' and the 'inspired' type.[16] The former include intellectual poets like Mallarmé and Valéry, whereas writers who express themselves in irrational or visionary imagery —Rimbaud, Apollinaire, Éluard—belong to the 'inspired' category. Other typologies are more broadly based. A Spanish critic believes that there are three essential ingredients of literary style: reason, feeling and imagination;[17] we thus have six cardinal types, according to the relative importance of each

---

[12]R. Wellek and A. Warren, *Theory of Literature* (1954), pp. 187 f.
[13]'Les Études de style et les différents pays', *Langue et Littérature. Actes du VIIIe Congrès de la Fédération Internationale des Langues et Littératures Modernes*, 1961, pp. 23-38.
[14]'Subordonner l'analyse stylistique à l'explication . . . d'œuvres particulières en tant *qu' organismes poétiques en soi,* sans recours à la psychologie' (ibid., pp. 27 f.).
[15]On this theory, propounded by Gaston Bachelard, see C. G. Christofides, 'Gaston Bachelard's Phenomenology of the Imagination', *Romantic Review,* lii, 1961, pp. 36-47.
[16]Ch. Bruneau, 'L'Image dans notre langue littéraire', *Mélanges A. Dauzat,* 1951, pp. 55-67.
[17]D. Alonso, *Poesía española; ensayo de métodos y límites estilísticos,* Madrid (1950).

of the three factors. A far more sophisticated scheme was put forward in 1959 by the Swiss scholar Henri Morier in his entertaining book, *La Psychologie des styles*. He distinguishes between no less than eight classes of style, each corresponding to a certain temperament and mental make-up: weak, delicate, balanced, positive, strong, hybrid, subtle, and defective. Each class has several subdivisions, yielding a grand total of seventy different styles. These essays in typology are certainly interesting and stimulating, but they are too abstract and schematic to be of much help in the stylistic study of particular texts or authors.

4. THE EVIDENCE OF KEY-WORDS

As early as 1832, Sainte-Beuve declared, in his essay on Sénancour: 'Each writer has his favourite word which frequently recurs in his style and inadvertently betrays some secret wish or some weakness of the user.'[18] It is possible that Baudelaire was referring to this passage when he wrote in *L'Art romantique:* 'I read in a review: "To discover the mind of a poet, or at least his main preoccupation, let us find out in his works which is the word or which are the words which occur most frequently. The word will express the obsession." '[19] In our own time, Valéry has spoken of 'words whose frequency in a writer shows that they possess for him a resonance and, therefore, a positively creative power far stronger than in ordinary usage', adding the interesting comment: 'This is an example of those personal evaluations, those *great private values,* which certainly play a significant part in a product of the mind where singularity is an element of prime importance.'[20] On this reading, a key-word is a purely statistical concept: it is a term whose frequency is significantly higher in a particular author than in his contemporaries.[21] It follows that key-words cannot be precisely identified until we have established the norm from which they deviate. Even so, the discovery of key-words will be a delicate operation. One must carefully avoid what have been called 'contextual words' whose frequency is due to the subject-matter rather than to any deep-seated stylistic or psychological tendency.[22] As Spitzer once remarked, the high frequency of terms like *love, heart, soul* or *God* in poetry is hardly more surprising than that of *car* in a report on motor racing or of *penicillin* in a medical journal.[23]

---

[18]'Chaque écrivain a son mot de prédilection, qui revient fréquemment dans le discours et qui trahit par mégarde, chez celui qui l'emploie, un vœu secret ou un faible' (*Portraits contemporains*, I, p. 162). I am indebted for this information to Professor P. Bénichou of Harvard University.

[19]'Je lis dans une critique: "Pour deviner l'âme d'un poëte, ou du moins sa principale préoccupation cherchons dans ses oeuvres quel est le mot ou quels sont les mots qui s'y représentent avec le plus de fréquence. Le mot traduira l'obsession".' (*L'Art romantique,* XXII, 7; p. IIII of the Pléiade ed.).

[20]'Il y a des mots dont la fréquence, chez un auteur, nous révèle qu'ils sont en lui tout autrement doués de résonance, et, par conséquent, de puissance positivement créatrice, qu'ils ne le sont en général. C'est là un exemple de ces évaluations personnelles, de ces *grandes valeurs-pour-un-seul,* qui jouent certainement un très beau rôle dans une production de l'esprit où la singularité est un élément de première importance' (*Variété V,* Paris 1944, ed., p. 318).

[21]See P. Guiraud, *Les Caractères statistiques du vocabulaire,* Paris (1954), pp. 64 ff.

[22]CF. Posner, loc. cit., p. 136.

[23]'Les Études de style et les différents pays', p. 36.

Most enquiries concerned with key-words are statistically orientated, but the concept can also be defined in qualitative terms. A linguist who makes extensive use of key-words in lexical studies has described them as 'lexicological units expressing a society . . . denoting a person, a feeling, an idea which are alive in so far as society recognizes in them its ideal'.[24] This approach can also be applied to individual authors. In this way, Corneille has been re-examined in the light of a small number of key-words epitomizing his ideals and aspirations: *mérite, estime, devoir, vertu, générosité*—and of course the famous *gloire* which, for a Cornelian hero, is the very breath of his nostrils.[25]

5. RECURRENT IMAGES

The range and nature of a writer's imagery will obviously be conditioned by various personal factors: his experiences, his reading, his environment, his circle of friends and acquaintances. An author without Proust's encyclopaedic culture and aesthetic sensibility could never have thought of the famous analogies from painting and other arts which run like *leit-motivs* through his cycle: the parallel between Odette and Botticelli's Zephora, between the kitchen-maid and Giotto's Charity, and many more. Some writers have obtained valuable effects by portraying their characters through their choice of imagery. A well-known example occurs at the end of Victor Hugo's poem, 'Booz endormi', which is based on the Book of Ruth. After a day spent working on the land, Ruth is gazing up at the night sky, but her mind is still full of the things she saw during the day: she wonders 'what god, what *harvester* of the eternal summer had, when leaving, casually thrown this golden *sickle* on the *field* of the stars'.[26] In the same way, the narrator in Gide's *L'Immoraliste,* a young historian and former student of the École des Chartes, sums up his quest for a deeper self in an image admirably attuned to his interests and his background: 'I compared myself to a palimpsest; I experienced the joy of the scholar who, underneath more recent writing, discovers on the same paper a very old and infinitely more valuable text.'[27]

Some critics have gone considerably further and have tried to interpret recurrent images as symptoms of a writer's deeply rooted likes and dislikes, aspirations, fixations and obsessions. The vogue of psychoanalysis in literary studies has naturally encouraged this tendency. On the other hand, the con-

---

[24]'L'unité lexicologique exprimant une société . . .. Le mot-clé désignera un être, un sentiment, une idée, vivants dans la mesure où la société reconnaît en eux son idéal' (G. Matoré, *LaMéthode en lexicologie,* Paris, 1953, p. 68).

[25]O. Nadal, *De quelques mots de la langue cornélienne,* Paris (1948).

[26]'Quel dieu, quel *moissonneur* de l'éternal été,
  Avait, en s'en allant, négligemment jeté
  Cette *faucille* d'or dans le *champ* des étoiles.'

[27]'Je me comparais aux palimpsestes; je goûtais la joie du savant qui, sous les écritures plus récentes, découvre sur un même papier un texte très ancien infiniment plus précieux' (Paris, 1926 ed., p. 83).

troversy to which Miss Spurgeon's book on Shakespeare's imagery gave rise[28] has cast considerable doubt on psychological inferences from images. There are many examples where an author's most crucial experiences, interests and preoccupations left no trace whatever in his similes and metaphors. The fourteenth-century composer Guillaume de Machaut used no images from music in his poetry, nor is there any analogy drawn from fishing in Izaac Walton's *Life of Donne*. In Camus's novels there is only one image connected with tuberculosis, an illness which played an important part in his life. It is worth noting that Proust, who was keenly interested in imagery —he once declared that 'metaphor alone can give a kind of eternity to style'[29] —clearly saw that there was no necessary connection between the tastes of an author and the images he uses: he maliciously pointed out that Sainte-Beuve was anything but attracted to sport, army life or the sea, although he did derive some of his metaphors from these spheres.[30]

At the same time it would be wrong to deny the existence of obsessive images rooted in some highly personal traumatic experience. Such cases are admittedly rare, but they do occur. An interesting example which has recently come to light is the frequent recurrence of insect images in Sartre. In *La Nausée*, a hand is likened to a crab, with the fingers moving like the animal's legs, whereas a human tongue is transformed into a centipede.[31] The same motif reappears in many of Sartre's later writings; in the play *Les Mouches (The Flies)*, it provides the central symbol enshrined in the title. The novel *La Mort dans l'âme*, which deals with the French collapse of 1940, is full of insect images, some of which have a hallucinatory and surrealist quality. In the account of the great exodus from Paris, the people and vehicles on the overcrowded roads are assimilated to painfully crawling insects: 'The long dark ants covered the whole road . . . Insects were crawling in front of them, huge, slow, mysterious. . . . The cars creaked like lobsters, chirped like crickets. Men have been turned into insects. . . . Now we are merely the legs of this endless vermin.'[32] The persistence of this theme is truly remarkable. In *Le Diable et le bon Dieu*, Goetz, the proud idealist, implores God to deliver him from his thoughts and turn him into an insect (VI,2), and even in such a recent play as *Les Séquestrés d'Altona* we find a Nazi war criminal pleading his case before an imaginary tribunal of crabs—the descendants of the human race—in the thirtieth century (II, I). Sartre himself has admitted that he was influenced by Kafka in some of this

---

[28]See especially L. H. Hornstein, 'Analysis of Imagery: a Critique of Literary Method', *PMLA*, lvii, 1942, pp. 638-53.
[29]'Je crois que la métaphore seule peut donner une sorte d'éternité au style' ('A propos du "style" de Flaubert', *Nouvelle Revue Française*, xiv, i, 1920, pp. 72-90).
[30]See Proust's preface to Paul Morand's *Tendres Stocks*.
[31]1st ed., Paris, Gallimard, pp. 128 and 199.
[32]'Les longues fourmis sombres tenaient toute la route . . . Les insectes rampaient devant eux, énormes, lents, mystérieux . . . Les autos grinçaient comme des homards, chantaient comme des grillons. Les hommes ont été changés en insects . . . Nous ne sommes plus que des pattes de cette interminable vermine' (Paris, 1949, pp. 20 f. and 24).

imagery, and there are various reasons, aesthetic and philosophical, which explain the frequency of these disturbing parallels between men and insects.[33] At the same time it is impossible to separate these images, and the specific forms in which they appear, from certain experiences recorded by Simone de Beauvoir in her autobiographical volume *La Force de l'âge*. Here we are told that, a few years before he wrote *La Nausée*, Sartre asked a doctor to give him an injection of mescaline so that he could watch the effect of the drug on himself. As a result he experienced all kinds of semi-hallucinatory states: 'he saw umbrellas turned into vultures, shoes which looked like skeletons, monstrous faces; and by his side, from behind, crabs, octopuses, grimacing creatures were crawling'; on several occasions he actually thought that he was being followed about by a lobster.[34] There can be little doubt that Sartre's obsession with insects is connected with these pathological experiences, though, needless to say, this has nothing to do with the philosophical validity or the artistic merits of the imagery.

Even this very selective and perfunctory survey will have shown that modern stylistics has begun to evolve some methods for studying an author's personality through his style. Neither of these is entirely satisfactory in itself: while each has at least a grain of truth, they all are tentative and have their inherent limitations, even though, on occasion, they can lead to interesting results. There are, however, two essential difficulties about the whole approach. Carried to unreasonable lengths, it may easily become a new form of the 'biographical fallacy', the naïve assumption that there must exist a close connection between the life of an author and his writings. One is reminded of what Dr. Johnson wrote about an admirer of the poet Thomson: 'She could gather from his works three parts of his character: that he was a great lover, a great swimmer, and rigorously abstinent; but, said (his intimate) Savage, he knows not any love but that of the sex; he was perhaps never in cold water in his life; and he indulges himself in all the luxury that comes within his reach.'[35]

There is also some danger that the critic, mesmerized by the connections, alleged or real, between the mind of an author and his style, may lose sight of what remains his chief task: the aesthetic evaluation of the text. Spitzer himself was keenly aware of this temptation and warned against it in the lecture, already referred to, which he gave shortly before his death:

> Even where the critic has succeeded in connecting one aspect of an author's work with some personal experience, it does not follow, it would even be wrong to assume, that such correspondence between life and work will always contribute to the artistic beauty of the latter.

---

[33] See S. John, 'Sacrilege and Metamorphosis: Two Aspects of Sartre's Imagery', *Modern Language Quarterly*, XX, 1959, pp. 57-66, and my *Style in the French Novel*, Oxford (1964) pp. 251 f. See also P. Thody's edition of *Les Séquestrés d'Altona* (1965), p. 196.

[34] 'Il avait vu des parapluies-vautours, des souliers-squelettes, de monstrueux visages et sur ses côtés, par derrière, grouillaient des crabes, des poulpes, des choses grimaçantes' (Paris, 1960, p. 216; cf. also pp. 217, 228, 282).

[35] Quoted by Wellek and Warren, op. cit., p. 214.

After all, experience is no more than the raw material of the work of art, in the same way as are, for example, its literary sources.[36]

The critic should therefore constantly remind himself that attempts to reach a writer's personality through his language will interest stylistics only if they can throw light on the aesthetic qualities of the text. The ultimate aim of style studies must be the one foreshadowed by Valéry: to investigate the 'strictly literary effects of language' and to examine the 'expressive and suggestive devices which have been invented in order to enhance the power and impact of speech'.[37]

ROGER FOWLER

Linguistics, Stylistics; Criticism?

Roger Fowler is lecturer in English literature at the University of East Anglia. He has recently published Essays on Style and Language *(1966). Like Stephen Ullmann, Professor Fowler has shown considerable interest in the application of linguistics to literary study. The opening essay in the volume mentioned above is a clear statement of his method. But Fowler does not found his stylistic theory upon a theory of syntax, something Ohmann claims necessary for a linguistic analysis of style. Such controversies as this are evidence of the rigor and vitality of language studies on both sides of the Atlantic. The article which follows is a persuasive argument for the use of linguistics in the critical analysis of style. As such, Fowler's essay provides a bridge to Part Three of this book, "Style and Criticism."*

". . . recently philologists have turned to the new science of linguistics to counter the Cambridge emphasis on literary appreciation".[1]

---

[36]'Même dans les cas où le critique a réussi à rattacher un aspect de l'œuvre d'un auteur à une expérience vécue, à une *Erlebnis,* il n'est pas dit, il est même fallacieux d'admettre que cette correspondance entre vie et œuvre contribue toujours à la beauté artistique de cette dernière. L'*Erlebnis* n'est en somme que la matière brute de l'œuvre d'art, sur le même plan que, par exemple, ses sources littéraires' (op. cit., p. 27).
[37]'La recherche des effets proprement littéraires du langage, l'examen des inventions expressives et suggestives qui ont été faites pour accroître le pouvoir et la pénétration de la parole' (*Introduction à la poétique,* quoted by R. A. Sayce, *Style in French Prose,* Oxford, 1953, p. 7).
From *Lingua,* XVI (1966), 153-165. Used by permission of the author and the publishers.
[1]C. B. Cox and A. E. Dyson, *Modern Poetry, Studies in Practical Criticism,* London, 1963, p. 14.

It is no new thing for the academic linguist to turn his attention to literature. For centuries written texts were his almost exclusive concern: often, texts which were written rather than literary—any records of a directly inaccessible language community; but as often again, literary pieces, from the highly treasured sacred documents analysed and annotated by the Indian grammarians before Christ to the indisputably literary remains of the Germanic cultures of the early centuries of this era, equally treasured by nineteenth century philologists. If all philology was not literary criticism, much of it, at least from the points of view of objects studied and motives for study, has to be granted that title.

The invention of scientific phonetics and the doctrine of the primacy of speech proved a temporary setback. Linguistics and philology drew apart, and a gulf also appeared between philology and literary studies in our universities. "Oral linguistics" as developed in America by the followers of Leonard Bloomfield, with its demand for rigorous consistency of approach, pushed "linguistic criticism" towards anthropology and the literatures of unlettered peoples. Paradoxically, literature had to be oral.

Significantly, linguistic criticism re-emerged as a phonetic thing. The beginning of this subject in its modern formulation can be traced to Trager and Smith's brilliant *Outline of English Structure*,[2] published in 1951. This is most compactly described as a sketch of a phonological grammar: an attempt to fuse structural, analytic syntax and morphology with the meaningful patterns of sound found in English. Harold Whitehall, in a review of the *Outline* in *Kenyon Review* (xiii [1951] pp. 710-714), pointed the way to the use of linguistics in criticism: "Trager and Smith have unwittingly assembled for the critic some of the necessary linguistic tools" (p. 713). He later expanded the implications of his comments in the same journal (xviii [1956] pp. 411-421), heading a special section "English verse and what it sounds like" which also contained an application of these analytic principles to Robert Frost's "Mowing" by Seymour Chatman.[3] This, then, linguistic analysis with a strong bias towards the "phono-grammatics" of poetry, marks the beginning of the contemporary movement to linguistic criticism.

Anyone today who reads those articles in *Kenyon Review* and *PMLA* must be struck by the narrow limitation of the position expounded there. How could this—the formal analysis of one aspect of the language of gramophone records of poetry—combine fruitfully with the new interest in literary language being shown by the exponents of Practical Criticism or by such critics as William Empson, Cleanth Brooks and Donald Davie? These are critics with a humbling range of linguistic interest, however impressionistic

---

[2]American Council of Learned Societies, Washington, 1951. There is an important review of the book by James Sledd in *Language* xxxi (1955) pp. 312-335. The ultimate development of the Trager-Smith version of Bloomfieldian linguistics is A. A. Hill, *Introduction to linguistic structures: from sound to sentence in English*, New York, 1958.

[3]"Robert Frost's "Mowing": an inquiry into prosodic structure", pp. 321-438. In the same vein is A. A. Hill's "An analysis of *The Windhover*: an experiment in structural method", *PMLA* lxx (1955) pp. 968-978. Structural metrics on these lines survived in Terence Hawkes, "The problems of prosody", *A Review of English Literature* iii (April, 1962) pp. 32-44. See also Chatman, *A theory of meter*, The Hague, 1964.

their techniques may be considered. Such students of literature offered an admirable environment for the contributions of linguists; but, since the fifties, it has taken an absolute revolution in linguistics to fit us in any degree for the role of linguistic critics. And I do not believe that we will be fully fitted until we can make ourselves become, once linguists, less of linguists. Linguistics, a subject noted for its efficient handling of first principles, has reached an impasse through considering no first principles for criticism, or only its own. Blind competence has produced many a fatuous or useless analysis: technical analysis without thought or sensitivity.

I shall elaborate on two aspects of linguistic criticism: the potentiality of its methods and approaches in the service of literary studies, and the adjustment in the linguists' views of their own contribution necessary before the contribution can become really worthwhile.

However inadequate the analyses of Chatman and Hill may seem as an approach to poetry, however suspect in their assumptions about the oral performance of poems, their technical merit as (partial) descriptions cannot be doubted. They are founded on a powerful and productive theory of language, and by reference to this (as documented in Trager and Smith and the tradition behind them) their terms and concepts can be understood and their statements utilised. The Trager-Smith analysis of English is now viewed as outmoded (but still, I think, often useful).[4] Now we have a range of techniques for description. The precision of the early fifties can still be achieved or bettered, and the repertoire of statements we can make about the language of literature is much wider. Two chief modes of analysis are now available, and not necessarily in opposition. The *transformational-generative* mode, propounded by Noam Chomsky and all-powerful in America, has already produced some very interesting discussion of poetry.[5] Admittedly, there is a strong suspicion that those transformationalists who have interested themselves in poetry have been using poetic utterances merely to test the efficiency of their grammatical concepts. But in their writings there has been a steady focus on utterances of a type highly likely to appear in poetry: *colourless green ideas sleep furiously, seven oceans answer from their dream, argumentative windows cook with their destinies, he danced his did, a grief ago,* utterances on the borderlines of poetry and nonsense, grammar and non-grammar, lexical decorum and anarchy of diction. Here is a conscientious attempt to make a grammar of English adequate to describe language outside normal (colloquial, casual, common, etc.) usage, and adequate to explain the place of *any* utterance within the

.[4]An interesting use of the Trager-Smith methods is John Thompson, *The Founding of English Metre,* London, 1961.

[5]The classic book is N. Chomsky, *Syntactic structures,* The Hague, 1957, and an elementary account of the method is E. Bach, *An introduction to transformational grammars,* New York, 1964. S. R. Levin proposed the application of T. G. to poetry in *Linguistic structures in poetry,* The Hague, 1962. See also his "Poetry and grammaticalness, in H. G. Lunt (ed.) *Proceedings of the ninth international congress of linguists,* The Hague, 1964, pp. 308-314; J. P. Thorne, "Stylistics and generative grammars", *Journal of Linguistics* i (1965) pp. 49-59; Richard Ohmann, "Generative grammars and the concept of literary style", *Word* xx (1964) pp. 423-439.

corpus of possible English sentences: to state not just that an utterance is "grammatical" or "ungrammatical" but that it has an understandable place on the scale of grammaticalness.

The second popular mode of analysis is the *levels-and-categories* method, based on the thought of J. R. Firth and developed by M. A. K. Halliday and others.[6] The [method] operates on the basis of a model of language which postulates the existence of the relevant levels *substance, form* and *context*. Substance is the physical matter of speech or writing, a "surface" or a "medium" without meaning. Form (linked to subtance by phonology, sound-patterning) is the level at which meaningful patterns are found. It is the primary level for analysis, and has two sub-levels, grammar and lexis. Here patterns are discovered and described. Context comprises all relevant things outside language. The connexion between context and particular linguistic forms ("contextual meaning") may be said to constitute the field for semantic analysis. One positive assertion of the theory, however, is that there is formal, as well as contextual, meaning. Language functions, and its manner of functioning is significant. The implications of this theory for the study of literary language are obvious. Linguists, when describing grammatical, lexical or metrical patterns, believe themselves to be making statements of meaning. Also important is the habit of separate recognition and description of the categories of literary language: the ability to say, for example, "this is a grammatical and not a lexical feature". Needless to say, sets of terms are available to aid analysis of features within these categories (although lexical analysis is still at a relatively primitive stage).

We must add to these two versions of linguistic analysis the older *structural* analysis associated with Bloomfield and his pupils and followers, only recently displaced by transformational grammar. As shown above, it first manifested itself in linguistic criticism in the form of phonological metrics, but its range is wider than that. It can still supply many useful and very precise analytic techniques.[7,8]

All I have wanted to show in the brief survey above is that a range of

---

[6]See J. R. Firth, *Papers in linguistics*, London, 1957; M. A. K. Halliday, "Categories of the theory of grammar", *Word* xvii (1961) pp. 241-292; Halliday, Angus McIntosh and Peter Strevens, *The linguistic sciences and language teaching*, London, 1964. John Spencer and Michael J. Gregory describe the Hallidayan position and its application to stylistics in "An approach to the study of style", *Linguistics and style*, London, 1964, pp. 59-105. Among literary descriptions on this basis are: Halliday, "The linguistic study of literary texts" in *Proceedings of the ninth international congress of linguists* pp. 302-307; Geoffrey Leech, "Language and interpretation", *A Review of English Literature* vi (April, 1965) pp. 66-75; J. M. Sinclair, "Taking a poem to pieces", in Roger Fowler (ed.) *Essays on Style and Language* (London, 1966) pp. 68-81.

[7]'Structural' linguistics is massively documented between 1930 and 1960. The important works (apart from those cited in fn. 2) are: L. Bloomfield, *Language*, New York, 1933; Bloch and Trager, *Outline of linguistic analysis*, Baltimore, 1942; Z. S. Harris, *Methods in structural linguistics*, Chicago, 1951; M. Joos, *Readings in linguistics*, New York, 1958; the journal *Language;* and a number of books by K. L. Pike and E. A. Nida.

[8]Other linguistic writings relevant to literary study include the books of Stephen Ullman on semantics and stylistics; Halliday, "The tones of English", *Archivum Linguisticum* xv (1963) pp. 1-28; A. McIntosh, "Patterns and ranges", *Language* xxxvii (1961) pp. 327-337; D. Abercrombie, "A phonetician's view of verse structure", *Linguistics* vi (June, 1964) pp. 1-13, "Syllable-quantity and enclitics in English", *In honour of Daniel Jones*, London, 1964, pp. 216-222.

very exact techniques for linguistic analysis is available. If one is interested in the grammar, metre, sound-structure, or vocabulary of a literary text, one has a wide choice of means to the understanding and discussion of the selected feature. Much space has been wasted by linguists justifying their methods: a necessary public-relations job that has now been done often enough. Nor is the applicability of linguistic analysis to literature a really fundamental issue worthy of discussion. Literature is (among other things, perhaps) language and evidently analysable: this is a presupposition of much modern criticism, and need not be set up as an assumption peculiar to linguistic criticism. We can say that modern descriptive linguistics is a natural companion to modern criticism because both are text-centred: both involve analysis, close reading, and both set a premium on accuracy and usefulness of description. It is arguable that explicit linguistics alone can provide a real basis for descriptive criticism, and that if descriptive criticism had succeeded in developing intelligent modes of analysis of its own, this whole problem would not exist: linguistic analysis would be detectable as a natural part of criticism.

I have affirmed the usefulness of linguistic methods as part of the critic's equipment. But is the contribution merely technical, just part of conscious method? In a publication which came into my hands during the writing of this article, Professor Jeffares asks (and I hope he knows the answer) "How much more, in fact, does [the linguist] offer beyond a new vocabulary, a jargon which gives him that sense of exclusiveness often beloved by new groups in academic society, a new system of analysis, a new set of categories, to set against those of his rival colleagues?"[9] In fact, the linguist offers something perhaps more important than technique and terminology: a set of attitudes which are reinforcement of, not substitutes for, those of descriptive criticism. He is practised in that essential of much modern criticism, close reading; in the recognition of what is language and what is not; in seeing what are the separately analysable parts of a text; in spotting patterns and meanings. These faculties—comprising a kind of mood for analysis —are summed up in an ideal honoured by linguists since the early years of this century, "the descriptive attitude". The linguist focuses automatically on what is the first concern of descriptive criticism: "what is "there" in the poem". That phrase is from the first sentence of a book whose method demonstrates the point I am making here: that criticism can benefit from the linguistic frame of mind as well as from the techniques and jargon of the linguist.[10] "Linguistic" criticism, as here, is often brilliant through the fact that its linguistics comes so naturally that it hardly appears at all. There are no morphemes, tagmemes, sememes within sight, but just a steady focus on the form of the text. The two extremes of linguistic explicitness are well illustrated by two essays by J. M. Sinclair. In "Taking a poem to pieces"

---

[9]*A Review of English Literature* vi (April, 1965) p. 7.
[10]The book is Winifred M. T. Nowottny, *The language poets use*, London, 1962.

(see fn. 6) he demonstrates an almost complete and very technical analysis of a poem; in "When is a poem like a sunset?"[11] his linguistics is simply a controlled and rational handling of language: there is an implication of analysis which carries respect.

For students, the techniques of linguistics should probably be kept largely out of sight. One of my duties as a linguist teaching literature and criticism is to teach, and direct practice in, Practical Criticism. In this context I can use a linguistic approach entirely compatible with a critic's "close reading". The aim is to stimulate reading habits and opinions which achieve a nice balance between response and analysis—which can allow rationalisation of response without its inhibition. This is met by concentration on form and by creating a mood which makes detailed linguistic analysis always possible but hardly ever practised. If I use terms like "sentence", "phoneme", "lexical item" occasionally, my students will not be shocked: their class-discussion provides a sympathetic environment for formal statements, which can arise naturally and be understood easily, without the students knowing that anything as "difficult" or "scientific" or "inhuman" as linguistics is in the air.

The "public" critic ought to operate in such a state of mind; but he will also need to have explicit linguistics (of whatever sort) at his fingertips. The good Practical Critic needs to be a very good linguistician. But even the most excellent linguisticians have failed to gain respect as critics, for technical virtuosity is not a guarantee of critical success. It is not, as I think linguists have tended to believe, that critics have failed to acknowledge the efficiency of linguistic techniques. Nor, except superficially, is it a question of interdisciplinary hostility, though we linguists have given enough cause for hostility. The fault is with the linguists: to be critics, we must be competent linguists and then become less of linguists. The development of precise techniques, and theorising in linguistic terms,[12] though essential, carry us only a short distance. A programme for linguistic criticism cannot be proposed in terms of a theory of language only. After the refinement of methods, and some thought on elementary questions (literature is basically a use of language, a literature is a part of a particular language, etc.), all remaining issues are critical problems. We should not ask "how can linguistic criticism be established as a branch of linguistics?" More proper and rewarding is "what is the place of objective formal description in literary studies?"

At this point there is a need for some scrutiny of our terminology. I have argued that there is an important part of criticism—and a prominent part in twentieth century criticism—which consists of the close examination of the

---

[11]*A Review of English Literature* vi (April, 1965) pp. 76-91.

[12]Æsthetic and other theory, put in terms of general linguistics, is very adequately represented in the literature of what has come to be called "linguistic stylistics". While much of it is essential to the adjustment of the linguists' and critics' attitudes to their disciplines, it has hardly penetrated into profitable critical theory and practice. For some discussion see T. A. Sebeok, *Style in language*, New York, 1960; Fowler, "Linguistic theory and the study of literature", *Essays on style and language* pp. 1-28.

language of literature *qua* language before statements are made about it as literature. Differences of method of analysis are more superficial than may appear. One method is *linguistic analysis,* described in the earlier part of this article. Another is *explication de texte,* defined by H. A. Hatzfeld as

> a close analysis of . . . lexicological and syntactic features, including the so-called figures of speech and rhythmical elements.[13]

Then we have "Practical Criticism" in the Cambridge sense—not a method, but an approach which *"involves* a minute scrutiny of the verbal detail of works of literature".[14] The "New Criticism" is another powerful approach which demands critical analysis or close reading.[15] At least these four historically definable phenomena—two methods and two approaches involving similar methods—can be identified. What needs to be named is the common element, focus on the text and analysis, for whatever critical uses or dependent on whatever aesthetic presuppositions. "Critical analysis", "practical criticism", "close reading" are best used for whole approaches, in which verbal study is only a part; "linguistic analysis" and "explication de texte" have too specific connotations. I propose "verbal analysis" as a term for the process of describing the language of literature: the analysis itself, not the criticism founded on it. I shall now consider the process of utilising verbal analysis, and specifically that form based on linguistics, in criticism.

The aims and assumptions of criticism will determine the most important aspects of verbal analysis, irrespective of particular techniques used. There are, in a sense, two "hows" of analysis: the "technical", with criteria such as objectivity, precision and flexibility of method, criteria which may select methods derived from general linguistics; the "critical", wholly determined by questions of a critical nature, problems largely concerned with what to select for analysis and how to select it. A further question is involved in the transition from verbal analysis to critical statement: what to add to the verbal analysis to make complete statements about the work being discussed.

Here I would like to suggest three "levels of achievement": description, stylistics and criticism. This tripartite division of the field incorporates—I believe most significantly for the confrontation between linguists and critics —a value scale, with criticism (including "evaluation", "interpretation", etc.) at the top. Linguists have already shown themselves to be most adroit at "mere description". A linguistic description of any text (literary or not) is, ideally, absolutely revealing: it can lay bare the formal structure of the language in more detail than any critic would want. We can find out about

---

[13]*A critical bibliography of the new stylistics applied to the Romance literatures, 1900-1952,* Chapel Hill, 1953, p. 1.

[14]A. C. Spearing, *Criticism and medieval poetry,* London, 1964, p. 1 (my italics). At this point one would cite (as Spearing quotes) the writings of Empson, Leavis and Brooks. For a clear exposition of the tenets of the Practical Criticism of today, see Cox and Dyson, op. cit. (fn. 1).

[15]See J. C. Ransom, *The new criticism,* Norfolk, Conn., 1941; Robert Wooster Stallman, *Critiques and essays in criticism,* 1920-1948, New York, 1949.

all aspects of grammatical structure from that of words to that of sentences; about lexical distribution, history and etymology; about phonological shape. The description is, in a technical sense, "meaningful": it reveals formal meaning. the meaning of information theory seen in patterns, contrasts, choices.[16] Completeness and revealingness (with simplicity and consistency) are ideals for linguistic description, and so one can understand why linguists seem to reverse the "scale" with which I began this paragraph. There has been an understandable defensive tendency to stay at the lower end of my scale, or to urge the ideals of description passionately. So Halliday:

> In talking of "the linguistic study" of literary texts we mean, of course, not "the study of the language" but "the study (of the language) by the theories and methods of linguistics". There is a crucial difference between the *ad hoc,* personal and arbitrarily selective statements offered, frequently in support of a preformulated literary thesis, as "textual" or "linguistic" statements about literature, and an analysis founded on general linguistic theory and descriptive linguistics. It is the latter that may reasonably be called "linguistic stylistics".[17]

In fact, however linguistically wholesome these sentiments may be, and however much apparently in accord with the views of modern criticism insofar as they are anti-impressionistic and anti-prejudice in spirit, the stubborn adoption of this position will be the very thing which disqualifies linguistic description from contributing significantly to literary criticism. Of course, any form of verbal analysis must take pains to ensure the validity and meaningfulness of its description. But verbal analysts, to become critics, must then renounce some part of their position. To pass on to stylistics, we must point to patterns which are meaningful not simply because they are efficient carriers of information, but because they are significant in a comparative context ("Browne's style is different from Burton's in these ways . . ."). To go farther up the scale still, we must acknowledge that the meaning of a poem is more than the sum of its cognitive and formal meanings, and that perhaps some of the causes of this meaning and value are inaccessible to verbal analysis. In both cases progress involves losing some of the description, or making it "impure" by invoking non-linguistic matters, or postulating the existence of an aesthetic area beyond the linguist's power to explore.

Mere description—whether linguistic, of literary or nonliterary texts, or any kind of verbal analysis conducted for its own sake—is of no great use, except possibly as an exercise to promote awareness of language or of method. And for a linguist to say that he will do the description, or show the critic how to do it, and leave the *using* of the description to the critic, is not

---

[16]For linguistics as the revelation of meaning by analysis, see the items by Firth and Halliday cited in fn. 6, especially Firth pp. 190-215 ("Modes of meaning"); Leech, *A Review of English Literature* vi (April, 1965) pp. 66-7.

[17]"The linguistic study of literary texts", *Proceedings of the ninth international congress of linguists*, p. 302.

constructive. It implies that description is nine-tenths of the critical task, and that interpretation has to, and can, follow directly on. No: the description itself must be purposeful. The crucial point is that linguistic study (in the sense given by Halliday) is essentially unselective. It describes everything, and all data are of equal significance. To analyse usefully (could one say "critically"?) one must know (or have some at least marginally positive clue) *why* one is undertaking verbal analysis: and this knowledge will inevitably direct the manner of the analysis. A "preformulated literary thesis" is essential in a very real way; to have this thesis, or hunch, or feeling, is the property of the sensitive critic or reader, and to have it is not to cheat.[18] Whether one is proceeding only to stylistics, or beyond the language to interpretative or evaluatory criticism, one must, and can without falsifying, select for description certain features which one feels to be significant.

The most obvious first use of verbal analysis is in stylistics. This is a tortured subject. The definition of "style" is of course a sitting target for the linguist, and too often he progresses no further.[19] However one defines style, pure verbal analysis is not the same thing as stylistic description. One is concerned to *characterise* a style, not simply list all the features of the language of a text. One seeks to provide objective evidence for feelings about the distinctive linguistic character of an author or a text. A feature, or group of features, is usually isolated as a result of asking not "what linguistic choices are made here?" but "what *sorts of* linguistic choices are made here?" These features are characteristic—they identify a text (or author) against a norm, a norm defined by reference to the language as a whole (a difficult concept) or that of some other text or author. Stylistics is comparative, for a stylistic feature has meaning or force only against a background of usage. Granted a hunch to make him select the significant feature(s), and the patience to describe the normative background, the linguist may be an extremely revealing stylistician. He still needs an educated reader's sensitivity, of course: but there are signs that, if he has this, his equipment for handling significant variation (*deviation* in his terms[20]) can be rewardingly productive.

The linguist's "formal meaning" perhaps provides a clue to the limits of stylistics as a branch of criticism. Stylistics examines the cause of only a narrow range of responses in the reading of literature: one's response to form and pattern. It may be a characteristic of literary expression that it draws attention to itself, is a significant artefact as well as a signifying medium: in any event, stylistics is concerned with the cause of this attention only. And for a handful of motives which are often connected with literary history rather than criticism.

---

[18]Spencer and Gregory speak of "a response to a work of literature which is a kind of hypothesis, a basis for further observation and testing" (p. 61).

[19]Notable tormentors are several of the contributors to Sebeok's *Style in Language;* M. Riffaterre, "Criteria for style analysis", *Word* xv (1959) pp. 154-174; N. E. Enkvist, "On defining style", in Spencer and Gregory, *Linguistics and style*, pp. 3-56; M. Joos, "The five clocks", *IJAL* xxviii (April, 1962).

[20]Discussion of "deviation" is to be found in Sebeok, op. cit., especially pp. 91-2, 420-22; in the article by Leech cited in fn. 6, and in his "Linguistics and the figures of rhetoric" in *Essays on style and language.*

To date, linguistics has tended to press no further than stylistics. A survey of the titles listed in the footnotes to this article reveals a limitation in labelling, if not in aim. Even the recent issue of *A Review of English Literature* (vi, April, 1965) calls itself "New Attitudes to Style", although the contents are manifestly of wider critical interest than just stylistics. There is probably a feeling in both camps that the contribution of linguistics to literary studies is too limited to go beyond stylistic description. The linguist is too politically cautious to claim too much, and the critic too jealous to admit too much. Of course, there is a limitation; but not that linguistic analysis has no part to play in higher criticism. Once linguistic description has become verbal analysis (in the sense I have proposed) by being selective and purposeful, its place in criticism beyond stylistics can be challenged only by arguments which will also throw out Practical Criticism and all similar and highly-respected modern critical approaches. The limitation is that verbal analysis, though vital, is only a part of criticism: and a smaller part than of stylistics. In evaluatory and interpretative criticism verbal analysis has a basic role, because language is at once the medium and the central focus. However, criticism, acknowledging that the total meaning of a text is more than the sum of its formal and referential meanings, and probably ultimately unanalysable by objective means, must exploit all the aids it knows: verbal analysis is only the chief among many.

PART THREE

Style
and Criticism

RICHARD OHMANN

Prolegomena to the Analysis of Prose Style

Richard Ohmann is represented here in "Style and Criticism" as well as in Part Two, "Style and Linguistics," not only because he has written so often and so informatively on style, but also because he has shown great interest in the interrelations of rhetoric, linguistics, and criticism. The essay reprinted here, a clear indication of that interest, begins with a consideration of style as analyzed by rhetoricians (I. A. Richards in particular), treating the problem of form and content in much the same way that Beardsley and Milic have presented it. Then, building on Richards' attempted refutation of J. S. Mill's notion of grammar, Ohmann introduces a series of problems which attempt to get at style from the point of view of the linguist. In the final section of his essay Ohmann extends the argument of the first two sections to encompass a critical theory of style for the analysis of prose. It should be noted that this essay was presented at the English Institute in 1958, before Noam Chomsky's Syntactic Structures *(1957) became well known. Section two of Ohmann's essay reflects the interest in semantics which seemed to dominate linguistic studies in the fifties.*

The considerations of this essay are of a very primitive sort. If they are prolegomena to the study of style, they are preliminary by several stages to the study of style in the novel. What is more, a few decades ago they would have seemed utterly superfluous to most rhetoricians, who were quite content to think of style as the verbal dress of disembodied thought. Yet now comes a school of criticism which aims to discredit the split between form and content, a school which argues that no two different utterances mean the same thing, and, more radically that, "every statement is a unique style of its own."[1] This organicist position, in spite of its stringency, has appealed increasingly to critic and linguist alike.[2] In fact it has nearly attained the status of dogma, of an official motto, voiced in the triumphant tones of reason annihilating error. Appealing as the idea is, commonplace though it has lately become in criticism, semantics, and linguistics, it would seem to render futile most extant stylistic analysis, if not to undercut the whole idea of style.

From *Style in Prose Fiction: English Institute Essays*, ed. Harold C. Martin, copyright 1959, pp. 1-24. Reprinted by permission of Columbia University Press.
[1]Andrews Wanning, "Some Changes in the Prose Style of the Seventeenth Century" (Ph.D. dissertation, University of Cambridge, 1938), p. 20.
[2]An example of the linguist's position: "It is a well-tried hypothesis of linguistics that formally different utterances always differ in meaning. . . ." Leonard Bloomfield, "Linguistic Aspects of Science," *International Encyclopedia of Unified Science*, I (Chicago, 1955), 253.

For if style does not have to do with *ways* of saying *something,*[3] just as style in tennis has to do with ways of hitting a ball, is there anything at all which is worth naming "style"? If not, most critics of style have really given us judgments about what writers mean, masquerading as judgments about manner. The critic can talk about what the writer says, but talk about style he cannot, for his neat identity—one thought, one form—allows no margin for individual variation, which is what we ordinarily mean by style. Style, then, becomes a useless hypothetical construct half way between meaning and the person who means, and the study of style would seem to be the moribund offspring of a prolific reification: the assumption that because there is a word "style," there must be a thing to match.

Confronted with this dilemma, the conscientious critic can only say, with Wittgenstein, "Whereof one cannot speak, thereof one must be silent," and rejoice at the elimination of another pseudo-discipline. The trouble with this ascetic solution is that the critic may still feel it useful to speak of style. If he *is* unwilling to see stylistics tossed into the positivist's scrap-heap, along with ethics and metaphysics, he may work out a compromise: the most common is to say that style is part of what we ordinarily call meaning,[4] that it is peripheral meaning, or subterranean meaning, or connotative meaning. Such a solution is fruitful, I think, but it leads to a new problem. If style exists, by courtesy of this redefinition, where are its boundaries? Which part of meaning is to be called style, and which is really meaning? In short, how can we tell style from not-style?

These difficulties are not, I hope, mere compliant straw men to be handily blown down. They are real, and they are crucial, for on their resolution depend answers to these questions: What is style? What kind of scrutiny will it reward? What can it show about the writer?

I

Let me begin the argument, unabashedly, where so many critical arguments begin—with I. A. Richards.

Socrates is wise.

Wisdom belongs to Socrates.

Mr. Richards offers these two sentences as a capsule demonstration of the way in which we "can put one thought form into many different word patterns."[5] He does not, as he may seem to do, neatly sever form and content; he is arguing a more subtle case, and one which ends by leaving form and

---

[3] Here, as with too many pseudo-philosophical problems, ordinary language seems to have been the villain. Our speech makes a separation between saying and thing said: one *says it.* And if expressing is an action that one performs on an idea, just as hitting is an action performed on a tennis ball, why not different *ways* of expressing an idea? The distinction works with vocal speech, for the same words can be spoken with different stress, pitch, tone, and so forth; but a moment's reflection shows that it does not apply to the written word, and that any approach to stylistics empowered by a split between form and content is in serious theoretical trouble.

[4] This is Mr. Wanning's theoretical justification for proceeding with his study.

[5] *Interpretation in Teaching* (New York, 1938), p. 285.

content neither quite joined nor totally separated—a happy compromise, seemingly, for the beleaguered would-be critic of style. Let us examine it.

Mr. Richards uses the example concerning the wisdom of Socrates in a discussion calculated to refute J. S. Mill's contention that "the principles and rules of grammar are the means by which the forms of language are made to correspond with the universal forms of thought."[6] On the contrary, argues Mr. Richards, anyone who wishes to predicate wisdom of Socrates may cast his thought in one of several molds. Conversely, in English, thoughts of incompatible forms often take the same syntactical shape: for example, "I see a tiger" and "I kick a tiger." It is obvious that to kick a tiger is to act on it, whereas to see a tiger is to be affected in a complicated way by it. Mr. Richards submits that the tiger would no doubt administer a terminal lesson in logic to the man who confused sentence forms with forms of thought in this disastrous fashion.

His contention that the two sentences about Socrates express *congruent* thoughts is not, however, a contention that they express the *same idea,* or mean the *same thing,* or are *equivalent.* In one statement Socrates is the given quantity; in the other, wisdom. One sentence works by limiting the denotation of "Socrates," by eliminating possible statements such as "Socrates is stupid," and "Socrates is foolish." The other sentence focuses on a set of attributes and ways of behaving called "wisdom," and tells of one point in space-time where we can find it, namely in Socrates. One sentence belongs in a context of curiosity about Socrates; it might come in answer to the question, "What sort of mind had Socrates?" The other might satisfy someone who is looking, not for an honest, but for a wise man. The two sentences differ in the type of information given, in pattern of emphasis, in the sort of expectation they satisfy. In short, they say different things.

Rather than artificially separating idea from expression, Mr. Richards suggests that ideas fall into a finite set of categories, according to logical shape or form. His medial position between a dualism of manner and matter which is currently heretical, and a monism which is orthodox but fatal, allows to style a tenuous existence as the manner of clothing ethereal forms of thought in neatly tailored word patterns.[7] Under the aegis of this theory the study of a writer's style becomes the examination of the formal changes he works on each group of ideas, of the metamorphoses through which he puts each form of thought.

Attractive as this theory may seem to the critic who wishes to talk about style, but is hard put to see what style is, I think it must be rejected, even at the cost, possibly, of a final lesson in logic from Mr. Richards's tiger. For one thing, these shadowy forms of thought are so indistinguishable from each other, so nearly hidden by overlapping word patterns, that, rather than implementing a rigorous criticism, they would make it inhumanly difficult.

---

[6]*Inaugural Lecture at St. Andrews,* quoted by Richards, p. 280.
[7]This rescue maneuver is my inference from Mr. Richards's position; *his* main aim is to debunk the monism of Mill's grammar.

Mr. Richards's distinction between seeing and kicking a tiger is easy enough to follow; one idea is of the form *"a receives sense data from b,"* and the other is of the form *"a acts on b."* But what of the sentence "I feel a tiger"? To which form of thought does it belong? A new form of thought must no doubt be established to contain this sentence. But the process is endless; as rapidly as the forms multiply, borderline sentences will rise up to plague the classifier, who may eventually find, as a result of his labors, that the number of forms precisely equals the number of sentences.

In raising this objection I have tentatively accepted the notion of "forms of thought," and merely questioned the practicability of their use by a critic. But the disconcerting proliferation of thought forms calls the whole theory into question. If there is a separate form for every thought, then the concept of "form" is identical with that of "thought," and we can dispense with one or the other. To look at the matter from another angle, let me press somewhat further the hypothetical meeting of man and tiger, attending to forms of thought. To an observer the tiger consists of certain sense data— color, texture, odor, shape, motion, sound—data related to each other in extremely complex ways, however simple and primitive an object the tiger may seem to the adult's highly integrated mind. The man is a similar complex. Both tiger and man are capable of receiving sensations from, say, the jungle around them, as well as from each other. And the jungle, like man and tiger, is a welter of surfaces, glints of light, disorderly movements, unmusical noises. In this tangle of sensation the man sees trees, plants, a tiger; but these *Gestalten* are not inherently *there;* they are arbitrary ways of breaking up the flux; arbitrary, that is, except that the man has in the past been rewarded for using them, to the extent that parts of his environment (e.g. the tiger) demand, with special persistence, recognition as separate things.[8] When the man kicks the tiger, an exceedingly intricate shift takes place in the arrangement of sense data, a shift which is indistinguishable *in type* from the shifts which are occurring every millionth of a second. There has been a change; something has happened, but something is always happening, and it is man who separates one phenomenon from another, both by seeing and by naming. Our habits of sorting and classifying are so ingrained that we cannot describe or imagine things as they appear to the tiger, or in the infant's "blooming, buzzing confusion." The world in itself, the infant's world, is barren of form, without order, mere raw material for man's perceptual and verbal manipulation. The forms of thought, then, are not inherent in things as they are. There is no logical or ontological reason why, on some tiger-infested tropical island, a people could not see man and tiger as one entity, and give a single name to this "object." Then "I kick the tiger" might run, "The tigerman coalesces footwise," and "I see the tiger"

---

[8]This view is, to the best of my knowledge, in accord with current perception theory. For instance: "perception is never a sure thing, never an absolute revelation of 'what is.' Rather, what we see is a prediction— our own personal construction designed to give us the best possible bet for carrying out our purposes in action. We make these bets on the basis of our past experience." W. H. Ittelson and F. P. Kilpatrick, "Experiments in Perception," *Scientific American Reader* (New York, 1953), p. 581.

could read, "The tigerman coalesces eyewise." Surely the two ideas are now of the same form, as are the two sentences.

In another section of *Interpretation in Teaching*,[9] Mr. Richards argues that communication depends on a sameness of experience—a uniformity offered from without and a uniformity as organized from within. His acceptance of "forms of thought" must depend on this "sameness," on a belief that experience affords common elements to all men. But if my analysis is correct, experience is not molded from without, except in so far as nature rewards certain of man's sorting responses to the passing show and punishes others. It is interesting to note that we may be led into a misconception partly by the very word "experience." A logician points out that "'experience' itself is a relational term masquerading as a thing-name; x is an experience if and only if there is some y (the experiencer) which stands in the experience relation to x."[10] Ordinary language urges us to think of experience as a constant, offered with impartial sameness to all experiencers, rather than as an infinite series of relations of which no two need be alike.

The conception of experience as a series of relations is damaging also to Mr. Richards's claim that experience has "uniformity as organized from within," for it seems extremely improbable that any experiencer should ever stand in exactly the same relation to a field of perception as any other experiencer, or, indeed, that any man should see the same way twice. I do not wish to peddle a crippling subjectivism; communication does take place, and we must act most of the time as if there were uniformity of experience. At the same time it seems more accurate to speak behavioristically and say that men often *respond* similarly to similar fields of perception—respond similarly, that is, either in words or in action.

Neither the external world, then, nor our "experience" of it offers any ready-made forms of thought to the analyst who wishes to see style as the way in which ideas get into words. What nature does offer to experience, however, and experience to language, is a constant *formlessness*. Just as, in the existentialist view, man is confronted in his search for ethical order by the indifference of the universe, man in his search for perceptual order faces a chaotic world-stuff which gives no hints as to the proper method of sorting. But Camus calls the world's moral anarchy benign, in that it allows us to consider man the maker of his own morality, and the chaos pictured by modern psychologists has a parallel advantage: the perceiver, according to this theory, shapes the world by choosing from it whatever perceptual forms are most useful to him—though most often the choice is unconscious and inevitable. The unfriendly behavior of tigers may, to be sure, coerce him in his perceptual sorting, and his choice of perceptual forms largely governs his choice of linguistic categories, but the selections are initially free, in an important sense.

---

[9]Page 68.

[10]Charles W. Morris, "Foundations of the Theory of Signs," *International Encyclopedia of Unified Science,* I, 123.

In these multifarious *ur*-choices, these preverbal and verbal pigeon-holings, style has its beginnings. If the critic is able to isolate and examine the most primitive choices which lie behind a work of prose, they can reveal to him the very roots of a writer's epistemology, the way in which he breaks up for manipulation the refractory surge of sensations which challenges all writers and all perceivers. In this Heraclitean flux, and not in the elusive forms of thought, is the common source of all perceptions, all sentences, all prose. The stream of experience is the background against which "choice" is a meaningful concept, in terms of which the phrase *"way* of saying *it"* makes sense, though "it" is no longer a variable. Form and content are truly separate if "content" is not bodiless ideas, but the formless world-stuff. And if such a hypothesis carries forward the analysis of style only a comfortless millimeter or so, at least it offers to that discipline a firm theoretical base, and a justification as well, inasmuch as it establishes an accessible and interesting connection between style and epistemology.

II

Before this hypothesis can be of use, however, it requires major refinement. The most obvious barrier to a fruitful consideration of these fundamental epistemic choices is the fact that most of them are irrevocably made for any given writer by the particular language he writes in. A James Joyce or a Gertrude Stein may reshuffle linguistic forms in an attempt to draw aside the curtain that English places between us and the world of psychic and physical phenomena, but most conventional writers permit English to govern their epistemologies, as do all who merely speak the language. In other words, writers in English deal with bare experience only as it is censored by their language; they manipulate linguistically a world which is already highly organized for them.

Take, for example, the question of grammatical case. In English, a language which, compared to its neighbors, is syntactically rigid and very slightly inflected, most contemporary linguists recognize two cases[11] (as opposed to the four, five, or six of earlier grammarians). Of these two, genitives are relatively uncommon, so that nearly all occurrences of nouns are in one case. This limitation of cases means that a noun standing by itself, say "dog," calls attention merely to the animal of that name, and tells us nothing about it, not even that it is *not* a dog seen in an attitude of possession, since we have many constructions such as "hair of the dog" which express the genitive idea without recourse to the genitive case. The isolated word "dog's" names an animal *seen as owning something;* that is, it conveys a somewhat different idea. It also creates a different set of expectations; to

---

[11]"Contemporary" in a loose sense: Otto Jespersen, whose semi-notional approach to grammar has made him seem old-fashioned to many later linguists, is one who argues against more than two cases in English; *The Philosophy of Grammar* (London, 1924), pp. 173-86. Writers of the Fries-Trager-Smith era also favor a two-case system, as for example, Paul Roberts in *Understanding Grammar* (New York, 1954), pp. 39-40, and Donald Lloyd and Harry Warfel in *American English in Its Cultural Setting* (New York, 1956), pp. 241-42.

say "dog" is probably to stimulate the question "What about a dog?"; but the word "dog's" leads to the question "Dog's what, and what about it?" Thus English offers the speaker or writer two different notions of a certain four-footed animal; it sees the canine beast in two different ways.

In French, by contrast, there is only one form of *chien*. That word in isolation tells nothing about the dog at all. At the atomic level of meaning English has two things where French has but one. When we turn to Latin, with its six cases, the difference becomes more obvious. To translate *canis* properly, we would have to use a term such as "dog-doing-something-or-having-something-predicated-of-it" (actually, a full translation would be much more complex even than this). *Canem* might be partially rendered "dog-being-acted-upon-or-seen-as-the-goal-of action." In Latin there is no conceivable way of expressing the English idea of "dog," untrammeled by ideas of position, agency, attitude, possession, mode of being perceived, and so forth. There is in Latin no symbol which is so free to be manipulated syntactically.

The writer in English, therefore, sees the universe through a verbal screen which divides it up less finely; classes are larger in English, because less subtly distinguished. What we conceive of as one thing, the writer of Latin must have conceived of, in some unquestioning, preverbal way, as six different things. These are the epistemic implications of case. The implications for style are equally significant: the importance of word order in English, the many possibilities of achieving emphasis in Latin by placement of a word, the greater dependence of the English writer on "function words." Epistemic differences of this sort run through the whole Indo-European family of languages, but within that family the similarities are more noticeable than the differences, and one must examine languages of other groups to find out how radically verbal environments can differ.

Benjamin Lee Whorf, a pioneer in metalinguistics, studied Western languages in juxtaposition with esoteric languages such as Hopi, and found that we treat the cosmos as much more segmented than do they—often artificially so.[12] We objectify time into a thing with boundaries and divisions instead of seeing it in terms of relations in lateness as Hopi does. We have "distributed nouns," such as "meat," "water," and "butter," whereas Hopi has none; nor does Hopi have abstract nouns. Evidently the Hopi language is in some sense closer to the raw material of perception than English is, with its complex and sophisticated system of categories.

It is notorious that Korzybski, Hayakawa, and other semanticists go further than Whorf, attacking Western languages for making inaccurate distinctions and concealing the functional relationships of nature.[13] Supposedly, Indo-European language structure was responsible for our long slavery to Aristotelian philosophy and Newtonian physics[14] and is to blame

[12]*Language Thought, and Reality* (Cambridge, Mass., and New York, 1956), esp. "The Relation of Habitual Thought and Behavior to Language" and "Languages and Logic."
[13]See, for example, "What Is Meant by Aristotelian Structure of Language?," in *Language, Meaning and Maturity*, ed. by S. I. Hayakawa (New York, 1954).
[14]According to this view it is not surprising that the Hopi have produced no Newton, but it is surprising that no Einstein has risen among the Pueblos.

for a good share of our present neuroses to boot. This criticism of ordinary language seems to me even more utopian than that leveled against it by the early positivists, and logically faulty as well. The semanticists use the very language which, according to them, hoodwinks us so severely to point out the fallacies of thought which it induces. Certainly a language which permits analysis of its own artificialities—which in effect transcends its own limitations—will suffice for most ordinary thinking.

Thus I find attacks on the cosmological limitations of English beside the point. What *is* relevant to the study of style is the fact that any language persuades its speakers to see the universe in certain set ways, to the exclusion of other ways. It thereby limits the possibilities of choice for any writer, and the student of style must be careful not to ascribe to an individual the epistemic bias of his language. A writer cannot escape the boundaries set by his tongue, except by creating new words, by uprooting normal syntax, or by building metaphors, each of which is a new ontological discovery. Yet, even short of these radical linguistic activities, an infinite number of meaningful choices remain to be made by the writer. A heavy dependence on abstraction, a peculiar use of the present tense, a habitual evocation of similarities through parallel structure, a tendency to place feelings in syntactical positions of agency, a trick of underplaying causal words: any of these patterns of expression, when repeated with unusual frequency, is the sign of a habit of meaning, and thus of a persistent way of sorting out the phenomena of experience. And even single occurrences of linguistic oddities, especially in crucial places, can point to what might be called temporary epistemologies.

Here, then, is one way in which the term "style" is meaningful, one kind of *choice* which really exists for the author. This view does not, of course, represent an entirely new departure from conventional stylistics, even though my formulation has been elicited by the chaos of past criticism. Style as epistemic choice may be what John Middleton Murry has in mind when he says that "a true idiosyncrasy of style [is] the result of an author's success in compelling language to conform to his mode of experience."[15] It probably is what W. K. Wimsatt refers to when he calls style "the last and most detailed elaboration of meaning."[16] New or not, this approach to style has the advantage of being philosophically defensible, as well as the advantage of yielding results that have to do with the literary work as a whole, not merely with its (nonexistent) window dressing. Finally, the method which I suggest saves the study of style from having to rely *only* on those impressionistic, metaphorical judgments which have too often substituted for analysis: dignified, grand, plain, decorative, placid, exuberant, restrained, hard, and the whole tired assortment of epithets which name without explaining.[17]

---

[15]*The Problem of Style* (London, 1922), p. 23.
[16]*The Prose Style of Samuel Johnson* (New Haven, 1941), p. 63. Mr. Wimsatt is one critic who has fruitfully approached style in this way, both in this book and in *Philosophic Words* (New Haven, 1948).
[17]Such terms may be legitimately used to name habits of meaning which have been described specifically; see, for instance, Mr. Wimsatt's discussion of "plain" and its opposite, *Prose Style of Johnson,* p. 101. The more usual procedure, however, is to use them as if they had clear a priori meaning.

Yet this account of style is not complete. The naive, common sense feeling that style is a *way* of saying *something* demands more than a cursory dismissal. For one thing, a discussion of style as epistemic choice can operate effectively only over wide areas of prose, where habitual kinds of choice become evident. There is little sense in comparing the epistemic decisions of a writer who is discussing a rowing match with those of a writer on Christian ideas of teleology. The very choice of subject matter precludes a large number of stylistic decisions: it can force the writer to be concrete or abstract, for instance. Thus the criticism of style requires a more manageable backdrop than the entire panorama of the world. If, as Wittgenstein says, "the world is the totality of facts, not of things,"[18] perhaps individual facts, or combinations of them, will serve the purpose.

This position is the one that I propose to take, and I shall use the term "proposition" to describe what is expressed by sentences. As before, Mr. Richards's remarks will provide a convenient starting place for the argument. During a discussion of logic[19] he lists these three sentences:

Mussolini is mortal.

Voltaire is witty.

Havelock Ellis is old.

A logician, he says, would claim that these sentences "express propositions of the same form," a contention which "is flagrantly not so." The first sentence, Mr. Richards says, means "Mussolini will die sometime"; the second means "Voltaire makes remarks which cause in certain people, a peculiar pleasure, and in others a peculiar annoyance"; the third, "Havelock Ellis has lived through many years." These sentences show that "the similar adjectives stand for very different forms." Mr. Richards's analysis is revealing, and the particular logician he has in mind[20] *had* made the error of assuming that syntactical structure is a key to the structure of propositions. But Mr. Richards makes precisely the same error in implying that his *translations* of the first three sentences reveal the structure of the propositions they express, for he takes the translations as showing that the propositions are of different forms. And by what superior right is the sentence "Mussolini will die sometime" a better indication of propositional form than the sentence "Mussolini is mortal"? Or for that matter, why not other sentences, such as "Mussolini's life will end," or "Mussolini will not live forever"? If the first two sentences express the same proposition, then there are many other sentences which do so, and these sentences are of many syntactical forms. I see no way of picking one of such a group of sentences as *the* mirror of the proposition it expresses.[21]

The difficulty, of course, is that a "proposition," as Mr. Richards uses the term and as I wish to use it, has no form at all. The form of a proposition,

---

[18]Ludwig Wittgenstein, *Tractatus Logico-Philosophicus,* trans. by C. K. Ogden (London, 1922), p. 31.
[19]*Interpretation in Teaching,* p. 370.
[20]Susan Stebbing, *A Modern Introduction to Logic* (London, 1930), p. 51.
[21]The truth is, I think, that most logicians would say that Mr. Richards's *sentences* are of the same form, and not the propositions they express.

like the forms of thought, is illusory, if I am right in what I take a proposition to be. It is the class of all sentences which are related to a fact or a cluster of facts in this way: if the fact (or cluster) exists, the sentences are all true; if the fact does not exist, the sentences are all false. In other words, they contain no parts which will not stand or fall with the fact. The process of determining, by observing facts, whether a sentence is true or false, is called "verification."[22] What may have led Mr. Richards to claim that his translations revealed the propositional forms which had been concealed by the original versions, is the fact that the restatements are more nearly descriptions of the facts which would go to *verify* the propositions involved.

Thus, for a sentence to express a proposition is for it to be a member of a group of sentences. But this class membership does not imply that a given sentence is one sub-form of a main propositional form. Rather, all members of the class have a most general form: the form "*x* is the case," or *f(x)*. And this form they have in common with *all* sentences, and with all propositions, for "the general propositional form is a variable."[23] This form distinguishes propositions from expletives, isolated words, commands, and so forth, none of which state that anything is the case, but it does not distinguish one proposition from another.

Propositions, then, offer a second locus for the analyst of style. Many sentences can express the same proposition; that is, they can be jointly verifiable by reference to the same fact. This is Bloomfield's contention when he states that "formally different utterances," though they always differ in meaning, may be equivalent "as to some partial phase of meaning." Equivalence covers "the phase of meaning which is observable indifferently by all persons," and "it is only the accompanying personal and social adjustments which differ."[24] These "adjustments" in language I would call "style," but it is worth noting again that they, as well as the root idea, are *meanings,* and not merely embellishment. Style is the hidden thoughts which accompany overt propositions; it is the highly general meanings which are implied

---

[22]See A. J. Ayer, *Language, Truth and Logic,* rev. ed. (New York, 1946), pp. 13, 35, for a positivist's account of the criterion of verifiability. See also Alfred Tarski, "The Semantic Conception of Truth and the Foundations of Semantics," *Semantics and the Philosophy of Language* (Urbana, Ill., 1952), esp. pp. 15-17. According to Tarski, whose article is a classic in the field, the general definition of "truth" is a logical conjunction of all equivalences of the form "*x* is true, if and only if *p*," where "*p*" is any "true" sentence and "*x*" is the name of that sentence (i.e., that sentence in quotation marks). Tarski's definition seems to bypass propositions altogether by applying the term "true" to sentences only; and in view of the long dispute over propositions among logicians and philosophers, Tarski's move may be a wise application of Occam's razor. But it has the disadvantage of throwing out a term which is in common use by both philosophers and laymen, and the more severe disadvantage of leaving no term at all to describe that which sentences express. For these reasons I follow Ayer, *The Foundations of Empirical Knowledge* (London, 1940), pp. 100-1, in retaining the term. But I am made uncomfortable by an identification of "proposition" and "sentences which are true or false" (as in Wittgenstein, *Tractatus,* pp. 61-103), and more uncomfortable by a gentleman's agreement to use the term "proposition" while confessing ignorance as to its meaning. My own definition (which I have not seen elsewhere) is somewhat odd in that it requires us to think of a *class* of sentences as being true or false. But it jibes reasonably well with most technical usage, and has notable advantages for the study of style, the main one being that it places something between sentences and the facts, thus allowing meaningful talk of what sentences express (propositions) as well as of what they describe (facts).
[23]Wittgenstein, *Tractatus,* p. 103.
[24]*International Encyclopedia of Unified Science,* I, 253.

by a writer's habitual methods of expressing propositions. Thus, as an aid to analyzing a writer's dissection of the entire universe, the critic may examine what the writer does with modest corners of that universe—that is, with particular facts and particular propositions.

Some theory such as the one I have been suggesting must be held by the modern critic who looks to style for insight into meaning, who believes that "the consideration of style is a consideration of complete meanings, and there is little of any importance that can be studied that is not a consideration of meanings."[25]

III

So far I have been outlining a theory of style which describes choices that I have called epistemic. These choices are important, for they are the critic's key to a writer's mode of experience. They show what sort of place the world is for him, what parts of it are significant or trivial. They show how he thinks, how he comes to know, how he imposes order on the ephemeral pandemonium of experience. These insights into a writer's world view are well worth pursuing, to whatever extent style can yield them. But an account of style which focuses on discursive content alone is only partial; style as it appears, for example, in the novel, I have left largely untouched. For the limits of speakable thought are not the boundaries of experience, or even of rational experience, and thoughts not included in the totality of verifiable propositions are nonetheless an integral part of style, as of knowledge. Thus argues Susanne Langer, who finds post-positivist man on "a tiny grammar-bound island" of human thought, in "the midst of a sea of feeling."[26] He wants to talk of good and evil, substance, beauty, and so forth, but whenever he does, he lapses into nonsense (according to the positivists). Mrs. Langer's method of egress from the narrow cage is well known. She calls symbolism of the sort tolerated by radical empiricists "discursive," and claims that even beyond its limits there is a possibility of genuine semantic. This semantic she calls "presentational symbolism," because its symbols "are involved in a simultaneous, integral presentation."[27] Of this sort is the symbolism of single words, or cries, or music and the visual arts. It is a symbolism of emotional configurations, Mrs. Langer contends, for feelings have contours just as do thoughts, though of a different kind. They are static, grasped in sudden gestalts, rather than formed by gradual accretions of meaning. And to presentational symbolism belongs a large part of what we call "style," a part with which I have yet to deal.

Mrs. Langer says elsewhere,[28] "A statement is always a formulation of an idea, and every known fact or hypothesis or fancy takes its emotional value largely from the way it is presented and entertained." For "idea" my

---

[25]Wanning, "Some Changes," p. 20.
[26]*Philosophy in a New Key* (New York: Mentor edition, 1948), pp. 70-71.
[27]*Ibid.*, p. 79.
[28]*Feeling and Form* (New York, 1953), p. 258.

term is "proposition," and this substitution brings Mrs. Langer's statement into close parallelism with my analysis of varying descriptions of facts—but with this exception: her point is that one proposition may be expressed in many different *emotional* forms. The claim is incontestable; a large portion of the submerged meaning in prose is presentational, and the constant shaping of emotions is an always audible counterpoint to the melodic line of discursive thought. The presentational part of prose does not, of course, get communicated by a special set of symbols or by a code of emotive punctuation marks. It is buried in an exceedingly complex set of relationships among the same symbols which transmit the discursive meaning. These relationships are what Bloomfield referred to as "accompanying personal and social adjustments."

Many critics see the emotional freight of literature as of primary importance, even in prose that is mainly discursive. Hence epigrams such as "Style is the man himself," or "Style is ingratiation."[29] Certainly the configurations of feeling which accompany any argument are vital in governing its reception by the reader. The writer must observe the amenities common to all human relationships, by "saying the right thing," as Kenneth Burke puts it, by showing himself a particular human being in a certain social relationship with his auditor.[30] Style adds the force of personality to the impersonal forces of logic and evidence, and is thus deeply involved in the business of persuasion. Students of rhetoric since Plato have been largely concerned, at one or another level of sophistication, with analyzing the role of emotion in inducing agreement, and with the methods of embodying it in writing.

But an analysis of tone, distance, dramatic situation, and the rest, solely as ways of persuading, is only a partial analysis, and one which can lead to the damaging distrust of rhetoric as tricky and insidious. Emotion enters prose not only as disguises for slipping into the reader's confidence, but as sheer expression of self. Complete honesty demands that the writer not only state his ideas accurately, but also take an emotional stance. A proposition is never held altogether dispassionately, nor can it be expressed without some indication of feeling (except in the artificial languages of logic and mathematics, where symbols and structural patterns have no connotations, no psychic contexts). This being so, the writer must either recreate in prose the emotional concomitants of his thinking, or be in some degree unfaithful to himself. To acknowledge the expressive value of tone, however, is not to say that it is isolated from the persuasive value. When a writer such as Newman creates a full picture of the frame of mind in which he approaches a problem and reader, he is being honest, certainly, but his self-revelation may have the effect of persuading the reader to follow the same emotional path. With Arnold and many other writers the two uses of tone are even more inextricably fused. Arnold argues for a temper of mind, rather than

---

[29]Kenneth Burke, *Permanence and Change* (New York, 1935), p. 71.
[30]See Reuben Arthur Brower, *The Fields of Light* (New York, 1951), chap. I, for this view of tone.

for a set of specific doctrines. In his prose, therefore, tone *is* the argument, in large measure: ingratiation and personality become one, for the case stands or falls depending on whether Arnold's feelings and attitudes are attractive to his readers.[31] His use of language is presentational in that a full understanding of his prose depends on a grasp of the emotional pattern which it presents.

Feeling enters discursive prose, then, as expression and as persuasion. In addition there is a third way, I think, which is almost beyond the power of language to describe. A sentence, at its inception, raises questions rather than answering them. The first word or two may limit the field of possible things-to-be-said, but they do not really transmit information. They may name something, or set an attitude toward something, or indicate a shift in direction from a previous sentence, but they always give rise to questions such as "What about it?" or "What am I to think of in that way?" These demands for completion of a sequence are of course subverbal; they are the vaguest sort of dissatisfaction with suspended thought, with a rational process not properly concluded. As the sentence progresses some of the demands are satisfied, others deferred, others complicated, and meanwhile new ones are created. But with the end of the sentence comes a kind of balance which results from something having been *said*. There may be a new set of indefinite expectations which remain for future sentences to gratify or disappoint, but one circle is completed, one temporary equilibrium gained. The very act of predication is an emotional act, with rhythms of its own. To state something is first to create imbalance, curiosity, where previously there was nothing, and then to bring about a new balance. So prose builds on the emotional force of coming to know, of pinning down part of what has previously been formless and resolving the tensions which exist between the human organism and unstructured experience. Mrs. Langer speaks of the

> feeling that naturally inheres in studious thinking, the growing intensity of a problem as it becomes more and more complex, and at the same time more definite and "thinkable," until the demand for answer is urgent, touched with impatience; the holding back of assent as the explanation is prepared; the cadential feeling of solution, and the expansion of consciousness in new knowledge.[32]

To emotion, then, as well as to epistemic choice, the stylistic critic must turn his attention. This part of the study is and always has been particularly enticing, perhaps because the individual character of a writer emerges with special clarity in the patterns of feeling which are habitual with him. The epistemic part of style, moreover—a writer's method of dissecting the universe, as expressed by the infinite number of choices he makes—is likely to seem indistinguishable from what he overtly *says*. Yet this is all the more

---

[31] I am indebted for this notion to John Holloway, *The Victorian Sage* (London, 1953), p. 207.
[32] *Feeling and Form*, p. 302.

reason for pursuing stylistic meaning through the maze of surface meaning. That which is not immediately obvious may be just as central to the spirit of the writer, and therefore just as valuable to know, as that which starts up unbidden from the page. And, finally, it should be said that a dichotomy between thought and emotion, though useful, is artificial. A writer's characteristic way of manipulating experience is organically related to his feelings about coming to know; his attitude toward the reader and toward the process of communicating is also part of the whole.

The view of style which I have been outlining clearly takes prose as a serious literary venture. What Leo Spitzer says of the purely imaginative forms is also true of good discursive prose: "the lifeblood of the poetic creation is everywhere the same, whether we tap the organism at 'language' or 'ideas,' at 'plot' or at 'composition.'"[33] This rather mystical theory makes good sense if "lifeblood" is translatable to "modes of experience and habits of feeling." Spitzer's dictum means only that a work of prose can be self-consistent just as a good poem is, its fabric all of a piece. Such a view is the direct antithesis of the older one, which saw style as sugar-coating; if my hypothesis is legitimate, style is just as useful a key to total meaning as is any other element. For this reason, and for no other, it is worth studying: to say something about style is to contribute fresh insight into the artistic contours of the work as a whole.

JOSEPHINE MILES

Language and Proportion

Josephine Miles is professor of English at the University of California, Berkeley. Among her many books are Eras and Modes in English Poetry *(rev. ed., 1964) and* Style and Proportion *(1967), from which the following essay is taken. Although Professor Miles has constructed her theory of style with an acute awareness of classical rhetoric and modern linguistics, her theory is based upon a statistical analysis of word and structure frequencies in the works of sixty prose writers and sixty poets; thus, her conclusions are highly original.*

Prose proceeds forward in time by steps less closely measured, but not less propelling, than the steps of verse. While every few feet, verse reverses, repeats, reassesses the pattern of its progression, prose picks up momentum

---

[33]*Linguistics and Literary History* (Princeton, 1948), p. 18.

toward its forward goal in strides variably adapted to its burdens and purposes. Both use steps; neither merely flows; each may be perceived and followed by its own stages of articulation. A printed text indicates such stages graphically by white spaces, the graphic representation of pauses in utterance, between words, between sentences, and between paragraphs, the spaces of increasing size representing increasing durational emphasis. Prose does not, however, make use of the additional white space of margins which represent the more regular rhythmic and thus typographical reversals of verse. Is this why a page of prose does not seem for the usual reader adequately posted, but rather a maze of print into which he must cast himself without such guidelines as verse supplies? And do many readers enjoy prose dialogue because the back and forth breaks in the print serve to provide the sort of pauses they need for recognition of emphasis? It is true that modern print especially provides additional guides in the form of punctuation: capital letters to begin steps, period marks to end them, with various lighter pauses in between. But verse makes use of all these and then, in addition, marks off its linear units as they coincide with, and cross over, its units of statement. Has prose no comparable guides?

I think it has, and I think the reason we have not recognized and used them as fully as we might in reading the sense of a page is that they are not external measures like line length but rather internalized, built into the content, the guideposts of explicit connective terms. Rather than milestones, they are road signs of varying content, indicating the contexts of statement by junctures like *on one hand* and *on the other; either, or; behind, ahead; now, then; to, from;* related less to recurrent measures than to the occurrent locuses of significance along the way. Poetry, while it works with these same explicit materials, using these same signs, has somewhat less frequent need for them because of the guidances given by measure; therefore, it uses consistently fewer explicit connectives than prose—by one in every two or three lines.

Suppose that printers shared my belief in the lively function of connective units to locate the steps by which prose moves forward; then they might well use their white spaces to aid in recognition, as in the following sentence.

Early in the morning,   in a small town   near the highway,   because he was hungry   and though he was   in danger,   the young boy, looking   neither to left   nor to right,   climbed the path   to the city hall.

The sentence takes a step: its verb locates itself in time and relation, *The boy climbed the path;* subject acts upon object, in past tense. The rest of the material of the sentence is additional: specifically linked by the links *in, near, because, though, neither, nor, to.* The only other terms not so linked are the words of modification, the single adverbs and adjectives *early, small, happy, looking, young.* First we get one of these, the single word *early,* then a phrase of time; then two phrases of place; then two contrasting clauses of consequence; then the subject qualified, first by an adjective and then by a participle controlling two disjunctive alternative phrases; finally, the verb, and its object with a qualifying phrase of location. All this variety can be ordered into three parts: the basic section, the predication of subject, *the boy climbed the path;* the qualifying phrases and clauses signalized by connectives *in, near, because,* and so on; and the adjectives that assume rather than predicate.

This is a moderately long sentence, about average for modern English; but note how much longer the wordage, though shorter the sentences, if it were to be transformed back to its root statements, from qualifiers and connectives back to their basic predications, from *a small town near the highway* to *the town was small, the town was near the highway.*

> The time was early. The time was morning. The place was a town. The town was small. The town was   near the highway. The boy was young. The boy was hungry. The boy was   in danger. The boy did not look   to the left. The boy did not look   to the right. The boy climbed the path. The path belonged   to the city hall.

Even without the further divisions possible, the text is half again as long. On the other hand, it can be shortened by the reduction of phrases and clauses to qualifiers.

> Early this morning   in a small highway town,   hungry   and in danger, the young boy, looking   neither left   nor right, climbed the city-hall path.

While the alternatives of qualifying and connective forms are plain, it is also plain that some alternatives are better suited to one purpose than to another. The sentence just varied seems to take to localizing subordinations better than it does to itemizations of process or of quality. More seriously, characteristic passages by admirable writers of prose exemplify the same sort of possible differences in choice of grammatical method for different purposes. In other words, the reader who can recognize the signifying sections of a prose passage and how they work together can recognize also what their alternatives may be, in structure as well as in content, and so can then more fully appreciate their purpose in their character. It is possible to recognize alternative modes of progression just because the alternatives are limited by grammatical possibility. In the roots of grammar, the stems of logic and the flowers of rhetoric take their being.

In statements small or large, from word to paragraph, the root of potentiality is the verb, as in "The boy climbed the path," the establishing of a relation in time by the verb root and its suffix of time and person. Verb implies noun, predicate implies subject, in a way that subject cannot in turn imply predicate, so the relation of the two is not isometric, not binary, not susceptible of two-part analysis. Topic is subsumed by theme. Even minimal statements like *He speaks,* where pronoun-substitute works with verb alone, establish the specific time of the suffix in relation to personal action, so that *speaks* is more grammatically complex than *he,* implying *he* as *he* does not imply *speaks,* and so establishing the sentence in a way that *he* cannot.

The augmentation of subject-verb into more amply loaded sentences is made by the addition of attributive words, like adjectives, adverbs, and nouns in apposition; or, more complexly, by the substitution of larger forms for these smaller. This is how prepositions and conjunctions function as connectives: to introduce the substantive forms that in phrasal or clausal structure serve in the place of adjectives, adverbs, and nouns. Only verbs cannot be substituted for. So a subject or nominative may be *The man* or *He* or *Whoever you think he is,* and a qualifier may be *The man is honest* or *The honest man speaks* or *The man who is honest speaks* or *The man in honesty speaks.* Both implicitness in order and explicitness in connective labels like *who* and *in* serve to signal the substitutions or transformations. Noam Chomsky has drawn upon examples used by the Port-Royal grammarians of the seventeenth century to illustrate how lucidly these various modes of structure have been recognized as substitutive or transformative. Three short sentences are *Dieu est invisible, Le monde est visible, Dieu a créé le monde. God is invisible, The world is visible, God has created the world.* From the first two, parts can be drawn to amplify the third, in substitutive phrasal and clausal form: *God who is invisible* or *in his invisibility, has created the world which is visible.* Or in more succinct modification, *Invisible God has created the visible world.*[1]

Of these, the first is more strongly predicative and sequenced with its three statements. The second is subordinative, like the boy on the path. The most loaded form is the adjectival: having cut away the predicates of attribution, it assumes the attributes and by such assumption can build a multiplicity of qualified nouns upon a single verb. Classically, such richness of condensation was recognized also in verse, in the "golden line" of which Dryden reminds us in his Preface to the *Fables.* In parallel to *Dieu invisible a créé le monde visible* is the Latin *ultima$_A$ cumaei$_A$ venitiam$_V$ carminis$_N$ aetas$_N$.* Both present a proportion of two adjectives and two nouns to one verb instead of three, and represent therefore an economy by relative paucity of assertion, relative generosity of assumption. Between these extremes are the partial assertions, partial assumptions of explicitly clausal and phrasal structure, working in forms not fully sentences yet not simply words.

These three alternative structures provide the chief possible choices in sentence-making in English; and, therefore, establish the grounds for the three styles distinguishable on the basis of structural choice: the predicative, the connective-subordinative, and the adjectival. Structure supports substance. In addition to the primary relation of *who* to *what,* the material

---

[1]Noam Chomsky, *Current Issues in Linguistic Theory* (The Hague: Mouton & Co., 1965), p. 15.

to be explicated, we have the material of our questions *where, when, how,* and *why;* questions, that is, of time and place, of manner and consequence, our normal settings of relation in context. Logic makes these same distributions in sentence structure: conjunctive *and . . . and,* with *then . . . then,* and *there . . . there* for time and place; *either . . . or* for alternatives; *if . . . therefore* for consequence; along with the correspondent disjunctive *but, nor, though.* Logic and grammar thus work with content and furnish out the situation of statement, allowing single words, subsentences, or extra sentences to do the work of specification. So just as a single word or a whole paragraph may serve the function of one sentence with its subject-verb and affixes, so also a single word, sentence, or paragraph may function as affix or adjunct to a primary assertion; that is, supply material of *where, when, how, why* to a basic predication of *who-what.*

A "characteristic passage" in prose must mean, therefore, not just any section of given length, inasmuch as we should not expect or wish for such homogeneity of character throughout a text, but rather a "passage," a progression which does actually move forward by a major predicate in ways, with segmentations or subordinations, representative of those habitual in the text when it is making such progress. A whole sentence or a whole long paragraph may take one main step: *I came;* where, why, or how. It may take three: *I came, I saw, I conquered;* where, when, why, how. Or it may take only part of one, a substep (I came): *The place I came to was distant and disturbed;* when, where, why, or how.

For these reasons of assumption and subordination, these powers of prose to expand and contract and shift its emphases, the criterion of length of word, sentence, or paragraph is an especially irrelevant one, much as it has been used by critics of prose style. Is a short word more economical than a long one, or must three be used as equivalent? Is a sentence that spares verbs more economical than one that spares assumptions? Economy must depend on intent. At least we may say, therefore, that a characteristic passage needs to be recognized in terms of a text's whole style of progression or its general habits of little leaps, heavy landings, or long articulated strides. Shall we carry the furniture to the new house by one trip in one large truck or by many trips in our own car. Or shall we take just the small items and leave the rest to a friend? A motor can move many different sizes and weights, one way or another. A defining feature is the delivery of the goods.

Now, with the aid of additional white space around connected sections, let us look at some passages of prose, which I suggest to be characteristic of the texts from which they come, and note how their differences in sentence-structures make for a perceptible difference in effect of manner, even of traditional styles. Then, later, we can turn to the larger and more abstract proportions in structure which these passages illustrate.

Consider D. H. Lawrence's command of many independent verbs in a paragraph from "The Spirit of Place" in *Studies in Classic American Literature.*

The real American day hasn't begun yet. Or at least, not yet sunrise. So far it has been the false dawn. That is, in the progressive American consciousness there has been the one dominant desire, to do away with the old thing. Do away with masters, to exalt the will of the people. The will of the people being nothing but a figment, the exalting doesn't count for much. So in the name of the will of the people get rid of masters. When you have got rid of masters, you are left with this mere phrase of the will of the people. Then you pause and bethink yourself, and try to recover your own wholeness.

The dozen verbs carry the line of thought: . . . *hasn't begun . . . so far it has been . . . that is, the desire to do away . . . to exalt . . . doesn't count . . . so get rid . . . you are left . . . pause and bethink,* and *try to recover. . . .* A persistent chronology supports the argument. *When . . . then . . .* with only one *so* to enforce the logic. The adjectives *real . . . false . . . dominant . . . mere . . . own* are thematic, too, but fewer and are in a supporting relation. Repetitions work also to support thematically, to do some of the work that subordinate connections might otherwise do; the repeated phrasal *will of the people* is thematically put down by the repeated imperative verb *get rid of.*

Characteristic as is such an active sequence in the prose of Lawrence, it is famed also as the early native English style: the active sequences of Tyndale's Biblical prose; the narrative arguments of More, Lyly, Sidney, Dryden; even to Joyce in our own day. Indeed, at least half of our best-known writers use this jaunting tone—the curt wit of predicative concept.

If we would call this a plain, a sequential style of process, then we could read in contrast the subordinating prose of Bertrand Russell's essay "Philosophy's Ulterior Motives," noting particularly the complexly related steps in its explicitly connected subordinations: *as opposed to . . . from . . . to . . . belief that . . . and that . . . but . . . such as . . .* and again *as opposed to.*

Philosophy, as opposed to science, springs from a kind of self-assertion: a belief that our purposes have an important relation to the purposes of the universe, and that, in the long run, the course of events is bound to be, on the whole, such as we should wish. Science abandoned this kind of optimism, but is being led towards another: that we, by our intelligence, can make the world such as to satisfy a large proportion of our desires: This is a practical, as opposed to a metaphysical, optimism. I hope it will not seem to future generations as foolish as that of Dr. Pangloss.

We sense here not just colorful references but their perspective at different levels in the fabric of connection. The careful subordinations in interior thought may develop partially from the state of prose language in Russell's time, which he accepts naturally and works with companionably, partially from his own biases of character and tone. The *that* clauses, the practical and metaphysical contrast, are to be found in paragraph after paragraph, in essay after essay by Russell, and reflect in their close design a weighing and arguing, an active and balancing mind and mode of thought, which makes use of the various alternatives that the language offers. In precise terms of proportions, we may say that this style balances adjectives and verbs, phrases and clauses, and that its explicit connectives are strong in the same way, balancing prepositions and conjunctions, with emphasis on the subordinating relative pronoun and on prepositions like *by* and *to* in phrases of motion.

We may call this style classical inasmuch as logic, subordination, and poise are its strong characteristics; we may also call it modern because it is used by so many of Russell's contemporaries: Churchill, Shaw, Read, and Orwell. If we look back in time, we will see it also in the work of Bacon, of Hobbes, of Milton, of Clarendon, of Locke, of Burke, of Alison and Arnold; and, inasmuch as many of these have been traditionally called both classical and modern, we may tentatively use both labels. The earlier writers share with Russell his moderate alternatives: his sense of balance on the one hand and on the other his strong substantial sense of nouns, phrases, and relative clauses. For example, Bacon's essay "Of Friendship" in its final form possesses a number of passages in style and structure similar to Russell's.

Both the free independent verb of Lawrence and the bound subordinate verb of Russell are modern as well as traditional, but they do not provide the only possible choices. A third style is characterized by the infrequent verb, heavily loaded with noun modifications, as in the highly adjectival style of Huxley's "Uniqueness of Man" in *Man in the Modern World.*

> Man's opinion   of his own position   in relation   to the rest   of the animals   has swung pendulum-wise   between too great   or too little a conceit   of himself,   fixing   now too large a gap   between himself   and the animals,   now too small. The gap, of course, can be diminished   or increased   at either the animal   or the human end. One can,   like Descartes,   make animals too mechanical,   or,   like most unsophisticated people, humanize them too much.   Or one can work   at the human end   of the gap,   and then   either dehumanize   one's own kind   into an animal species   like any other,   or superhumanize it   into being a little lower   than the angels.

The many epithets—*too great, too little, too large, too small, animal, human, mechanical*—are crucial to the thought and overweigh the fewer verbs, themselves nearly adjectival—*has swung, can be diminished, can work, dehumanize, superhumanize.* Such proportioning is accentuated by a choice of participial modifiers like *fixing* instead of verb clauses with *which.* So, even though this paragraph deals with the kind of balance of contrasts we think of as classical, its procedure is not classical. Its choices are not subordinative; it slights clauses for phrasal *of, in, at, to, like,* and it explicitly compares, with *either, or, than,* setting up contrasting structures.

In other traits, this style of Huxley's is to be contrasted rather to Lawrence's than to Russell's. What for Huxley and Russell is one sentence, for Lawrence is two or three. Like Russell, Huxley does not progress temporally, with Lawrence's sense of immediate process, but works within the generality of a pendulum swing. The point of view of Huxley's general *one* is closer to Russell's *we* than to Lawrence's *you,* though all are talking about human nature. Other scientists and pre-scientists—Darwin, Adam Smith, Gibbon, Browne, Ascham—write in this mode of Huxley's.

Not subject merely, but attitude, purpose, and sense of verbal tradition establish these distinctions in expression. Out of varieties of choice, persistent nuclei of choice recur. The tongue twists; the hand, the *stylus* or pen, slants in ways perceivably guided by language as by spirit. We find an interplay, with its flexibility disconcerting to causal analysis, between the singularity and community of a work of literature as between the singularity and community of a person.

Happily, there is good Greek precedent for grounding personal rhetorical choice in general grammatical structure. Demetrius in Alexandria in the third century B.C. characterized styles by rhetorics of purpose within the potentialities of certain grammatical constructions. The plain style, he said, is simple, using many active verbs and keeping its subjects spare. Its purposes include lucidity, clarity, familiarity, getting its work done crisply and well; so it uses few difficult compounds, coinages, or qualifications; avoids harsh sounds or odd orders; employs helpful connective terms and clear series with firm endings; and in every way tries to be natural, following the order of events themselves with moderation and repetition as in dialogue.

The eloquent style, in contrast, changes the natural order of materials in order to effect control over them even before predication. So the style may be called, in a form of *pathos,* passive in contrast to active. As strong assumptions are made, subjects are tremendously amplified without the activity of predication, because inherent qualities rather than new relations are stressed. Sentences are lengthy, rounded, suspended, with a great deal of elaborately connected material. Words can be unusual, coined, figured; sounds can be mouth-filling, even harsh; and meanings can be implied, oblique, symbolic.

The modern student of prose may quickly praise plainness and condemn the eloquent, which he often calls high or flowery, but after consideration may remember that purposes differ and that if he wishes to move, to enhance, to persuade, some language of flowers, some structure of suspense and excitement, may be valuable, in contrast to a plain naturalness.

Demetrius cut across this contrast with another—one between styles energetic on the one hand and polished on the other: between short and harsh phrases, broken, loose, and spontaneous, as if under great stress, with a choice of terms symbolic like the eloquent, though not so elaborated, and without interconnected qualifying structures; and the polished, smoothly connected, aesthetically pleasant in reference and tone, which embellishes the familiar with charm and grace. Two centuries later, Dionysius of Halicarnassus characterized Pindar by this contrast: his harmony natural, stately, spacious, articulated by pauses rather than smoothly polished and joined by connectives; naturally off-balance, not rounded and symmetrical.

Note that this contrast is another version of the first, between an art of naturalness and an art of inventiveness: the first contrast grammatically stressing the choice between predication or qualification; the second, between implicit or explicit connection; these grammatical choices providing the structural basis for choices of reference, reason, and tone. Gradually the choices, in certain combinations, settled into three—plain, middle, and high—because, though the high could not easily descend or blend, the plain could easily be somewhat energetic, somewhat polished, even somewhat eloquent and thus effect a middle style. In grammatical terms, the predicative style could be either implicitly or explicitly connected, abrupt or smooth; while the high qualifying style, because of its greater mass and extension, could not so easily get along with the abruptness of connectives merely implied. For the high style, the terms of reference are implicative of further qualities rather than of further active relations. The gamut in choice between sparest and fullest materials of qualification is mediated by the choice along the way of sparest or fullest signals of relation. The sentence is a synthesis; a composition; an arrangement of sounds, references, and structures; put to a purpose of showing, weighing, moving, and of pleasing along with these. From the high style of Aeschylus and Demosthenes and the smooth of Isocrates to the moderate fullness of Cicero and to the loose or intense brevity of the Stoics, classic prose tradition came into English with all its variations still possible in the new language, so that More, Ascham, and Bacon all within one century could well disagree on what different styles would be appropriate even to similar subject matter. Still today all three basic styles and their variations are useful and are, indeed, still discernible by the measures of the most technical linguistic analysis, as beneath the differing surfaces of procedure may be seen the simple kernel forms for the plain style and what we now call the further levels of transformations for the high.

The work of authorship in its rhetoric involves not only the horizontal ordering, or disposition, but also the vertical ordering, or invention, of the hierarchies of emphasis: the selecting, from any set of possible transformations, what is chosen to be predicated and what to be modified in what form of modification. In such selectivities of substance and structure, we may vividly recognize the functioning of choice, which, when habitual, becomes style, closely limited by its material into certain kinds and developments, yet profoundly variable in individual identity.

Metaphysically, one may speculate a little about these styles, what attitudes they may be concerned with. Most simply, the predicative style is statement-making. It has much to say and says it sequentially, leaving context to establish relations between statements, making the most important relation the statable one between verb and noun. In other words, it creates situations. The adjunctive style, on the other hand, assumes situations and therefore is able to express them in form of additive words and phrases— *old Jacob . . .* or *Jacob, one of the oldest . . .* rather than *Jacob ages* or *Jacob is old.* This is the spatial attitude—as distinguished from the temporal —which Joseph Frank, for example, considers characteristic of the modern novel; and, inasmuch as we note the strong decline of the use of connectives, especially conjunctions, in the English essay also, we may surmise a central defining characteristic of the present-day literary prose style. I have recently read in newspapers supposedly word-of-mouth reports so suspensive, substantive, and adjectival, so lacking in the many verbs which normally, according to Fries, characterize the colloquial, that I have wondered whether even everyday speech was being affected by the attitude of assumption and was moving in the same direction as literary prose, toward "presenting" in preference to "stating." Perhaps also a central problem in writing may be put in this way: writers are far more adept at assuming, at naming and presenting, than at stating and connecting. The freer they are to do either one, the freer they may be to choose.

The balanced and adjunctive style, which Russell used, has the advantage of complexity, in making direct statements in the express terms of subordinate assumptions and thus weighing the evidence. It lacks, however, the simplicity both of the rapid-fire statement with which English began and the noncommittal naming toward which, at times, we seem to move. At any rate, we may see that stating, naming, and connecting are not only forms but functions of the language. More than part of speech, they are parts of thought.

We may suggest as ideas important for fuller analysis of prose styles: The participating nature of art makes it simple to analyze without distortion; clear strands of agreement run through it, from form to form, from time to time, and from individual to individual. On the other hand, each form and time, even each individual work, has its own structures of relevance that need to be fairly discerned, so as not to be subordinated to others. In the language in which art works, certain patterns are given by speech and certain patterns are formalized by prose and poetry; for example, in complex discursive writing, word, phrase, and clause structures play across sentence structures in ways that build certain clear types of recognizable wholes. The artist's choices are not atomistic and infinitely various, but already shapely when he comes to them in the language. By recognizing the general proportion and continuity of these choices, we may sooner recognize what we value in the artist's specific integrity.

Proportion is a concept important for the analytical study of an art because it concerns not only the structure in the discernible parts of the material and not only the content or reference of the parts but also the relation between material and structure, the relation between *what* and *how* in *how much what?* So, for example, an architect will care not only about the character or function of the room he is designing and not only about its links to other rooms but also about its own proportions and its proportionate relations, in shape, size, and arrangement. Or a cook will care not only about the order of combination of salt and sugar in a sauce but also about the amounts of salt and sugar, the proportion of one to the other for very different effects.

Proportion is, so to speak, an aesthetic, a sensory interest, as this relates to interest in identity and function. It is the relation of the old *quadrivium* of geometry, music, architecture, astronomy, with its patterns in numbers, to the *trivium* of grammar, rhetoric, logic, with its patterns in letters. The figures 235 can mean a sum checkable in fact or a sum functionable for a purpose or within itself have an aesthetic relevance of shape, an ascending pattern of 235 as distinguished, for example, from a balanced one of 232. Many theories of beauty have their basis, as they did for Pythagoras and for Leonardo da Vinci, and still do today, in a consciousness of "right" proportions. So in language, for the Romans, a recommended proportion for language in verse was the two nouns and two adjectives to one verb, which they called the "golden line." Interest in the interworking of parts in structure leads also to interest in proportioning of parts.

Modern grammar, with its emphasis on functioning parts, aids in the discerning of proportions in the use of language and thus in the discerning of some of the choices in prose and poetry as arts of language. Asking such questions as whether prose is similar to poetry in its uses and whether the histories of the two run parallel in continuity and change, I have found more and more illumination in their grammars as well as in their vocabularies, in the ways that proportionings of materials reflect proportionings of structures.

Certain more commonly discussed characteristics of style I examine less systematically either because they have already been thoroughly treated or because they will be subsumed under topics here. For sentence structure, as an instance, writers have often treated sentence lengths and sentence rhythms without treating sentence parts and groups. Their findings have therefore seemed to me too atomic. True, Macaulay's sentences are half Milton's in length; but how much of the difference is punctuational? What is a sentence unit? Macaulay's lesser use of clausal connectives and thus of bound interior verb forms seems to me the more helpful clue to the difference. Again, rhythms are treated as cadences, as ends of sentences, without an overview of varying sentence structures. As for diction, the common distinction, by Quayle and others from Aristotle down, is between rare and usual terms or between Saxon, Norman, and Latin terms, with a tendency to assume norms never explicated and thus to emphasize oddity apart from patterns of usage.

There is perhaps a feeling that long Latinate words, much affixed, make for long, periodic sentences, much balanced and subordinated; while, in contrast, short, crisp sentences are pronounced in short, crisp monosyllables. But there are a number of difficulties in such a dualism. One is that the chief short, crisp monosyllables (the Englishness of which Dryden complained of) are the connectives, as distinguished from affixed forms; subordinating and phrasal structures, therefore, in all their complexity, can be as English as Latin. On the other hand, short, simple sentences may easily use multisyllables for weight. The contrasts are not one but many: content, order, subordination, generality, abstraction, figurativeness, connotation, and the complexities of reference—all supply their multiple interrelations. My purpose therefore is to follow out the main lines provided by proportion in both content and structure, and then to see how these are variable in individual combinations in individual texts.

An important objection to the literary relevance of proportion is that it is not specific, that it is expressible as an average or norm, not as descriptive of actualities of prose. The important answer is that it is both general and specific; that is, I have not yet found a text of which the general proportions are alien to central specific passages. Of course, no writer is apt to write in monotone without variation. But if a proportion shows many connectives, for example, then paragraphs illustrating just this ratio of connectives come immediately to view. The most fundamental part of the objection is that proportion is abstracted from order, from context. True, it is by such abstraction that I hope to follow out certain main lines of emphasis; but these abstractions need ultimately to be seen in order and context again, the specific adjectives with their specific nouns, the emphasis and choices in their correlative progressing.

The advantage of thinking about grammar, logic, and rhetoric together is to see their interconnections more plainly. This *trivium* of letters, as distinguished from the *quadrivium* of numbers, establishes the full relations of letter to letter, letter to reference, and letter to intent and effect, which a system of symbols makes pertinent. As representing sound and syllable, unit of meaning from morpheme to word and utterance, the letter of *logos* conveys spirit in the signs of speech. Each specialist sees the proliferations of complexity in the process, the exceptions and ambiguities that make the borderlines of distinctions; the subtle differences between one verb form and another, the habits of tautology, the artifices of rhetoric as device. But the contemplation of lettered, of literary, language in general can afford to blur these distinctions for the sake of focusing upon the whole use of the medium in a paragraph or stanza, to learn how one sentence, one word, one syllable fits with another, and how all fit the pattern of their intent. Not a geometer, musician, astronomer, or architect, I nevertheless think that proportion, the basis of the *quadrivium,* is pertinent to language as well as to structural forms. Properties of sound, syllable, grammatical unit, and rhetorical scheme in composed language are just as significant as properties of perceived design in stone or constellation.

Specifically, the pattern of proportions I present in concentrated form on pp. 204, 205 is the proportion of adjectives, nouns, verbs, and connectives used by sixty poets and sixty prose writers in English in the past five centuries. Because my earlier interest was in frequencies of reference in the major vocabulary of poetry, I paid little attention in *Eras and Modes* and the *Continuity of Poetic Language* to questions of syntactic proportion, to connectives, and to prose structures. Then, when I recognized the close relations between syntactic structures and the proportioning of parts of speech, I supposed that prose would differ in its uses especially by an emphasis on connectives. As can be seen, this idea did not turn out to be wholly true. But it led to the selective emphases of the present study: upon certain parts of speech and upon poetry and prose in parallel through the centuries.

First, to be more specific about the parts of speech: the terms commonly called terms of reference or content are nouns, adjectives, verbs. Words used chiefly for linking and connecting, prepositions and conjunctions, then are usually grouped as "grammatical terms." These two kinds of terms, referential and grammatical, constitute the language of our study. Of the other parts of speech, the pronouns, and the articles or determiners so neatly treated by Rostrevor-Hamilton, both are so closely related to the noun that they belong to a fuller study of the noun itself; their absence here limits the validity of what is indicated about the noun's functions in other forms as the absence of adverbs limits the view of the verbs.

The chief specified pattern then is the proportion, in a sequential text of one thousand lines of poetry (six to eight thousand words) and eight thousand words of prose, of adjective to noun to verb, the referential pattern; and of these to connectives, the grammatical pattern. These proportions, simply established, allow us to see the overall structure of the text—its dominant subordination or its dominant qualification, for example—more easily than a close structure-by-structure scrutiny would do. It allows us to see the trees within the forest.

Note needs to be made of inclusion in categories: in a simpleminded way, all nouns and gerunds as nouns; numerical or limiting adjectives and present and past participles as adjectives when used so, as in *sparkling broken glass;* infinitives as verbs; all connectives, prepositional and conjunctival, together as connectives. As Jespersen says, "The difference between the various functions of one and the same word, e.g., *before* in . . . 'using this before my marriage,' and 'many times before I was married,' is not important enough to cause it to be placed in different categories."[2] Of the seventy most used connectives, half, like *before,* are used as either prepositions or conjunctions, so that the tendency of the language seems to relate the two; and this relation simplifies the habit of the reader to note all connective material as of a kind, whatever the further possible subdivisions. In the distinguishing of verbs, it seems to me that the forms *I go, he goes, he is going, he has gone, he hopes to go* all share a predicative force which the assumptive form, a *going* or *gone concern,* lacks. At any rate, it has turned out that adjectival writers are the large users of participial adjectives, so that they seem to concur in my feeling of affinity in such parallelism as that of *England's green and pleasant land.*

---

[2]Otto Jespersen, *Essentials of English Grammar* (London: Allen & Unwin, 1933), p. 12.

The two pages which follow give an overview of English poetry and English prose in their pattern of structural variation. Most immediately visible is the similarity of the two patterns. On both pages, the writers cluster first at lower left, then at upper center, then at middle right, with an effect of motion through five centuries from one extreme through midpoints to another extreme and then back to midpoint. The great difference between the two is that the prose motion first leads, then follows the poetic, developing a middle style earlier than poetry, but then not moving into the adjectival heights until a century later, coming in the twentieth century to much the same agreement with which it had begun, though closer to mid level.

In closer detail, the reader may note, starting at the left, that each century-column contains the names of the ten writers publishing in that century, in order, from bottom to top, of the dominance of verb over adjective: strongest verbs at bottom, balance in the middle, least verbs at top. So in prose Tyndale's Bible, More, Sidney, and others, like the Ballads, Wyatt, and Sidney in poetry, use the active English of three verbs to every one or two adjectives; while a few experimenters, Bacon and Ascham in prose, like Spenser, Shakespeare, and Sylvester in poetry, try a stronger set of attributions. Connectives, somewhat more numerous for prose, tend to follow nouns in number; that is, to relate to the extra noun called for in phrase or clause. The average sixteenth-century proportion for prose is $2-4-3-5$, for poetry $2-4-3-4$, as these numbers represent reduction by the least common denominator of four hundred, of proportions such as $800-1000-1200-2000$ adjectives, nouns, verbs, connectives in $6000-8000$ cursive words of text.

If read across the bottom of the page, the averages reflect the similarities of tendencies in the two forms: for prose, the seventeenth-, eighteenth-, and nineteenth-century decrease of verbs with increase of nouns; the nineteenth-century increase of adjectives; the twentieth-century increase of verbs, which with lessening of connectives would seem to be not clausal but independent. Nearly the same pattern for poetry: a similar portioning at first and last, and in between a later lessening of verbs, an earlier gain and then loss of adjectives, a persistently smaller number of connectives except in the present day; in America, more oddity of meagerness in poetry than in prose.

These pages are full of amazement for me both because they show in their fundamental likenesses the whole basis of the art in the language and because they show in their differences the power of literary forms and of individuals working within those forms to vary even the chief characteristics of structure in the medium through which they work.

Our prose has moved in good array from much clausal subordination to much phrasal subordination to much adjectival assumption, through three standard styles—plain, middle, and high. Our present day has made the change, noted by many commentators, toward a variant, a lessening of connectives while the referential forms are at their height: a device of juxtaposition, it would seem, in relation to strong statement and assumption. Through

TABLE 1A   PROPORTIONS IN ENGLISH POETRY*

	BRITISH					AMERICAN
	16th century A-N-V-C	17th century A-N-V-C	18th century A-N-V-C	19th century A-N-V-C	20th century A-N-V-C	19th & 20th centuries A-N-V-C
Adjectival	Sylvester 3-5-2-3p	Blackmore 3-5-2-4 Milton 3-4-2-4	Thomson 4-5-2-4p Blake 3-6-2-6cp Bowles 3-5-2-4 Collins 3-5-2-4 Gray 3-5-2-3 Cowper 3-4-2-4c	Keats 4-6-2-5cp Swinburne 4-6-3-6crp Tennyson 3-4-2-3	Thomas 3-6-2-4p Spender 3-5-2-4p	Whitman 3-7-2-5p Crane 3-5-2-4 Dwight 3-5-2-4
Balanced	Shakespeare 3-4-3-4cr Spenser 3-4-3-4r	Waller 3-5-3-4r	Pope 3-5-3-4 Johnson 2-5-2-3 Wordsworth 2-4-2-4	Shelley 2-5-2-4p Hopkins 2-5-2-3 Yeats 2-4-2-4c	Lawrence 3-4-3-4c Sitwell 2-6-2-5cp Nicholson 2-5-2-4p	Bryant 2-4-2-4 Emerson 2-4-2-3 Eliot 2-4-2-3 Roethke 2-4-2-2 Robinson 2-3-2-2
Predicative	Dunbar 1-3-1-3 Sidney 2-5-3-4r Gascoigne 2-5-3-4cr Surrey 2-4-3-4r Wyatt 2-3-3-3 Coverdale 1-2-2-3 Ballads 1-3-3-3	Dryden 2-5-2-4 Jonson 2-4-3-4cr Herrick 2-4-3-4c Herbert 2-4-3-3 Donne 2-3-3-6cr Marvell 2-3-3-3 Vaughan 2-3-3-3	Crabbe 2-4-2-3	Coleridge 2-4-3-4c Byron 2-4-3-4 Browning 2-4-3-3 Hardy 1-3-2-3	Graves 2-4-2-3 Jennings 2-4-3-4 Gunn 2-4-3-3 Muir 2-4-3-3 Auden 2-4-3-3	Lowell 2-5-3-3 Dickinson 1-3-2-2
	2-4-3-4	2-4-3-4	3-5-2-4	2-5-2-4	2-5-3-4	2-4-2-3

A-N-V-C Adjective-Noun-Verb-Connective
c clausal or phrasal
r relative
p phrasal

*Note that proportions for Pindar's *Odes* (Olymp. 1, 2; Pyth. 1, 8, 9; Ist. 5, 6, 7) are 1260-2050-760-970. For other proportions in other languages, see Appendix, *Eras and Modes*, rev. ed. 1964.

TABLE 1B PROPORTIONS IN ENGLISH PROSE

| | BRITISH | | | | | AMERICAN |
	16th century	17th century	18th century	19th century	20th century	19th & 20th centuries
	A-N-V-C	A-N-V-C	A-N-V-C	A-N-V-C	A-N-V-C	A-N-V-C
Adjectival	Ascham 3-4-2-5c	Browne 3-5-2-4p	Gibbon 3-6-2-5p	Macaulay 3-5-2-5p	Huxley 3-5-2-4	Whitman 3-5-3-4
			Smith 3-5-2-5p	Ruskin 3-5-2-6cpr		
				Pater 3-5-2-5		
				Carlyle 3-4-2-4		
				Darwin 3-4-2-3p		
				De Quincey 2-4-1-3p		
Balanced	Bacon 2-4-2-5cpr	Hobbes 2-5-2-5	Alison 2-5-2-5p	Arnold 2-5-2-4	Russell 3-5-5-5p	Twain 3-5-3-4
		Burnet 2-5-2-5	Burke 2-5-2-5p	Shaw 2-5-2-4	Orwell 3-4-3-4	Eliot 3-4-3-4
		Clarendon 2-4-2-5	Godwin 2-4-2-4p		Churchill 2-5-2-4	Paine 2-5-2-4
		Milton 2-4-2-5cr	Swift 2-4-2-4		Read 2-5-2-4p	
		Locke 2-3-2-5cr			Wain 2-5-2-4	
Predicative	Holinshed 2-5-3-5p	Donne 2-4-3-5	Addison 2-5-3-5	Hazlitt 2-5-3-5	Connolly 2-5-3-4	Lardner 2-6-3-4
	Hooker 2-4-3-5c	Jonson 2-4-3-5	Johnson 2-5-3-4	Frazer 2-5-3-4p	Lawrence 2-5-3-3	Emerson 2-5-3-4
	Dekker 2-4-3-5c		Shaftesbury 2-4-3-4p		Joyce 2-4-3-4	Baldwin 2-5-3-4
	Sidney 2-4-3-4	Dryden 2-4-3-4	Berkeley 2-4-3-4		West 2-4-3-4	Edwards 2-4-3-5
	Lyly 2-4-3-4					Santayana 2-4-3-4
	More 2-4-3-4c	Bunyan 1-4-3-5cpr				Hemingway 2-4-3-4
	Latimer 1-4-3-4c					
	Tyndale 1-4-3-5cpr					
	2-4-3-5	2-4-2-5	2-5-2-5	3-5-2-4	2-5-3-4	2-5-3-4

A-N-V-C Adjective-Noun-Verb-Connective   r relative

c clausal or phrasal   p phrasal

the temporal stages of general usage, the types are to be found, whether in general favor or not, in individual practice. For example, the simpler statement in favor now, as in the work of Lawrence, was early emphasized by Hazlitt and still earlier by Lyly and Sidney. In the midst of the early predicative stress we yet find Ascham's complex modificational bent, notable in the prose of Sir Thomas Browne, before its cumulative force in Gibbon in the eighteenth century. The balanced choice too has its range of use, early in the work of Bacon and of Milton, as well as late in Orwell; for all of whom the poise of adjective and verb, of phrase and clause, presents equivalent emphases before and after the chief time of classical strength. As a whole we may say that about half the writers favor the early clausal qualification; a fifth, the nineteenth-century phrasal qualification; and the rest, between and at present, some variety of balance, now tending toward the simple. Yet again we may note writers who move out from any of these possibly generalizable types to further extremes. Ben Jonson is such a one, who, even in literary criticism, employs such a variety of verbs that one might think he was writing the narrative of Bunyan or Joyce; while many more actual narrative writers, as in the histories, do not so predicate.

Condensation of proportions provides a still recognizable view of English prose. In its terms, the traditional three styles are visible: the early increase of noun phrases and and recent decline of connectives; the accepted contrasts, between More and Ascham, for example, or between Donne and Browne or between Hazlitt and De Quincey; and the accepted comparisons between Hooker and Milton, Hobbes and Russell, Burke and Churchill, Swift and Shaw.

On the other hand, some less familiar lines of relation come into view. The likeness of Lyly's and Sidney's so-called euphuistic and "curt" juxtapositions to Dryden's, Johnson's, and the moderns'; the clear difference between Dryden's and Addison's modernity; the striking relation of Julian Huxley to Adam Smith and the technical writers as well as the dreamers.

Analysis works to support and invite intuition. Often today we hear skepticism of the analytic because we ask it to do more than it can do. It does not create, invent, imagine, lead to values; but given values, it clarifies and discerns, helping us to understand the relation between what we feel and what we know.

A generation ago, most criticism was not analytical. It was discovering and rediscovering values through aesthetic impression and, if historical, was historical in a general sense, in studies of what were called sources and analogues. Now, after a generation of close criticism of individual and autonomous texts, we may find that criticism has still further steps to take, to reach poetry as well as poems, extensions as well as intensions, participations as well as isolations. Though my first purpose in studying the language of poetry was to be able to recognize a poem of any poet by the singularity of his choices, now I have learned that singularity of choice is a part of the commonality of choice that serves a poet in the making of poetry. Both in kinds of substance and in kinds of arrangement, one work is like, as well as different from, another; they share great stores of interest and assumption, from artist to artist, throughout an era, throughout a tradition, and even throughout a literature in a specific language. It is impossible to treat the autonomy of the work without considering also its patrimony and hegemony. The intrinsic criteria and extrinsic criteria, though they are separated in such an established work as Wellek and Warren's *Theory of Literature,* extend in strands through the work from outside to inside, from inside to outside again, so that their pattern is not static but dynamic in its effect. In the metaphors of R. S. Crane and others, an object may be both an icon and a message; a construct, at once a gift, a mirror, and a lamp; a poem, a part of poetry.

Poets and prosaists work in the same language: the same sentence structures, the same references, even the same terms of value. But thus far we have learned less about prose's procedures than about meter and other intensifying poetic structures. Relatively few studies of prose style have been made, and these have been either in poetic terms of cadence or in rhetorical terms of figure or in quantitative terms of sentence length, but all with little attention to the working wholes we have come to appreciate in poetry.

In recent years, two philosophical schools, the ordinary-language philosophers and the structural linguists, have been raising new and different questions: the first covering the reaches of usage, in relation to specific lexical definition, and the second concerning the structure of basic minimal sentence units. The one so subjective *a priori,* the second so objective and universal, their divisions are yet part of one larger whole. My suggestions for analysis work in the no-man's-land that theorists have encouraged to stretch between them unexplored—the realm of art. This realm, as it gives us our best direct experience of generality in particularity can serve to close the gap between the infinite particulars of the ordinary-language theorists and the generated laws of transformation theorists, by showing the actual structures of evaluative choice and the way particulars do actually work within them. In such a realm, we need not limit our questions to utterances either as speech in ordinary-language phrases or as all the possible sentences of a language.

Rather we can start at the other end, the complex realm of values already uttered and recorded in writing, with an intricacy alien to the precise formalities of our predecessors, yet susceptible of just that degree of working and observable generality that is provided by the common agreements of artists in language when they make choices of materials and structures; that is, a generality not rigorously generated but freely observed, a particularity not infinitely variable but focused in patterns of actual choice. When we speak, we paraphrase and reparaphrase our statements, seldom echoing statements in exact repetition, but using different words and different forms each time, so that by a sort of cumulative redundancy, if not by simple clarity of situation, we may make ourselves understood. But in literature the writer is responsible for constructing both the situation and its phrasing, and must find patterns that will stand fixed to do the work for many readers in many times. There is in literature a normative function, a preserving of choices that will hold good.

That the normative function is present and that it functions for more than mere analysis is testified to by the tradition of comedy or joke on this subject of tone in grammar. Comedy enjoys pulling the chair from under that very person who most fully assumes its stability. So, much of the comedy of language plays upon the contrast between adjectival assumptions and verbal assertions, assertions and assumptions that we have been noting in styles. "Why does Uncle Sam wear red, white, and blue suspenders?" The puzzled responder is hung up on those adjectives because he assumes their importance. The more straightforward listener gets to the actual predicate and replies, "To keep his pants up." Pliny supposedly reported just such a joke: "How would you like to be shaved, sir?" asks the barber. "In silence," replies the customer, shifting the assumption of manner from passive to active. Even the ambiguity of qualification itself can be played upon; does the phrase qualify noun, verb, or predication in "Would you hit a woman with a child?" "No, I'd hit her with a brick." The shift is double: from *woman with* to *hit with,* turning upon the predicate *would you hit?*

Such jokes play upon and across the breaks of the language: the breaks between nucleus and adjunct, between assertion and assumption, between the act of sitting on a chair and the assumption that it is there to sit on. In their humor, they seem to me a trustworthy guide to art in language, both in what they suggest about the usable segments of language and in what they suggest about the bases of emphasis.

RICHARD BRIDGMAN

From *The Colloquial Style in America*

Richard Bridgman teaches American literature at the University of California, Berkeley. In his book The Colloquial Style in America *(1966), Professor Bridgman traces the emergence of a distinctively American prose style, which is characterized by "outlining and elevating single words."*

Several observers have noted that modern American prose appears to give unusual prominence to single elements within its sentences. Harold Whitehall, expanding his sense of the difference between American and British English, wrote:

> In the most typical American writing, sentences seem to be constructs in which the key words function as isolated counters of expression . . . [while] in British English, individual words, even the key words, seem to be far more submerged into the larger syntactical units of expression. The sense hovers over the whole phrase or sentence, not over the word. . . .[1]

Malcolm Cowley also described the colloquial American style as composed of sentences which focused on a key word. That word, he thought, gained its conspicuous position by appearing repeatedly in a context of flat assertions made with simple, monosyllabic words.[2] More recently, Northrop Frye has distinguished three basic rhythms of verbal expression: that of verse with a regularly recurring pattern of speech; that of prose based upon the unit of the sentence; and that of ordinary speech, which he regards as centered upon a short phrase which contains the essential idea or word upon which the speaker is concentrating. The surrounding verbal sounds, he believes, "are largely rhythmic filler."[3] Frye, Whitehall, and Cowley all agree that there is a certain style of verbal communication, especially associated with North America (although Frye is establishing universal categories), which emphasizes single words or phrases at the expense of the larger verbal structure. The jewel is displayed against a plain, featureless background; the pearl is located in the formless viscosity of the oyster. What accounts for this colloquial propensity for outlining and elevating single words?

Some vernacular words had always drawn more than normal attention to themselves as words, often abetted by the writer's attitude toward their informality. When writers first began to introduce questionable diction into their prose, they quarantined it with quotation marks, or put it in italics to emphasize its alien identity, or introduced it with a phrase that designated its origin and dissociated the writer from intimacy with it. John Neal, whom one twentieth-century critic has called "the first in America to be natural in his diction,"[4] prided himself on the colloquial vigor of his language. In a series of articles he wrote during 1824 and 1825 for *Blackwood's Magazine* on the subject of American writers, Neal remarked: "We have continued, as we began—using *low* words, unless they were wholly beneath us, whenever the subject required it; whenever they were more suitable, ex-

---

[1]"Linguistic Patriot," *The Kenyon Review* (Winter, 1946), VIII, 159-60.
[2]"The Middle American Style," *The New York Times Book Review,* July 15, 1945, pp. 3, 14.
[3]*The Well-Tempered Critic* (Bloomington: Indiana University Press, 1963), p. 21. [See pp. 222-226 of this collection.]
[4]F. L. Pattee in the introduction to Neal's *American Writers,* p. 12.

pressive, or vigorous, than *high* words."[5] But as late as 1869, in his autobiography, *Wandering Recollections,* Neal still formally set off his colloquial expressions:

> He had written, or *made,* as he termed it, an article for the "North-American Review."

> I had to put up with a "glittering generality" as we politicians would call it.

> When a boy, I was always a bungler, not being sure of hitting a barn-door—I might say of *fetching* a two-story house.

> Most of us tried our hand at what our secretary called *ex-trumpery* speaking.

> I came to be talked about as rather an "ugly customer."[6]

The writer's attitude toward his vernacular material can give it the double prominence that anything reaches which, in addition to being odd, is declared odd. Neal's behavior is altogether typical of many writers who were attracted to the vernacular yet unwilling to commit themselves wholly to it. Whether rhetorical or typographical, procedures such as Neal employed in 1834 caged the vernacular and, by caging it, drew attention to it:

> With this, the hunter "squared himself, and sot his triggers," fully determined either to hunt the disputed game, or be vanquished in combat.[7]

Deep-seated social attitudes are reflected in this use of quotation marks with the vernacular. Certain words, like certain clothes, schools, and professions, are proper for the educated and others are not. On a reduced scale, such quarantining of the vernacular resembles the humorist's frequent use of a frame of standard English to enclose vernacular stories. The presence of a literate narrator to introduce the vernacular speaker permitted the reader to enjoy colorful informality, yet be assured that the hierarchy of social values still stood, that the vulgar were still under control.

On such occasions, the robust candor of the vernacular threatened the legitimacy of standard literary English. For example, when George, the educated narrator who normally introduces Sut Lovingood's tales, has translated a passage of Sut's "English," Sut bursts out: "Now why the devil

[5]*American Writers,* pp. 185-6.

[6]*Wandering Recollections of a Somewhat Busy Life: An Autobiography* (Boston: Roberts Brothers, 1869), pp. 235, 261, 315, 44, 71.

[7]James Hall, "Pete Featherton," *The Cyclopedia of Wit and Humor,* ed. William E. Burton (New York, 1870, originally 1858), p. 111. Hereinafter, *Cycl.*

can't I 'splain myself like yu? I ladles out my words at random, like a calf kickin at yaller-jackids; yu jis' rolls 'em out tu the pint, like a feller a-layin bricks—every one fits. How is it that bricks fits so clost enyhow? Rocks won't ni du hit."[8] Even as Sut expresses his exasperation with the clumsiness of his diction, he is exposing standard prose to criticism. Rocks make up the vernacular world—hard, individual, rough, heavy, intractable. Bricks are a product of an organized social world. That is why they fit so well. They are manufactured, artificial, uniform, and capable of being manipulated without difficulty. And when a rock appeared in a brick wall, even if it was not formally set off, its very incongruity drew the reader's attention to it. Vernacular life offered details simply alien to standard prose, whether from the diction of steam-boating, bear-hunting, or courting, or such idiomatic expressions as "I'm married folks," or the metaphorical comparison, "green as a jimson weed." Even as the power of the printed obscene word attests, the mind is arrested by the appearance of a word it has not seen before, however familiar it may otherwise be. In an extreme way, the shock of four-letter words suggests the power of the vernacular term encountered for the first time in a normal context.

Misspellings also emphasized individual words by so disguising them that, even if the words were not newly encountered, they were encountered for the first time looking as they did. The motives for misspelling varied, and as we shall see in the following chapter, it makes a difference whether the writer's goal was accuracy or buffoonery. Sometimes the word is spelled phonetically by a semi-literate writer: *fite, enuf, jist* or *jest, strate.* At other times the malformation is not an error in spelling, but reproduces a dialect pronunciation, although sometimes one cannot distinguish naïve phonetic literalness from scientific accuracy, since the spellings *larn, fellers,* and *sartin* could result from ignorance or a wish to represent the sounds. Barbarisms are also spelled "correctly" in the sense that their rendering accurately represents usage: *onst* (once), *seed* (seen), *hearn* (heard). Such errors resemble those misspellings where the actual construction of a word is mistaken. Sometimes in these cases plain distortion takes place—*norate* for *narrate;* sometimes folk etymology is at work—*cowcumbers* for *cucumbers;* sometimes malapropisms occur in which the known word is inadvertently substituted for another: "Tha found him requitted of murder, but tha found him gilty of salt an batter."[9] Finally, there are occasional instances of the kind of revelation associated with the portmanteau economy of the language of *Finnegans Wake.* So Huck Finn describes one of the subjects taught by the duke and the king as "yellocution" (ch. 31).

These vernacular tricks with language arouse various responses in the reader: superiority, amusement, curiosity, the pleasure of mimetic recognition. The point, however, is that the reader's mind is more than normally

[8]"Mrs. Yardley's Quilting," in George Washington Harris, *Sut Lovingood* (New York, 1867), p. 134. Hereinafter, *Sut.*
[9]*A Quarter Race in Kentucky and Other Sketches,* ed. William T. Porter (Philadelphia, 1846), pp. 182, 174, 46.

engaged by the actual structure of the vernacular word, and, depending upon the nature of the disguise it is given, the adjustment necessary to translate it may be quite complicated. *Norate* is no word, *cowcumber* is a partially familiar one, *salt an batter* are familiar words in the wrong context, and *yellocution* is at once no word and a neologism superior to the proper one. The effort to understand in each of these instances accentuates the word itself.

In the more rudimentary stages of vernacular writing, the disguised word is not only misspelled, but italicized as well so that none may miss the joke. When an ailing woman is told by her doctor that she must be cupped on the sternum, she shrieks, "What! . . . you cup me on de *starn!*" A rural matron reassures a traveler spending the night in her home that he may undress without trepidation: "You can un*kiver* now, stranger; I'm *married folks, you ain't afeard o' me,* I reckon!" An appeal for a drink of whiskey is rendered: "Colonel, let us have some of your *byled* corn." In short, comic punch lines contain punch words, and the blow is always a vernacular one.[10]

If one major preoccupation of those using the vernacular was to render the words as they actually sounded, another was to determine what those words meant. This again focused attention on the single word. Sometimes this was done quite baldly, as when Cooper in *The Prairie* refers to "the brown and party-colored livery of the fall," then footnotes it: "The Americans call the autumn the 'fall' from the fall of the leaf" (ch. 8). As late as 1887 in *Zury* Joseph Kirkland was doggedly defining his vernacular terms:

"Chuck-holes" is the expressive Western name for the short, sharp depressions which use makes in unworked country roads.

The "prairie flowers" (blue gentian) gave to the whole award a tinge of pale azure.

"Puncheons" or "slabs" are the side-cuts from logs squared for sawing.[11]

Overt definition also frequently occurs in the narrative itself when opposed points of view come into conflict. With at least an upper and a lower linguistic world recognized in the United States, a good deal of inter-translation was necessary. Sometimes the genteel narrator served as the interpreter, either furnishing a paraphrase of the vernacular, or actually defining the troublesome word. Sut Lovingood's heavy dialect required frequent explanation. George was his sympathetic but sometimes puzzled interlocutor:

"What have you been doing, Sut?"
"Helpin tu salt ole Missis Yardley down."

[10]Ibid., pp. 186, 59, 14.
[11]*Zury: The Meanest Man in Spring County* (Boston, 1887), pp. 2, 10, 21.

"What do you mean by that?"

"Fixin her fur rotten cumfurtably, kiverin her up wif sile, tu keep the buzzards frum cheatin the wurms."

"Oh, you have been helping to bury a woman."[12]

Only after Sut has provided several ugly versions of his activity can George understand and translate his idiom into acceptable decency. Sometimes the translation proceeds in the other direction, from standard down to coarse. Sut, for example, tells of a young blacksmith so smitten with love "he splotch'd his whiskers wif foam," whereupon he is asked:

"What was the matter with this Mr. Mastin? I cannot understand you, Mr. Lovingood; had he hydrophobia? . . ."

"What du yu mean by high-dry-foby? . . ."

"A madness produced by being bit by some rabid animal. . . ."

"Yas, hoss, he hed high-dry-foby *orful,* an' Mary McKildrin . . . hed gin him the complain."[13]

The one occasion when George, the representative of normality, lapses into a sentimental idiom occurs, appropriately enough, when he begins to recount a youthful escapade. Hypnotized by nostalgia, George soon reflects: "'Tis strange how faithfully memory paints the path and places belonging to our boyhood—happy, ragged, thoughtless boyhood." Sut knows that George's memory is anything but faithful, so as George muses on about "the Bluff with its triple echo . . . the Dardis lot, and its forbidden grapes . . . the old church and its graveyard," all stock ingredients of sentimental fiction, Sut exclaims, "Oh, komplikated durnashun! That hain't hit. . . . Yu's drunk, ur yure ashamed tu tell hit."

The actual incident in George's "happy, ragged, thoughtless boyhood" involved terror, violence, and a repellent conclusion in which young George splashes through an uncovered privy hole. Sut being familiar with the incident calls for a drink. "Arter I'se spunged my froat, I'll talk hit all off in English, an' yu jis watch an' see ef I say 'echo,' ur 'grapes,' ur 'graveyard' onst." Again, a specific dictional critique brings an uncustomary stress to bear upon individual words.[14]

The interchanges between Sut and George involve gross alternatives. Their misunderstandings and disputes over diction were a staple of comic writing so long as dialects existed in the United States. But as the nineteenth century progressed, this same process of criticism and redefinition began to take place within the arena of the norm. Henry James dramatizes innumerable clashes over words and the tone in which they are used:

---

[12]"Mrs. Yardley's Quilting," *Sut,* p. 134.
[13]"Rare Ripe Garden-Seed," *Sut,* p. 231.
[14]"Eaves-Dropping a Lodge of Free-Masons," *Sut,* pp. 115-16.

Richard Bridgman 213

> "I don't like the way you say that," she declared. "It's too imperious."
>
> "I beg your pardon if I say it wrong. The main point's to give you an idea of my meaning."

The linguistic issue here is no longer the crude one of decorum facing vulgarity. Now the most familiar of words come under scrutiny. One's words stand for one's experience, and as one's experience changes, the words one uses become crucial.

> "Did you ever hear anything so quaint?"
> "So 'quaint,' my dear?"

As standards and the certainties that bolster them disintegrate, the meaning of words becomes less certain. The lengthy fencing matches between Henry James's men and women represent their attempts to define themselves and their companions by defining what they say.

> "You're old enough, dear Miss Miller, to be talked about."
> Daisy wondered to extravagance. "Talked about? What do you mean?"

The defining impulse, which concentrates upon the word, is integral with the stylistic shift toward the colloquial.[15]

Definition, whether explicitly carried out or accomplished by translation or by the confrontation of two conflicting meanings for a single term, is but another way for words to achieve abnormal prominence. Still another occurs in lists of things. Lists define by proximity, by implicitly comparing similarities and contrasting differences. Lists, possessing little visible organization, are common in American vernacular writing. The natural sequence of objects as they are found in life or in the unconscious associative processes of the mind of the narrator determine the order in which the items of the list will be named.

Sut Lovingood describes the contents of an overturned cupboard:

> Pickil crocks, preserves jars, vinegar jugs, seed bags, yarb bunches, paragorick bottils, aig baskits, an' delf war—all mix'd dam permiskusly. . . .[16]

Lacking awareness of any principle of imposed order, Sut lists things as they appear—"dam permiskusly." But what then constitutes the special interest of each item in such a list? I can discern three answers, each peculiar to the vernacular tradition. First, the things in themselves are colorful and unfamiliar to conventional literature. Second, the distorted spelling forces

---

[15]"Daisy Miller," *Selected Fiction*, ed. with intr. by Leon Edel (New York: Dutton, 1953), pp. 44, 40, 48.
[16]"Sicily Burns's Wedding," *Sut*, p. 92.

extra attention on the word to decipher and to hear it. To object that the added attention required is so minimal as to be meaningless is, I think, to underestimate the sensitivity of man as a reading mechanism. Like the other irregularities common to the colloquial situation, such as italics, incomplete phrases, alliteration, repetition, word play, each misspelling makes an impression on the mind. The third distinctive feature of the list is its artful juxtaposition of things for humorous effect. Humor—and emphasis—can be achieved by placing the dandy in a frontier setting. So here Sut's list is principally composed of receptacles for foods and medicines, but he ends with Delftware smashed together with the more homely containers—crocks, jars, jugs, bags, bottles and baskets—to make a pottery version of the prim schoolmar'm suddenly thrown into the crude violence of the far West.

At the end of the century Mr. Dooley contributed another list that interests us in the same way as does Sut's list. Its terms, odd, misspelled and ironically juxtaposed, lead to a satiric climax:

> An' th' invintions—th' steam-injine an' th' bicycle an' th' flyin' machine an' th' nickel-in-th'slot machine an' th' Croker machine an' th' sody fountain an'—crownin' wur-ruk iv our civilization—th' cash ray-gisther.[17]

The atomizing effect of such a list is increased because the conjunctions serve not only as connectors but also as buffers. In the Dooley example, the reiterated "an' th'" separates the items visually as well as aurally. The conjunctions establish an exclusive territory for each noun. The effect is that of a line of people on a darkened stage, each in turn being caught by a spotlight. Or, reading such a list resembles watching a long freight train pass by, the items being the cars, the conjunctions the couplings. Each item is independent, yet joined to the whole. The conjunctions are also unifiers in their unobtrusive and monotonous way. As the separate cars roll by, an underlying rhythmic beat is felt. The variety of a list is notable, yet there is a basic regularity to it which can be worked by the skilled writer. In the following sentence from *Huckleberry Finn* Mark Twain repeats "I took" three times, then discards "I," in the next unit, and finally discards "took" to move into a crescendo of physical items:

> *I took* all the coffee and sugar there was, and all the ammunition; *I took* the wadding; *I took* the bucket and gourd; *took* a dipper and a tin cup, and my old saw and two blankets, and the skillet and the coffee-pot. (ch. 7, italics added)

In lists of physical objects, and in sentences like this where the verbs are muted, things are displayed in themselves. They do nothing; they are merely

[17]Finley Peter Dunne, "On the Victorian Era," in Walter Blair, *Native American Humor* (San Francisco: Chandler Publications, 1960), p. 461. Hereinafter, *NAH*.

available for inspection as objects at rest. Such static displays also heighten the importance of the individual word.

The compound sentence characteristic of colloquial prose is basically a list—a list of actions. The vernacular speaker offers those actions in an unsubordinated series, just as he does physical objects. He seems to display only the crudest awareness of how the actions are related, not because of stupidity, but because he literally recounts the events in the order in which they occurred. This focuses attention upon the single unit of action as it is caught and isolated between commas and conjunctions. One can observe the increased technical proficiency with which the compound sentence is managed by beginning with the irregular extravagance of an 1843 dialect story, then moving to the fluent simplicity of *Huckleberry Finn* in the 1880's, and finally to the deliberately angular rhythm of a Hemingway sentence written in the 1930's. First, "Mike Hooter's Bar Story":

> Torectly I see Ike take down the ole shooter, AND kinder kersamine [examine] the lock, AN' when he done that, he laid her on his shoulder, AND shook his fist at the bar, AND walked towards home, AN' the bar he shuk his fist, AN' went into the cane brake, AND then I cum off.[18]

Then Huck Finn:

> I went out in the woods AND cooked a supper, AND I had about made up my mind I would stay there all night when I heard a *plunkety-plunk, plunkety-plunk,* AND says to myself, horses coming, AND next I hear people's voices. (ch. 8, capitals added)

And finally, a Hemingway drifter speaks:

> I could see her floating plain AND I hit the glass twice with the wrench hard AND I heard the noise clink in my ears BUT it wouldn't break AND I had to come up.[19]

Such compound sentences originate naturally in the psychology of the colloquial situation. Because the speaker lacks the time to distribute the events in synthetic categories, he produces a linear sequence, moving from event to event, observing democratic equality in the arrangement of his clauses. The most repeated phrase in *Huckleberry Finn* is "by-and-by" which is no more than a vernacular alternative to "and then. . . ." Actions enumerated but barely related constitute the basic sentence of the colloquial style.

The enumeration of events is but the last of the many ways we have discovered in which the psychology of speech separates and emphasizes the

---

[18]William Hall, *Cycl.,* p. 220. (Capitals added.)
[19]"After the Storm," *The Short Stories of Ernest Hemingway* (New York: Modern Library, 1938), p. 472. (Capitals added.) Hereinafter, *Short Stories.*

single word and phrase. The word may be deformed for dialectal accuracy. It may represent an instance of word-play, a malapropism, or a pun. The word may be drawn from unfamiliar jargon, or it may be coined for the occasion. It may be italicized, repeated, defined, discussed, or argued about. Moreover, the colloquial prose surface is fragmented by the cut-and-thrust of dialogue, by the rhetorical emphases of one speaker, and by the groping hesitancy of another. And, as the stylization of colloquial prose continued, its ground was cleared of the underbrush of qualification. The subject-verb-object relationship was made as direct as possible, and then, with the burden on each word heavier than ever before, each word took on an added importance. But even as individual words achieved increased independence, the basic unifying elements among them also emerged into prominence.

The propensity of colloquial prose to fragment is compensated for by its innate repetitiveness. It is true that instances of repetition occur in all writing, but not to the degree that they do in colloquial prose. The colloquial writer will retain, and at the pitch of stylization even cultivate, repetition. It begins in the simplest possible way, with single letters and syllables— "a-quaking and shaking"—and extends on up through full independent clauses—"She loved to fish. She loved to fish with Nick."[20] The repetitions are visual and semantic as well as aural. Their source often appears to be below the level of consciousness, although in the later stages of colloquial writing, heightened technical awareness diminishes the incidence of inadvertent repetition.

Repetition often turns up when the action is crucial, or where the writer-speaker is in some way thoroughly engaged. With the mind diverted, one combination of letters summons up a similar combination. Extemporaneous speakers such as the revivalist depend upon the repetition of phrases to hold the audience, but they themselves become mesmerized by the rhythms of their speech. "Oh, come to the mourners' bench! come, black with sin! (*amen!*) come, sick and sore! (*amen!*) come, lame and halt, and blind! (*amen!*) come, pore and needy, sunk in shame! (*a-a-men!*) (*HF,* ch. 20). Here meaning plays a distinctly secondary role to patterned noise.

Any kind of distraction or mutiny of the intellectual monitor may increase verbal echoes. A journalist keeping a day-to-day account of the deliberations of the U.S. Senate describes "Cordell Hull's very hush-hush huddle."[21] The stupor of fatigue and narcotics in which Norman Mailer testifies he revised *The Deer Park* may be responsible for such phrases as "men lacquered with liquor" and a "painful jail of jealousy."[22] Or, to take a quite

---

[20]*Huckleberry Finn,* ch. 13; and "The End of Something," *Short Stories,* p. 206.
[21]Allen Drury, *A Senate Journal: 1943-1945* (New York: McGraw-Hill Book Co., 1963), p. 119.
[22]*The Deer Park* (New York: Putnam, 1955), pp. 4, 257. In *Advertisements for Myself* (New York: Putnam, 1959), pp. 238-9, Mailer describes the writing of *The Deer Park:* "I worked by tricks, taking marijuana the night before and then drugging myself into sleep . . . benzedrine entered the balance."

different example, Beatrix Potter's first story of Peter Rabbit displays un-
mistakable sound associations not present in her other work, probably
because she improvised the original story in a letter to a child. So, the
onomatopoetic sound of a hoe determines the verb that follows: "the noise
of a hoe—SCR-R-RITCH, SCRATCH, SCRATCH, SCRITCH. Peter SCUTTERED
underneath the bushes." When Peter emerges, his vantage point calls up
the next verb: "He came out, and climbed upon a WHEELBARROW, and
PEEPED over."[23] The improvisation, haste, and distraction evidenced in
these quotations constitute an integral part of the colloquial situation.

We can never determine absolutely what the author's state of awareness
was at the time of composition, but the distinction between conscious and
unconscious sound association can be demonstrated in three passages
from Harriet Beecher Stowe's "The Minister's Wooing." When Mrs. Stowe
writes,

> They fussed and fuzzled and wuzzled till they'd drinked up all the
> tea in the teapot,

one is confident that she deliberately encouraged the alliteration for the
reader's amusement. But in a second sentence marked by a high incidence
of the letter "p," one cannot ascertain with any confidence how conscious
the alliteration was:

> Huldy . . . showed 'em her pantries, and her cakes, and her pies, and
> her puddin's, and took 'em all over the house; and they went peekin'
> and pokin' . . .

Finally, when Mrs. Stowe catalogues some flowers to lend color rather than
humor to her story, the syllable "-ar" dominates her list. But it seems improbable that she deliberately assembled the unobtrusive internal rhymes:

> Huldy planted marigolds and larkspurs, pinks and carnations . . . and
> trained up mornin' glories and scarlet runners round the windows.[24]

The repeated syllable either emanates from the unconscious or represents
a case of sheer coincidence.

Fits of alliteration and other sound repetitions and associations may be
brought on then when the writer is more preoccupied with the imagined experience than with the surface of his prose. This is no more than to say that
instances of repetition arise more often in speech than in writing, and more
often in colloquial writing than in other prose. The writer may be excited,
he may be pleasurably relaxed, he may be writing in a hurry, but the result
will be an increase in sound associations. Henry Nash Smith has pointed

---

[23]*The Tale of Peter Rabbit* (New York: Warne, 1904), pp. 48, 49. (Capitals added.)
[24]*The Humour of America*, ed. James Barr (London and New York, 1894), pp. 63, 69, 69. Hereinafter, *HA*.

out that "when Mark Twain is working up a rhetorical effect, he resorts to conspicuous alliteration ('winding rivers, and weary wastes')."[25] Mark Twain alliterates not only when he himself is straining for an effect, but also when circumstances strain his character Huck Finn. When the crowd disinters Peter Wilks, Huck's tension heightens the alliteration, the rhyme, and the repetition of whole words:

> So they *dug* and *dug* like everything; and it got awful *dark,* and the rain *started,* and the wind *swished* and *swushed* along, and the lightning came *brisker* and *brisker.* . . . At last they got out the coffin and begun to un*screw* the lid, and then such another *crowding* and *shouldering* and *shoving* as there was, to *scrouge* in and get a *sight,* you never *see.* . . . (ch. 29, italics added)

Rhetorical control for the colloquial writer begins in repetition and controlled variation. Even as he jettisons conventional arrangements for his prose, he begins to build new ones in his own medium. The listing of food at a Tennessee frolic is threaded through with the sound "uh."

> The SUPPER is made UP by the fellers; every one fetches SUMTHIN; SUM A lick of meal, SUM A middlin of bacon, SUM A hen, SUM A POSSUM, SUM A PUNKIN, SUM A grab of taters, or a pocket of peas, or dried apples, an SUM only fetches a good appetite and a skin chock FULL of particular deviltry.[26]

The effect is one of casually managed variety. The serpentine sentence, made up like this one of a series of separate images, each of which emerges to take on a peculiar brilliance, the whole unified by the droning regularity of the narrator's tone and supplemented by the alliterative rhythm, is common to the colloquial.

> Well, the eyes KEP COMIN' CLOSER and CLOSER. and gettin BIGGER and BRIGHTER, and the fust thing I know'd ther was a whole grist of 'em all follerin' right after the fust ones, and DODGIN' up and DOWN in the DARK like they was so many DANCIN' DEVILS.[27]

Even when the repetition is not exact, one word conjures up a compatible partner. Threaded throughout *Huckleberry Finn* are such phrases as

> squirming and scrouging
> moaning and mourning
> sobbing and swabbing

[25]*Mark Twain: The Development of a Writer* (Cambridge: Harvard University Press, 1962), p. 17.
[26]"S —— L" of Tennessee, "Dick Harlan's Tennessee Frolic," *Quarter Race,* p. 83. (Capitals added.)
[27]W. T. Thompson, "The Fire-Hunt," *Cycl.,* p. 243. (Capitals added.)

Richard Bridgman 219

                    fretted and sweated
                    thinking, and wrinkling
                    warmed up and went warbling and warbling
                    chipping in a little Scripture (chs. 21, 23, 25, 31, 31, 29, 28)

Mark Twain's sensibility responded with unusual acuteness to the stimuli
of sounds, especially in this book. These minute repetitions and a thousand
others constitute the musical murmur of Huck's voice. From time to time
it breaks into overt but diversified repetition. The form of

                    dug and dug
        and
                    brisker and brisker
        is varied by the comma in
                    he drank, and drank;
        and by the italics in
                    and begged and *begged*
        and
                    well, go on, *go* on:
        and it lengthens into
                    and listened, and listened, and listened
        as well as
                    always moving back, and back, and back
        and
                    told me to say it *again,* say it *again,* say it *again!* (chs. 29, 29, 6,
                    25, 27, 40, 21, 28)

As some of these quotations suggest, the eye makes associations, too.
In the phrase, "It STOOD on her BACKSTOOP, minus a HOOP,"[28] one passes
from the "stoo-" in *stood* to its visual repetition in *stoop;* then on to the
aural repetition of "-oop" in *hoop.* In *Huckleberry Finn* the "oh" sound is
mixed with the "ow" look:

        . . . besides some TOW. I TOTED up a LOAD, and went back and set
        down on the BOW of the skiff to rest. (ch. 6, capitals added)

Nor need the associations literally repeat. They may only approximate
the original. Consider these three sentences from *Huckleberry Finn:*

        It was all grass clear to the canoe; so I hadn't left a track. I followed
        around to see. I stood on the bank and looked out over the river. All
        safe. (ch. 7)

Can there be any doubt that "all grass" produced "all safe"? Or when Huck
sees a canoe "riding high like a duck," does not that observation of aquatic

---

[28]J. M. Bailey, "Tempest in a Tub," *HA*, p. 128.

wild life give rise to the figure of speech with which he describes his next action?—"I shot head first off the bank, like a frog" (ch. 7).

The associations may reveal a pictorial or semantic connection as well as a visual or aural one. The vision of a log calls up the idiom "fit to split" when Mike Hooter finds himself in a state of high amusement: "I never see ennything so funny in all my life! There was I layin' down behind er log, fit to split. . . ."[29] A newspaper reviewer of the novel *Candy* observed that although it had "sold like hotcakes," any public discussion of its subject necessarily called for "fudging."[30] Another reviewer of a biography of Lord Alfred Douglas fittingly enough referred to a "pugnacity, marked by the Queensberry rules."[31]

The level at which such associations are created may often be below what we would deem conscious; so in fact may be their reception. But the point is that all of these various repetitions and associations go to make up the unity of form in colloquial prose. They join company with the frequent occurrence of co-ordinating conjunctions, which Walt Whitman sometimes brought to the fore in his verse.

> I believe in those wing'd purposes,
> And acknowledge red, yellow, white, playing within me,
> And consider green and violet and the tufted crown intentional
> And do not call the tortoise unworthy because she is not
>   something else,
> And the jay in the woods never studied the gamut, yet trills pretty
>   well to me,
> And the look of the bay mare shames silliness out of me.[32]

Compare this with a sentence from *Huckleberry Finn*, similarly arranged:

> Then she got to talking about her husband,
> And about her relations up the river,
> And her relations down the river,
> And about how much better off they used to was,
> And how they didn't know but they'd make a mistake coming to our
>   town, instead of letting well alone—
> And so on and so on,
> Till I was afeard *I* had made a mistake coming to her to find out what
>   was going on in the town;
> But by-and-by she dropped onto pap and the murder,
> And then I was pretty willing to let her clatter right along.
>   (ch. 11)

---

[29]William Hall, "Mike Hooter's Bar Story," *Cycl.*, p. 219.
[30]Donald Stanley, "The Sex Revolution," *People* in *The California Weekly*, San Francisco *Examiner*, June 28, 1964, p. 15.
[31]Richard Ellmann, "In Lord Alfred's Camp," *The New York Review of Books*, II, No. 6 (April 30, 1964), 7.
[32]"Song of Myself," sec. 13.

These co-ordinating conjunctions furnish the beat for long colloquial sentences. The sense may wander, the meaning may cloud over, and clarification may never come (since cloudiness is the truest vision of the moment), but underneath it all pulsates that monotonous, barely noticeable rhythm of the conjunctions, sufficiently dependable to sustain equilibrium and to provide the confidence and comfort that go with it.

The resemblance between Whitman and the colloquial prose writer is no more coincidental than the frequent references to the poetic quality of modern American prose. When the distractions of the abnormal, the clownish, and the awkward handling of the colloquial manner were eliminated, what remained was a highly rhythmic prose with frequent internal rhyme and alliteration, making concentrated statements with concrete images. In the first flush of colloquial stylization, the following sentence from Hemingway's "My Old Man" was the rule rather than the exception:

"He won't win," George says very low, leaning
over and buttoning the bottoms of his breeches.[33]

Colloquial writers had to become aware of the repetition inherent in their prose and of what use they might make of it. In the process of stylizing the colloquial traits learned in dialogue, American writers seized on repetition to restore a coherence threatened by that fragmentation which was in turn produced by the stress of individual words and phrases. The way of fragmentation led toward incoherence, the way of repetition toward verse. Discretion and practice were needed to reach a prose compromise.

NORTHROP FRYE

From *The Well-Tempered Critic*

Northrop Frye holds the chair of Professor of the University at Toronto. Among his many books are Anatomy of Criticism *(1957) and* The Well-Tempered Critic *(1963), from which the following selection has been taken. Professor Frye's critical theories have had a more profound effect on literary criticism than those of any other recent critic. In* The Well-Tempered Critic *Frye distinguishes three verbal rhythms: "the verse rhythm dominated by recurring beat, the prose rhythm dominated by the sentence with its subject-*

---

[33]*Short Stories*, p. 295.
From *The Well-Tempered Critic* by Northrup Frye, copyright 1963, pp. 57-66. Reprinted by permission of Indiana University Press.

predicate relation, and the associative rhythm dominated by the short and irregular phrase. Of these, the verse rhythm belongs, now, entirely to literature, and the prose rhythm both to literature and to ordinary speech. The associative rhythm belongs, in its pure form, to undeveloped ordinary speech or to the representing of such speech in fiction or drama. . . ." The following is an analysis of the prose rhythm.

Let us begin with normal prose, the language of exposition and description which can be used for either literary or non-literary purposes. Here is a passage from Darwin's *Origin of Species:*

> The great and inherited development of the udders in cows and goats, in countries where they are habitually milked, in comparison with these organs in other countries, is probably another instance of the effects of use. Not one of our domestic animals can be named which has not in some country drooping ears; and the view which has been suggested, that the drooping is due to the disuse of the muscles of the ear, from the animal's being seldom alarmed, seems probable.

I have chosen this passage partly because it is prose at some distance from an associative rhythm. It is, in other words, emphatically written prose: anyone who talked like this would be thought pedantic. Still, it is solidly built in a Victorian model, and does not lack either rhythm or readability. Its rhythm is based on the sentence, and it is readable because that rhythm is consistent. We notice a bit of alliteration in it ("the drooping is due to the disuse"), and the alliteration gives a touch of a slightly more vigorous stress accent. The touch is welcome: Darwin has not tried to avoid it, and such a feature, if it appeared in dull or incompetent prose, would not have such a function. Yet we are confident that it is purely "accidental": if we felt it was deliberate we should be annoyed with Darwin. There is an associative trace with the repetition in "probable": this is not good prose style, but again it is unconscious, and so helps to assure us that we are proceeding with the right kind of scientific caution.

Now let us take a passage from Gibbon's *Decline and Fall of the Roman Empire:*

> Every circumstance of the secular games was skilfully adapted to inspire the superstitious mind with deep and solemn reverence. The long interval between them exceeded the term of human life; and as none of the spectators had already seen them, none could flatter themselves with the expectation of beholding them a second time. The mystic sacrifices were performed, during three nights, on the banks of the Tiber; and the Campus Martius resounded with music and dances, and was illuminated with innumerable lamps and torches . . . A chorus of twenty-seven youths, and as many virgins, of noble families, and whose parents were both alive, implored the propitious gods in favour

of the present, and for the hope of the rising generation; requesting, in religious hymns, that, according to the faith of their ancient oracles, they would still maintain the virtue, the felicity, and the empire of the Roman people.

This is still expository prose, designed to convey information. But here we are aware of deliberate tricks of style, such as the doubling of adjectives and the antithetical balancing of clauses. If we feel annoyed with these devices, we should avoid reading Gibbon: they are his conventions, inseparable from his kind of readability. Gibbon is writing not direct prose but consciously rhetorical prose; or, as we say, he is a "stylist." The stylizing of his sentences indicates a more self-conscious bid for literary fame. He expects to be read for entertainment, in the genuine sense, as well as instruction, and he expects this quality to keep him alive after his work as a historian has been superseded. As part of this he is asking us to develop a *meditative* interest in the theme of the decline of the world's greatest ancient empire. It is the meditative quality in his work that makes his book a permanent possession of literature and not simply a contribution to scholarship: a quality of wisdom and insight rather than merely of learning, and one which may range in the mood of its expression from solemnity to irony. This meditative quality manifests itself in prose sentences with a distinctive roll in them which is unmistakably metrical. If we stop a sentence of Darwin's in the middle, we feel chiefly that certain words are needed to complete the sense: if we stop a sentence of Gibbon's in the middle, we feel that there is also a rhythmical space to be filled up, as we should if we interrupted the reading of verse.

The rhetorical quality of Gibbon's prose puts him close to oratory, and in oratory, though the controlling form is still prose, the chief appeal is to the emotions or the imagination, so that the meditative element is considerably increased. There is a corresponding increase in the metrical influence, especially in the repetitive passages that form the climaxes of so many orations. In (for instance) the Gettysburg address and in Churchill's 1940 speeches, we see how the sentence rhythm breaks up into balanced clauses, or, in moments of emotional climax, into a series of phrase-units, with a recurring accentual pattern that brings it close to verse. We remember Lincoln's "of the people, by the people, for the people," and Churchill's "We shall fight on the beaches; we shall fight in the hills." Here is a similar example from Samuel Johnson's letter to Chesterfield:

The notice which you have been pleased to take of my labours, had it been early, had been kind; but it has been delayed until I am indifferent, and cannot enjoy it; till I am solitary, and cannot impart it; till I am known, and do not want it.

In more than one sense these are "measured" words. We noticed a similar phrase-unit in the monologues of Jingle and Bloom, but these are quite different in effect, because rhetorical, fully aware of a present and an invisible audience. It is possible, of course, to have a more introverted prose rhetoric with the same kind of rhythm, where the author pretends to be talking to himself but is actually working out a stylistic or rhetorical exercise, as in Sir Thomas Browne's *Urn Burial* or Jeremy Taylor's *Holy Dying*. Oratory and metrical rhythm are as evident in Browne's great meditation on death as they are in a contemporary baroque prose form, the *oraison funèbre* of Bossuet:

> The spirits put off their malice with their bodies, and Caesar and Pompey accord in Latin Hell, yet Ajax in Homer endures not a conference with Ulysses; and Deiphobus appears all mangled in Virgil's Ghosts, yet we meet with perfect shadows among the wounded ghosts of Homer.

Oratory, then, and rhetorical prose generally, is one of our secondary or mixed forms, a form of prose which shows a considerable influence from verse. One important influence on English rhetorical prose, Biblical parallelism, is a Hebrew verse form reproduced in prose.

But suppose, now, that a more restless and experimental writer were to take a further step, and produce an extreme form of prose, as strongly affected by the characteristics of verse as it could be and still remain prose. This would give us what is known as euphuism, a form of prose in which all the rhetorical devices of verse, rhyme, alliteration, assonance and a half-metrical balancing of phrases and clauses, are employed. Such a prose would contain all the features that a normal prose writer would do his best to eliminate. Here is a euphuistic sentence from Robert Greene's *Card of Fancy:*

> This loathsome life of Gwydonius, was such a cutting corrasive to his father's careful conscience, and such a hapless clog to his heavy heart, that no joy could make him enjoy any joy, no mirth could make him merry, no prosperity could make him pleasant, but abandoning all delight, and avoiding all company, he spent his doleful days in dumps and dolours, which he uttered in these words.

We are not surprised to learn that euphuism is of rhetorical origin, deriving partly from sermons, and a euphuistic story, true to its rhetorical ancestry, tends to keep breaking down into a series of harangues. The passage just quoted, as its final phrase indicates, leads up to a harangue, and in Greene's story the hero and heroine eventually settle down to writing letters at each other, each letter a rhetorical exercise. Thus the increase of meditative and rhetorical elements in metrical prose tends to make for discontinuity. We noticed that "primary" forms of prose and verse, like the treatise and the epic, are continuous. One either reads or does not read the *Origin of Species;* but the *Decline and Fall,* with its greater meditative and literary interest, one can read more discontinuously, stopping here and there or going back, if one is familiar with it, to certain passages. In euphuism the discontinuity has begun to affect the structure.

Along with discontinuity there comes a certain sense of paradox. Euphuism, as we remember from Falstaff, is easy to parody, but in euphuism itself there is a curious quality that is really a kind of self-parody. Its ingenuity makes it witty, and the wit may be conscious or, at times, unconscious: one wonders which it is in Lyly's "which I cannot without blushing behold, or without blubbering utter." Euphuism was an experimental style, and so had its vogue and then quickly went out of fashion, as experimental styles usually do. But what euphuism represents, the ornamenting of a prose rhythm with as many of the features of verse as possible, is a permanent technical resource of style, and will reappear whenever occasion seems to call for it. Here, handled with great tact and skill, is a passage of modern euphuism: the familiar opening of Dylan Thomas's *Under Milk Wood:*

> It is Spring, moonless night in the small town, starless and bible-black, the cobblestreets silent and the hunched, courters'-and-rabbits' wood limping invisible down to the sloeblack, slow, black, crowblack, fishingboat-bobbing sea.

When oratorical prose is pushed to the limit of euphuism, an associative element begins to make itself felt in the writing. But here we discover a whole area of associative rhythm which we have not yet touched on. It is clear that associative speech, if sufficiently confused and off its guard, will often produce the unconscious wit of malapropism, a nice derangement of epitaphs. One step further takes us into the poetic process itself, the largely subconscious free association of words by sound out of which the schemata of poetry develop. In euphuism, where the underlying rhythm is that of prose, such associations are not subconscious but are deliberately added ornament, and this deliberate quality is the reason for the sense of self-parody in euphuism, as though, on Freudian principles, a normally suppressed mental process were made humorous by being openly displayed.

WALKER GIBSON

Tough Talk:
The Rhetoric of Frederic Henry

Walker Gibson is professor of English at the University of Massachusetts. He has written widely and informatively on rhetoric and criticism. One of his early essays, "Authors, Speakers, Readers, and Mock Readers"(College English, XI [February 1950], 265-269) has had a significant influence on such rhetorical critics as Wayne Booth, who records his debt to Gibson in The Rhetoric of Fiction *(1961). In "Authors, Speakers, Readers, and Mock Readers" Gibson argues that in every literary work an author creates a speaker who "is made of language alone," but at the same time the author also creates a particular reader who is the "new person"—the mock reader—we become each time we imaginatively enter a literary work. Gibson's most recent book,* Tough, Sweet and Stuffy *(1966) is an application of the rhetorical theory presented in his early essay to the problem of style. In this book Gibson identifies the three dominant styles of modern American prose. Tough style, which is discussed in the selection below, presents us with a speaker who is "a hard fellow who has been around in a violent world and who pays us very little mind." Sweet style creates a speaker who is "an affable fellow who is familiar with us and knows just who we are." Stuffy style creates a speaker who withdraws into an "omniscient and polysyllabic detachment."*

I did not say anything. I was always embarassed by the words . . . .

When a new style swims into our ken, as Hemingway's did in the 1920s, it is new, or was new, in respect to a historical situation. People brought to their reading, just as they still do of course, a set of assumptions about how books ought to be written. No novelist would be interested in a reader who had never read a novel, or who had never experienced, as *he* has experienced, the going literature of the recent past. So Hemingway's assumed reader of the 1920s had an ear tuned to nineteenth-century rhythms and attitudes; it was in their light that Hemingway's style appeared so fresh and exciting. It is still exciting, if not exactly fresh, a generation later, which is testimony enough to the power of a great writer.

But in order to remind ourselves of some of the stylistic expectations against which Hemingway was first read, and to some extent must still be read, it will be useful to contrast the opening of *A Farewell to Arms* (1929) with the opening of a standard sort of American novel of forty years earlier. The opening I have chosen, from W. D. Howells' *A Modern Instance* (1888), has some superficial resemblance in stage setting to Hemingway's opening that may make the contrast in style the more striking. In each case a narrator is introducing us to a scene as well as to himself, and both scenes include a *village* on a *plain,* in the *summer,* with a view of *mountains* and a *river.*

PASSAGE A (HOWELLS)

The village stood on a wide plain, and around it rose the mountains. They were green to their tops in summer, and in the winter white through their serried pines and drifting mists, but at every season serious and beautiful, furrowed with hollow shadows, and taking the light on masses and stretches of iron-grey crag. The river swam through the plain in long curves, and slipped away at last through an unseen pass to the southward, tracing a score of miles in its course over a space that measured but three or four. The plain was very fertile, and its features, if few and of purely utilitarian beauty, had a rich luxuriance, and there was a tropical riot of vegetation when the sun of July beat on those northern fields. They waved with corn and oats to the feet of the mountains, and the potatoes covered a vast acreage with the lines of their intense, coarse green; the meadows were deep with English grass to the banks of the river, that, doubling and returning upon itself, still marked its way with a dense fringe of alders and white birches.

PASSAGE B (HEMINGWAY)

In the late summer of that year we lived in a house in a village that looked across the river and the plain to the mountains. In the bed of the river there were pebbles and boulders, dry and white in the sun, and the water was clear and swiftly moving and blue in the channels. Troops went by the house and down the road and the dust they raised powdered the leaves of the trees. The trunks of the trees too were dusty and the leaves fell early that year and we saw the troops marching along the road and the dust rising and leaves, stirred by the breeze, falling and the soldiers marching and afterward the road bare and white except for the leaves.

The plain was rich with crops; there were many orchards of fruit trees and beyond the plains the mountains were brown and bare. There was fighting in the mountains and at night we could see the flashes from the artillery. In the dark it was like summer lightning, but the nights were cool and there was not the feeling of a storm coming.

Who are these two people talking to us?

The narrator in Passage A (Howells) is concerned with making us see and know the landscape surrounding the village, and he can do this because he can occupy a position where *he* sees and knows this landscape intimately.

Let us begin by locating this position, which is expressible in respect to both space and time. Physically, the narrator can speak as from a cloud, a balloon, floating wide-eyed over the plain. He sees large features of the scene—the mountains, the course of the winding river, the fields with their crops. It is a bird's-eye view. He also occupies a favorable position in time. He has been here before, he *knows*. He knows, for example, how the mountains look not only in summer (the *then* of the opening scene), but in winter as well. (Sentence A-2.) He knows (A-3), even though it is not at present visible, that the river slips away "through an unseen pass" to the southward. This is a speaker whose particular rhetorical personality, which would look very strange in a novel of the second half of the twentieth century, serves to inspire our confidence, partly from its very antiquity. Note that as assumed readers we date the speaker immediately, however vaguely, and date ourselves as well, by ruling out some twentieth-century suspicions and expectations. We are introduced to a familiar kind of traditional gentlemanly voice whose tones we associate with Standard Literature, and whose word we accept absolutely. This man knows what there is to know about this scene. We are in good hands.

The man talking in Passage B speaks to us from an utterly different position. As he thinks back on his experience in the village—and note that it is *his* experience that he thinks back on—the positions he occupies are drastically more limited than those of our airborne observer in A. Everything described in B can be seen (or almost seen) from one place, the house where *he* lived. The language keeps reminding us of this limitation by returning to the speaker and his companions (*we*) and their vantage point for seeing and feeling. The house "looked across the river"; "we saw the troops"; "we could see the flashes"; "there was not the feeling of a storm coming." The speaker's range is similarly limited in time; all he tells us about is the way things looked during one particular late summer as it became autumn. The other seasons, before he came to live in the village, or after he left, he presumably doesn't know about. We hear the familiar "flatness" of the voice addressing us, the speaker's refusal to say more than he knows from ordinary human experience. He is close-lipped. The simplicity of his style, the apparent simplicity of it, is of course notorious. You would not call this man genial. He behaves rather as if he had known us, the reader, a long time and therefore doesn't have to pay us very much attention. He is more tense, more intense, than A. And after all, we should observe, he is dealing with images of war, and not with a peaceful New England landscape.

So much for one reader's quick first impression of the two personalities addressing us and the positions from which they speak. But I propose a longer look at some grammatical and rhetorical peculiarities of these two speakers, returning often to their personalities and positions to ask how these have been created, and how we may refine our first impressions. How are these impressions justified by the language, if they are? How do details of wording force us to certain conclusions about the man we're being introduced to? If some of what follows seems alarmingly statistical and detailed, I would argue that only by such devices can we begin to understand the effort that went into these two creative acts.

Words, their size. Everybody knows that Hemingway's diction is characterized by short, simple, largely Anglo-Saxon words. Howells' vocabulary is more conventionally extensive. Actually, in the Howells passage, almost three-quarters of the words are monosyllables, while only one word out of twenty is longer than two syllables. It is hardly an elaborate or affected diction. Yet we recognize in Howells that there are particular words, especially the longer words, which for various reasons would be unthinkable in Hemingway. Among them are *beautiful, utilitarian, luxuriance*—and I shall have more to say about them below. For the present, we note that in passage B, the Hemingway passage, over four-fifths of the words (82 per cent) are of one syllable only, an extremely high proportion. What is more remarkable, only two words, or about one in a hundred, are more than two syllables in length. (These two are *afterward* and *artillery,* neither of them very formidable.) The rigorous selection, or limitation, in vocabulary that these figures imply is drastic, and certainly contributes largely to our sense of a laconic, hard-bitten, close-talking fellow. He is literally *curt.*

Modifiers. An important distinction in the way the two speakers choose words has to do with the frequency of their modifiers. What would we expect of a man who knows, who is magically airborne over the landscape, as against a speaker who is laconically reporting the facts of his own limited experience? We would expect that the former would be more free with his modifiers, would be, that is, willing to name the qualities and virtues of things, not just the things themselves. Actually there are about twice as many modifiers in the Howells as in the Hemingway. Some of Howells' adjectives, in particular, have obvious implications of value: *serious, beautiful, rich, utilitarian.* While many others are simply descriptive (if that is possible), such as *green, deep, dense,* every one of the modifiers in B is of the type that purports to avoid value and simply state facts, especially physical facts: *dry, white, blue, dusty, swiftly,* and so on.

Nouns and repetition. A count of nouns in the two passages results in almost identical figures. But because of a great difference in repetition of nouns, there is a difference in the actual repertoire the two writers use. There are 47 appearances of nouns in A, and because repetition is negligible there are 43 different nouns used. In Hemingway I count 46 noun appearances with a remarkable refrain of repetition. Fourteen nouns appear twice or three times; only 32 different nouns are to be found in the passage. The effect of this rather astonishing contrast is worth speculating on. It helps us, again, to understand why we could call the B narrator "close-lipped." He simply doesn't use many words! There is a critical suggestion to the speaker's personality, as if he were saying, I'm not one of your fancy writers, always scrabbling around for elegant variation. I say what I mean. If I mean the same thing twice, I *say* the same thing twice, and I don't care if it offends the so-called rules of so-called graceful prose.

Imagery, abstract and concrete. It is a commonplace about modern writers, and it may seem to be borne out by our analysis up to this point, that the more recent writers are concerned hardheadedly with things-as-they-are, with precise description rather than with the evaluative blur that we like to think characterizes the older literature. Everybody's passion nowadays for being "concrete" rather than "abstract" represents a fashionable general attitude. But, judging from the present evidence, the commonplace may not be true. Nobody knows, I suspect, how to distinguish concrete words from abstract in any very satisfactory way, but suppose we apply in all innocence this rule of thumb: which of our two speakers tells us more about the scene, supposing we wanted to paint a picture of it? There is no doubt that it is Howells. It is not simply Hemingway's paucity of nouns and modifiers that handicaps him as a scene-painter. It is his very choice of the nouns and modifiers that he does use. Where Hemingway writes *trees*, Howells names them—*alders, birches*. Where Hemingway refers to *crops* and *orchards*, Howells gives us *corn, oats*, and *potatoes*. It is true that Howells includes some words normally thought of as "abstract" (*features, beauty, luxuriance*), while Hemingway gives us plenty of "concrete" nouns, *pebbles* and *boulders, mountains, orchards, soldiers*. But the result is what matters, and in this case the result is that the language creates, in A, a narrator who *cares* about telling us what the landscape looked like, and in B we sense a narrator who cares about something else.

What else does he care about? Why does he, in spite of his superficial and apparent concreteness, tell us so little specifically about the scene? Because the scene, from his position, is not important except as it contributes to his own feelings, his remembered feelings. His recurrences to the act of personal viewing mentioned earlier (*We saw, we could see*) are reminders of the highly personal interest of this speaker. He is not concerned with having us see the landscape, but in having us understand *how he felt*. This is a very different aim; all his devices of grammar and rhetoric are chosen to achieve this aim.

Sentences, their size and structure. Again the short sentence in Hemingway is a commonplace observation, and it no doubt contributes to the curtness we have been noticing. Actually, in these two passages, the difference is only between an average length of 38 words and of 28 words—nothing very spectacular. Much more interesting is the grammatical structure of the sentences of each passage. In A we have both compound and compound-complex sentences, with considerable subordination of clauses. In B we have largely compound sentences made up of coordinate clauses strung together with *and*. (Sentence B-4 is a good example.) When we count up subordinate clauses in the two passages, we discover that in B there are only two, and they are informal and inconspicuous. "The dust they raised," for instance, gives us a modifying clause without the signal *that*, an omission common in oral speech. We are reminded that the narrator knows us, speaks familiarly, doesn't in fact go out of his way for us much. Modifying clauses in A, on the other hand, are crucially different. Here their formal qualities are directed not toward maintaining a pose of familiarity with a reader, but instead toward seriously clarifying for the reader, whom the speaker has only just met, what the landscape looked like. The second half of Sentence A-5, for example, offers us a subordinate clause of some elegance and considerable skill.

> . . . the meadows were deep with English grass to the banks of the river, that, doubling and returning upon itself, still marked its way with a dense fringe of alders and white birches.

One may not wish to go so far as to say that the very phrasing here, in its leisurely meandering, doubles and returns upon itself like the river, but one would have to say, at least, that a subordinate clause of this kind, punctuated in this way, would look very odd in Hemingway. You do not talk this way to someone you know easily and intimately.

More spectacular in the Hemingway style, of course, are the successions of coordinate clauses linked by *and*. It is a highly significant grammatical expression, and its significance can be grasped if one tries irreverently to rewrite a coordinate Hemingway sentence in more traditional patterns of subordination. Here is the original sentence B-4, for instance:

> The trunks of the trees too were dusty and the leaves fell early that year and we saw the troops marching along the road and the dust rising and leaves, stirred by the breeze, falling and the soldiers marching and afterward the road bare and white except for the leaves.

Now here is a version attempting to subordinate some of the clauses:

> The leaves fell early that year, which revealed the dusty trunks of the trees and the marching troops on the road; when the troops went by, we saw the dust rise, while the leaves fell, stirred by the breeze, but after the soldiers had gone the road was bare and white except for the leaves.

The original B-6 reads this way:

> There was fighting in the mountains and at night we could see the flashes from the artillery.

If we subordinate one of these clauses, we must state a relation between them—for example the relation of logical cause:

> We knew there was fighting in the mountains, for at night we could see the flashes from the artillery.

Now the damage done to the original, in both cases, is of course catastrophic. In the original B-6, the speaker doesn't say how he knew there was fighting in the mountains. It was just there, ominous, baldly stated. The awareness of the fighting and the seeing of the flashes are all part of a huge complex of personal feeling, and the connections between the various sensations are left (deliberately of course) ambiguous. This is a highly refined example of the leave-it-up-to-the-reader technique that I found so irritating in "Private World" of the preceding chapter.

> This is why so many people do not know how to read. They have been taught to turn books into abstractions.

There, as in Hemingway, the logical connection between the two unconnected independent structures was unstated. But there is a difference. In "Private World," the intended connection is plain. What in Hemingway was a suggestive technique for implying several possible connections while stating none, becomes merely a rhetorical gimmick for forcing the reader to supply an obvious meaning. This is what we mean by the Misuse of a Style.

The definite article. I have mentioned a difference in relation with their assumed readers that the two speakers suggest. Whereas the speaker in A keeps his distance, using what we think of as fairly formal discourse, the speaker in B seems to have known the reader before and doesn't trouble himself to explain things as one must for an acquaintance one has just met. A possible cause of this difference between the two speakers can be found in the different ways they use a simple three-letter word—the word *the*. To be statistical again, the incidence of the definite article in the Howells paragraph comes to about 8 per cent; in the Hemingway passage it is about 18 per cent, or almost one word out of every five. It is clearly the Hemingway passage that is unconventional, labeling every other noun with *the*.

What is the effect of such an extraordinary preoccupation?

> In the late summer of that year we lived in a house in a village that looked across the river and the plain to the mountains.

One's first naive response to that sentence might be some perfectly pardonable questions. "What year? What river, what plain, what mountains? I don't know what you're talking about." Precisely: the *real* reader doesn't know what the speaker is talking about, but the assumed reader doesn't bother about that. *He* has been placed in a situation where he is expected to assume that he does know what the speaker is talking about. It is as if, for the assumed reader, a conversation had been going on before he opened the book, a conversation that laid the groundwork for all this assumed intimacy. Or it is as if—another analogy—we were suddenly plopped down in a chair listening to a man who has begun telling a story to another man who has just left the room. Curiously the storyteller confuses us with the friend who has just departed, and we find ourselves taking the place of this friend, yoked to the teller as he was. And of course, as always, we can't talk back.

The difference can be realized if again we try an irreverent revision, excising most of the definite articles:

> Late in 1915, when I was an officer in the Italian army, my unit lived in a house in a northern Italian village that looked across a river toward some mountains.

In this version, the speaker makes no such assumptions about the common knowledge shared by himself and his assumed reader. Now he names the year and the locale, he defines who "we" are, and his consistent indefinite articles maintain a more distant posture with his reader.

My revision again, naturally, is disastrous. It does more than create distance between reader and speaker. Reading it, one has the impression that the narrator doesn't care much about what he's saying. It starts off like any old war reminiscence. But in Hemingway's version, for many more reasons than I've been able to express here, we feel already the excitement, or what I have to call the intensity, of the narrator. He is deeply involved in his feelings about what he is going to tell us, and perhaps one reason he can give that impression is that he can pretend not to have to worry very much about us, about cueing us in in the conventional way.

The first word of the Howells passage is *The,* but the quickest reading reveals the difference. Here the narrator is describing a scene as if we had never seen it before—as indeed we have not. We need not assume the same kind of intimate relation with the narrator; he keeps us relatively at a distance, and he does not use (as Hemingway does) the first person pronoun. Yet even the Howells narrator launches us somewhat *in medias res,* assuming we will not ask, of his first two words, "What village?" Again the removal of the definite article will show how a speaker can back off even further from his reader, beginning a wholly new relationship with new information: A village stood on a wide plain, and around it rose mountains. One feels, of that sentence, that it should be prefaced by "Once upon a time," and it may be that in telling a fairy story, part of the trick is to assume very little from your reader. Nor is there any effort, in the fairy story, to make the narrator or his tale sound "real." In fact the effort must be just the other way. In the Hemingway kind of story, quite a lot is implied, through intensity of tone, about how seriously, how real, we are to take all this. There is a scale of pretension we could trace, something like this:

> Fairy story: Here's a little tale of something that (let's pretend) might have happened a long, long time ago in the Land of Nod.
> Howells: Here is a story about people behaving much as people in life do behave; I hope you enjoy it.
> Hemingway: This is how it really felt to me when it all happened. (Oh yes, if you insist, it's a *story.*)

My passages can't possibly justify all that. But if there is anything to such a scale, then the Hemingway rhetoric has the effect of including, as part of its fiction, the fiction that all this really happened to a narrator who felt intensely about it, and the reader is maneuvered into a position of sympathy with a person whose principal concern is not with the reader, not with the scene he is describing, but with himself and his own feelings. There is a consequent lift of the voice, a tension in the vocal chords. That is no armchair, relaxed and comfortable, that the Tough Talker occupies.

It will be useful now to summarize the Tough Talker's manner by means of a tentative definition of his personality and rhetoric. In doing so, we remember that our source is only the first 189 words of one Hemingway novel. Nor should we assume that the character described here is absolutely new to literature. What we do have here is an identifiable speaker (Frederic Henry by name), defined in an identifiable rhetoric, some of whose qualities we will be able to recognize in later prose.

A description of a Tough Talker. Frederic Henry is a hard man who has been around in a violent world, and who partially conceals his strong feelings behind a curt manner. He is in fact more concerned with those feelings than he is with the outward scenes he presents, or with cultivating the good wishes of the reader to whom he is introducing himself. He can ignore these traditional services to the reader because he assumes in advance much intimacy and common knowledge. (We are beyond explanations, beyond politenesses.) He presents himself as a believable human character, without omniscience: he knows only what he knows, and is aware of his limitations.

His rhetoric, like his personality, shows its limitations openly: short sentences, "crude" repetitions of words, simple grammatical structures with little subordinating. (I have no use for elegant variation, for the worn-out gentilities of traditional prose.) His tense intimacy with his assumed reader, another man who has been around, is implied by colloquial patterns from oral speech and by a high frequency of the definite article. He lets his reader make logical and other connections between elements. (You know what I mean; I don't have to spell it all out for *you*.) He prefers naming things to describing them, and avoids modification, especially when suggestive of value. All these habits of behavior suggest that he is self-conscious about his language—even about language generally. He is close-lipped, he watches his words.

This suspiciousness about language, only implied in our passage, deserves amplification particularly because it will concern us again later, in other writers. Part of the violent world that the Tough Talker has been around in is the violent verbal world, where words have been so abused that they have lost their lives. In a famous passage later on in *Farewell to Arms* Frederic Henry makes the point explicitly:

> I did not say anything. I was always embarrassed by the words sacred, glorious, and sacrifice, and the expression in vain. We had heard them, sometimes standing in the rain almost out of earshot, so that only the shouted words came through, and had read them, on proclamations, now for a long time, and I had seen nothing sacred, and the things

that were glorious had no glory and the sacrifices were like the stock-
yards at Chicago if nothing was done with the meat except to bury it.
There were many words that you could not stand to hear and finally
only the names of places had dignity. Certain numbers were the same
way and certain dates and these with the names of the places were all
you could say and have them mean anything. Abstract words such as
glory, honor, courage, or hallow were obscene beside the concrete
names of villages, and the numbers of roads, the names of rivers, the
numbers of regiments and the dates.

Such a negative attitude toward language, however understandable and
right in this novel, becomes deadly in later and less skillful hands. For some
members of the Beat Generation all language became meaningless—a
conviction peculiarly difficult for a writer to live with. The conviction may
have had something to do with the poverty of beat style, and with the early
demise of that movement. In any event, a self-conscious anxiety about the
very reliability of words has become one of the crosses the modern writer
has to bear. Fortunately it can be borne in many ways, from comedy to
despair.

DONALD P. COSTELLO

The Language of
The Catcher in the Rye

*Donald P. Costello teaches English at the University of Notre Dame. In
"The Language of* The Catcher in the Rye" *Costello studies the style of
Holden Caulfield's narrative "as an example of teenage vernacular in the
1950's." By centering his attention on the narrator's style, Costello is applying a rhetorical theory of style similar to Walker Gibson's. Gibson, however,
is concerned with the relationship of the speaker to the work itself, while
Costello is interested in Holden Caulfield's speech as a reflection of the
actual language habits of teenagers.*

A study of the language of J. D. Salinger's *The Catcher in the Rye* can be
justified not only on the basis of literary interest, but also on the basis of

From *American Speech,* XXXIV (October 1959), 172-181. Reprinted by permission of Columbia University Press.

linguistic significance. Today we study *The Adventures of Huckleberry Finn* (with which many critics have compared *The Catcher in the Rye*) not only as a great work of literary art, but as a valuable study in 1884 dialect. In coming decades, *The Catcher in the Rye* will be studied, I feel, not only as a literary work, but also as an example of teenage vernacular in the 1950s. As such, the book will be a significant historical linguistic record of a type of speech rarely made available in permanent form. Its linguistic importance will increase as the American speech it records becomes less current.

Most critics who looked at *The Catcher in the Rye* at the time of its publication thought that its language was a true and authentic rendering of teenage colloquial speech. Reviewers in the Chicago *Sunday Tribune*, the London *Times Literary Supplement*, the *New Republic*, the New York *Herald Tribune Book Review*, the New York *Times*, the *New Yorker*, and the *Saturday Review of Literature* all specifically mentioned the authenticity of the book's language. Various aspects of its language were also discussed in the reviews published in *America*, the *Atlantic*, the *Catholic World*, the *Christian Science Monitor*, the *Library Journal*, the Manchester *Guardian*, the *Nation*, the *New Statesman and Nation*, the New York *Times Book Review*, *Newsweek*, the *Spectator*, and *Time*.[1] Of these many reviews, only the writers for the *Catholic World* and the *Christian Science Monitor* denied the authenticity of the book's language, but both of these are religious journals which refused to believe that the 'obscenity' was realistic. An examination of the reviews of *The Catcher in the Rye* proves that the language of Holden Caulfield, the book's sixteen-year-old narrator, struck the ear of the contemporary reader as an accurate rendering of the informal speech of an intelligent, educated, Northeastern American adolescent.[2]

In addition to commenting on its authenticity, critics have often remarked —uneasily—the 'daring,' 'obscene,' 'blasphemous' features of Holden's

---

[1]See reviews in *America*, LXXV (August 11, 1951), 463, 464; *Atlantic*, CLXXXVIII (1951), 82; *Catholic World*, CLXXIV (1951), 154; Chicago *Sunday Tribune*, July 15, 1951, Part 4, p. 3; *Christian Science Monitor*, July 19, 1951, p. 9; *Library Journal*, LXXVI (1951), 1125; *Times* [London] *Literary Supplement*, September 7, 1951, p. 561; Manchester *Guardian*, August 10, 1951, p. 4; *Nation*, CLXXIII (September 1, 1951), 176; *New Republic*, CXXV (July 16, 1951), 20, 21; *New Statesman and Nation*, XLII (August 18, 1951), 185; New York *Herald Tribune Book Review*, July 15, 1951, p. 3; New York *Times Book Review*, July 15, 1951, p. 5; New York *Times*, July 16, 1951, p. 19; *New Yorker*, XXVII (August 11, 1951), 71-76; *Newsweek*, XXXVIII (July 16, 1951), 89, 90; *Saturday Review of Literature*, XXXIV (July 14, 1951), 12, 13; *Spectator*, CLXXXVII (August 17, 1951), 224; *Time*, LVIII (July 16, 1951), 96, 97.

[2]If additional evidence of the authenticity of the book's language is required, one need only look at the phenomenal regard with which *The Catcher in the Rye* is held by today's college students, who were about Holden's age at the time the book was written. In its March 9, 1957, issue, the *Nation* published a symposium which attempted to discover the major influences upon the college students of today. Many teachers pointed out the impact of Salinger. Carlos Baker, of Princeton, stated: 'There is still, as there has been for years, a cult of Thomas Wolfe. They have all read J. D. Salinger, Wolfe's closest competitor.' Stanley Kunitz, of Queens College, wrote: 'The only novelist I have heard praised vociferously is J. D. Salinger.' Harvey Curtis Webster, of the University of Louisville, listed Salinger as one of the 'stimulators.' R. J. Kaufman, of the University of Rochester, called *The Catcher in the Rye* 'a book which has complexly aroused nearly all of them.' See 'The Careful Young Men,' *Nation*, CLXXXIV (March 9, 1957), 199-214. I have never heard any Salinger partisan among college students doubt the authenticity of the language of their compatriot, Holden.

Donald P. Costello   237

language. Another commonly noted feature of the book's language has been its comic effect. And yet there has never been an extensive investigation of the language itself. That is what this paper proposes to do.

Even though Holden's language is authentic teenage speech, recording it was certainly not the major intention of Salinger. He was faced with the artistic task of creating an individual character, not with the linguistic task of reproducing the exact speech of teenagers in general. Yet Holden had to speak a recognizable teenage language, and at the same time had to be identifiable as an individual. This difficult task Salinger achieved by giving Holden an extremely trite and typical teenage speech, overlaid with strong personal idiosyncrasies. There are two major speech habits which are Holden's own, which are endlessly repeated throughout the book, and which are, nevertheless, typical enough of teenage speech so that Holden can be both typical and individual in his use of them. It is certainly common for teenagers to end thoughts with a loosely dangling 'and all,' just as it is common for them to add an insistent 'I really did,' 'It really was.' But Holden uses these phrases to such an overpowering degree that they become a clear part of the flavor of the book; they become, more, a part of Holden himself, and actually help to characterize him.

Holden's 'and all' and its twins, 'or something,' 'or anything,' serve no real, consistent linguistic function. They simply give a sense of looseness of expression and looseness of thought. Often they signify that Holden knows there is more that could be said about the issue at hand, but he is not going to bother going into it:

> . . . how my parents were occupied and all before they had me (5.)[3]
> . . . they're *nice* and all (5.)
> I'm not going to tell you my whole goddam autobiography or anything (5.)
> . . . splendid and clear-thinking and all (6.)

But just as often the use of such expressions is purely arbitrary, with no discernible meaning:

> . . . he's my *brother* and all (5.)
> . . . was in the Revolutionary War and all (6.)
> It was December and all (7.)
> . . . no gloves or anything (7.)
> . . . right in the pocket and all (7.)

Donald Barr, writing in the *Commonweal,* finds this habit indicative of Holden's tendency to generalize, to find the all in the one:

---

[3]Whenever *The Catcher in the Rye* is substantially quoted in this paper, a page number will be included in the text immediately after the quotation. The edition to which the page numbers refer is the Signet paperback reprint.

Salinger has an ear not only for idiosyncrasies of diction and syntax, but for mental processes. Holden Caulfield's phrase is 'and all'—'She looked so damn *nice,* the way she kept going around and around in her blue coat and all'—as if each experience wore a halo. His fallacy is *ab uno disce omnes;* he abstracts and generalizes wildly.[4]

Heiserman and Miller, in the *Western Humanities Review,* comment specifically upon Holden's second most obvious idiosyncrasy: 'In a phony world Holden feels compelled to reenforce his sincerity and truthfulness constantly with, "It really is" or "It really did."'[5] S. N. Behrman, in the *New Yorker,* finds a double function of these 'perpetual insistences of Holden's.' Behrman thinks they 'reveal his age, even when he is thinking much older,' and, more important, 'he is so aware of the danger of slipping into phoniness himself that he has to repeat over and over "I really mean it," "It really does."'[6] Holden uses this idiosyncrasy of insistence almost every time that he makes an affirmation.

Allied to Holden's habit of insistence is his 'if you want to know the truth.' Heiserman and Miller are able to find characterization in this habit too:

> The skepticism inherent in that casual phrase, 'if you want to know the truth,' suggesting that as a matter of fact in the world of Holden Caulfield very few people do, characterizes this sixteen-year-old 'crazy mixed up kid' more sharply and vividly than pages of character 'analysis' possibly could.[7]

Holden uses this phrase only after affirmations, just as he uses 'It really does,' but usually after the personal ones, where he is consciously being frank:

> I have no wind, if you want to know the truth. (8.)
> I don't even think that bastard had a handkerchief, if you want to know the truth. (34.)
> I'm a pacifist, if you want to know the truth. (44.)
> She had quite a lot of sex appeal, too, if you really want to know. (53.)
> I was damn near bawling, I felt so damn happy, if you want to know the truth. (191.)

These personal idiosyncrasies of Holden's speech are in keeping with general teenage language. Yet they are so much a part of Holden and of the flavor of the book that they are much of what makes Holden to be Holden. They are the most memorable feature of the book's language. Al-

---

[4]Donald Barr, 'Saints, Pilgrims, and Artists,' *Commonweal,* LXVII (October 25, 1957), 90.
[5]Arthur Heiserman and James E. Miller, Jr., 'J. D. Salinger: Some Crazy Cliff,' *Western Humanities Review,* X (1956), 136.
[6]S. N. Behrman, 'The Vision of the Innocent,' *New Yorker,* XXVII (August 11, 1951), 72.
[7]Heiserman and Miller, *op. cit.,* p. 135.

though always in character, the rest of Holden's speech is more typical than individual. The special quality of this language comes from its triteness, its lack of distinctive qualities.

Holden's informal, schoolboy vernacular is particularly typical in its 'vulgarity' and 'obscenity.' No one familiar with prep-school speech could seriously contend that Salinger overplayed his hand in this respect. On the contrary, Holden's restraints help to characterize him as a sensitive youth who avoids the most strongly forbidden terms, and who never uses vulgarity in a self-conscious or phony way to help him be 'one of the boys.' *Fuck,* for example, is never used as a part of Holden's speech. The word appears in the novel four times, but only when Holden disapprovingly discusses its wide appearance on walls. The Divine name is used habitually by Holden only in the comparatively weak *for God's sake, God,* and *goddam.* The stronger and usually more offensive *for Chrissake* or *Jesus* or *Jesus Christ* are used habitually by Ackley and Stradlater; but Holden uses them only when he feels the need for a strong expression. He almost never uses *for Chrissake* in an unemotional situation. *Goddam* is Holden's favorite adjective. This word is used with no relationship to its original meaning, or to Holden's attitude toward the word to which it is attached. It simply expresses an emotional feeling toward the object: either favorable, as in 'goddam hunting cap'; or unfavorable, as in 'ya goddam moron'; or indifferent, as in 'coming in the goddam windows.' *Damn* is used interchangeably with *goddam;* no differentiation in its meaning is detectable.

Other crude words are also often used in Holden's vocabulary. *Ass* keeps a fairly restricted meaning as a part of the human anatomy, but it is used in a variety of ways. It can refer simply to that specific part of the body ('I moved my ass a little'), or be a part of a trite expression ('freezing my ass off'; 'in a half-assed way'), or be an expletive ('Game, my ass.'). *Hell* is perhaps the most versatile word in Holden's entire vocabulary; it serves most of the meanings and constructions which Mencken lists in his *American Speech* article on 'American Profanity.'[8] So far is Holden's use of *hell* from its original meaning that he can use the sentence 'We had a helluva time' to mean that he and Phoebe had a decidedly pleasant time downtown shopping for shoes. The most common function of *hell* is as the second part of a simile, in which a thing can be either 'hot as hell' or, strangely, 'cold as hell'; 'sad as hell' or 'playful as hell'; 'old as hell' or 'pretty as hell.' Like all of these words, *hell* has no close relationship to its original meaning.

Both *bastard* and *sonuvabitch* have also drastically changed in meaning. They no longer, of course, in Holden's vocabulary, have any connection with the accidents of birth. Unless used in a trite simile, *bastard* is a strong word, reserved for things and people Holden particularly dislikes, especially 'phonies.' *Sonuvabitch* has an even stronger meaning to Holden; he uses it only in the deepest anger. When, for example, Holden is furious with Strad-

---

[8]See H. L. Mencken, American Profanity,' *American Speech,* XIX (1944), 242.

later over his treatment of Jane Gallagher, Holden repeats again and again that he 'kept calling him a moron sonuvabitch' (43).

The use of crude language in *The Catcher in the Rye* increases, as we should expect, when Holden is reporting schoolboy dialogue. When he is directly addressing the reader, Holden's use of such language drops off almost entirely. There is also an increase in this language when any of the characters are excited or angry. Thus, when Holden is apprehensive over Stradlater's treatment of Jane, his *goddams* increase suddenly to seven on a single page (p. 39).

Holden's speech is also typical in his use of slang. I have catalogued over a hundred slang terms used by Holden, and every one of these is in widespread use. Although Holden's slang is rich and colorful, it, of course, being slang, often fails at precise communication. Thus, Holden's *crap* is used in seven different ways. It can mean foolishness, as 'all that David Copperfield kind of crap,' or messy matter, as 'I spilled some crap all over my gray flannel,' or merely miscellaneous matter, as 'I was putting on my galoshes and crap.' It can also carry its basic meaning, animal excreta, as 'there didn't look like there was anything in the park except dog crap,' and it can be used as an adjective meaning anything generally unfavorable, as 'The show was on the crappy side.' Holden uses the phrases *to be a lot of crap* and *to shoot the crap* and *to chuck the crap* all to mean 'to be untrue,' but he can also use *to shoot the crap* to mean simply 'to chat,' with no connotation of untruth, as in 'I certainly wouldn't have minded shooting the crap with old Phoebe for a while.'

Similarly Holden's slang use of *crazy* is both trite and imprecise. 'That drives me crazy' means that he violently dislikes something; yet 'to be crazy about' something means just the opposite. In the same way, to be 'killed' by something can mean that he was emotionally affected either favorably ('That story just about killed me.') or unfavorably ('Then she turned her back on me again. It nearly killed me.'). This use of *killed* is one of Holden's favorite slang expressions. Heiserman and Miller are, incidentally, certainly incorrect when they conclude: 'Holden always lets us know when he has insight into the absurdity of the endlessly absurd situations which make up the life of a sixteen-year-old by exclaiming, "It killed me."'[9] Holden often uses this expression with no connection to the absurd; he even uses it for his beloved Phoebe. The expression simply indicates a high degree of emotion —any kind. It is hazardous to conclude that any of Holden's slang has a precise and consistent meaning or function. These same critics fall into the same error when they conclude that Holden's use of the adjective *old* serves as 'a term of endearment.'[10] Holden appends this word to almost every character, real or fictional, mentioned in the novel, from the hated 'old Maurice' to 'old Peter Lorre,' to 'old Phoebe,' and even 'old Jesus.' The only pattern

---

[9]Heiserman and Miller, *op. cit.*, p. 136.
[10]*Ibid.*

that can be discovered in Holden's use of this term is that he usually uses it only after he has previously mentioned the character; he then feels free to append the familiar *old*. All we can conclude from Holden's slang is that it is typical teenage slang: versatile yet narrow, expressive yet unimaginative, imprecise, often crude, and always trite.

Holden has many favorite slang expressions which he overuses. In one place, he admits:

> 'Boy!' I said. I also say 'Boy!' quite a lot. Partly because I have a lousy vocabulary and partly because I act quite young for my age sometimes. (12.)

But if Holden's slang shows the typically 'lousy vocabulary' of even the educated American teenager, this failing becomes even more obvious when we narrow our view to Holden's choice of adjectives and adverbs. The choice is indeed narrow, with a constant repetition of a few favorite words: *lousy, pretty, crumby, terrific, quite, old, stupid*—all used, as is the habit of teenage vernacular, with little regard to specific meaning. Thus, most of the nouns which are called 'stupid' could not in any logical framework be called 'ignorant,' and, as we have seen, *old* before a proper noun has nothing to do with age.

Another respect in which Holden was correct in accusing himself of having a 'lousy vocabulary' is discovered in the ease with which he falls into trite figures of speech. We have already seen that Holden's most common simile is the worn and meaningless 'as hell'; but his often-repeated 'like a madman' and 'like a bastard' are just about as unrelated to a literal meaning and are easily as unimaginative. Even Holden's nonhabitual figures of speech are usually trite: 'sharp as a tack'; 'hot as a firecracker'; 'laughed like a hyena'; 'I know old Jane like a book'; 'drove off like a bat out of hell'; 'I began to feel like a horse's ass'; 'blind as a bat'; 'I know Central Park like the back of my hand.'

Repetitious and trite as Holden's vocabulary may be, it can, nevertheless, become highly effective. For example, when Holden piles one trite adjective upon another, a strong power of invective is often the result:

> He was a goddam stupid moron. (42.)
> Get your dirty stinking moron knees off my chest. (43.)
> You're a dirty stupid sonuvabitch of a moron. (43.)

And his limited vocabulary can also be used for good comic effect. Holden's constant repetition of identical expressions in countless widely different situations is often hilariously funny.

But all of the humor in Holden's vocabulary does not come from its unimaginative quality. Quite the contrary, some of his figures of speech are entirely original; and these are inspired, dramatically effective, and terribly funny. As always, Salinger's Holden is basically typical, with a strong overlay of the individual:

He started handling my exam paper like it was a turd or something. (13.)

He put my goddam paper down then and looked at me like he'd just beaten the hell out of me in ping-pong or something. (14.)

That guy Morrow was about as sensitive as a goddam toilet seat. (52.)

Old Marty was like dragging the Statue of Liberty around the floor. (69.)

Another aspect in which Holden's language is typical is that it shows the general American characteristic of adaptability—apparently strengthened by his teenage lack of restraint. It is very easy for Holden to turn nouns into adjectives, with the simple addition of a -y: 'perverty,' 'Christmasy,' 'vomity-looking,' 'whory-looking,' 'hoodlumy-looking,' 'show-offy,' 'flitty-looking,' 'dumpy-looking,' 'pimpy,' 'snobby,' 'fisty.' Like all of English, Holden's language shows a versatile combining ability: 'They gave Sally this little blue butt-twitcher of a dress to wear' (117) and 'That magazine was some little cheerer upper' (176). Perhaps the most interesting aspect of the adaptability of Holden's language is his ability to use nouns as adverbs: 'She sings it very Dixieland and whorehouse, and it doesn't sound at all mushy' (105).

As we have seen, Holden shares, in general, the trite repetitive vocabulary which is the typical lot of his age group. But as there are exceptions in his figures of speech, so are there exceptions in his vocabulary itself, in his word stock. An intelligent, well-read ('I'm quite illiterate, but I read a lot'), and educated boy, Holden possesses, and can use when he wants to, many words which are many a cut above Basic English, including 'ostracized,' 'exhibitionist,' 'unscrupulous,' 'conversationalist,' 'psychic,' 'bourgeois.' Often Holden seems to choose his words consciously, in an effort to communicate to his adult reader clearly and properly, as in such terms as 'lose my virginity,' 'relieve himself,' 'an alcoholic'; for upon occasion, he also uses the more vulgar terms 'to give someone the time,' 'to take a leak,' 'booze hound.' Much of the humor arises, in fact, from Holden's habit of writing on more than one level at the same time. Thus, we have such phrases as 'They give guys the ax quite frequently at Pency' and 'It has a very good academic rating, Pency' (7). Both sentences show a colloquial idiom with an overlay of consciously selected words.

Such a conscious choice of words seems to indicate that Salinger, in his attempt to create a realistic character in Holden, wanted to make him aware of his speech, as, indeed, a real teenager would be when communicating to the outside world. Another piece of evidence that Holden is conscious of his speech and, more, realizes a difficulty in communication, is found in his habit of direct repetition: 'She likes me a lot. I mean she's quite fond of me.' (141), and 'She can be very snotty sometimes. She can be quite snotty.' (150). Sometimes the repetition is exact: 'He was a very nervous guy—I mean he was a very nervous guy.' (165), and 'I sort of missed them. I mean I sort of missed them.' (169). Sometimes Holden stops specifically to interpret slang terms, as when he wants to communicate the fact that Allie liked Phoebe: 'She killed Allie, too. I mean he liked her, too' (64).

There is still more direct evidence that Holden was conscious of his speech. Many of his comments to the reader are concerned with language. He was aware, for example, of the 'phony' quality of many words and phrases, such as 'grand,' 'prince,' 'traveling incognito,' 'little girls' room,' 'licorice stick,' and 'angels.' Holden is also conscious, of course, of the existence of 'taboo words.' He makes a point of mentioning that the girl from Seattle repeatedly asked him to 'watch your language, if you don't mind' (67), and that his mother told Phoebe not to say 'lousy' (160). When the prostitute says 'Like fun you are.' Holden comments:

> It was a funny thing to say. It sounded like a real kid. You'd think a prostitute and all would say 'Like hell you are' or 'Cut the crap' instead of 'Like fun you are.' (87.)

In grammar, too, as in vocabulary, Holden possesses a certain self-consciousness. (It is, of course, impossible to imagine a student getting through today's schools without a self-consciousness with regard to grammar rules.) Holden is, in fact, not only aware of the existence of 'grammatical errors,' but knows the social taboos that accompany them. He is disturbed by a schoolmate who is ashamed of his parents' grammar, and he reports that his former teacher, Mr. Antolini, warned him about picking up 'just enough education to hate people who say, "It's a secret between he and I"' (168).

Holden is a typical enough teenager to violate the grammar rules, even though he knows of their social importance. His most common rule violation is the misuse of *lie* and *lay,* but he also is careless about relative pronouns ('about a traffic cop that falls in love'), the double negative ('I hardly didn't even know I was doing it'), the perfect tenses ('I'd woke him up'), extra words ('like as if all you ever did at Pency was play polo all the time'), pronoun number ('it's pretty disgusting to watch somebody picking their nose'), and pronoun position ('I and this friend of mine, Mal Brossard'). More remarkable, however, than the instances of grammar rule violations is Holden's relative 'correctness.' Holden is always intelligible, and is even 'correct' in many usually difficult constructions. Grammatically speaking, Holden's language seems to point up the fact that English was the only subject in which he was not failing. It is interesting to note how much more 'correct' Holden's speech is than that of Huck Finn. But then Holden is educated, and since the time of Huck there had been sixty-seven years of authoritarian schoolmarms working on the likes of Holden. He has, in fact, been overtaught, so that he uses many 'hyper' forms:

> I used to play tennis with he and Mrs. Antolini quite frequently. (163.)
> She'd give Allie or I a push. (64.)

I and Allie used to take her to the park with us. (64.)

I think I probably woke he and his wife up. (157.)

Now that we have examined several aspects of Holden's vocabulary and grammar, it would be well to look at a few examples of how he puts these elements together into sentences. The structure of Holden's sentences indicates that Salinger thinks of the book more in terms of spoken speech than written speech. Holden's faulty structure is quite common and typical in vocal expression; I doubt if a student who is 'good in English' would ever create such sentence structure in writing. A student who showed the self-consciousness of Holden would not *write* so many fragments, such after-thoughts (e.g., 'It has a very good academic rating, Pency' [7]), or such repetitions (e.g., 'Where I lived at Pency, I lived in the Ossenburger Memorial Wing of the new dorms' [18]).

There are other indications that Holden's speech is vocal. In many places Salinger mildly imitates spoken speech. Sentences such as 'You could tell old Spencer'd got a big bang out of buying it' (10) and 'I'd've killed him' (42) are repeated throughout the book. Yet it is impossible to imagine Holden taking pen in hand and actually writing 'Spencer'd' or 'I'd've.' Sometimes, too, emphasized words, or even parts of words, are italicized, as in 'Now *shut up,* Holden. God damn it—I'm *warn*ing ya' (42). This is often done with good effect, imitating quite perfectly the rhythms of speech, as in the typical:

> I practically sat down on her *lap,* as a matter of fact. Then she *really* started to cry, and the next thing I knew, I was kissing her all over— *any*where—her eyes, her *nose,* her forehead, her eyebrows and all, her *ears*—her whole face except her mouth and all. (73.)

The language of *The Catcher in the Rye* is, as we have seen, an authentic artistic rendering of a type of informal, colloquial, teenage American spoken speech. It is strongly typical and trite, yet often somewhat individual; it is crude and slangy and imprecise, imitative yet occasionally imaginative, and affected toward standardization by the strong efforts of schools. But authentic and interesting as this language may be, it must be remembered that it exists, in *The Catcher in the Rye,* as only one part of an artistic achievement. The language was not written for itself, but as a part of a greater whole. Like the great Twain work with which it is often compared, a study of *The Catcher in the Rye* repays both the linguist and the literary critic; for as one critic has said, 'In them, 1884 and 1951 speak to us in the idiom and accent of two youthful travelers who have earned their passports to literary immortality.'[11]

---

[11]Charles Kaplan, 'Holden and Huck: the Odysseys of Youth,' *College English,* XVIII (1956), 80.

BURNHAM CARTER, JR.

President Kennedy's Inaugural Address

Burnham Carter, Jr., is professor of English and Dean of Briarcliff College. The following essay is an analysis of word choice, sentence construction, and emotional appeal in President Kennedy's Inaugural Address.*

After John Fitzgerald Kennedy had delivered his Inaugural Address on January 20, 1961, many hailed it as "a great speech" (*Life*) or as "distinguished for its style and brevity as well as for its meaty content" (*The New York Times*). A few commentators denigrated it as mere "mood music" for a new administration (*The Reporter*). In the last year I have asked several groups of students to study it as a piece of rhetoric. On each occasion the class has enjoyed working with a piece of contemporary prose by a man of eminence, and they are pleased to discover so much to discuss about Mr. Kennedy's word choice, figurative language, phrase-making, and variety of appeals.

Alliteration offers an easy start: "Civility i*s* not a *s*ign of weakne*ss*, and *s*incerity i*s* alway*s s*ubject to proof" is a fine instance, although the smoothness of the phrasing will lead some to overlook the host of *s*'s. When the President says he hopes to enlarge the area in which the UN's "writ may run," many will not see the economy and force of this example until they try a paraphrase, such as "until its decisions may have the force of law." Along the same lines, an alert reader will enjoy an internal rhyme like "the st*ea*dy spr*ea*d of the d*ea*dly atom."

In considering connotations, one notices right away that Mr. Kennedy uses the word *pledge* seven times in a row (the last two with slight variations, to avoid monotony). *Promise* would never do here, for "promises, promises, always promises" has become a cant phrase for us. The reasons for his choice are clear when we remember the happy contexts in which we use *pledge:* swearing allegiance to the flag, making a gift to the church or other charity, drinking a friend's health, and even in the marriage ceremony ("and thereto I plight thee my troth"). The final use of this key word shows a nice distinction. To Soviet Russia Mr. Kennedy offers "not a *pledge* but a *request*," for one's enemy does not deserve the same promise of support as do one's allies. *Request* will suffice. Lest he seem petulant, he dignifies the U.S.S.R. as "those nations who would make themselves our *adversary*," a designation that recalls the high seriousness of Milton's virtue that "sallies

From *College Composition and Communication*, XIV (February 1963), 36-40. Reprinted with the permission of the National Council of Teachers of English and Burnham Carter, Jr.
*The text of the speech appears in Appendix A, p. 299.

out and seeks her *adversary*," or the word's use in the Sermon on the Mount and elsewhere in Scripture.

The address is full of richly connotative words. Consider the force of "*unleashed* powers of destruction" as opposed, say, to *released,* or the refurbishing of the tired phrases *balance of power* and *iron curtain* with fresh variants, "balance of *terror*" and "iron *tyranny.*" With such changes the President calls upon an echo in the reader's mind yet avoids the cliché.

It is as a phrasemaker that Mr. Kennedy has made his strongest mark in both his formal and informal speeches. The two best known epigrams in the Inaugural Address are "Let us never negotiate out of fear, but let us never fear to negotiate" and "Ask not what your country can do for you, but what you can do for your country." These inversions sound deceptively easy and inevitable, as do all such concise and pointed expressions. The writer uses few and simple words; he changes the order or alters the wording only slightly; and the result is memorable because it is short, witty and precise. In his September 25th speech to the UN, the President employs a similar reversal when he asserts, "Mankind must put an end to war, or war will put an end to mankind."

Mr. Kennedy is fond of paradox; witness the following two examples: "Only when our arms are sufficient beyond doubt can we be certain beyond doubt that they will never be employed" (from the Inaugural Address), and terror will always fail as a policy weapon because "men are not afraid to die for a life worth living" (from the UN address). The first of these points up the inescapable irony of any massive defensive effort. The triple walls of Carcassonne were a major reason why it was rarely attacked and, after 1240, never taken; similarly the United States is to spend billions for defense to make sure, hopefully, that none of it will ever be used. How absurd, and yet how true—that is the calculated effect of paradox. The second example relies on the ancient and honorable concept of dying in order that another might live better, of giving up one's life to "save" it. In each instance the writer must produce a statement that is self-contradictory on the surface but in a larger sense correct.

Wit of this sort is risky. It demands attention, and listeners to political speeches are notoriously slack. It depends on the reader's catching on to the allusion, irony, or contradiction quickly, and often the writer receives only incomplete comprehension, as Dean Swift learned with *A Modest Proposal.* In his Inaugural Address Mr. Kennedy requests that new nations remember that "in the past, those who foolishly sought power by riding the tiger end up inside." Whether the allusion is to a folk saying of the sort Mr. Khrushchev favors, or to the old limerick of the lady from Niger,[1] Mr.

---

[1]There once was a lady from Niger
Who smiled as she rode on a tiger.
They came back from the ride
With the lady inside
And the smile on the face of the tiger.

Kennedy's witty analogy may miss the listeners who have never heard of it or annoy others who distrust all cleverness. Those who know the allusion or have a taste for the wry epigram, however, will enjoy this touch of the sardonic. That the President himself savors a bit of sarcasm is evident from the following dinner party parody he gave of his own famous address.

> We observe tonight not a celebration of freedom but a victory of party, for we have sworn to pay off the same party debt our forebears ran up nearly a year and three months ago. Our deficit will not be paid off in the next hundred days, nor will it be paid off in the first one thousand days, nor in the life of this Administration. Nor, perhaps, even in our lifetime on this planet. But let us begin—remembering that generosity is not a sign of weakness and that ambassadors are always subject to Senate confirmation. For if the Democratic party cannot be helped by the many who are poor, it cannot be saved by the few who are rich. So let us begin. (*The New York Times* magazine, Feb. 25, 1962, p. 70.)

Not all of Mr. Kennedy's care for phrasing is for elegance. Much of it is for clarity and emphasis, especially the repetitions, which are of course intentional and not (like many of our own) the result of inattention or an impoverished vocabulary. The President uses them to give order and balance to a series of thoughts, as in the five paragraphs beginning "*To those* old allies . . . , *to those* new states," etc. Such repetition of a minor word in the construction allows the listener to rest as he follows the steps in the speaker's program. Later Mr. Kennedy's four repetitions of "let both sides" stress the mutual responsibility of the U.S.A. and the U.S.S.R., and at the same time organize his proposals so that the millions in his audience can follow him easily.

Parallelism and antithesis are major devices in the President's style. He describes the new generation of Americans as "born in this country, tempered by war, disciplined by a hard and bitter peace, proud of our ancient heritage . . ." Studied parallelism should hardly become an earmark of every writer's style—such a return to euphuism would be appalling—but it is important for him to recognize it when he sees it and to be able to use it himself when the occasion demands. The same is true for Mr. Kennedy's fondness for antithesis. His opening sentence, "we observe today *not a* victory of party *but a* celebration of freedom," employs the same careful contrast as "I come to bury Caesar, not to praise him." Throughout the Inaugural Address one finds *not because, not because, but because,* or "*not as a call* to bear arms . . . , *not as a call* to battle . . . , *but a call* to bear the burden . . ." In part this device is definition of an idea by elimination, but it also offers a welcome simplicity of argument. "If a free society cannot help the many who are poor, it cannot save the few who are rich," regardless of its position, is a good example of a phrasing that is tidy, balanced, and easy on the ear. A sentence that seems to say so much in so little is always likely to be persuasive. Mr. Kennedy's poet laureate, Robert Frost, has a similar penchant for gnomic utterances, as in "We dance around in a ring and suppose,/ But the secret sits in the middle and knows," or "I never dared be radical when young/ For fear it would make me conservative when old." As a final example of Mr. Kennedy's balanced style, the conclusion of his address to the UN is notable:

> Together we shall save our planet or together we shall perish in its flames. Save it we can and save it we must, and then shall we earn the eternal thanks of mankind and, as peacemakers, the eternal blessings of God.

Here the repetition in the first sentence allows the contrast of *save* versus *perish* to shine forth, just as the repetition of *save it we* stresses the double obligation of *can* and *must*. Seldom do most of us think to reverse the order of subject and verb, as the President effectively does here.

President Kennedy relies on metaphor throughout his address. "The bonds of mass misery . . . , the chains of poverty . . . , a beachhead of cooperation [pushing back] the jungles of suspicion . . ." We need to ask, "Is this comparison correct?" and then "How effective do I find it?" In his third paragraph Mr. Kennedy says that "the torch has been passed to a new generation of Americans." As a symbol of freedom, of any light we use to hold back the dark, be it physical or spiritual, *torch* has a traditional value. To some it may even be a cliché, however honored by the wind and weather of time, like the Statue of Liberty. Perhaps the listener will recall Olympic runners bringing the divine flame from Mt. Olympus to the meeting of the competitors. *Torch* is surely correct enough here, for the parallel is clear; whether or not it is wholly successful depends on the degree of literary sophistication of the audience.

A similar reliance on a traditional symbol occurs in the President's peroration, when he announces that "now the trumpet summons us again," for bugles have been used in times of crisis since the days of Charlemagne or even Joshua. A more direct metaphor occurs later in the reference to the four "common enemies of mankind: tyranny, poverty, disease, and war itself." With the trumpet having already established a Biblical context, it is not much of a leap to associate these four adversaries with a similar quartet, the four horsemen of the Apocalypse: conquest, slaughter, famine, and death. Unfortunately, mention of "the four horsemen" in a Midwestern classroom is liable to produce only "Miller, Crowley, Layden, and Stuhldreher," the lethal backfield of Notre Dame in the twenties.

Lastly, the various appeals of the Inaugural Address are designed to call upon all the ideals of the listener. The opening paragraph urges a new unity, a closing of ranks after the campaign, by reference to the common tradition of Presidents taking office in the last 171 years. Mr. Kennedy speaks of "our forebears . . . nearly a century and three quarters ago," just as Mr. Lincoln cited "our forefathers . . . four score and seven years ago." Unity established, the President speaks of Americans as *tempered, disciplined* and *proud,* as men willing to *pay any price, bear any burden, meet any hardship, support any friend, oppose any foe.* Such an appeal to stoicism and courage insures an optimistic attitude toward the obligations which he will list next. Finally, for over two thirds of the speech Mr. Kennedy speaks only of *we,* from the opening words, "We observe today," to "But let us begin." Only when his sense of our unified strength has been well established does he switch to "in *your* hands" and "will *you* join in that historic effort?" By way of encouragement he speaks briefly of his own attitude: "*I* do not shrink from this responsibility—*I* welcome it." Then quickly he returns to "the devotion which *we* bring to this endeavor," and the final, overriding emphasis is on *our* reward, *our* deeds and *our* work.

The last paragraph of the Inaugural Address illustrates almost all the rhetorical techniques noted so far: the alliteration, the simple yet precise wording, the inverted sentences, the intentional repetitions, the sense of community and tradition. All are here, plus another, as yet unmentioned element. The subject matter of this address is foreign policy, but the aim is not only to reassure other nations of our plans but to encourage Americans to implement them. Many a speaker makes his cause a crusade, for "if God be on our side, who can be against us?" A religious motif runs through this speech, from the reference to "Almighty God" and "the hand of God," to the quotations from Isaiah 58:6 and Romans 12:12, the allusion to Armageddon in "mankind's final war," that trumpet call, and "the faith, the devotion" stressed in the final paragraphs and especially in the last sentence:

> With a good conscience our only sure reward, with history the final judge of our deeds, let us go forth to lead the land we love, asking His blessing and His help, but knowing that here on earth God's work must truly be our own.

Few will miss the echo here of Lincoln's "With malice toward none, with charity toward all," and the phrase "God's work must truly be our own" has a Puritan ring. Such company is highly honorific.

As these religious and historical allusions are ticked off, a danger arises that threatens the integrity of the entire speech. The familiarity of a religious or idealistic appeal may lead to the superficial conclusion that a successful speech is pure semantics. The easily cynical will sneer that political speeches are all "hokum," "political propaganda," or "Fourth of July oratory." A careful analysis of this address, however, ought not to persuade the writer that now he has the inside story, that now, like Mr. Barnum, he can fool some of the people some of the time. Instead, he should see in this address a craftsman at work, but not let his sophomoric glee at discovering how words are used lead him to scoff at the idealism present, however familiar its form. Such a reader should be asked to look at his own last piece of writing. Can he, like Mr. Kennedy, vary his sentence length from 80 words to 4, yet average a mature 26? Can he successfully echo his opening stand in his conclusion, as the President does with "Let us go forth"? And would he be willing to submit a statement of his beliefs to the scrutiny of the entire world? Few of us risk as much in a lifetime of speaking and writing as does the President in a single day.

The 1961 Inaugural Address offers an appealing entry into the world of word choice, sentence construction, and emotional appeals. And as we watch a young, successful and highly literate man like Mr. Kennedy work successfully to convince others, perhaps we will become more concerned with our own ability to express ourselves. The Inaugural Address forms a good exercise in close reading, and the student will find in it more to write about than he has time for. A cynical few will demur at parts of the speech as old bromides, but by far the majority will conclude, as Dr. Johnson did with Gray's *Elegy,* that here we meet "images which find a mirror in every mind, and sentiments to which every bosom returns an echo."

CHARLOTTE WATKINS SMITH

Carl Becker's Practice of Writing

Charlotte Watkins Smith has taught history at Iowa State College and Rockford College. She is the author of Carl Becker: On History and the Climate of Opinion *(1956), from which the selection below has been taken. In this article Mrs. Smith studies the stylistic effects of four revisions on the final draft of a passage from Becker's book,* Eve of the Revolution.

> One whose ear is sensitive to the subtler, elusive harmonies of expression, one who in imagination hears the pitch and cadence and rhythm of the thing he wishes to say before he says it, often makes a sad business of public speaking. . . . He instinctively wishes to cross out what he has just said, and say it over again in a different way. . . . In writing he can cross out and rewrite at leisure, as often as he likes, until the sound and the sense are perfectly suited—until the thing composes.[1]

One of the few handwritten first drafts which remains in Becker's files is a part of Chapter V of his *Eve of the Revolution.* This particular chapter, "A Little Discreet Conduct," is a model of Becker's literary virtues; it shows to the full the happy perfection that can occasionally be attained in the con-

---

Reprinted from C. W. Smith: *Carl Becker: On History and the Climate of Opinion.* © 1956 by Cornell University. Used by permission of Cornell University Press.
[1]Becker, *Declaration of Independence*, p. 195.

struction of a chapter. It is unified and coherent; it flows from paragraph to paragraph through faultless transitions. This chapter exhibits at once Becker's chief interest in history and his greatest historical gifts. In a letter to William E. Dodd in 1920, Becker indicated his theme:

> The conclusion I draw [from the World War, 1914-1918] is not that the world is divided into good men and bad, intelligent and ignorant, and that all will be well when the bad men are circumvented and the ignorant are enlightened. This old eighteenth century view is too naive and simple. Neither good men nor bad wanted *this* war . . . yet neither were able to prevent it. . . . For good men and bad, ignorant and enlightened (even as enlightened as Mr. Wilson), reason and aspiration and emotion—what we call principles, faith, ideals—are without their knowing it at the service of complex and subtle instinctive reactions and impulses. This is the meaning, if it has any, of my book on the Eve of the Revolution, and particularly of the chapter on Adams and Hutchinson.[2]

"A Little Discreet Conduct" is chiefly a portrayal of the fateful lack of discreet conduct on the part of two men—Thomas Hutchinson and Samuel Adams. The brilliant contrast Becker drew between these two men of Massachusetts illuminates the path to revolution during the relatively quiet years between the Boston Massacre and the Boston Tea Party. Becker later wrote the studies of Adams and Hutchinson for the *Dictionary of American Biography,* expanding and developing his analysis of the relations between the two men a good deal further, but both biographies are outlined in this chapter.

In *The Eve of the Revolution,* which conveys "not a record of what men did, but a sense of how they thought and felt about what they did,"[3] Becker disclaimed any attempt at writing orthodox history based entirely on verifiable references. But the scholarly authority behind the book was recognized at once, even though at that time (1918) "scientific history" was a great deal more attempted and more honored than it is today. Perhaps critics were disarmed by Becker's own genial admission that the book might not be history, but they would not have been so disarmed if "the illusion of the intellectual atmosphere of past time" had not been utterly convincing.[4]

The "reproduction of the thought and feeling" of past days had the ring of truth to the scholar and the expert not less than to the uninitiated.[5] It had it, I think, because after knowledge of documents left off, Becker used "those fainter powers of apprehension and surmise and sensitiveness, by which after all, most high truth has been reached as well as most high art and po-

---

[2]Becker to Dodd, June 17, 1920.
[3]*Eve of the Revolution,* p. vii.
[4]*Ibid.,* pp. vii-viii.
[5]Cf. review by C. H. Van Tyne, *AHR,* XXIV, 734-735.

etry."[6] Still, a look into his files—and even more into his doctoral dissertation—shows that behind the "rather free paraphrase of what some imagined spectator or participant might have thought or said"[7] lay an immense detailed knowledge of what, in fact, a great many actual persons had said and written. Becker's thesis, *The History of Political Parties in the Province of New York, 1760-1776,* was a thoroughly documented, scholarly study of the formation of revolutionary parties. He was absorbed in the mental processes by which the revolutionist was gradually differentiated from the loyalist. For this study he read a vast amount of primary source material on the first phase of the revolution—letters, diaries, newspapers, minutes of committee meetings, and pamphlets. Unfortunately the notes for this study are not now in the Becker files. The only large collection of research notes on American history remaining is the set done for his book *The Beginnings of the American People.* The reading Becker did for his first two books gave him an intimate acquaintance with men and ideas in the last half of the eighteenth century in America and in England. Information he had in quantity; *The Eve of the Revolution* is evidently the result of recollecting it in tranquillity after years in which his memory had performed the sure task of sifting and selecting from the mass of facts those most vivid and meaningful to Carl Becker. It added something new to the history of the American Revolution, not because it was an "original contribution to knowledge," but because it was a unique interpretation of old facts. Not a competent organization of 3 by 5 slips, but the creation of individual imagination, which therefore had to be new. "Be yourself; it is the only thing nobody else can be" was a rule for writing history as well as anything else.

So completely was *The Eve* a presentation of what interested Carl Becker in 1918 about the years from 1763 to 1776 that in the original draft it did not include (or only barely mentioned) such famous and stirring events as the Stamp Act Congress, the Boston Massacre, and the battles of Lexington and Concord. Descriptions of these were added on the request of the editor of the series who thought that the readers who expected these things ought not to be disappointed.[8] The book is about events in the minds of men, not overt actions, for the most part.

Although Chapter V presents most effectively the thoughts and feelings of Samuel Adams and Thomas Hutchinson, neither of these character sketches brings out any new facts or corrects any previous study. For Hutchinson, at least, Becker apparently relied entirely on secondary sources. The quotations from Hutchinson's letters are almost entirely taken from those quoted in James K. Hosmer's *Life of Thomas Hutchinson.*[9] Becker

[6]Gilbert Murray, *Five Stages of Greek Religion* (Oxford, 1925), p. 206.
[7]*Eve of the Revolution,* p. vii.
[8]Allen Johnson to Carl Becker, March 15, 1918.
[9]James K. Hosmer, *Life of Thomas Hutchinson* (Boston: Houghton Mifflin, 1896). Becker's notes and the MS of the *Eve of the Revolution* show this. Becker read the unpublished Hutchinson papers before writing the *DAB* article (see his Notes, drawer 16) but not before writing *The Eve.* He also used P. O. Hutchinson's *Diary and Letters of Thomas Hutchinson* (2 vols.; Boston: Houghton Mifflin, 1884-86).

did not set out to correct Hosmer; he accepted his work, but he refocused it. Not by research but by reflection, by bringing his acute imagination to bear upon the old, well-known facts of the colonial governor's career Becker was able to bring him to life in a portrait that is intensely human and poignant. The struggle between the governor, who "possessed the efficient mind" but was often wrongheaded, and the "Great Incendiary," who "had the soul of a Jacobin," is as gripping as a novel because it is told with as much artistry.

His first concern—and this is in accord with the rules he worked out for himself—was to get clear organization. His transitions linked paragraph to paragraph, chapter to chapter, so firmly that the whole is a faultless chain—perfectly distinguishable, link from link, yet unbroken. Chapter V of *The Eve of the Revolution* is a superb example of his technique. The quotations at the head of the chapter form the prelude:

> It has been his [Thomas Hutchinson's] principle from a boy that mankind are to be governed by the discerning few, and it has been ever since his ambition to be the hero of the few.—Samuel Adams.

> We have not been so quiet these five years. . . . If it were not for two or three Adamses, we should do well enough.—Thomas Hutchinson.[10]

These quotations are precisely suitable because they not only show the deep gulf between Adams and Hutchinson, but they also are fairer remarks than they usually made about each other and they forecast very well Becker's own judgment of each man. Each said much more violent things about the other at times, but Becker did not seek merely vivid contrasts; he was introducing strains that would be developed further.

The first paragraph states the theme. He shows that things were indeed quiet; Horace Walpole thought in December, 1771, that all the storms were happily blown over; and the Connecticut agent, Mr. Johnson, wrote to Wedderburn in October, 1771: "A little discreet conduct on both sides would perfectly reestablish that warm affection and respect toward Great Britain for which this country was once remarkable."

Still, that affection had been strained and we are reminded that "Discreet conduct was nowhere more necessary than in Massachusetts." The deliberate mention, one by one, of a few of the chief men of the colony reveals why that was so: John Adams, James Otis, John Hancock, Governor Francis Bernard, and, above all, Samuel Adams and Thomas Hutchinson.

The third paragraph begins the sketch of Samuel Adams, which continues through eleven pages to the point where the sketch of Hutchinson begins. Since the first draft of the chapter is fragmentary up to the beginning of the description of Thomas Hutchinson, let us begin a comparison of the rough draft and the printed version at this point. The closing paragraph of the

---

[10]*Eve of the Revolution*, p. 150.

Adams sketch ends with this sentence: "Of all these restless adversaries and infamous plotters of ruin, the chief in the mind of Samuel Adams, was probably Mr. Thomas Hutchinson."

Beginning there the rough draft reads:

> Judged only by what he said and did, and by such other superficial sources of information as are open to the historian, Mr. Th. Hutchinson does not appear to have been, at any time in his life, an Enemy of the Human Race.

The final version is:

> Judged only by what he did and said and by such other sources of information as are open to the historian, Thomas Hutchinson does not appear to have been, prior to 1771, an Enemy of the Human Race.

There are four changes in this sentence—each one attesting to the care and sensitivity with which Becker's revisions were made. First, the order is reversed from the hackneyed "said and did" to "did and said"; after all, by any pragmatic test a man's actions rank ahead of his words. Second, the "superficial" is omitted. Besides other possible objections, it made the line too sibilant. Third, the "Mr." is dropped because it repeated the "Mr. Thomas Hutchinson" of the previous sentence, and this was particularly undesirable because there it carried the sneering tones of Samuel Adams. The last and greatest improvement was changing "at any time in his life" to "prior to 1771." The irony is sharpened by dry accuracy.

None of these changes is indicated on the original draft. All were made in some intermediate copy or (more likely) copies which are no longer in his files. This original draft, like all the others, indicates that Becker wrote "with ease and rapidity," no more "constructing his sentences with slow and painful effort" than Jefferson did.[11] There are many changes, crossed out words and slashed out paragraphs, but signs of really difficult writing are absent. There are few places where repeated false starts to a sentence appear; crossed out lines never fill up more space on the page than accepted lines. There are no indications that he was ever simply stuck and unable to get going. His words run together as if they flowed from a flying pen seldom lifted from the paper. Becker made endless changes: substituting the more exact word for the less, the simpler statement for the more complex, one word where there had been two before; revising always away from the conventional, the stereotyped, the pretentious; but his original drafts (by 1918 at least) were not crude productions as they stood. His original sentences have all the characteristic flavor. Where whole sentences or paragraphs are crossed out, it is usually done to change or clarify the organization or to compress a thought by omitting details.

---

[11]*Declaration of Independence*, p. 198.

His characterization of Hutchinson completes the statement of the main theme of the chapter: an unaccustomed quiet prevailed in the colonies even in Massachusetts; if it could be prolonged and deepened the colonies would be saved for the empire, but some powerful forces were making for dissension. It was not yet clear which would triumph. Then Adams and Hutchinson are shown as the principals—two determined men out to build inconsistent worlds. We see then that they do not wish to compromise and do not know how.

The climax of the book is here, in the middle of chapter five. Suspense is turned into premonition in one crucial paragraph. Structurally this paragraph forms the link between the long flashback portrayals of Adams and Hutchinson and the continuing narrative. A transition paragraph both in form and in emotional tone, it represents Becker's most painstaking work. Seldom indeed, if the evidence of his few remaining first drafts be taken as typical, did Becker labor so long to perfect one small section. It is interesting to see how he brought it, bit by bit, to its final shape.

The organization must have been perfectly clear in his mind from the beginning: from the first draft to the printed copy the position of this paragraph was not changed, nor the general burden of it. It developed one clear idea: the reconciliation which seemed to be in the offing in 1771 was not going to come because Adams and Hutchinson were fated to keep on widening the breach instead of narrowing it. Becker's tragic sense of life and of history became almost explicit here. The war came not because of the actions of bad men, but because "for good men and bad, ignorant and enlightened . . . reason and aspiration and emotion—what we call principles, faith, ideals—are without their knowing it at the service of complex and subtle instinctive reactions and impulses."[12] Knowing as deeply as any poet that "words have an aura as well as a core,"[13] he kept rewriting until his meaning was conveyed in the very pitch and cadence of the words, until the reader could hear in the distance the slow, sure step of impending doom. Succeeding paragraphs then would detail how Adams and Hutchinson between them brought about the final break.

The Hutchinson sketch closed with a letter the governor wrote denouncing Samuel Adams as a "Great Incendiary." In one paragraph Becker wanted to bring us back to the line of marching events and at the same time let us see where that line must end. This was his first attempt:

FIRST DRAFT—A

The letter undirected and undated, in which ~~Gov~~ Th. H. pronounced

this judgment of S. Adams, was probably written about the time ~~when~~

---

[12]Becker to Dodd, June 17, 1920.
[13]Joseph Wood Krutch, "The Indispensable Century," *Saturday Review of Literature,* XXXIII (Sept. 2, 1950), 7.

~~he~~ of his accession to the governorship; about the time, that is to say

when Mr. Johnson was writing to Wedderburn that "a little discreet

conduct on both sides would perfectly reestablish that warm aff. &

respect for Gt. B for which this country was once remarkable." This

was no doubt true advice, and perhaps practicable to follow, on both

sides, so far as both sides were on opposite sides of the Atlantic. Lord

North did not irritate John Adams and John Adams ~~was~~ not being
    a member of the House
~~the daily companion of the minister~~ was not a persistent thorn in ~~his~~

the side of the first minister. ~~With M In the case of Mr. H and S Adams~~

~~it was otherwise different.~~ These men might grow ~~tired of controversy~~

~~& be willing~~ weary of altercations, and willingly let the controversy

subside. In the case of Mr. H. & Samuel Adams, it was not so.
    They were on opposite sides to be sure; but of necessity
~~They~~ lived together in the little town of Boston, were ~~brought~~
        the performance of
bound to come together in virtue of official functions, & ~~were~~
    come face to face round the corner in some or other
likely any day to ~~meet in the~~ narrow streets. ~~In the case of S.~~

~~Adams and Mr. H.~~ Under these circumstances, & each holding so
        both
      ~~neither~~ xxxx [illegible] xxxx Human Race
low an opinion of the other's honesty, a little discreet conduct, even

a very little, was scarcely to be looked for from ~~Sam~~ Samuel Adams or

Mr. Hutchinson. And in fact both men, during the years 1771 & 1772

when if ever there was a prospect that the controversy would subside,

did what they could to perpetuate it: wittingly or unwittingly they ~~did~~

~~their~~ labored to push the continent into a rebellion, giving and taking

occasion to recall ancient grudges, to renew useless ~~arguments~~ debates,

Charlotte Watkins Smith   257

daily keeping the dying embers alive against the time when some

chance wind might blow them to a devouring flame.

Notice how the logical sequence from paragraph to paragraph was provided in this first draft. The beginning and ending of this passage remained
the same except for slight verbal changes through every revision. Nevertheless, much of the passage as it stands is awkward and overwritten, and it
comforts us to see that even Becker had to fight those ubiquitous and meaningless "in the case of's." Not satisfied with the sound of it, Becker reached
for a clean sheet of paper and tried rewriting the last third:[14]

SECOND DRAFT—B

~~his Enemy & the chief Enemy~~ and each holding so low an opinion of

the other's honesty,—under these circumstances, discreet conduct,

even a little, was scarcely to be looked for. ~~Under the circumstances~~

~~No conduct on the part of either man could be thought of as discreet~~
                                         wittingly or unwittingly
~~on the pa by the other.~~ Both men, in fact, did what they could, during

the ~~two years~~ 1771 and 1772, ~~to keep the great controversy alive, to~~

~~perpetuate that~~ perpetuate the quarrel, giving & taking occasion ~~to~~

~~renew useless arguments~~ to recall ~~old grudges~~ ancient differences &

renew useless arguments, keeping as it were the dying embers alive

against the time when some chance wind might blow them once more

into devouring flame.

Although he rearranged the last two sentences several times, he still failed
to achieve what he was after, so he slashed it out, turned the sheet over and
rewrote the paragraph entirely:

[14]My assumption has been that Becker wrote all the drafts given here (A-D) at one sitting and that a final
revision (or more than one) was made before the book was printed. It is possible, however, that Becker
did each one at a separate sitting with considerable time in between.

The letter, undated and undirected, in which Th H pronounced this deliberate judgment of S Adams, was probably written about the time of his accession to the Governorship; about the time, that is to say, when Mr. Johnson, the Conn Agent, was writing to Wedderburn that a "little discreet conduct on both sides" would ~~fully re-establish~~ restore the former cordial relations between Gt. B & the colonies. This was not good advice, and perhaps practicable to be followed, "on both sides," so far as ~~both sides.~~ the parties to the controversy were ~~sufficiently~~ in a physical sense, sufficiently separated. ~~Lord~~ Lord North did not irritate John Adams, at least not excessively; and John Adams, not ~~be present daily~~ being in daily attendance in the House of Commons, on the opposition benches, was not a persistent thorn in official the side of the first Minister. These men and perhaps even Mr. Wed-derburn himself, might have grown weary of altercations carried on under so great disadvantages ~~at a distance of 3000 miles~~ & without the stimulus of mutual reciprocal exasperation ~~engendered~~ engendered by reasonable propinquity: ~~therefore~~ ~~These men~~ might conceivably have let the controversy subside. But Samuel Adams & Mr. H. were differently situated. Both men, unfor-tunately, lived in Boston, which was ~~not a~~ smaller then, and in some ways more provincial, than it is now: necessarily, ~~requirements of the~~ ~~perform~~ in the performance of official functions, their ~~conflicting~~ keen & incomperable [sic] minds were brought to bear upon ~~matters~~ the same matters: & they were likely, any day, to come face to face round

the corner in some or other narrow street. From S. Adams & Th H,

seeing that neither had a high opinion of the other's honesty a "little

discreet conduct," even a very little, was scarcely to be looked for

under the circumstances.—And in fact both men, during the years

1771 & 1772, when if ever there was ~~a~~ good prospect that the controv.

might subside, did what they could to perpetuate it. Giving & taking

occasion to ~~keep~~ recall ancient grudges or renew useless debates, and

so during those calm days keeping the dying embers alive against the

time when some chance wind might fan them into devouring flames.

The first thing he did in this third draft was to shorten the quotation from Johnson's letter giving just enough to recall the passage cited earlier with the key phrase "a little discreet conduct." The sentence, already a long one, was thus simplified and improved. The first real difficulty was tackled in the next five sentences where he had repeatedly used the word *side* or *sides*. To be sure, the sentences were intelligible enough upon a careful reading, but the repetition of "both sides" . . . "both sides," . . . "opposite sides" . . . "thorn in the side" . . . "subside" . . . "opposite sides" did not come off as a device for emphasis and without that it was merely flat or even confusing. After this was smoothed out, a number of small changes were made through the rest of the paragraph, and some of the phrases introduced in draft B were incorporated.

After that, Becker evidently reread this third draft (C) testing its clarity and cogency. Anything which confused or blurred the main point had to be eliminated. I think that was the reason for his subsequent dropping of the lines about Lord North and John Adams. These lines made a colorful illustration of his point, one which intrigues the imagination. Too much so, perhaps. It conjures up pictures of persons and situations that are not properly a part of this particular tale and is more distracting than helpful. Moreover, it breaks the passage in two distinct halves which might well have been two separate paragraphs—the first ending with "might conceivably have let the controversy subside"; the second beginning: "But Samuel Adams and Mr. Hutchinson were differently situated." By the omission of the two sentences on North and John Adams, in spite of the nice contrast they made with Hutchinson and Sam Adams, the unity of the paragraph was preserved and the structure tightened:

The letter, undated & undirected, in which ~~Mr. H~~ Th H pronounced

this deliberate judgment of S. Adams, was probably written about the

time of his accession to the Governorship; that is to say, about the

time when Mr. Johnson, the Conn. agent, was writing to W- that "A

little discreet conduct on both sides" would perfectly restore cordial

In the way of

relations between ~~Eng.~~ B. & her colonies. ~~Of~~ discreet conduct, even

~~either~~

a very little, not much was to be ~~exp~~ hoped from Governor H or S

Adams in their dealings with each other; ~~seeing that they each had so~~

~~low an opinion of the other's honesty~~ Unfortunately, they had dealings

with each other; their incomparable minds were necessarily, in the per-

formance of official functions, brought to bear on the same matters &

~~personally they were likely, any day~~ Unfortunately they both lived in

~~Boston the small town of~~ Boston, and were likely, any day, to come

face to face round the corner of some or other narrow street of that

small town. ~~Each~~ The ~~stimulus of~~ reciprocal exasperation engendered

by reasonable propinquity, so necessary to the maintenance of ~~per-~~

~~petual~~ altercations, was a perpetual stimulus to both men, confirming

each in his low opinion of the others honesty of purpose. And there-

fore, both men, preeminent as leaders on either side, did what they

could during the years 1771 and 1772, when if ever ~~there was good~~

~~prospect~~ it appeared that others were "growing weary of altercations,"

to perpetuate the controversy: by giving and taking occasion to recall

Charlotte Watkins Smith   261

ancient grudges or revive fruitless ~~debate~~ disputes, they managed ~~to~~

~~keep~~ during this time of calm to keep the dying embers alive against

the day when some ~~chance~~ rising wind might blow them into a de-

vouring flame.

Whatever was irrelevant was omitted, even when it was only a trifling matter of a short clause like the one about eighteenth-century Boston, which was "smaller, and in some ways more provincial, than it is now." The smallness of Boston in 1771 was relevant to the point he was making; the provinciality of Boston, then or subsequently, was, alas, not relevant and so that part was suppressed.

The change in the last sentence from "some chance wind" to "some rising wind" was really admirable. With one word we are reminded that the wind, however low it gets, never dies. It is inevitable, not a chance, that it will blow again, and the embers of disaffection kept alive by Samuel Adams will flame into rebellion.

Draft D is close to the final form of the paragraph as it appears on pages 175-177 of *The Eve of the Revolution,* but some more changes were made in later revisions which are not now among the Becker Papers. Perhaps the most noticeably unsatisfactory spot remaining in the fourth draft was the phrase "their incomparable minds." "Incomparable" was first substituted for "conflicting" in draft C; it stayed in draft D, although such an ambiguous word must have been only a makeshift until the right word came to mind. Or possibly Becker really wished to use the word in its primary sense—"impossible of comparison"—and only gave it up reluctantly after reflecting that the derived meaning of "fine beyond comparison" has become so much more common that he could not escape it. Several other phrases were not quite satisfactory either. For example, "preeminent as leaders on either side" is awkward. These and other flaws, discernible, perhaps, only to Becker's sensitive ear, disappeared in the final version:

> The letter, undated and undirected, in which Thomas Hutchinson pronounced this deliberate judgment on Samuel Adams, was probably written about the time of his accession to the Governorship; that is to say, about the time when Mr. Johnson, the Connecticut Agent, was writing to Wedderburn that "the people seem to grow weary of altercations," and that "a little discreet conduct on both sides" would perfectly restore cordial relations between Britain and her colonies. In the way of "a little discreet conduct," even a very little, not much was to be hoped for from either Governor Hutchinson or Samuel Adams in their dealings with each other. Unfortunately, they *had* deal-

ings with each other: in the performance of official functions, their incommensurable and repellent minds were necessarily brought to bear upon the same matters of public concern. Both, unfortunately, lived in Boston and were likely any day to come face to face round the corner of some or other narrow street of that small town. That reciprocal exasperation engendered by reasonable propinquity, so essential to the life of altercations, was therefore a perpetual stimulus to both men, confirming each in his obstinate opinion of the other as a malicious and dangerous enemy of all that men hold dear. Thus it was that during the years 1771 and 1772, when if ever it appeared that others were "growing weary of altercations," these honorable men and trusted leaders did what they could to perpetuate the controversy. By giving or taking occasion to recall ancient grudges or revive fruitless disputes, wittingly or unwittingly they together managed during this time of calm to keep the dying embers alive against the day when some rising wind might blow them into devouring flames.[15]

The first difference between draft D and the printed version is in the quotation from Johnson. In the final reading the first part of the quotation—"the people seem to grow weary of altercations," is included. This balances the paragraph more perfectly, and is needed as a reminder that Adams and Hutchinson were at that moment somewhat out of step with many of their contemporaries. The next change—inserting the words "a little" into the beginning of the second sentence: "In the way of 'a little discreet conduct'"—is typical of Becker's careful attention to emphasis.

Two small additions follow—"either" is inserted before Governor Hutchinson in the same sentence, and "had" is italicized in the following one. Italics seem desirable and justifiable in that place, but italics were rarely used by Becker. He used them here purely for emphasis and not to try to rouse the reader's emotions, of course, which was the use he deprecated so strongly in Jefferson's "philippic against slavery."[16]

The next notable alteration occurs in the same sentence. The semicolon after "Unfortunately, they had dealings with each other;" was changed to a colon—a common (in fact a highly characteristic) construction in Becker's writing. Typically the rest of the sentence illustrates, explains, and makes specific the general statement preceding the colon. Here he made another improvement by transposing the phrase "in the performance of official functions" to stand ahead of the main clause instead of in the middle of it, where it separated subject from verb. Then for the ambiguous word "incomparable" he has happily substituted the clear and precise words "incommensurable and repellent." So the sentence reads finally: "Unfortunately, they *had* dealings with each other: in the performance of official functions, their

---

[15]*Eve of the Revolution*, pp. 175-177.
[16]*Declaration of Independence*, pp. 220-221.

incommensurable and repellent minds were necessarily brought to bear upon the same matters of public concern."

Several one-word changes follow. "Life" for "maintenance" improves that irritating sentence which begins "The reciprocal exasperation engendered by reasonable propinquity . . ." (though, to my mind, it remains too irritating for its worth as onomatopoeia). Then comes another change worth noting. Draft D reads "confirming each in his low opinion of the other's honesty of purpose." See how much better the final version is: "confirming each in his obstinate opinion of the other as a malicious and dangerous enemy of all that men hold dear."

Most interesting of all, perhaps, is the revision of the last sentence of draft D, which becomes two sentences in the final reading. First, it becomes much more sonorous by being put into indirect construction. The opening "Thus it was that" reminds us of the Biblical "And so it came to pass that." Then again the adverbial clause "during the years 1771 and 1772, when if ever it appeared that others were 'growing weary of altercations'" is transposed so that the subject and verb stand together. The subject, by an inspired change, from "both men, preeminent as leaders on either side" becomes "These honorable men and trusted leaders." The connotations of "these honorable men" are grim and full of tragedy for us, though we find in the next paragraph that Samuel Adams openly wished to make "Brutuses of the men of Boston." The last sentence continues the somber rhythm, the falling cadence which tells us as clearly as the words themselves that there will be not peace but a sword.

It remained for the rest of the chapter to show how Adams and Hutchinson dealt with each other, how Adams (conscientiously) and Hutchinson (in the vain endeavor to say the last word) kept the quarrel going. Becker has prepared us to understand why they act as they do and to appreciate at once how each man's action will affect the other and ultimately will affect the relations between Great Britain and the colonies. In this chapter "even the blind can see the two countries drifting into war,"[17] William E. Dodd wrote to Becker.

What was more important from Becker's point of view, they can see why. "This is precisely the task of the historian, to explain why," Becker protested in an exasperated note on Madelin's treatment of the fall of the Bastille.[18] Madelin, instead of explaining why the fall of the Bastille became a great event, treats it as a sham. "This is not writing history, it is merely complaining about the way things happen in history," Becker commented. Given a somewhat similar situation in the affair of the Hutchinson letters, he does not treat it that way. He explains with delicious irony just how it was that Samuel Adams made the publication of the letters into an exposé that ended the governor's influence on his countrymen forever, and how

---

[17] Dodd to Becker, Jan. 23, 1919.
[18] Louis Madelin, *The French Revolution* (New York: Putnam, 1916), p. 85. Cited in Becker's Notes, box 2.

Adams did it in spite of the fact, bewildering to the logical governor, that "in these letters there was no statement of fact or expression of opinion not already well known."[19] Becker's closing paragraph on the letter incident is a typical example of his work. Here he was doing what he thought was his proper task, explaining how a mere affair of words (and not very amazing ones either) had become a great event:

> His Majesty did not remove Mr. Hutchinson; but the Governor's usefulness, from every point of view, was at an end. When the notorious letters were finally printed, it appeared that there were seventeen in all, of which six were written by Mr. Hutchinson in the years 1768 and 1769. These latter documents did not in fact add anything to the world's stock of knowledge; but they had been so heralded, ushered in with so much portentous explication that they scarcely needed to be read to be understood. "Had they been Chevy Chase," the Governor said, the people would have believed them "full of evil and treason." It was indeed the perfect fruit of Samuel Adams's labors that the significance of Mr. Hutchinson's letters had in some manner become independent of their contents. So awake were the people to the danger of being deceived, that whatever the Governor now said or ever had written was taken to be but the substance of things hoped for, the evidence of things not seen.[20]

Becker saw that Samuel Adams' great undertaking was to create a climate of opinion in which any loyally conservative crown officer would be judged an Enemy of the Human Race. Hence, for Becker, the victory of the Great Incendiary was proved, not in December, 1773, when the mob at his signal boarded the East India Company's ships and threw tea worth £14,000 into the Boston harbor, but six months earlier, when the men of Boston read treason in their governor's letters. Accordingly Becker spent six pages on the letter episode, "the perfect fruit of Samuel Adams' labors," and disposed of the Tea Party, a far more tangible fruit of his labors, in a dozen lines.[21]

After the affair of the governor's letters, the duel between Adams and Hutchinson was really over; the time when discreet conduct might have counted was past. Becker swiftly brought his chapter to a close, without even mentioning Hutchinson's last indiscretion, his refusal of return clearance papers to the tea ships, which precipitated the final train of crises. By that time it did not matter who did it, Becker implies. A final revealing glimpse of Hutchinson ends the chapter:

> It was a limitation of Thomas Hutchinson's excellent administrative mind that he was wholly unaware of this crisis. In February of the

---

[19]*Eve of the Revolution*, p. 195.
[20]*Ibid.*, p. 198.
[21]*Ibid.*, pp. 199, 206.

next year, finding that "a little discreet conduct," or indeed any conduct on his part, was altogether without good effect, the Governor
announced that he had "obtained leave from the King to go to England." . . . It was his expectation that after a brief absence, when General Gage by a show of military force should have brought the province
to a reasonable frame of mind, he would return and assume again the
responsibilities of his office. He never returned, but died in England
on June 3, 1780, an unhappy and a homesick exile from the country
which he loved.[22]

IAN WATT

The First Paragraph
of *The Ambassadors:*
An Explication

Ian Watt is professor of English at Stanford. He is the author of The Rise
of the Novel *(1957), a pioneer sociological study of the eighteenth-century
novel. The article included here is also a pioneer study, for in this essay
Professor Watt applies to prose the techniques of close explication usually
applied only to poetry. Watt's syntactic analysis leads him to conclude that
"All the details are scrupulously presented as reflections from the novel's
essential centre—the narrator's patterning of the ideas going forwards and
backwards in Strether's mind." Both Watt and Walker Gibson, then, see
style as psychological revelation: Gibson as a psychological revelation of
the speaker, and Watt as a psychological revelation of the relationship between speaker and subject.*

When I was asked if I would do a piece of explication at this conference,
I was deep in Henry James, and beginning *The Ambassadors:* so the passage chose itself; but just what was explication, and how did one do it to
prose?[1] I take it that whereas explanation, from *explanare*, suggests a mere

---

[22]*Ibid.*, p. 199.
From *Essays in Criticism,* X (July 1960), 250-274. Reprinted by permission of the publisher.
[1]A paper given at the Ninth Annual Conference of Non-Professorial University Teachers of English, at
Oxford on April 5th, 1959. I am very grateful for the many criticisms and suggestions made in the course
of the subsequent discussion; in preparing the paper for publication I have taken as much account of them
as was possible, short of drastic expansion or alteration. I also acknowledge my debt to Dorothea Krook,
Frederick C. Crews, and Henry Nash Smith.

making plain by spreading out, explication, from *explicare,* implies a progressive unfolding of a series of literary implications, and thus partakes of our modern preference for multiplicity in method and meaning: explanation assumes an ultimate simplicity, explication assumes complexity.

Historically, the most developed tradition of explication is presumably that which developed out of medieval textual exegesis and became the chief method of literary instruction in French secondary and higher education in the late nineteenth century. *Explication de texte* in France reflects the rationalism of nineteenth-century Positivist scholarship. At its worst the routine application of the method resembles a sort of bayonet drill in which the exposed body of literature is riddled with etymologies and dates before being despatched in a harrowingly insensitive *résumé.* At its best, however, *explication de texte* can be solidly illuminating, and it then serves to remind us that a piece of literature is not necessarily violated if we give systematic attention to such matters as its author, its historical setting, and the formal properties of its language.

Practical Criticism, on the other hand, as it was developed at Cambridge by I. A. Richards, continues the tradition of the British Empiricists. Inductive rather than deductive, it makes a point of excluding linguistic and historical considerations, so as to derive—in appearance at least—all the literary values of a work empirically from the words on the page. In the last thirty years the emphasis of Practical Criticism on the autonomy of the text has revolutionised the approach to literary studies, and has proved itself a technique of supreme value for teaching and examining students; I myself certainly believe that its use should be expanded rather than curtailed. Yet, at least in the form in which I picked it up as a student and have later attempted to pass it on as a teacher, both its pedagogical effects and its basic methodological assumptions seem to me to be open to serious question. For many reasons. Its air of objectivity confers a spurious authority on a process that is often only a rationalisation of an unexamined judgment, and that must always be to some extent subjective; its exclusion of historical factors seems to authorise a more general anti-historicism; and—though this objection is perhaps less generally accepted—it contains an inherent critical bias in the assumption that the part is a complete enough reflection of the literary whole to be profitably appreciated and discussed in isolation from its context. How far this is true, or how far it can be made to appear so by a well-primed practitioner, is a matter of opinion; but it is surely demonstrable that Practical Criticism tends to find the most merit in the kind of writing which has virtues that are in some way separable from their larger context; it favours kinds of writing that are richly concrete in themselves, stylistically brilliant, or composed in relatively small units. It is therefore better suited to verse than to prose; and better suited to certain kinds of either than to others where different and less concentrated merits are appropriate, as in the novel.

As for its pedagogical effects—and here again I have mainly my own past experience in mind—Practical Criticism surely tends to sensitise us towards objects only within a certain range of magnitude: below that threshold it becomes subjective and impressionist, paying very little attention to the humble facts of the grammar and syntax of the words on the page; while, at the other extreme, it often ignores the larger meaning, and the literary and historical contexts of that meaning.

As a practical matter these restrictions may all be necessary for the pupil and salutary for the teacher; and I mention them mainly to justify my present attempt to develop the empirical and inductive methods of Practical Criticism in such a way as to deal with those elements in a literary text whose vibrations are so high or so low that we Ricardian dogs have not yet been trained to bark at them.

It is mainly in these penumbral areas, of course, that the French *explication de texte* habitually operates; but its analysis of grammar and of the literary and historical background are usually a disconnected series of discrete demonstrations which stop short of the unifying critical synthesis that one hopes for. Until fairly recently the same could have been said, and perhaps with greater emphasis, about the German tradition of literary scholarship, with its almost entirely independent pursuit of philology and philosophy. More recent trends in *Stilforschung* however—of which Wolfgang Clemen's *The Development of Shakespeare's Imagery* (Bonn, 1936), was an early example—come closer to, and indeed partly reflect, the more empirical Anglo-American models of literary criticism; while, even more promising perhaps for the study of prose, though seemingly quite independent of the influence of Practical Criticism, is the development, mainly from Romance philology, of what has come to be called 'stylistics'.

For my purposes, however, it remains not so much a method as a small group of isolated, though spectacular, individual triumphs. I yield to no one in my admiration for Leo Spitzer's *Linguistics and Literary History* (Baltimore, 1948), or for the continual excitement and illumination offered in Erich Auerbach's *Mimesis* (1946: trans. Willard Trask, Princeton, N.J., 1953); their achievements, however, strike me mainly as tributes to the historical imagination and philosophical understanding of the German mind at its best; I find their brilliant commentaries on words or phrases or passages essentially subjective; and if I am tempted to emulate the *bravura* with which they take off from the word on the page to leap into the farthest empyreans of *Kulturgeschichte,* I soon discover that the Cambridge east winds have condemned me to less giddy modes of critical transport.

Yet what other models are there to help one to analyse a paragraph of Jamesian prose? Some of the historical studies of prose style could, conceivably, be applied; but I am fearful of ending up with the proposition that James was a Ciceronian—with Senecan elements, of course, like everyone else. As for the new linguistics, the promises as regards literary analysis seem greater than the present rewards: the most practical consequence of my exposure to Charles Fries's *The Structure of English: An Introduction to the Construction of English Sentences* (New York, 1952), for example, was to deprive me of the innocent pleasure that comes from imagining you know the names of things. Structural linguistics in general is mainly (and rightly) concerned with problems of definition and description at a considerably more basic level of linguistic usage than the analysis of the literary effect of Henry James's grammatical particularities seems to require.

Perhaps the most promising signs of the gaps being filled have come from what are—in that particular area—amateurs: from Francis Berry's *Poets' Grammar* (London, 1958), or Donald Davie's *Articulate Energy* (London, 1955). But they don't help much with prose, of course, and they aren't basically concerned with grammatical structure in the ordinary sense; although Davie's notion that the principle of continuity in poetry is, after all, primarily grammatical and rational, at least lessens the separation between the stylistic domains of poetry and prose, and suggests some ways of studying how syntax channels expressive force.

Virtually helpless,[2] then, I must face the James passage alone as far as any fully developed and acceptable technique for explicating prose is concerned; but there seem to be good reasons why practical criticism should be supplemented by some of the approaches of French and German scholarship, and by whatever else will lead one from the words on the page to matters as low as syntax and as high as ideas, or the total literary structure.

I

Strether's first question, when he reached the hotel, was about
his friend; yet on his learning that Waymarsh was apparently not
to arrive till evening he was not wholly disconcerted. A telegram
from him bespeaking a room 'only if not noisy', reply paid, was
5 produced for the inquirer at the office, so that the understanding
they should meet at Chester rather than at Liverpool remained
to that extent sound. The same secret principle, however, that had
prompted Strether not absolutely to desire Waymarsh's presence
at the dock, that had led him thus to postpone for a few hours his
10 enjoyment of it, now operated to make him feel he could still
wait without disappointment. They would dine together at the
worst, and, with all respect to dear old Waymarsh—if not even,
for that matter, to himself—there was little fear that in the sequel
they shouldn't see enough of each other. The principle I have just
15 mentioned as operating had been, with the most newly disembarked
of the two men, wholly instinctive—the fruit of a sharp sense that,
delightful as it would be to find himself looking, after so much
separation, into his comrade's face, his business would be a trifle

---

[2]This was before the appearance of the English Institute's symposium *Style in Prose Fiction* (New York, 1959), which offers, besides two general surveys and a valuable bibliography of the field, stylistic studies of six novelists, including one by Charles R. Crow, of 'The Style of Henry James: *The Wings of the Dove.*'

bungled should he simply arrange for this countenance to present
20 itself to the nearing steamer as the first 'note' of Europe. Mixed
with everything was the apprehension, already, on Strether's part,
that it would, at best, throughout, prove the note of Europe in
23 quite a sufficient degree.[3]

It seems a fairly ordinary sort of prose, but for its faint air of elaborate
portent; and on second reading its general quality reminds one of what
Strether is later to observe—approvingly—in Maria Gostrey: an effect of
'expensive, subdued suitability'. There's certainly nothing particularly
striking in the diction or syntax; none of the immediate drama or rich description that we often get at the beginning of novels; and certainly none of
the sensuous concreteness that, until recently, was regarded as a chief
criterion of good prose in our long post-imagistic phase: if anything, the
passage is conspicuously un-sensuous and un-concrete, a little dull perhaps,
and certainly not easy reading.

The difficulty isn't one of particularly long or complicated sentences:
actually they're of fairly usual length: I make it an average of 41 words; a
little, but not very much, longer than James' average of 35 (in Book 2, ch. 2.
of *The Ambassadors*), according to R. W. Short's count, in his very useful
article 'The Sentence Structure of Henry James' (*American Literature,*
XVIII [March 1946], 71-88.)[4] The main cause of difficulty seems rather to
come from what may be called the delayed specification of referents:
'Strether' and 'the hotel' and 'his friend' are mentioned before we are told
who or where they are. But this difficulty is so intimately connected with
James's general narrative technique that it may be better to begin with purely
verbal idiosyncrasies, which are more easily isolated. The most distinctive
ones in the passage seem to be these: a preference for non-transitive verbs;
many abstract nouns; much use of 'that'; a certain amount of elegant varia-

---

[3]Henry James, *The Ambassadors* (Revised Collected Edition, Macmillan: London, 1923). Since there are
a few variants that have a bearing on the argument, it seems desirable to give a collation of the main editions; P is the periodical publication (*The North American Review,* clxxvi, 1903); 1A the first American
edition (Harper and Brothers, New York, 1903); 1E the first English edition (Methuen and Co., London,
1903); N.Y., the 'New York Edition,' New York and London, 1907-9 (the London Macmillan edition used
the sheets of the American edition); CR the 'Collected Revised Edition,' London and New York, 1921-31
(which uses the text of the New York Edition). It should perhaps be explained that the most widely used
editions in England and America make misleading claims about their text: the 'Everyman' edition claims
to use the text 'of the revised Collected Edition', but actually follows the 1st English edition in the last
variant; while the 'Anchor' edition, claiming to be 'a faithful copy of the text of the Methuen first edition',
actually follows the first American edition, including the famous misplaced chapters.
1.4.   *reply paid* NY, CR; *with the answer paid* P, 1A, 1E.
1.5.   *inquirer* P, 1A, 1E, CR; *enquirer* NY.
1.5-6. *Understanding they* NY, CR; *understanding that they* P, 1A, 1E.
1.10. *feel he* NY, CR; *feel that he* P, 1A, 1E.
1.14. *Shouldn't* CR; *shouldn't* NY; *should not* P, 1A, 1E.
1.15. *Newly disembarked,* all eds. except P: *Newly-disembarked.*
1.19. *arrange that this countenance to present* NY, CR; *arrange that this countenance should present*
       P, 1A, 1E.
1.20. *'note' of Europe* CR; *'note', for him, of Europe,* P. 1A, 1E; *'note', of Europe,* NY.
1.22. *that it would* P, 1A, NY, CR; *that he would,* 1E.
[4]I am also indebted to the same author's 'Henry James's World of Images', *PMLA* LXVIII (Dec., 1953),
943-960.

tion to avoid piling up personal pronouns and adjectives such as 'he', 'his' and 'him'; and the presence of a great many negatives and near-negatives.

By the preference for non-transitive verbs I mean three related habits: a great reliance on copulatives—'Strether's first question *was* about his friend'; '*was* apparently not to arrive': a frequent use of the passive voice—'*was* not wholly *disconcerted*'; 'a telegram . . . *was produced*'; 'his business *would be* a trifle *bungled*': and the employment of many intransitive verbs—'the understanding . . . remained . . . sound'; 'the . . . principle . . . operated to'. My count of all the verbs in the indicative would give a total of 14 passive, copulative or intransitive uses as opposed to only 6 transitive ones: and there are in addition frequent infinitive, participial, or gerundial uses of transitive verbs, in all of which the active nature of the subject-verb-and-object sequence is considerably abated—'on his learning'; 'bespeaking a room'; 'not absolutely to desire'; 'led him thus to postpone'.

This relative infrequency of transitive verbal usages in the passage is associated with the even more pronounced tendency towards using abstract nouns as subjects of main or subordinate clauses: 'question'; 'understanding'; 'the same secret principle'; 'the principle'; 'his business'. If one takes only the main clauses, there are four such abstract nouns as subjects, while only three main clauses have concrete and particular subjects ('he', or 'they').[5]

I detail these features only to establish that in this passage, at least, there is a clear quantitative basis for the common enough view that James's late prose style is characteristically abstract; more explicitly, that the main grammatical subjects are very often nouns for mental ideas, 'question', 'principle', etc.; and that the verbs—because they are mainly used either non-transitively, or in infinitive, participial and gerundial forms,—tend to express states of being rather than particular finite actions affecting objects.

The main use of abstractions is to deal at the same time with many objects or events rather than single and particular ones: and we use verbs that denote states of being rather than actions for exactly the same reason—their much more general applicability. But in this passage, of course, James isn't in the ordinary sense making abstract or general statements; it's narrative, not expository prose; what need exploring, therefore, are the particular literary imperatives which impose on his style so many of the verbal and syntactical qualities of abstract and general discourse; of expository rather than narrative prose.

Consider the first sentence. The obvious narrative way of making things particular and concrete would presumably be 'When Strether reached the hotel, he first asked "Has Mr. Waymarsh arrived yet?"' Why does James say it the way he does? One effect is surely that, instead of a sheer stated event, we get a very special view of it; the mere fact that actuality has been

---

[5] Sentences one and four are compound or multiple, but in my count I haven't included the second clause in the latter—'there was little fear': though if we can talk of the clause having a subject it's an abstract one —'fear'.

digested into reported speech—the question 'was about his friend'—involves a narrator to do the job, to interpret the action, and also a presumed audience that he does it for: and by implication, the heat of the action itself must have cooled off somewhat for the translation and analysis of the events into this form of statement to have had time to occur. Lastly, making the subject of the sentence 'question' rather than 'he', has the effect of subordinating the particular actor, and therefore the particular act, to a much more general perspective: mental rather than physical, and subjective rather than objective; 'question' is a word which involves analysis of a physical event into terms of meaning and intention: it involves, in fact, both Strether's mind and the narrator's. The narrator's, because he interprets Strether's act: if James had sought the most concrete method of taking us into Strether's mind—'"Has Mr. Waymarsh come yet?" I at once asked'—he would have obviated the need for the implied external categoriser of Strether's action. But James disliked the 'mere platitude of statement' involved in first-person narrative; partly, presumably, because it would merge Strether's consciousness into the narrative, and not isolate it for the reader's inspection. For such isolation, a more expository method is needed: no confusion of subject and object, as in first-person narration, but a narrator forcing the reader to pay attention to James's primary objective—Strether's mental and subjective state.

The 'multidimensional' quality of the narrative, with its continual implication of a community of three minds—Strether's, James's, and the reader's—isn't signalled very obviously until the fourth sentence—'The principle I have just mentioned as operating . . .'; but it's already been established tacitly in every detail of diction and structure, and it remains pervasive. One reason for the special demand James's fictional prose makes on our attention is surely that there are always at least three levels of development—all of them subjective: the characters' awareness of events: the narrator's seeing of them; and our own trailing perception of the relation between these two.

The primary location of the narrative in a mental rather than a physical continuum gives the narrative a great freedom from the restrictions of particular time and place. Materially, we are, of course, in Chester, at the hotel—characteristically 'the hotel' because a fully particularised specification—'The Pied Bull Inn' say—would be an irrelevant brute fact which would distract attention from the mental train of thought we are invited to partake in. But actually we don't have any pressing sense of time and place: we feel ourselves to be spectators, rather specifically, of Strether's thought processes, which easily and imperceptibly range forwards and backwards both in time and space. Sentence three, for example, begins in the past, at the Liverpool dock; sentence four looks forward to the reunion later that day, and to its many sequels: such transitions of time and place are much easier to effect when the main subjects of the sentences are abstract: a 'principle' exists independently of its context.

The multiplicity of relations—between narrator and object, and between the ideas in Strether's mind—held in even suspension throughout the narrative, is presumably the main explanation for the number of 'thats' in the passage, as well as of the several examples of elegant variation. There are 9 'thats'—only two of them demonstrative and the rest relative pronouns (or conjunctions or particles if you prefer those terms); actually there were no less than three more of them in the first edition, which James removed from the somewhat more colloquial and informal New York edition; while there are several other 'thats' implied—in 'the principle [that] I have just mentioned', for instance.

The number of 'thats' follows from two habits already noted in the passage. 'That' characteristically introduces relative clauses dealing not with persons but with objects, including abstractions; and it is also used to introduce reported speech—'on his learning that Waymarsh'—not 'Mr. Waymarsh isn't here'. Both functions are combined in the third sentence where we get a triple definition of a timeless idea based on the report of three chronologically separate events 'the same secret principle that had prompted Strether not absolutely to desire Waymarsh's presence at the dock, that had led him thus to postpone for a few hours his enjoyment of it, now operated to make him feel that he could still wait without disappointment'.

Reported rather than direct speech also increases the pressure towards elegant variation: the use, for example, in sentence 1 of 'his friend', where in direct speech it would be 'Mr. Waymarsh' (and the reply—'*He* hasn't come yet'). In the second sentence—'a telegram . . . was produced for the inquirer'—'inquirer' is needed because 'him' has already been used for Waymarsh just above; of course, 'the inquirer' is logical enough after the subject of the first sentence has been an abstract noun—'question'; and the epithet also gives James an opportunity for underlining the ironic distance and detachment with which we are invited to view his dedicated 'inquirer', Strether. Later, when Strether is 'the most newly disembarked of the two men', we see how both elegant variation and the grammatical subordination of physical events are related to the general Jamesian tendency to present characters and actions on a plane of abstract categorisation; the mere statement, 'Mr. Waymarsh had already been in England for [so many] months', would itself go far to destroy the primarily mental continuum in which the paragraph as a whole exists.

The last general stylistic feature of the passage to be listed above was the use of negative forms. There are 6 'noes' or 'nots' in the first 4 sentences; four implied negatives—'postpone'; 'without disappointment'; 'at the worst'; 'there was little fear': and two qualifications that modify positiveness of affirmation—'not wholly', and 'to that extent'. This abundance of negatives has no doubt several functions: it enacts Strether's tendency to hesitation and qualification; it puts the reader into the right judicial frame of mind; and it has the further effect of subordinating concrete events to their mental reflection; 'Waymarsh was not to arrive', for example, is not a concrete statement of a physical event: it is subjective—because it implies an expectation in Strether's mind (which was not fulfilled); and it has an abstract quality—because while Waymarsh's arriving would be particular and physical, his *not* arriving is an idea, a non-action. More generally, James's great use of negatives or near-negatives may also, perhaps, be regarded as part of his subjective and abstractive tendency: there are no negatives in nature but only in the human consciousness.

II

The most obvious grammatical features of what Richard Chase has called Henry James's 'infinitely syntactical language' (*The American Novel and its Tradition,* New York, 1957), can, then, be shown to reflect the essential imperatives of his narrative point of view; and they could therefore lead into a discussion of the philosophical qualities of his mind, as they are discussed, for example, by Dorothea Krook in her notable article 'The Method of the Later Works of Henry James' (*London Magazine,* I [1954], 55-70); our passage surely exemplifies James's power 'to generalise to the limit the particulars of experience', and with it the characteristic way in which both his 'perceptions of the world itself, and his perceptions of the logic of the world . . . happen simultaneously, are part of a single comprehensive experience'. Another aspect of the connection between James's metaphysic and his method as a novelist has inspired a stimulating stylistic study—Carlo Izzo's 'Henry James, Scrittore Sintattico' (*Studi Americani,* II [1956], 127-142). The connection between thought and style finds its historical perspective in John Henry Raleigh's illuminating study 'Henry James: The Poetics of Empiricism' (*PMLA,* LXVI [1951], 107-123), which establishes connections between Lockean epistemology and James's extreme, almost anarchic, individualism; while this epistemological preoccupation, which is central to Quentin Anderson's view of how James worked out his father's cosmology in fictional terms (*The American Henry James,* New Brunswick, 1957), also leads towards another large general question, the concern with 'point of view', which became a crucial problem in the history and criticism of fiction under the influence of the sceptical relativism of the late nineteenth-century.

In James's case, the problem is fairly complicated. He may be classed as an 'Impressionist', concerned, that is, to show not so much the events themselves, but the impressions which they make on the characters. But James's continual need to generalise and place and order, combined with his absolute demand for a point of view that would be plastic enough to allow him freedom for the formal 'architectonics' of the novelists' craft, eventually involved him in a very idiosyncratic kind of multiple Impressionism: idiosyncratic because the dual presence of Strether's consciousness and of that of the narrator, who translates what he sees there into more general terms, makes the narrative point of view both intensely individual and yet ultimately social.

Another possible direction of investigation would be to show that the abstractness and indirection of James's style are essentially the result of this characteristic multiplicity of his vision. There is, for example, the story reported by Edith Wharton that after his first stroke James told Lady Prothero that 'in the very act of falling . . . he heard in the room a voice which was distinctly, it seemed, not his own, saying: "So here it is at last, the distinguished thing".' James, apparently, could not but see even his own most fateful personal experience, except as evoked by some other observer's voice in terms of the long historical and literary tradition of death. Carlo Izzo regards this tendency as typical of the Alexandrian style, where there is a marked disparity between the rich inheritance of the means of literary expression, and the meaner creative world which it is used to express; but the defence of the Jamesian habit of mind must surely be that what the human vision shares with that of animals is presumably the perception of concrete images, not the power to conceive universals: such was Aristotle's notion of man's distinguishing capacity. The universals in the present context are presumably the awareness that behind every petty individual circumstance there ramifies an endless network of general moral, social and historical relations. Henry James's style can therefore be seen as a supremely civilised effort to relate every event and every moment of life to the full complexity of its circumambient conditions.

Obviously James's multiple awareness can go too far; and in the later novels it often poses the special problem that we do not quite know whether the awareness implied in a given passage is the narrator's or that of his character. Most simply, a pronoun referring to the subject of a preceding clause is always liable to give trouble if one hasn't been very much aware of what the grammatical subject of that preceding clause was; in the last sentence of the paragraph, for example, 'the apprehension, already, on Strether's part, that . . . it would, at best, . . . prove the "note" of Europe,' 'it' refers to Waymarsh's countenance: but this isn't at first obvious; which is no doubt why, in his revision of the periodical version for the English edition James replaced 'it' by 'he'—simpler, grammatically, but losing some of the ironic visual precision of the original. More seriously, because the narrator's consciousness and Strether's are both present, we often don't know whose mental operations and evaluative judgments are involved in particular cases. We pass, for instance, from the objective analysis of sentence 3 where the analytic terminology of 'the same secret principle' must be the responsibility of the narrator, to what must be a verbatim quotation of Strether's mind in sentence 4: 'with all respect to dear old Waymarsh' is obviously Strether's licensed familiarity.

But although the various difficulties of tense, voice, and reference require a vigilance of attention in the reader which some have found too much to give, they are not in themselves very considerable: and what perhaps is much more in need of attention is how the difficulties arising from the multiplicity of points of view don't by any means prevent James from ordering all the elements of his narrative style into an amazingly precise means of expression: and it is this positive, and in the present case, as it seems to me, triumphant, mastery of the difficulties which I want next to consider.

Our passage is not, I think, James either at his most memorable or at his most idiosyncratic: *The Ambassadors* is written with considerable sobriety and has, for example, little of the vivid and direct style of the early part of *The Wings of the Dove,* or of the happy symbolic complexities of *The Golden Bowl.* Still, the passage is fairly typical of the later James; and I think it can be proved that all or at least nearly all the idiosyncrasies of diction or syntax in the present passage are fully justified by the particular emphases they create.

The most flagrant eccentricity of diction is presumably that where James writes 'the most newly disembarked of the two men' (lines 15-16). 'Most' may very well be a mere slip; and it must certainly seem indefensible to any one who takes it as an absolute rule that the comparative must always be used when only two items are involved.[6] But a defence is at least possible. 'Most newly disembarked' means something rather different from 'more newly disembarked'. James, it may be surmised, did not want to compare the recency of the two men's arrival, but to inform us that Strether's arrival was 'very' or as we might say, 'most' recent; the use of the superlative also had the advantage of suggesting the long and fateful tradition of transatlantic disembarcations in general.

The reasons for the other main syntactical idiosyncrasies in the passage are much clearer. In the first part of the opening sentence, for example, the separation of subject—'question'—from verb—'was'—by the longish temporal clause 'when he reached the hotel', is no doubt a dislocation of normal sentence structure; but, of course, 'Strether' must be the first word of the novel: while, even more important, the delayed placing of the temporal clause, forces a pause after 'question' and thus gives it a very significant resonance. Similarly with the last sentence; it has several peculiarities, of which the placing of 'throughout' seems the most obvious. The sentence has three parts: the first and last are comparatively straightforward, but the middle is a massed block of portentous qualifications: 'Mixed with everything was the apprehension—already, on Strether's part, that he would, at best, throughout,—prove the note of Europe in quite a sufficient degree.' The echoing doom started by the connotation of 'apprehension'—reverberates through 'already', ('much more to come later') 'on Strether's part' ('even he knows') and 'at best' ('the worst has been envisaged, too'); but it is the final collapse of the terse rhythm of the parenthesis that isolates the rather awkwardly placed 'throughout', and thus enables James to sound the fine full fatal note; there is no limit to the poignant eloquence of 'throughout'. It was this effect, of course, which dictated the preceding inversion which places 'apprehension' not at the start of the sentence, but in the middle where, largely freed from its syntactical nexus, it may be directly exposed to its salvos of qualification.

The mockingly fateful emphasis on 'throughout' tells us, if nothing had before, that James's tone is in the last analysis ironic, comic, or better, as

---

[6]Though consider *Rasselas*, ch. xxviii: 'Both conditions may be bad, but they cannot both be worst'.

I shall try to suggest, humorous. The general reasons for this have already been suggested. To use Maynard Mack's distinction (in his Preface to *Joseph Andrews,* Rinehart Editions, New York, 1948), 'the comic artist subordinates the presentation of life as experience, where the relationship between ourselves and the characters experiencing it is a primary one, to the presentation of life as a spectacle, where the primary relation is between himself and us as onlookers'. In the James passage, the primacy of the relation between the narrator and the reader has already been noted, as has its connection with the abstraction of the diction, which brings home the distance between the narrator and Strether. Of course, the application of abstract diction to particular persons always tends towards irony,[7] because it imposes a dual way of looking at them: few of us can survive being presented as general representatives of humanity.

The paragraph, of course, is based on one of the classic contradictions in psychological comedy—Strether's reluctance to admit to himself that he has very mixed feelings about his friend: and James develops this with the narrative equivalent of *commedia dell'arte* technique: virtuoso feats of ironic balance, comic exaggeration, and deceptive hesitation conduct us on a complicated progress towards the foreordained illumination.

In structure, to begin with, the six sentences form three groups of two: each pair of them gives one aspect of Strether's delay; and they are arranged in an ascending order of complication so that the fifth sentence—72 words —is almost twice as long as any other, and is succeeded by the final sentence, the punch line, which is noticeably the shortest—26 words. The development of the ideas is as controlled as the sentence structure. Strether is obviously a man with an enormous sense of responsibility about personal relationships; so his first question is about his friend. That loyal *empressement,* however, is immediately checked by the balanced twin negatives that follow: 'on his learning that Waymarsh *was not* to arrive till evening, he *was not* wholly disconcerted': one of the diagnostic elements of irony, surely, is hyperbole qualified with mock-scrupulousness, such as we get in 'not wholly disconcerted'. Why there are limits to Lambert Strether's consternation is to transpire in the next sentence; Waymarsh's telegram bespeaking a room 'only if not noisy' is a laconic suggestion of that inarticulate worthy's habitual gloomy expectations—from his past experiences of the indignities of European hotel noise we adumbrate the notion that the cost of their friendly *rencontre* may be his sleeping in the street. In the second part of the sentence we have another similar, though more muted, hint: 'the understanding that they should meet in Chester rather than at Liverpool remained to that extent sound'; 'to that extent', no doubt, but to *any other?* —echo seems to answer 'No'.

In the second group of sentences we are getting into Strether's mind, and we have been prepared to relish the irony of its ambivalences. The

---

[7]As I have argued in 'The Ironic Tradition in Augustan Prose from Swift to Johnson', *Restoration and Augustan Prose,* (Los Angeles, 1957).

negatived hyperbole of 'not absolutely to desire', turns out to mean 'postpone'; and, of course, a voluntarily postponed 'enjoyment' itself denotes a very modified rapture, although Strether's own consciousness of the problem is apparently no further advanced than that 'he could still wait without disappointment'. Comically loyal to what he would like to feel, therefore, we have him putting in the consoling reflection that 'they would dine together at the worst'; and the ambiguity of 'at the worst' is followed by the equally dubious thought: 'there was little fear that in the sequel they shouldn't see enough of each other'. That they should, in fact, see too much of each other; but social decorum and Strether's own loyalties demand that the outrage of the open statement be veiled in the obscurity of formal negation.

By the time we arrive at the climactic pair of sentences, we have been told enough for more ambitious effects to be possible. The twice-mentioned 'secret principle', it appears, is actually wholly 'instinctive' (line 16); but in other ways Strether is almost ludicrously self-conscious. The qualified hyperbole of 'his business would be a trifle bungled', underlined as it is by the alliteration, prepares us for a half-realised image which amusingly defines Strether's sense of his role: he sees himself, it appears, as the stage-manager of an enterprise in which his solemn obligations as an implicated friend are counterbalanced by his equally ceremonious sense that due decorums must also be attended to when he comes face to face with another friend of long ago—no less a person than Europe. It is, of course, silly of him, as James makes him acknowledge in the characteristic italicising of 'the "note" of Europe';[8] but still, he does have a comically ponderous sense of protocol which leads him to feel that 'his business would be a trifle bungled' should he simply arrange for this countenance to present itself to the nearing steamer as the first 'note' of Europe. The steamer, one imagines, would not have turned hard astern at the proximity of Waymarsh's sacred rage; but Strether's fitness for ambassadorial functions is defined by his thinking in terms of 'arranging' for a certain countenance at the docks to give just the right symbolic greeting.

Strether's notion of what Europe demands also shows us the force of his aesthetic sense. But in the last sentence the metaphor, though it remains equally self-conscious, changes its mode of operation from the dramatic, aesthetic, and diplomatic, to something more scientific: for, although ten years ago I should not have failed to point out, and my readers would not, I suppose, have failed to applaud, the ambiguity of 'prove', it now seems to me that we must chose between its two possible meanings. James may be using 'prove' to mean that Waymarsh's face will 'turn out to be' the 'note of Europe' for Strether. But 'prove' in this sense is intransitive, and 'to be' would have to be supplied; it therefore seems more likely that James is using 'prove' in the older sense of 'to test': Waymarsh is indeed suited to the role of being the sourly acid test of the siren songs of Europe 'in quite a sufficient degree', as Strether puts it with solemn but arch understanding.

---

[8]See George Knox, 'James's Rhetoric Quotes,' *College English,* XVII (1956), 293-297.

The basic development structure of the passage, then, is one of progressive and yet artfully delayed clarification; and this pattern is also typical of James's general novelistic method. The reasons for this are suggested in the Preface to *The Princess Casamassima,* where James deals with the problem of maintaining a balance between the intelligence a character must have to be interesting, and the bewilderment which is nevertheless an essential condition of the novel's having surprise, development, and tension: 'It seems probable that if we were never bewildered there would never be a story to tell about us.'

In the first paragraph of *The Ambassadors* James apprises us both of his hero's supreme qualities and of his associated limitations. Strether's delicate critical intelligence is often blinkered by a highly vulnerable mixture of moral generosity towards others combined with an obsessive sense of personal inadequacy; we see the tension in relation to Waymarsh, as later we are to see it in relation to all his other friends; and we understand, long before Strether, how deeply it bewilders him; most poignantly about the true nature of Chad, Madame de Vionnet—and himself.

This counterpoint of intelligence and bewilderment is, of course, another reason for the split narrative point of view we've already noted: we and the narrator are inside Strether's mind, and yet we are also outside it, knowing more about Strether than he knows about himself. This is the classic posture of irony. Yet I think that to insist too exclusively on the ironic function of James's narrative point of view would be mistaken.

Irony has lately been enshrined as the supreme deity in the critical pantheon: but, I wonder, is there really anything so wonderful about being distant and objective? Who wants to see life only or mainly in intellectual terms? In art as in life we no doubt can have need of intellectual distance as well as of emotional commitment; but the uninvolvement of the artist surely doesn't go very far without the total involvement of the person; or, at least, without a deeper human involvement than irony customarily establishes. One could, I suppose, call the aesthetically perfect balance between distance and involvement, open or positive irony: but I'm not sure that humour isn't a better word, especially when the final balance is tipped in favour of involvement, of ultimate commitment to the characters; and I hope that our next critical movement will be the New Gelastics.

At all events, although the first paragraph alone doesn't allow the point to be established fully here, it seems to me that James's attitude to Strether is better described as humorous than ironical; we must learn like Maria Gostrey, to see him 'at last all comically, all tragically'. James's later novels in general are most intellectual; but they are also, surely, his most compassionate: and in this particular paragraph Strether's dilemma is developed in such a way that we feel for him even more than we smile at him. This balance of intention, I think, probably explains why James keeps his irony in such a low key: we must be aware of Strether's 'secret' ambivalence towards Waymarsh, but not to the point that his unawareness of it would verge on fatuity; and our controlling sympathy for the causes of Strether's ambivalence turns what might have been irony into something closer to what Constance Rourke characterises as James's typical 'low-keyed humor of defeat' (*American Humor,* 1931).

That James's final attitude is humorous rather than ironic is further suggested by the likeness of the basic structural technique of the paragraph to that of the funny story—the incremental involvement in an endemic human perplexity which can only be resolved by laughter's final acceptance of contradiction and absurdity. We don't, in the end, see Strether's probing hesitations mainly as an ironic indication by James of mankind's general muddlement; we find it, increasingly, a touching example of how, despite all their inevitable incongruities and shortcomings, human ties remain only, but still, human.

Here it is perhaps James's very slowness and deliberation throughout the narrative which gives us our best supporting evidence: greater love hath no man than hearing his friend out patiently.

III

The function of an introductory paragraph in a novel is presumably to introduce: and this paragraph surely has the distinction of being a supremely complex and inclusive introduction to a novel. It introduces the hero, of course, and one of his companions; also the time; the place; something of what's gone before. But James has carefully avoided giving us the usual retrospective beginning, that pile of details which he scornfully termed a 'mere seated mass of information'. All the details are scrupulously presented as reflections from the novel's essential centre—the narrator's patterning of the ideas going forwards and backwards in Strether's mind. Of course, this initially makes the novel more difficult, because what we probably think of as primary—event and its setting—is subordinated to what James thinks is—the mental drama of the hero's consciousness, which, of course, is not told but shown: scenically dramatised. At the same time, by selecting thoughts and events which are representative of the book as a whole, and narrating them with an abstractness which suggests their larger import, James introduces the most general themes of the novel.

James, we saw, carefully arranged to make 'Strether's first question', the first three words; and, of course, throughout the novel, Strether is to go on asking questions—and getting increasingly dusty answers. This, it may be added, is stressed by the apparent aposiopesis: for a 'first' question when no second is mentioned, is surely an intimation that more are—in a way unknown to us or to Strether—yet to come. The later dislocations of normal word-order already noted above emphasise other major themes; the 'secret principle' in Strether's mind, and the antithesis Waymarsh-Europe, for instance.

The extent to which these processes were conscious on James's part cannot, of course, be resolved; but it is significant that the meeting with Maria Gostrey was interposed before the meeting with Waymarsh, which James

In Dickens, characteristically, we get a loud note that sets the tone, rather than a polyphonic series of chords that contain all the later melodic developments, as in James. And either the Dickens method, or the 'mere seated mass of information', seem to be commonest kinds of opening in nineteenth-century novels. For openings that suggest something of James's ambitious attempt to achieve a prologue that is a synchronic introduction of all the main aspects of the narrative, I think that Conrad is his closest rival. But Conrad, whether in expository or dramatic vein, tends to an arresting initial vigour that has dangers which James's more muted tones avoid. In *An Outcast of the Islands* (1896), for example:

> When he stepped off the straight and narrow path of his peculiar honesty, it was with an inward assertion of unflinching resolve to fall back again into the monotonous but safe stride of virtue as soon as his little excursion into the wayside quagmires had produced the desired effect. It was going to be a short episode—a sentence in bracket, so to speak, in the flowing tale of his life. . . .

[C]onrad's sardonic force has enormous immediate impact; but it surely gives [t]o much away: the character, Willems, has been dissected so vigorously [th]at it takes great effort for Conrad—and the reader—to revivify him later. [Th]e danger lurks even in the masterly combination of physical notation and [sy]mbolic evaluation at the beginning of *Lord Jim* (1900): 'He was an inch, [pe]rhaps two, under six feet . . .': the heroic proportion is for ever missed, [by] an inch, perhaps two; which is perhaps too much, to begin with.

[I]t is not for me to assess how far I have succeeded in carrying out the [gen]eral intentions with which I began, or how far similar methods of analy[sis] would be applicable to other kinds of prose. As regards the explication [of t]he passage itself, the main argument must by now be sufficiently clear, [alth]ough a full demonstration would require a much wider sampling both of [othe]r novels and of other passages in *The Ambassadors*.[9] The most obvious [and] demonstrable features of James's prose style, its vocabulary and syntax, [are] direct reflections of his attitude to life and his conception of the novel; [and t]hese features, like the relation of the paragraph to the rest of the novel, [and t]o other novels, make clear that the notorious idiosyncrasies of Jamesian [prose] are directly related to the imperatives which led him to develop a nar[rativ]e texture as richly complicated and as highly organised as that of poetry. [No] wonder James scorned translation and rejoiced, as he so engagingly [confe]ssed to his French translator, Auguste Monod, that his later works [were 'l]ocked fast in the golden cage of the *intraduisible*'. Translation could [hardl]y do justice to a paragraph in which so many levels of meaning and [evalu]ation are kept in continuous operation; in which the usual introductory

---

[A] analysis of eight other paragraphs selected at fifty page intervals revealed that, as would be ex[pected] there is much variation: the tendency to use non-transitive verbs, and abstract nouns as subjects, [hen]ce, seems to be strong throughout the novel, though especially so in analytic rather than narrative [passages,] but the frequent use of 'that' and of negative forms of statement does not recur significantly.

had originally planned as his beginning in the long (20,000) word
of the plot which he prepared for *Harper's*. The unexpected me
many advantages; not least that James could repeat the first pa
pattern of delayed clarification in the structure of the first chapter a
On Strether's mind we get a momentously clear judgment at the
second paragraph: 'there was detachment in his zeal, and curic
indifference'; but then the meeting with Maria Gostrey, and its
tunities for a much fuller presentation of Strether's mind, inter
Waymarsh himself finally appears at the end of the chapter;
the joke behind Strether's uneasy hesitations in the first paragr
to its hilariously blunt climax: 'It was already upon him ever
tance—Mr. Waymarsh was for *his* part joyless'.

One way of evaluating James's achievement in this paragrap
would be to compare the opening of James's other novels, a
of previous writers: but it would take too long to do more th
possibilities of this approach. James's early openings certai
of the banality of the 'mere seated mass of information': in *Rc
(1876), for example: 'Rowland Mallet had made his arran
for Europe on the 5th of September, and having in the int
to spare, he determined to spend it with his cousin Cecilia
nephew of his father. . . .' Later, James showed a much mor
notion of what the introductory paragraph should attempt:
tively simple and concrete opening of *The Wings of the L
waited, Kate Croy, for her father to come in, but he kept he
and there were moments at which she showed herself, in
mantle, a face positively pale with irritation that had t
point of going away without sight of him. . . .' 'She waite
odd parenthetic apposition artfully contrived to prefigur
out the novel—to wait.

One could, I suppose, find this sort of symbolic pre
of earlier novelists; but never, I imagine, in associatic
levels of introductory function that James manages to
paragraph. Jane Austen has her famous thematic iro
Pride and Prejudice (1813): 'It is a truth universally
single man in possession of a good fortune must be i
pride and prejudice must come later. Dickens can h
into *Bleak House* (1852-3), into its time and place a
characters and opening action have to wait:

> London. Michaelmas Term lately over, and the
> in Lincoln's Inn Hall. Implacable November,
> in the streets, as if the waters had but newly
> the earth, and it would not be wonderful to m
> feet long or so, waddling like an elephantine
> Smoke lowering down from chimney-pots. . .

exposition of time, place, character, and previous action, are rendered through an immediate immersion in the processes of the hero's mind as he's involved in perplexities which are characteristic of the novel as a whole and which are articulated in a mode of comic development which is essentially that, not only of the following chapter, but of the total structure. To have done all that is to have gone far towards demonstrating the contention which James announced at the end of the Preface to *The Ambassadors,* that 'the Novel remains still, under the right persuasion, the most independent, most elastic, most prodigious of literary forms'; and the variety and complexity of the functions carried out in the book's quite short first paragraph also suggest that, contrary to some notions, the demonstration is, as James claimed, made with 'a splendid particular economy'.

LOUIS T. MILIC

Against the Typology
of Styles

In the following article Louis T. Milic is writing as a critic interested in literary style rather than a teacher interested in his students' development of stylistic techniques, the problem with which his essay appearing in the first part of this book was concerned. In the essay below, by stating categorically the bases for his own assumptions about style, Professor Milic rejects what he sees as the baseless impressionism which has dominated the study of prose style in the past.

A typology is a classification and a typology of styles is an arrangement of styles into categories, such as periods of time (Elizabethan, Restoration, Victorian or modern), kinds of influence or derivation, such as Euphuistic, Senecan, Ciceronian, or of impression, such as ornate, formal, learned, simple, plain and casual. Such classifications are based on the belief that groups of writers have styles that are alike and that any single member of such a group is typical of it. I am convinced that this model, which has a certain antiquity in literary history, is false and unnecessary. It cannot contribute anything to our understanding of literary style. Moreover, we can explain stylistic phenomena without the aid of such categories.

   The assumptions on which I base my disagreement are the following:

1. A writer's style is the expression of his personality.
2. A writer must write in his own style.
3. A writer can be recognized in his style.
4. No writer can truly imitate another's style.
5. The main formative influences on a writer are his education and his reading.
6. A writer's language is governed by the practice of his own time.
7. Language changes gradually with time.

There is nothing very revolutionary here. Much of it is summed up in Buffon's aphorism: 'Le style, c'est l'homme même."

I shall illustrate my thesis by reference to Restoration prose. Let me begin by quoting an authority, Professor James Sutherland:

> . . . Can we talk . . . about "Restoration prose," or are the two words merely a convenient way of referring to the prose that was written in England between 1660 and the closing years of the century? For myself, I believe that there *is* a prose style that is characteristic of the Restoration . . . and that this style is the genuine expression of a particular and definite type of culture.[1]

Professor Sutherland's studies of English prose need no encomia. I have selected his work because it is quite representative of typological *Stilforschung* in its assumptions and superior to most in originality and scholarship. My intention in singling out his work is to point to some limitations of this tradition.

The problem that I am interested in discussing will come into focus if we ask where this prose is to be found. Here is his answer:

> The prose I have in mind was written to perfection by Dryden and Halifax; with individual variations by such men as Robert South, Bishop Burnet, and Jeremy Collier; by Etherege and Rochester in their letters; with further variations by Roger L'Estrange in his pamphlets and translations; by Walter Pope in his *Life of Seth Ward* and by Robert Wolsey in his Preface to Rochester's *Valentinian;* by Thomas Sprat in his *History of the Royal Society* and by Robert Hooke in his *Micrographia;* and by many other minor writers. I do not think I should seriously confuse the issue if I added Cowley in his Essays and perhaps Stillingfleet in his *Origines Sacrae.* But I have got to admit that if there *is* such a thing as Restoration prose, not all the writers living in that period wrote it. There are a few of the greatest prose writers of the time whom I obviously cannot possibly include: one of these is John Bunyan, and another is Clarendon, and for various reasons I would exclude Isaac Barrow, the Hon. Robert Boyle, John

---

[1]James R. Sutherland, "Restoration Prose," *Restoration and Augustan Prose,* Los Angeles, 1956, pp. 1-2.

Evelyn, Richard Baxter, Thomas Rymer, and such eccentrics as Thomas Burnet, the author of *The Sacred Theory of the Earth*. And I don't know what to do with Samuel Pepys.[2]

This is a very select list, almost an eccentric one. It says yes to Dryden but no to Bunyan, yes to Burnet and no to Clarendon, yes to Collier and no to Rymer. It mentions Robert Wolseley [sic] and Walter Pope, who are rare birds indeed, and yet talks of minor writers. Moreover, it leaves out altogether John Dennis, Thomas Traherne, Andrew Marvell, William Congreve, Sir William Temple, Samuel Butler and John Locke, all of whom wrote prose of some distinction. Such a process of selection seems to suggest that writers of Restoration prose were not in the majority during the Restoration. In other words only some, perhaps a minority, of the writers of this time wrote Restoration prose. The typological criterion then is not merely chronological; there seems to be something else.

This new quality is sometimes called plain prose or the plain style. This well-known notion—that a change occurred in English prose style during the seventeenth century, in the direction of plainness or simplicity—has been present in the writings of literary historians for some time. A. A. Tilley, for example, in 1911, observed:

> Perhaps the most important literary achievement within this period is the creation of a prose style which, in structure if not in vocabulary, is essentially the same as that of today . . . possessing before all things, the homely virtues of simplicity, correctness, lucidity and precision.[3]

The change can be illustrated very simply. The most dramatic way to sense its real force is to read ten pages of Milton's polemical prose and to follow this with ten pages of Dryden's critical prose. To most modern readers, this is like coming out of a tunnel into the sunshine. The typical response is, How did this happen, that is, How did the English come to write so simply, so clearly, so informally after having written so much the other way? The implication of this form of the question is that before 1660 everyone wrote like Milton and after that date like Dryden.

To promote this feeling or impression into a theory, it is necessary only to group a few extreme cases around our two antagonists in order to produce two schools. On Milton's side, we put Browne, Clarendon, Taylor, Lancelot Andrewes . . . ; Dryden is teamed with Swift, Steele, Addison, Shaftesbury, Defoe. . . . Examples are easily come by. The following pair of citations would find few to disagree that the first of the two passages is less plain than the second:

---

[2]*Ibid.*, p. 2.
[3]"The Essay and the Beginning of Modern English Prose," *The Cambridge History of English Literature,* ed. Sir A. W. Ward and A. R. Waller, Cambridge, 1911, Vol. VIII, p. 368.

Not to insist upon the examples of Moses, Daniel, and Paul, who were skilful in all the learning of the Egyptians, Chaldeans, and Greeks, which could not probably be without reading their books of all sorts, in Paul especially, who thought it no defilement to insert into Holy Scripture the sentences of three Greek poets, and one of them a tragedian, the question was notwithstanding sometimes controverted among the primitive doctors, but with great odds on that side which affirmed it both lawful and profitable, as was then evidently perceived, when Julian the Apostate and subtlest enemy to our faith made a decree forbidding Christians the study of heathen learning: for, said he, they wound us with our own weapons, and with our own arts and sciences they overcome us.[4]

For there is a perpetual dearth of wit; a barrenness of good sense and entertainment. The neglect of the readers will soon put an end to this sort of scribbling. There can be no pleasantry where there is no wit; no impression can be made where there is no truth for the foundation.[5]

The second is in fact three sentences of Dryden, but together they take up less than half the space of Milton's single sentence.

If the case were always so clear, we should have no problem in characterizing plain prose and I would have no argument. Matter, however, does not follow categories. So for example, Isaac Barrow, who is relegated to Professor Sutherland's NO list, is described in the *Cambridge History of English Literature* as noted for "the clearness and simplicity which under his influence began to mark the prose of the later seventeenth century." His general manner "is an anticipation of Addison."[6] To show the practical difficulties of this sort of classification, I shall give a passage from Robert South from the YES list as well as one from Isaac Barrow.

We are all naturally endowed with a strong appetite to know, to see, to pursue Truth; and with a bashfull abhorrency from being deceived, and entangled in mistake. And as success in enquiry after Truth affords matter of joy and triumph; so being conscious of error, and miscarriage therein, is attended with shame and sorrow. These desires Wisdom in the most perfect manner satisfies, not by entertaining us with dry, empty, fruitless theories, upon mean and vulgar subjects; but by enriching our minds with excellent and useful knowledge, directed to the noblest objects, and serviceable to the highest ends.[7]

---

[4]John Milton, "Areopagitica," *Prose Selections,* ed. Merritt Y. Hughes, New York, 1947, pp. 218-219.
[5]John Dryden, "A Discourse Concerning the Original and Progress of Satire," *Essays,* ed. W. P. Ker, Oxford, 1900, Vol. II, p. 81.
[6]Vol. VIII, p. 296.
[7]Isaac Barrow, "The Pleasantness of Religion," *Seventeenth-Century Verse and Prose,* ed. Helen C. White, Ruth C. Wallerstein and Ricardo Quintana, New York, 1952, Vol. II, p. 178.

Now for the second passage:

> As nothing can be of more moment; so few things, doubtless, are of more difficulty, than for men to be rationally satisfied about the estate of their souls, with reference to God and the great concerns of eternity. In their judgment about which if they err finally it is like a man's missing his cast when he throws dice for his life; his being his happiness and all that he does or can enjoy in the world is involved in the error of one throw. And therefore it may very well deserve our best skill and care to enquire into those rules by which we may guide our Judgment in so weighty an affair both with safety and success.[8]

I wonder how many readers would be able to pick out the work of the Restoration prose writer from the other. Barrow's does not seem to be distinguishable from South's by means of the criterion of plainness. I am not suggesting that the Cambridge History is correct in placing Barrow in the plain group and Sutherland wrong in excluding him. I do not believe there is much evidence for either side and neither has offered anything like an incontestable or even a workable criterion. Calling it the plain style is not enough.

What is this plain style? According to Sutherland it is an English "simpler, less ornate, more colloquial, more practical."[9] A linguist might describe the syntax of Milton as nested or embedded and that of Dryden as linear. But neither of these descriptions will really help us when we come to average cases, such as those of South and Barrow, rather than extreme ones. The typological procedure is not very enlightening in this kind of problem. It tends to deal in impressionistic generalities, which may be adequate for getting a vague sense of the difference between two modes of expression but not adequate for analyzing the difference between two particular examples.

Whether one examines the claims of one set of theorists who try to account for the emergence of plain prose in terms of the influence of pulpit oratory, or whether one is willing to accept the views of those who attribute it to the influence of the Royal Society and its desire for scientific writing, or accepts the opinion that it derives from the conversation of well-bred aristocratic gentlemen, who prized easy informality, lack of affectation and a stress on the colloquial, does not matter very much. All three of these explanations and any others that may arise are attempts to explain with ingenuity what can be explained without it.

I am prepared to concede without any reservation that the English of nearly any writer of the eighteenth century sounds different from that of

---

[8]Robert South, "An Account of the Nature and Measures of Conscience," *Seventeenth-Century Verse and Prose*, Vol. II, p. 186-187.
[9]*On English Prose*, Toronto, 1957, p. 57.

most writers of the seventeenth. I am also willing to grant that the writing of many writers of the Restoration is easier to read than that of the subjects of the early Stuarts. What I am not willing to grant is that we need a theory of types in order to explain this development. The matter can be explained quite satisfactorily with some of the axioms cited earlier. On the scientific principle that an economical explanation based on opinions generally held is better than one requiring a number of dubious assumptions, I would suggest that the typological explanation of the plain style represented by Professor Sutherland be dismissed. I shall summarize the grounds.

Consider what we need to believe in order to accept a typological explanation of Restoration prose. First, we must believe that there is a hypothetical entity called Restoration prose, whose characteristics can be defined only generally. Second, we must agree that this entity is the common property of a certain number of writers of that period but not of some others, admittedly first-rank writers, and not only the work of a minority but of that minority only in certain works which can be specified. Third, we are invited to agree that the writers who partake of the mystic entity represent a significant subculture within the society, one which presumably is closer to the real work of the society than those outside it, however great the writers excluded may be.

The last of these points, that the writers who are thus isolated represent a significantly dominant aspect of the culture cannot detain us long. Both common sense and statistics tell us that lists of members of an in-group tend to be fallacious. The real members of the group may only be known to the truly *in* people, who keep their identities secret, like the Gray Eminence. Apart from the evident difficulty of at this distance assembling a group of writers who will constitute the spirit of the Restoration, it would seem even more hazardous to prefer the claims of one group over those of others. The courtiers no doubt had influence, but was it literary? The scientists, dissenters, the merchants, all had competing claims, not to mention the dramatists and the pamphleteers.

The constitution of the group representing the spirit of the Restoration raises insistent questions of logic. If Etherege and Rochester were members of the significant minority, why did this fact only make itself known when they wrote letters? Why was L'Estrange only *in* in his pamphlets and Cowley in his essays? More mysterious still, why was Walter Pope only part of the circle in a single *Life* and Wolseley in a preface to someone else's work? The inconsistency of such an argument requires no deep searching to detect.

The most interesting point is the first, the problem of describing the characteristics of Restoration prose. Description proceeds by the accumulation of detail, a sound procedure in dealing with style. But descriptions of style usually proceed by generalization, by abstraction of qualities from masses of detail. Style is difficult to handle simply because it is a mass of detail. To classify a particular set of such details by means of an abstraction is to make a claim that these details are more important than others, that they fall into a configuration and that this abstraction outweighs others that might be constructed out of the same materials. For example, when following the trend of modern comment we call today's prose colloquial or informal, we are constructing a category of informality with certain characteristics and are implicitly claiming that most of today's writing conforms to those characteristics. Both of these steps are more difficult than appears at first. Since we cannot examine all writing, how can we determine that today's prose is indeed informal? We cannot examine more than a fraction of it and that fraction may not be a true random sample. It is based on our preferences. The reader of the *Christian Century*, the *Journal of the History of Ideas* and *Victorian Studies* will get a different idea of the state of modern prose than will the reader of the *New York Times*, the *New Republic* and the *New Yorker* or for that matter the reader of *Playboy, Mad* and the *Evergreen Review*. Unless we take special precautions to be objective and cross-sectional, our evidence will be hopelessly biased and we shall be making generalizations which, however perceptive, will be inapplicable to more than a segment of the population.

The problem of criteria is even more difficult: how do we decide what makes a prose informal? Many critics do this intuitively. Without pointing to anything in the language, they say it sounds informal to them. This kind of impressionism is equivocal: another critic may say it does not sound informal to him. There is no way to settle so metaphysical a dispute. A better procedure is to particularize informality by means of a set of indicia. When they are present, the prose can be called informal; when they are absent, the reverse. Unfortunately, this leaves a great many cases unsettled, when some of the indicia are present and some not, when some sentences are informal and some are not. No consistent classification can emerge from this kind of disorder. Unless a policy on such questions is established in advance, no statements of description can be made with reliability.

In other words, one important objection to the typology of styles is the matter of method or procedure. It is *practically* impossible to make an accurate generalization about an abstraction so remote and inchoate as the dominant feeling or quality of the writings of a group of people expressing themselves on every subject during a period of forty years. The human animal is too various to be so categorized. Group personalities of this kind have no reality, any more than national languages have a character, as once was thought. Only individuals have personalities and therefore only individuals can have a style.

Style has many definitions but most of them are merely casual variations on a theme. On the basis of the uncontroversial axioms I offered at the beginning of this paper, I would now claim that an individual's style is his habitual and consistent selection from the expressive resources available in his language. In other words, his style is the collection of his stylistic options. Options or choices are not always exercised consciously; they are often habitual practices of which the practitioner is as unconscious as he is of the way that he bends his leg in walking or the way that he ties his shoelace. His reading, the way he has been taught to write, the bent of his mind have all influenced him in the direction of a particular uniqueness. To this may be added the ingredient of conscious rhetorical choice. The net effect is an individual style, which be it noted may be as individual among literary hacks as among literary geniuses. Milton and Dryden each write in their unique individual styles because of who and what they are. What divides them is personality; what unites them is chronology.

The language changes all the time, but it changes very slowly, at times so imperceptibly that it gives the illusion of being stable, so that speakers who become aware of changes raise passionate outcries about corruption and decay. All speakers are bound by these changes but not all writers are chronologically at the same point in time. At any given moment, there are writers imbued with the lexical choices and the syntactical options of a previous era. And there are some who are on the frontier of change, coining new words like any teen-ager. Thus the co-existence of several chronological states of the language at one time provides the medium within which the rich variety of individuals can express itself. Between these two poles, the changing language and the individual writer, all the facts of style can be satisfactorily accounted for.

The individual's style is the aggregate of his stylistic selections from the particular state of the language that he construes as the real one of his time. The consistent choices that he makes from it to serve his own expressive requirements constitute his style, his literary personality. It is evident that the writer's choices will be determined by certain fashions in education, in rhetoric and in literature, but the main tendency of writers in a given time is to be unlike rather than alike. The notion of period styles underrates this tendency and implies a uniformity of expression which is wildly at variance with the facts.

The writers of plain prose or what has been called the clear stream— Dryden, Addison, Swift, Fielding &c.[10]—are granted by this typology a uniformity which is quite foreign to their practice. A selection of passages might be made from the works of any single writer to support the claim that he prefers short sentences or long sentences, few adjectives or many and so on. Similarly, the plain style is not the prerogative of a given period; it is a rhetorical tendency which is present in all ages. A history of the plain style might be written showing that it arose in the sixteenth century and was practiced by writers from Bacon to E. B. White. The history of ornate prose would show a similar line, ending let us say with Churchill or Walter Lippmann.

The division of eighteenth-century prose into the clear stream and the ornate one oversimplifies the problems it is striving to solve. Most people in Johnson's time did not regularly write balanced Johnsonian prose, not even Johnson himself. Balanced prose, employing the devices of antithesis and parallelism, has been in some degree a feature of formal writing in all periods,

---

[10]James Sutherland, "Some Aspects of Eighteenth-Century Prose," *Essays on the Eighteenth Century Presented to David Nichol Smith,* Oxford, 1945, p. 94.

including our own. It is my conviction that such classes as plain style, ornate style, balanced style, may only be useful to describe individual sentences, paragraphs or perhaps even whole compositions, whenever they may have been written. But when such classes are tied to chronology and culture, they imply more than can be justified by a strict examination of the facts.

The dominant modern style, according to some observers, is the plain or casual or informal style. Many teachers and writing advisors recommend the following of this model. Yet we know that many highly admired writers of the present day do not do so. Writers of great reputation practice more elaborate forms, not to mention the esoteric language of the social scientists.[11] Whatever may be the central characteristics of modern prose style, they are not likely to tell us much about modern writing because the average of a very large number tends to iron out interesting peculiarities. That is a great danger of excessive typology.

The typology of styles seems to have descended to us from the practice, standard in literary history, of grouping writers in schools of drama or poetry, such as the Georgic poets, the bourgeois dramatists, the graveyard poets, whose subject matter and formal manner coincided significantly. But types of styles, schools of styles, genres of styles, and periods of styles are not analogous entities. A writer's style emerges from the tension between the state of the language that he uses and the demands of his individuality striving to express itself with the same materials as other individuals and struggling against the restraining powers of fashion, tradition and rhetoric.

Rhetorical training conditions both the writer and the reader and in that way may come to affect the language itself. The rhetorical inversion of one era is the normal word-order of another. But the scope of rhetoric is limited and affects mainly the more visible outward aspects of the repertory of stylistic resources provided by a language. To be sure, some writers have more or less consciously emphasized certain rhetorical features in their writing (Gibbon, Johnson, Macaulay), but these are not by themselves significant. Rhetoric becomes significant when it can be related to the writer's unconscious expressive mechanism, when it represents the controlling power, both limiting and enabling, of outer form upon idea and meaning. In that sense, it becomes one of the contributing factors to the totality we call an author's style. The contribution of conscious rhetorical adornment to the total style of an author is put into proper perspective when his theoretical pronouncements about style are compared with his actual performance. When Swift tells us about the ideals of style, he is not giving an accurate description of what he actually does. His own practice is some distance away from what he thought he was doing or what he would have liked to do. In fact, in the words of one scholar, Swift was always struggling against a tendency to write in just the way he disliked.[12] If this is true, it

---

[11]A number of critics, including Cyril Connolly and Roland Barthes, have expressed concern about the modern stress on a plain, featureless prose.

[12]Jonathan Swift, *An Enquiry into the Behavior of the Queen's Last Ministry,* ed. Irvin Ehrenpreis, Bloomington, 1956, p. xxxi.

surely refutes the arguments of those who would credit a writer with the power to alter his style at will, as if he had a wardrobe—or a stable—of different styles for different occasions.[13] The extent of his ability to adapt his style is probably limited to certain superficial aspects, among which are included rhetorical devices and diction.

In sum, the proper subject of stylistic speculation is the individual writer. To understand the style of the individual, we must concern ourselves first with the individual's writings and second with the linguistic resources from which his peculiar style is a selection. Typologies attract our attention to specious and minor similarities among authors. They are misleading because they take us away from what is really significant, the individual author's own peculiarity, his difference from his contemporaries, which is what is truly his style.

---

[13]This is the so-called *persona* theory. See, for example, Paul Fussell, Jr. "Speaker and Style in *A Letter of Advice to a Young Poet* (1721), and the Problem of Attribution," *Review of English Studies,* X (1959), 63-67.

APPENDIX A

JONATHAN SWIFT

A Modest Proposal for Preventing the Children of Ireland from Being a Burden to Their Parents or Country

This essay, written in 1729, is the subject for Edward P. J. Corbett's analysis on p. 81 of this volume.

1. It is a melancholy object to those who walk through this great town or travel in the country, when they see the streets, the roads, and cabin-doors crowded with beggars of the female sex, followed by three, four, or six children, all in rags, and importuning every passenger for an alms. These mothers, instead of being able to work for their honest livelihood, are forced to employ all their time in strolling to beg sustenance for their helpless infants, who, as they grow up, either turn thieves for want of work, or leave their dear native country, to fight for the Pretender in Spain, or sell themselves to the Barbadoes.

2. I think it is agreed by all parties, that this prodigious number of children in the arms, or on the backs, or at the heels of their mothers, and frequently of their fathers, is in the present deplorable state of the kingdom a very great additional grievance; and therefore whoever could find out a fair, cheap, and easy method of making these children sound and useful members of the common-wealth, would deserve so well of the public as to have his statue set up for a preserver of the nation.

3. But my intention is very far from being confined to provide only for the children of professed beggars; it is of a much greater extent, and shall take in the whole number of infants at a certain age, who are born of parents in effect as little able to support them, as those who demand our charity in the streets.

4. As to my own part, having turned my thoughts, for many years, upon this important subject, and maturely weighed the several schemes of other projectors, I have always found them grossly mistaken in their computation. It is true, a child just dropt from its dam, may be supported by her milk for a solar year with little other nourishment, at most not above the value of two shillings, which the mother may certainly get, or the value in scraps, by her lawful occupation of begging; and it is exactly at one year old that I propose to provide for them in such a manner, as, instead of being a charge upon their parents, or the parish, or wanting food and raiment for the rest of their lives, they shall, on the contrary, contribute to the feeding and partly to the clothing of many thousands.

5. There is likewise another great advantage in my scheme, that it will prevent those voluntary abortions, and that horrid practice of women mur-

dering their bastard children, alas! too frequent among us—sacrificing the poor innocent babes, I doubt, more to avoid the expense than the shame—which would move tears and pity in the most savage and inhuman breast.

6. The number of souls in this kingdom being usually reckoned one million and a half, of these I calculate there may be about two hundred thousand couples whose wives are breeders; from which number I subtract thirty thousand couples, who are able to maintain their own children, although I apprehend there cannot be so many, under the present distresses of the kingdom; but this being granted, there will remain an hundred and seventy thousand breeders. I again subtract fifty thousand, for those women who miscarry, or whose children die by accident or disease within the year. There only remain an hundred and twenty thousand children of poor parents annually born: The question therefore is, How this number shall be reared, and provided for? which, as I have already said, under the present situation of affairs, is utterly impossible by all the methods hitherto proposed; for we can neither employ them in handicraft or agriculture; we neither build houses (I mean in the country) nor cultivate land: They can very seldom pick up a livelihood by stealing till they arrive at six years old, except where they are of towardly parts, although, I confess, they learn the rudiments much earlier; during which time they can however be properly looked upon only as probationers; as I have been informed by a principal gentleman in the county of Cavan, who protested to me, that he never knew above one or two instances under the age of six, even in a part of the kingdom so renowned for the quickest proficiency in that art.

7. I am assured by our merchants, that a boy or a girl before twelve years old, is no saleable commodity, and even when they come to this age, they will not yield above three pounds, or three pounds and half a crown at most, on the exchange; which cannot turn to account either to the parents or kingdom, the charge of nutriment and rags having been at least four times that value.

8. I shall now therefore humbly propose my own thoughts, which I hope will not be liable to the least objection.

9. I have been assured by a very knowing American of my acquaintance in London, that a young healthy child well nursed is at a year old a most delicious nourishing and wholesome food, whether stewed, roasted, baked, or boiled; and I make no doubt that it will equally serve in a fricassee, or a ragout.

10. I do therefore humbly offer it to publick consideration, that of the hundred and twenty thousand children, already computed, twenty thousand may be reserved for breed, whereof only one fourth part to be males; which is more than we allow to sheep, black cattle, or swine, and my reason is, that these children are seldom the fruits of marriage, a circumstance not much regarded by our savages; therefore, one male will be sufficient to serve four females. That the remaining hundred thousand may at a year old be offered in sale to the persons of quality and fortune, through the kingdom, always advising the mother to let them suck plentifully in the last month, so

as to render them plump, and fat for a good table. A child will make two dishes at an entertainment for friends, and when the family dines alone, the fore or hind quarter will make a reasonable dish, and seasoned with a little pepper or salt will be very good boiled on the fourth day, especially in winter.

11. I have reckoned upon a medium, that a child just born will weigh 12 pounds, and in a solar year, if tolerably nursed, encreaseth to 28 pounds.

12. I grant this food will be somewhat dear, and therefore very proper for landlords, who, as they have already devoured most of the parents seem to have the best title to the children.

13. Infant's flesh will be in season throughout the year, but more plentiful in March, and a little before and after; for we are told by a grave author, an eminent French physician, that fish being a prolifick dyet, there are more children born in Roman Catholick countries about nine months after Lent, than at any other season; therefore reckoning a year after Lent, the markets will be more glutted than usual, because the number of popish infants, is at least three to one in this kingdom, and therefore it will have one other collateral advantage, by lessening the number of papists among us.

14. I have already computed the charge of nursing a beggar's child (in which list I reckon all cottagers, labourers, and four fifths of the farmers) to be about two shillings per annum, rags included; and I believe no gentleman would repine to give ten shillings for the carcass of a good fat child, which, as I have said will make four dishes of excellent nutritive meat, when he hath only some particular friend, or his own family to dine with him. Thus the squire will learn to be a good landlord, and grow popular among his tenants; the mother will have eight shillings neat profit, and be fit for work till she produces another child.

15. Those who are more thrifty (as I must confess the times require) may flay the carcass; the skin of which, artificially dressed, will make admirable gloves for ladies, and summer boots for fine gentlemen.

16. As to our city of Dublin, shambles may be appointed for this purpose, in the most convenient parts of it, and butchers we may be assured will not be wanting; although I rather recommend buying the children alive, and dressing them hot from the knife, as we do roasting pigs.

17. A very worthy person, a true lover of his country, and whose virtues I highly esteem, was lately pleased, in discoursing on this matter, to offer a refinement upon my scheme. He said, that many gentlemen of this kingdom, having of late destroyed their deer, he conceived that the want of vension might be well supplied by the bodies of young lads and maidens, not exceeding fourteen years of age, nor under twelve; so great a number of both sexes in every country being now ready to starve, for want of work and service: And these to be disposed of by their parents if alive, or otherwise by their nearest relations. But with due deference to so excellent a friend, and so deserving a patriot, I cannot be altogether in his sentiments; for as to the males, my American acquaintance assured me from frequent experience, that their flesh was generally tough and lean, like that of our schoolboys, by continual

exercise, and their taste disagreeable, and to fatten them would not answer the charge. Then as to the females, it would, I think with humble submission, be a loss to the publick, because they soon would become breeders themselves: And besides it is not improbable that some scrupulous people might be apt to censure such a practice (although indeed very unjustly) as a little bordering upon cruelty, which, I confess, hath always been with me the strongest objection against any project, how well soever intended.

18. But in order to justify my friend, he confessed, that this expedient was put into his head by the famous Psalmanazar, a native of the island Formosa, who came from thence to London, above twenty years ago, and in conversation told my friend, that in his country when any young person happened to be put to death, the executioner sold the carcass to persons of quality, as a prime dainty, and that, in his time, the body of a plump girl of fifteen, who was crucified for an attempt to poison the Emperor, was sold to his Imperial Majesty's prime minister of state, and other great mandarins of the court, in joints from the gibbet, at four hundred crowns. Neither indeed can I deny, that if the same use were made of several plump young girls in this town, who, without one single groat to their fortunes, cannot stir abroad without a chair, and appear at a play-house and assemblies in foreign fineries which they never will pay for; the kingdom would not be the worse.

19. Some persons of a desponding spirit are in great concern about that vast number of poor people, who are aged, diseased, or maimed, and I have been desired to employ my thoughts what course may be taken, to ease the nation of so grievous an encumbrance. But I am not in the least pain upon that matter, because it is very well known, that they are every day dying, and rotting, by cold, and famine, and filth, and vermin, as fast as can be reasonably expected. And as to the younger labourers, they are now in almost as hopeful a condition. They cannot get work, and consequently pine away for want of nourishment, to a degree, that if at any time they are accidentally hired to common labour, they have not strength to perform it, and thus the country and themselves are happily delivered from the evils to come.

20. I have too long digressed, and therefore shall return to my subject. I think the advantages by the proposal which I have made are obvious and many, as well as of the highest importance.

21. For *first,* as I have already observed, it would greatly lessen the number of papists, with whom, we are yearly over-run, being the principal breeders of the nation, as well as our most dangerous enemies, and who stay at home on purpose with a design to deliver the kingdom to the Pretender, hoping to take their advantage by the absence of so many good Protestants, who have chosen rather to leave their country, than stay at home, and pay tithes against their conscience to an episcopal curate.

22. *Secondly,* the poorer tenants will have something valuable of their own which by law may be made liable to distress, and help to pay their landlord's rent, their corn and cattle being already seized, and money a thing unknown.

23. *Thirdly,* whereas the maintenance of an hundred thousand children, from two years old, and upwards, cannot be computed at less than ten shillings a piece per annum, the nation's stock will be thereby increased fifty thousand pounds per annum, besides the profit of a new dish, introduced to the tables of all gentlemen of fortune in the kingdom who have any refinement in taste, and the money will circulate among our selves, the goods being entirely of our own growth and manufacture.

24. *Fourthly,* the constant breeders, besides the gain of eight shillings sterling per annum, by the sale of their children, will be rid of the charge of maintaining them after the first year.

25. *Fifthly,* this food would likewise bring great custom to taverns, where the vintners will certainly be so prudent as to procure the best receipts for dressing it to perfection; and consequently have their houses frequented by all the fine gentlemen, who justly value themselves upon their knowledge in good eating; and a skilful cook, who understands how to oblige his guests, will contrive to make it as expensive as they please.

26. *Sixthly,* this would be a great inducement to marriage, which all wise nations have either encouraged by rewards, or enforced by laws and penalties. It would encrease the care and tenderness of mothers towards their children, when they were sure of a settlement for life to the poor babes, provided in some sort by the publick, to their annual profit instead of expence; we should soon see an honest emulation among the married women, which of them could bring the fattest child to the market. Men would become as fond of their wives during the time of their pregnancy, as they are now of their mares in foal, their cows in calf, or sows when they are ready to farrow, nor offer to beat or kick them (as is too frequent a practice) for fear of a miscarriage.

27. Many other advantages might be enumerated. For instance, the addition of some thousand carcasses in our exportation of barreled beef: the propagation of swine's flesh, and improvement in the art of making good bacon, so much wanted among us by the great destruction of pigs, too frequent at our tables, which are no way comparable in taste or magnificence to a well grown, fat yearling child, which roasted whole will make a considerable figure at a Lord Mayor's feast, or any other publick entertainment. But this, and many others, I omit, being studious of brevity.

28. Supposing that one thousand families in this city, would be constant customers for infant's flesh, besides others who might have it at merry meetings, particularly at weddings and christenings, I compute that Dublin would take off annually about twenty thousand carcasses, and the rest of the kingdom (where probably they will be sold somewhat cheaper) the remaining eighty thousand.

29. I can think of no one objection, that will possibly be raised against this proposal, unless it should be urged, that the number of people will be thereby much lessened in the kingdom. This I freely own, and 'twas indeed one principal design in offering it to the world. I desire the reader will observe, that I calculate my remedy for this one individual kingdom of Ireland,

and for no other that ever was, is, or, I think, ever can be upon earth. Therefore let no man talk to me of other expedients: of taxing our absentees at five shilling a pound: of using neither cloths, nor household furniture, except what is of our own growth and manufacture: of utterly rejecting the materials and instruments that promote foreign luxury: of curing the expensiveness of pride, vanity, idleness, and gaming in our women: of introducing a vein of parsimony, prudence and temperance: of learning to love our country, wherein we differ even from Laplanders, and the inhabitants of Topinamboo: of quitting our animosities, and factions, nor act any longer like the Jews, who were murdering one another at the very moment their city was taken: of being a little cautious not to sell our country and consciences for nothing: of teaching landlords to have at least one degree of mercy towards their tenants. Lastly, of putting a spirit of honesty, industry, and skill into our shopkeepers, who, if a resolution could now be taken to buy only our native goods, would immediately unite to cheat and exact upon us in the price, the measure, and the goodness, nor could ever yet be brought to make one fair proposal of just dealing, though often and earnestly invited to it.

30. Therefore I repeat, let no man talk to me of these and the like expedients, till he hath at least some glimpse of hope, that there will ever be some hearty and sincere attempt to put them in practice.

31. But as to my self, having been wearied out for many years with offering vain, idle, visionary thoughts, and at length utterly despairing of success, I fortunately fell upon this proposal, which as it is wholly new, so it hath something solid and real, of no expense and little trouble, full in our own power, and whereby we can incur no danger in disobliging England. For this kind of commodity will not bear exportation, the flesh being of too tender a consistence, to admit a long continuance in salt, although perhaps I could name a country, which would be glad to eat up our whole nation without it.

32. After all, I am not so violently bent upon my own opinion, as to reject any offer, proposed by wise men, which shall be found equally innocent, cheap, easy, and effectual. But before something of that kind shall be advanced in contradiction to my scheme, and offering a better, I desire the author or authors, will be pleased maturely to consider two points. *First,* as things now stand, how they will be able to find food and raiment for a hundred thousand useless mouths and backs. And *Secondly,* there being a round million of creatures in human figure throughout this kingdom, whose whole subsistence put into a common stock would leave them in debt two millions of pounds sterling, adding those—who are beggars by profession, to the bulk of farmers, cottagers and labourers, with their wives and children, who are beggars in effect; I desire those politicians, who dislike my overture, and may perhaps be so bold to attempt an answer, that they will first ask the parents of these mortals, whether they would not at this day think it a great happiness to have been sold for food at a year old, in the manner I prescribe, and thereby have avoided such a perpetual scene of misfortunes as they have since gone through, by the oppression of landlords, the impossibility of pay-

ing rent without money or trade, the want of common sustenance, with neither house nor clothes to cover them from the inclemencies of the weather, and the most inevitable prospect of entailing the like, or greater miseries, upon their breed for ever.

33. I profess in the sincerity of my heart, that I have not the least personal interest in endeavouring to promote this necessary work, having no other motive than the publick good of my country, by advancing our trade, providing for infants, relieving the poor, and giving some pleasure to the rich. I have no children by which I can propose to get a single penny; the youngest being nine years old and my wife past child-bearing.

JOHN F. KENNEDY

Inaugural Address of the President: Friday, January 20, 1961

Burnham Carter's analysis of this speech is found on p. 246 of this volume.

Mr. Chief Justice, President Eisenhower, Vice President Nixon, President Truman, reverend clergy, fellow citizens, we observe today not a victory of party, but a celebration of freedom—symbolizing an end, as well as a beginning—signifying renewal, as well as change. For I have sworn before you and Almighty God the same solemn oath our forebears prescribed nearly a century and three quarters ago.

The world is very different now. For man holds in his mortal hands the power to abolish all forms of human poverty and all forms of human life. And yet the same revolutionary beliefs for which our forebears fought are still at issue around the globe—the belief that the rights of man come not from the generosity of the state, but from the hand of God.

We dare not forget today that we are the heirs of that first revolution. Let the word go forth from this time and place, to friend and foe alike, that the torch has been passed to a new generation of Americans—born in this century, tempered by war, disciplined by a hard and bitter peace, proud of our ancient heritage—and unwilling to witness or permit the slow undoing of those human rights to which this Nation has always been committed, and to which we are committed today at home and around the world.

Let every nation know, whether it wishes us well or ill, that we shall pay any price, bear any burden, meet any hardship, support any friend, oppose any foe, in order to assure the survival and the success of liberty.

This much we pledge—and more.

To those old allies whose cultural and spiritual origins we share, we pledge the loyalty of faithful friends. United, there is little we cannot do in a host of cooperative ventures. Divided, there is little we can do—for we dare not meet a powerful challenge at odds and split asunder.

To those new States whom we welcome to the ranks of the free, we pledge our words that one form of colonial control shall not have passed away merely to be replaced by a far greater iron tyranny. We shall not always expect to find them supporting our view. But we shall always hope to find them strongly supporting their own freedom—and to remember that, in the past, those who foolishly sought power by riding the back of the tiger ended up inside.

To those peoples in the huts and villages across the globe struggling to break the bonds of mass misery, we pledge our best efforts to help them help themselves, for whatever period is required—not because the Communists may be doing it, not because we seek their votes, but because it is right. If a free society cannot help the many who are poor, it cannot save the few who are rich.

To our sister republics south of our border, we offer a special pledge— to convert our good words into good deeds, in a new alliance for progress, to assist free men and free governments in casting off the chains of poverty. But this peaceful revolution of hope cannot become the prey of hostile powers. Let all our neighbors know that we shall join with them to oppose aggression or subversion anywhere in the Americas. And let every other power know that this hemisphere intends to remain the master of its own house.

To that world assembly of sovereign states, the United Nations, our last best hope in an age where the instruments of war have far outpaced the instruments of peace, we renew our pledge of support—to prevent it from becoming merely a forum for invective—to strengthen its shield of the new and the weak—and to enlarge the area in which its writ may run.

Finally, to those nations who would make themselves our adversary, we offer not a pledge but a request: that both sides begin anew the quest for peace, before the dark powers of destruction unleashed by science engulf all humanity in planned or accidental self-destruction.

We dare not tempt them with weakness. For only when our arms are sufficient beyond doubt can we be certain beyond doubt that they will never be employed.

But neither can two great and powerful groups of nations take comfort from our present course—both sides overburdened by the cost of modern weapons, both rightly alarmed by the steady spread of the deadly atom, yet both racing to alter that uncertain balance of terror that stays the hand of mankind's final war.

So let us begin anew—remembering on both sides that civility is not a sign of weakness, and sincerity is always subject to proof. *Let us never negotiate out of fear. But let us never fear to negotiate.*

Let both sides explore what problems unite us instead of laboring those problems which divide us.

Let both sides, for the first time, formulate serious and precise proposals for the inspection and control of arms—and bring the absolute power to destroy other nations under the absolute control of all nations.

Let both sides seek to invoke the wonders of science instead of its terrors. Together let us explore the stars, conquer the deserts, eradicate disease, tap the ocean depths, and encourage the arts and commerce.

Let both sides unite to heed in all corners of the earth the command of Isaiah—to "undo the heavy burdens and to let the oppressed go free."

And if a beachhead of cooperation may push back the jungle of suspicion, let both sides join in creating a new endeavor, not a new balance of power, but a new world of law, where the strong are just and the weak secure and the peace preserved.

All this will not be finished in the first 100 days. Nor will it be finished in the first 1,000 days, nor in the life of this administration, nor even perhaps in our lifetime on this planet. But let us begin.

In your hands, my fellow citizens, more than in mine, will rest the final success or failure of our course. Since this country was founded, each generation of Americans has been summoned to give testimony to its national loyalty. The graves of young Americans who answered the call to service are found around the globe.

Now the trumpet summons us again—not as a call to bear arms, though arms we need; not as a call to battle, though embattled we are; but a call to bear the burden of a long twilight struggle, year in, and year out, "rejoicing in hope, patient in tribulation"—a struggle against the common enemies of man: tyranny, poverty, disease, and war itself.

Can we forge against these enemies a grand and global alliance, North and South, East and West, that can assure a more fruitful life for all mankind? Will you join in that historic effort?

In the long history of the world, only a few generations have been granted the role of defending freedom in its hour of maximum danger. I do not shrink from this responsibility—I welcome it. I do not believe that any of us would exchange places with any other people or any other generation. The energy, the faith, the devotion which we bring to this endeavor will light our country and all who serve it—and the glow from that fire can truly light the world.

And so, my fellow Americans, ask not what your country can do for you: Ask what you can do for your country.

My fellow citizens of the world: Ask not what America will do for you, but what together we can do for the freedom of man.

Finally, whether you are citizens of America or citizens of the world, ask of us the same high standards of strength and sacrifice which we ask of you. With a good conscience our only sure reward, with history the final judge of our deeds, let us go forth to lead the land we love, asking His blessing and His help, but knowing that here on earth God's work must truly be our own.

John F. Kennedy 301

APPENDIX B

PAUL C. DOHERTY

Stylistics—A Bibliographical Survey

Paul C. Doherty teaches English at Boston College. His bibliographical survey of the scholarship on style is an excellent guide for students who wish to pursue the subject beyond the materials available in this collection. For an even more intensive bibliography, see Richard W. Bailey and Dolores M. Burton's English Stylistics: A Bibliography *(1968), or Louis T. Milic's* Style and Stylistics: An Analytical Bibliography *(1967).*

INTRODUCTION

Style means and has meant many things, and both Ohmann (1964) and Enkvist list some of the ways in which the word has been used. Three attributes are common to most definitions of style: 1) that it is a quality of language existing both within and beyond the limits of the sentence; 2) that it is somehow related to meaning; and 3) that it is the result of linguistic choices made by the speaker or writer.

The extremes in attempts to define the nature of style are epitomized by the contrasting definitions of Swift ("Proper words in proper places makes the true definition of style.") and Buffon ("Le style est l'homme même."). Definitions of the first type are concerned with the effect of style, and suggest that style is normative and that it may be considered independently of the thought of the discourse in which it occurs. The second type of definition points toward the cause of style, and suggests that it is an individual quality, inseparable from thought. These extremes are well understood, and most definitions may be grouped under one or the other.

The basis for this division may be understood by reference to Ferdinand de Saussure's distinction between language ("la langue") and speech ("la parole"). If style is regarded as a phenomenon within "la langue," that is, within the total expressive system of the culture, it will be seen comparatively, as a collection of linguistic choices visible against the context of the totality of the language. If style is regarded as "la parole," the linguistic means used by an individual to express his ideas, it will be described in terms of its individual characteristics.

Historically, the first attitude toward style (style as normative) is the older, and was a part of classical rhetoric. Abrams has placed the breakup of this attitude at the beginning of the Romantic movement, and most Romantic and post-Romantic students of style have preferred to think of style as an individual quality. Gibson suggests that the study of style is more necessary today than is the study of rhetoric.

However, this general historical view must be weighed against the fact that both extremes seem to have been present consistently. LaDrière has shown that Aristotle stands at the beginning of the normative theory of style, Plato at the beginning of the individual theory. Richard Puttenham, the sixteenth-century rhetorician, recognizes both attitudes toward style; for him style is "many times natural to the writer, many times his peculiar by election and arte." The persistence of the individual theory of style during the largely rhetorical eighteenth century is pointed out by Wimsatt; and among modern critics, who, taken as a whole, regard style as individual, there are those (Riffaterre, for example) who study style effects in terms of the total resources of the language.

Normative definitions of style often include classificatory and exemplificative material, as ancient as the use of Virgil's *Bucolics, Georgics,* and *Aeneid* to illustrate low, middle and high styles, as recent as current composition handbooks, in which more modern selections illustrate the same norms. The second view of style, which regards it as individual, of course lacks such objective norms. As a result, stylistic criticism from this basis is frequently impressionistic in its description and evaluation ("X's style is virile and energetic, Y's baroque, Z's supple."). The development of linguistics, however, through its emphasis on popular speech as the source of language and linguistic change, has provided not only a more accurate and detailed vocabulary (or vocabularies) with which to describe style, but also a theoretical basis for the individual view of style. The application of linguistic methods to the study of style has come to be called stylistics.

There are two main sources of modern stylistics. The first is the work of Charles Bally and his successors in what has been called the French school of stylistics. Drawing on de Saussure's distinction between language and speech, Bally was concerned with those aspects of speech which have value beyond their basic notational power, which are, in his terms, expressive. That is, certain words, because of their contextual position (a word used ironically, for example) or because of extra-textual value (a word associated with a particular occupation, class or region, for example) have a value greater than their lexical meaning.

The second source of modern stylistics has been called the German school because of the influence of Karl Vossler, Leo Spitzer, and others, though its source may be seen clearly in Benedetto Croce's *Aesthetics.* Unlike Bally, who was not concerned with literature, for Croce expressive language *is* art; the poem and its language are identical. The German school of stylistics, then, is concerned with the totality of a work of art, its wholeness, rather than with certain "expressive" elements in it. In de Saussure's terms, the French school utilizes "la langue," the total system of language, the German school, "la parole," an individual unit of speech, whether a single work of art, the work of a single author, a single epoch or a single nation.

Paul C. Doherty   303

The two sources of stylistics have not remained apart. Many of Bally's successors, Sayce and Ullmann (1957), for example, have applied the concept of expressiveness to literature, and Leo Spitzer, in his later work, admitted the dangers of his intuitive approach to style. British and American stylisticians tend to be eclectic, choosing the French idea of expressiveness as a starting point, and the German goal of using literature as the object of style study. But there are not just two schools of stylistics; their number is closer to a dozen. Hatzfeld (1955) lists eight others which he feels may be validly employed; often these represent the merger of other disciplines (poetics, psychology, art, history, statistics, for example) with stylistics.

There is no more agreement about the method and end of stylistics than there is about the nature of style. Methods of stylistic investigation vary. First of all, there is no consensus concerning what part of language is to be used as the stylistic unit. Until now, phonetic stylistics has largely been restricted to poetry, but Ullmann (1964) believes that sound as well as word and syntax may be studied to find stylistic characteristics of prose. The most common area of language studied in stylistics is the word, both word forms and word meanings. The word is the unit for statistical analysis of style and for stylistic study of imagery. As Ullmann (1964) points out, phonetic and syntactic choices are limited, but lexical choices are practically unlimited and hence a better indication of individual style. Ohmann (1964) claims that style reveals itself most clearly through a study of syntax, especially as explained by transformational grammar. The explanation of the semantic component of a transformational grammar, developed by Katz and Postal (1964), is the basis for Ohmann (1966). Many English stylisticians, such as Frith and Halliday, employ not only linguistic but also semantic units in stylistics.

Also, the process of stylistic investigation is not agreed upon. When what is "style" is considered objectively ascertainable, that is, when style is regarded as knowable expressive elements, the process of style begins with noting style elements. Riffaterre (1959), for example, identifies as features of style those elements which produce "defeated expectancy." Wellek also regards style elements as immediately knowable. On the other hand, McIntosh argues that stylistic features are not always evident.

Where stylistic elements are not considered as objectively ascertainable, stylistic analysis must either begin intuitively or completely describe the work using statistical methods (cf. Herdan and Vincent). The most well-known example of the intuitive approach is Leo Spitzer's "philological circle," in which the author approaches the work without preconceptions until he finds some verbal characteristics beginning to strike him. From this characteristic he attempts to find the work's "creative principle," and then to support his thesis with other stylistic observations. More recently, Spencer has also made the suggestion that the starting point must be the critic's intuition.

The traditional goal of style study has been evaluation, and for many modern stylisticians this goal has not changed. Riffaterre, Wellek, and Sayce hold that the final task of the stylistician is to render aesthetic judgment. Ullmann (1957) believes that stylistics which studies expressiveness should merely describe, but that which studies literature must evaluate. Spencer, however, considers comparison, often used as a basis for evaluation, to be the final task of stylistics; for Hill stylistics explains variations not otherwise accounted for. Ohmann (1964) insists that for the present, at least, stylistics must content itself with "the humble task of description."

The value of stylistics to the teacher of composition can hardly be univocally expressed. Traditionally, style has been taught by imitation of correct models; Milic holds that this is still the best method. Indeed, it is hard to imagine a method of teaching composition which would not involve showing the student the choices which his language allows. On the other hand there is something to be said for the approach to style which points out in a student's writing characteristics which are *his,* which may be said to form his style. The teacher who believes that style and content are not separable will of course use this approach to teaching style. Whichever theory forms the basis for a study of style, the greater descriptive power of modern linguistics should allow for more accurate analysis of style phenomena.

BIBLIOGRAPHY

The following bibliography is selective, and restricted for the most part to theories of stylistics as they apply to prose style. It lists only works published in English. Other bibliographies of stylistics may be found in Hatzfeld (1953), Spencer, Wellek and Warren, and annually in *The Year's Work in Foreign Language Studies.*

Abrams, M. H. *The Mirror and the Lamp: Romantic Theory and the Critical Tradition.* New York: Oxford U. Press, 1953.

Alonso, Amado. "The Stylistic Interpretation of Literary Texts," *MLN,* LVII (November, 1942), 489-96.

Auerbach, Eric. *Mimesis: The Representation of Reality in Western Literature.* Trans. Willard Trask. Princeton: Princeton U. Press, 1953.

Barish, Jonas A. "The Prose Style of John Lyly," *ELH,* XXIII (March, 1956), 14-35.

Carroll, John B. "Vectors of Prose Style," *Style in Language.* Thomas A. Sebeok, editor. Cambridge, Mass.: M.I.T. Press, 1960. Pp. 283-92.

Craddock, Sister Claire Eileen, C.C.V.I. *Style Theories as Found in Stylistic Studies of Romance Scholars (1900-1950).* Washington, D. C.: The Catholic U. of America Press, 1952.

Enkvist, Nils Erik. "On Defining Style: An Essay in Applied Linguistics," *Linguistics and Style.* John Spencer, editor. London: Oxford U. Press, 1964. Pp. 3-56.

Frith, J. R. *et al.* "Linguistics and the Problem of Meaning," *Proceedings of the Seventh International Congress of Linguists.* F. Norman, editor. London: [no pub.], 1956. Pp. 179-233.

————. "Modes of Meaning," *Essays and Studies* IV. London: John Murray, 1951. Pp. 118-49.

Gibson, Walker. "A Note on Style and the Limits of Language," *The Limits of Language*. Walker Gibson, editor. New York: Hill and Wang. Pp. 104-13.

Halliday, Michael A. K. "The Linguistic Study of Literary Texts," *Proceedings of the Ninth International Congress of Linguists*. Horace G. Lunt, editor. The Hague: Mouton and Company, 1964. Pp. 302-7.

Hatcher, Anna G. "Syntax and the Sentence," *Word*, XII (August, 1956), 234-50.

Hatzfeld, Helmut. *A Critical Bibliography of the New Stylistics Applied to the Romance Literatures, 1900-1952*. Chapel Hill: U. of North Carolina Press, 1953.

————. "Methods of Stylistic Investigation," *Literature and Science*. S. C. Aston *et al.*, editors. Oxford: Basil Blackwell, 1955. Pp. 44-51.

————. "Stylistic Criticism as Art-Minded Philology," *Yale French Studies*, II (Spring-Summer, 1949), 62-70.

Herdan, G. *Quantitative Linguistics*. Washington, D.C.: Butterworth, Inc., 1964.

Hill, Archibald A. *Introduction to Linguistic Structures*. New York: Harcourt, Brace and Company, 1958.

Katz, Jerrold J., and Paul M. Postal. *An Integrated Theory of Linguistic Descriptions*. Cambridge: The M.I.T. Press, 1964.

LaDrière, Craig. "Rhetoric and 'Merely Verbal' Art," *English Institute Essays, 1948*. D. A. Robertson, Jr., editor. New York: Columbia U. Press, 1949. Pp. 123-52.

McIntosh, Angus. "Saying," *Review of English Literature*, VI (April, 1965), 9-20.

Milic, Louis T. "Theories of Style and Their Implications for the Teaching of Composition," *College Composition and Communication*, XVI (May, 1965), 66-9, 126.

Morris, Edward P. "A Science of Style," *Transactions and Proceedings of the American Philological Association*, XLVI (1915), 103-18.

Ohmann, Richard. "Generative Grammars and the Concept of Literary Style," *Word*, XX (December, 1964), 423-39.

————. "Literature as Sentences," *College English*, XXVII (January, 1966), 261-7.

————. "Prolegomena to the Analysis of Prose Style," *Style in Prose Fiction: English Institute Essays, 1958*. Harold C. Martin, editor. New York: Columbia U. Press, 1958. Pp. 1-24.

————. *Shaw, the Style and the Man*. Middletown, Conn.: Wesleyan U. Press, 1962.

Posner, Rebecca. "The Use and Abuse of Stylistic Statistics," *Archivum Linguisticum*, XV (1963), 111-39.

Riffaterre, Michael. "Criteria for Style Analysis," *Word*, XV (April, 1959), 154-74.

————. Review of S. Ullmann, *Style in the French Novel, Word,* XV (August, 1959), 404-13.

————. "Stylistic Context," *Word,* XVI (August, 1960), 207-18.

————. "The Stylistic Function," *Proceedings of the Ninth International Congress of Linguists.* Horace G. Lunt, editor. The Hague: Mouton and Company, 1964. Pp. 316-22.

Sayce, R. A. *Style in French Prose.* Oxford: The Clarendon Press, 1953.

Spence, N. C. W. "A Hardy Perennial: The Problem of 'la langue' and 'la parole'," *Archivum Linguisticum,* IX (1957), 1-27.

Spencer, John, and Michael Gregory. "An Approach to the Study of Style," *Linguistics and Style.* John Spencer, editor. London: Oxford U. Press, 1964. Pp. 57-105.

Spitzer, Leo. *Linguistics and Literary History: Essays in Stylistics.* Princeton: Princeton U. Press, 1948.

Stutterheim, C. F. P. "Modern Stylistics," *Lingua,* I (1947-8), 410-26, III (1952-3), 52-68.

Ullmann, Stephen. *The Image in the Modern French Novel.* Cambridge, Eng.: Cambridge U. Press, 1960.

————. *Language and Style.* Oxford: Basil Blackwell, 1964.

————. *Style in the French Novel.* Cambridge, Eng.: Cambridge U. Press, 1957.

————. "Style and Personality," *Review of English Literature,* VI (April, 1965), 21-31.

Vincent, E. R. "Mechanical Aids for the Study of Language and Literary Style," *Literature and Science.* C. S. Aston *et al.,* editors. Oxford: Basil Blackwell, 1955. Pp. 56-60.

Wellek, René, and Austin Warren. "Style and Stylistics," *Theory of Literature,* 2nd ed. New York: Harcourt, Brace and Company, 1949, Pp. 163-74.

Wells, Rulon. "Nominal and Verbal Style," in *Style in Language,* Thomas A. Sebeok, editor. Cambridge, Mass.: M.I.T. Press, 1960. Pp. 213-20.

Wimsatt, W. K., Jr. *The Prose Style of Samuel Johnson.* New Haven: Yale U. Press, 1941.

* Bridgeman – American style; composed of sentences which focus on a key word. 3 basic rhythms of verbal expression: ① Verse with a regularly recurring pattern of speech ② Prose based on the unit of the sentence ③ Ordinary speech – short phrase which contains the essential idea or word upon which the speaker is concentrating. Surrounding verbal sounds "are largely rhythmic filler." Pg. 216→ Drawing attention techniques ① Portmanteau: putting 2 words together ② Vernacular words = draw reader's attention: (ex: 4 letter words). Lists, colloquial speech, (writing the way one speaks), repetition

* Christenson – "generative approach" will "generate" more writing. Pg. 341→ Cummulative / Rt. Branch sentences long flowing introduction before you get to kernel. Periodic, left branch sentence; subject & verb first.

* Embedding: Pg. 343 CR adding verb & adjective clauses, "gives life giving details & describing, displays syntactic richness.

* Co-ordinate sentence = equal, extending the meaning, adding to it, clauses can be used interchangeability. Sub-ordinate sentence: one more impt. then the other.

* Restrictive modifier – restricts the scope, uses no commas. (Ex: Motorists wearing eyeglasses are given a special driving test).

* Non-restrictive or free modifier: gives information, doesn't restrict (Ex: We had supper at the old forge, which was built in 1760).

* Mellon – suggests that the "competance level" is already there by the 4th grade. Syntactic maturity- ability to write fluently as time goes by, beginning to embed & becoming aware.

* Embedding- 2 distinct sentences combined into one.

* Beardsly: Pg. 3-4P → 3 concepts of style: ① "a style" – a set of stylistic features ② Style itself - part or aspect of the discourse ③ "a good style" - make the style better. Pg. 5-6P → Style - detail of explict mean-ing. Our "implict" meaning must agree with our "explicit" meaning. A difference of Style is a difference of meaning: to change words is to change meaning. Style not good, not bad – but just there. Style student choses is impt. is presenting ideas in a logical order so all parts fit together providing an explicite meaning.

*Millie P.15-4P⇒ Style is a starting block for teacher.

① Rhetorical dualism - find best words available, make meaning clearer by changing words.

② Crocean aestetic - no distinction bet. form or style (refers back to Plato), revealing inner self.

Good writing refers back to depending upon being aware of the best choices available & choosing them.

* Bad tests themselves produce bad scores. Tests compiled from what machines can score - things that can be tested, not what should be tested.

History of Rhetoric:

* First formal rhetorician: Corax (5th century) trained ordinary people on how to argue effectively in court to get their property back.
① Proem / Introduction ② Presentation / Narration ③ Argument ④ Peroration

* 2nd. rhetorician - Gorgias, Greek 425 B.C. One of first to use "emotional appeal." Used an ornate style & became famous for this.

* Isocrates - a sophist, didn't believe in anything, argued for the money. Sophists became deceitful later. Isocrates first sophist, was idealist.

* In order to become good rhetorician one had to be a virtuous man. Birth of liberal arts — "the whole men."

* Plato - look thru our eyes & see the deception of this world, (illusions), to the truth beyond. Plato created the Republic. Banned artists, poets, etc. Thought they could deceive thru writing. Saw thru the sophists - thought they were too interested in deceit instead of truth. Plato said: "suit yourself & your elements to your audience, (arrangement also impt.). Closer to the truth more than the others.

* Aristotle - pupil of Plato's, 333 B.C., most famous for arguing that a rhetorician should use any way possible to win. Use any means of persuasion - "the end justifies the means." Not just to deceive, but to win. Used 3 types argumentation: ① Logos (appeal to reason) ② Pathos (appeal to emotion ③ Ethos (appeal to ethics, authority).

* Cicero - practitioner / rhetoric. Used: ① Asiatic flowery style ② Attic - plain & simple style. He had 3 purposes: ① To teach ② To study persuade ③ To delight (The Study of Rhetoric)

* Middle ages: 4 courses of school
① Trivium - B.A. - 4 yrs. undergraduate, grammar logic, rhetoric
② Quadrivium - music, arithmetic, geometry astronomy. 2 3 4 5 6 7 8 9 10 11 12 13 14 15 16 17 18 19 20 21 22 23 24 25 RM 74 78 92 70

* 16th century - put stop to flowery rhetoric - use of plain style come in.

* John Dryden - language must fit occasion, subject & persons. Syntax became more natural because of him. Latin dropped off considerably.